Birdwatching
on Spain's Southern Coast

John R. Butler

Birdwatching on Spain´s Southern Coast
Is published in Spain by Ediciones Santana S.L.,
Apartado 422, Fuengirola 29640 Fuengirola (Málaga).
Tel: 952 485 838. Fax: 952 485 367.
E-mail: info@santanabooks.com
www.santanabooks.com

First edition 2001.

Design by Tina Bradley.
Illustrations by Rebecca Butler.
Maps by John R.Butler.
Cover design by Tina Bradley.
Cover illustration of a Golden Oriole
by Rebecca Butler.

Printed and bound in Spain by
Gráficas San Pancracio S.L.
Pol. Ind. San Luis, C/. Orotava 17, Málaga.

Depósito Legal: MA-1.576/2001 ISBN: 84-89954-20-8

Acknowledgement

I would like to express my gratitude to my wife, Rebecca, for the hundreds of hours spent researching, proof-reading and illustrating this book.

Contents

Introduction

This book deals mainly with the western Costa del Sol which includes a stretch of Mediterranean coastline, with inland sites, running some 135 kilometres from Málaga to Algeciras, just beyond Gibraltar. This is my specialized area but also included are sites in the province of Almería and sites along the 50 kilometre stretch of Atlantic coast (*Costa de la Luz*) between Gibraltar and the town of Bolonia.

These stretches of coastline benefit from the close proximity to the main migration routes to and from Africa, which are centred around the Strait of Gibraltar. The Strait offers the shortest sea crossing from Europe to the African continent and the legendary twin pillars of Hercules - Mount Abyla in Morocco and the Rock of Gibraltar - are obvious landmarks for migrating birds.

Apart from these coastal sites, there is a great diversity of other habitats that harbour a wide variety of resident and migrant species. These include rivers, reservoirs, wetlands, forests, mountains and areas of agricultural land, all of which are reasonably accessible by car from whichever point along the coast you start.

Here, in this part of Spain, you can regularly find over fifty different bird species that are classed as rarities in "The British Bird List", together with over thirty more that have never been recorded in Britain or in other northern European countries. This makes the area a veritable treasure trove for visiting birders.

Being a very popular holiday destination, the Costa del Sol is subject to a continued increase in tourism and a constant demand for more holiday homes and hotels which has resulted in much of the coastline becoming a concrete jungle. The outcome of this is that many natural habitats suitable to birds and other wildlife have been lost. It is not until you get beyond Sotogrande, travelling south-westward, that you will find untouched coastal areas, but even here the development is starting to spread. Fortunately, there are still havens where bird and animal life can still be seen to be thriving.

For some of the inland sites the prospects appear much better, but even here great swathes of land are being given up to the endless demands for villas, country clubs and golf courses. In the past, little attention has been paid to conservation but, thankfully, there is a growing awareness that not every tourist is only interested in golf and the beaches. The old areas that had been given the status of

protected sites, which for years had been neglected, are now being made more attractive and accessible to the public.

A prime example of this is the Paraje Natural (natural area) at Sotogrande. It is a very important marsh area with a lagoon, beside the estuary of the Río Guadiaro. For many years it had been neglected and its protection was never enforced but, in 1999, the Andalusian Government invested 213 million pesetas on erecting fences and gates to keep vehicles out, building elevated boardwalks giving access to the centre of the marsh, and constructing a bird observation hide overlooking the lagoon and an observation platform that offers excellent views of the marsh and the estuary. Together with this, a large scale re-vegetation programme was undertaken. The area is now a model of how a natural park should look and the birds and other wildlife are thriving. I hope the success of this project will be repeated elsewhere because wetland sites such as this are of vital importance to wildlife in general.

Away from the coast, much of the area is dominated by mountain ranges and agricultural land and is sparsely populated, except for the picturesque white villages that nestle in the hills. Some of these villages offer wonderful opportunities to view vultures, eagles and other raptors at close range as they often pass, quite literally, just metres overhead.

Numerous rivers flow through the area, although many of these tend to dry up in the summer or after prolonged periods without rain. The major rivers which normally flow throughout the year include the Río Guadalhorce in Málaga, the Río Verde near Marbella and the Ríos Guadiaro, Guadacorte, Hozgarganta and the Palmones, which are all in the province of Cádiz.

With the exception of the massive water catchment areas fed by the Río Guadalhorce that supply water to Málaga, embalses (reservoirs) are few and far between. The main ones that are reasonably accessible are the Embalse de la Concepción at Istán, the Embalse de Guadarranque at Castellar de la Frontera, the Embalse de la Leche at Benahavís and the Embalse del Taraje at Cancelada. Of these the Cancelada reservoir, although only small, is by far the best site for both numbers and species of birds.

The forests of the area are mostly of conifer or cork-oak and are usually well above sea-level in the hills and mountains. Los Reales, the mountain directly behind Estepona, is the stronghold of the Pinsapo pine, which is exceedingly rare anywhere else in Spain. Most forests normally shelter a good selection of raptors and passerines, along with other wildlife.

Eucalyptus trees are very common along most rivers and near to the coast, and are the favoured trees of the three species of parakeets that can be found in this part of Spain. The Monk Parakeet, although regarded as a rarity for the country as a whole, has quickly colonized this area and is now a common sight, nesting communally in the eucalyptus. The Black-hooded and the Ring-necked Parakeets are much scarcer and tend to be seen only singly or in very small groups.

Broadleaved woodlands similar to an English wood are very scarce here. However, there is an excellent little wood at San Enrique de Guadiaro which runs alongside a river. It has a good selection of both deciduous and evergreen trees and shrubs and is populated by most of the woodland birds you would expect to find in England, plus a few more exotic species such as Hoopoe, Golden Oriole, Penduline Tit, Melodious Warbler and Serin.

All along the coast at regular intervals are ancient watchtowers that today play host to nesting birds, especially colonies of Lesser Kestrels. You can enter the tower situated on a small headland between two beaches along the N-340 coastal road at km 147 and climb the steps to a flat observation roof some 10 metres above the ground. It has its resident population of kestrels but, equally important, it provides wonderful opportunities for watching off-shore seabirds.

Evidence of the Roman and Moorish occupations of Andalucía can be found scattered throughout the area. One of the better preserved sites is the the Roman baths near Manilva (*Baños Romanos de Hedionda*), which is situated in a valley beside the Río Manilva and is still used by people who believe in the health giving properties of the sulphurous water. The valley, river and surrounding hills attract a wide range of birds.

The opportunities for watching seabirds are endless in this part of the country. Every beach, clifftop, estuary and harbour wall is suitable for this purpose, though the areas near the Strait of Gibraltar offer the best views and the maximum number of species. In the province of Cádiz, the better areas are at Punto Carnero, Punta Secreta, Tarifa and Sotogrande. In Málaga province, the sea wall at Estepona port and the estuaries of the Río Guadalmansa and the Río Guadalhorce are recommended.

In the spring and summer, a visit to one or two of the sites described in this book can easily produce a list of 60 or 70 species in just a few hours of watching, including many species that you would probably never see elsewhere.

Offshore Seabird Watching

Although the opportunities for seawatching exist from any point along the coast, the stretches of coastline covered by this book are not ideal for this aspect of birdwatching. Gibraltar, due to its geographical location, and a few sites on the Atlantic coast offer the best chances of seeing seabirds at a reasonably close range. The Strait is the most reliable place to see shearwaters, petrels, auks, and skuas.

The observation site at Europa Point in Gibraltar provides excellent views across the Strait to the Moroccan coast. Easy parking, bench seating and usually the presence of other watchers with whom you can share experiences and compare notes, makes this an enjoyable place to visit.

Other sites in the area are also rewarding, but generally the distances are greater. In Cádiz province, Punto Carnero and Punto Secreta near Algeciras can offer good views, as can the sea wall at Tarifa and Los Lances beach. The estuary of the Río Guadiaro at Sotogrande is also very good and this and another area close by are described in this book.

In Malága province the best site, undoubtedly, is the estuary of the Río Guadalhorce, which over the years has produced a very impressive bird list. Also, I can recommend the harbour wall at Estepona port. It offers good views and is fairly reliable for Gannets and shearwaters along with both Black-necked and Great Crested Grebes, Razorbill, Redbreasted Merganser and sea ducks.

Stork and Raptor Migration

As with seawatching, the prime place for watching the migration of storks and raptors is undoubtedly Europa Point in Gibraltar. However, within the area there are other locations that are ideal to watch from without having to queue to get in and out of Gibraltar.

Obviously, the strength and direction of the wind will play a large part in determining where migrating birds, especially those that rely on soaring flight, will actually cross over the Spanish coast. To the east of Gibraltar, we benefit from westerly winds, as the birds are then carried toward us. In easterly winds, the birds tend to be blown away from us and the skies here can be empty. If you intend to watch the migration during prolonged periods of easterly winds, you should plan on travelling beyond the town of Algeciras, perhaps as far as the mountainous regions near Tarifa, or even further.

A good spot to watch migrating birds is the municipal park at El Rinconcillo, situated on the west bank of the Río Palmones, just above the estuary. The river flows into the Bay of Algeciras some seven kilometres from Gibraltar. The park has a large bird observatory with an open air viewing terrace offering excellent opportunities to watch the migrating birds arriving from Africa, especially on calm days, or when there is a westerly wind.

The hills above the town of La Linea can also be very rewarding, as it is over these hills that many of the raptors find the thermals to enable them to regain the height lost during the sea crossing. Also, many of the birds arriving later in the day often roost here overnight before continuing their journey.

The Honey Buzzards, which do not rely so much on soaring flight due to their flying prowess, seem to ignore the more direct routes taken by the other raptors and are likely to cross the coast at any point within the region, usually during the first week of May.

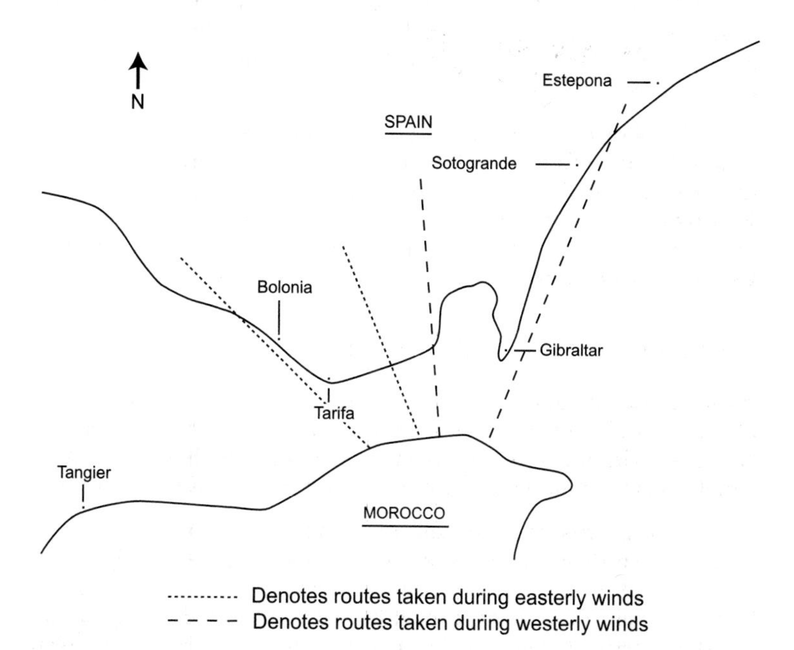

Honey Buzzards cross on a wide front and can be seen at any point on this map

The northward passage is by far the most spectacular as the birds tend to arrive at low levels, thereby giving the watcher much better

views. During the southward passage, the birds have generally gained great heights in preparation of the sea crossing long before they reach the coast, making identification much harder.

Although there is significant movement in both directions across the Strait throughout the year, the optimum time for viewing is from late February until the end of May. The map opposite gives an indication of the routes taken by migrating birds during the northward passage and should be used as reference only after you have determined the wind direction.

How to use this Book

The sites selected for this book have all been visited by me on many occasions, either during my guided birdwatching tours or on my own personal birding trips. I have always found them to be very reliable sites at which to see a wide variety of species at any time of the year.

The sites are varied and include rivers, coasts, forests, mountains, woods, estuaries, wetlands and farmland. Most benefit from having three, four, or even more types of habitat in the same general area. Most can be easily reached from any point along the coast, or from inland, by a first class road system.

Site descriptions

Each of the site descriptions include the following information to assist you:

1. a detailed map of the site, highlighting the main features of the area, points of interest and all access roads, tracks and footpaths.

2. precise directions on how to reach the site. The text will guide you around the area, tell you what you can expect to find in any particular spot, point out the feeding and, where appropriate, the nesting sites of certain birds, and give you any other pieces of local knowledge that could make your visit more rewarding and enjoyable.

3. the times of year that are the most productive for the site in question, the best times of the day to visit and the times to avoid visiting, for example at weekends and public holidays when the site may be very busy with picnickers or very noisy.

4. a complete list of all the birds that I have personally identified at

the site. I will make no claim for any species that have supposedly been seen by any other person unless there is documented evidence to support the sighting. This will normally include all rarities that have been reported to and accepted by the Iberian Rarities Committee (*Comité Ibérico de Rarezas*) of the Sociedad Española de Ornitología (SEO).

The species that can be seen all year will come under the heading of Resident, even if their numbers increase or decrease at any time of the year. The migratory birds that remain in the area throughout the summer will come under the heading of Summer / Breeding. Those that are generally seen only in the winter will naturally be found under that heading. The other heading will be for those species classed as Passage Migrants. These are birds that pass through the area at some time of the year but do not normally remain here. Many offshore seabirds, although present for most of the year, are constantly moving and may be classed here.

5. the accessibility of the site for wheelchair users and people with other mobility/health problems so that valuable time and money can be saved by not travelling to a site that is totally unsuitable for them.

General Information

When to visit

If you are planning a holiday mainly for birdwatching in this area, you need to know something about the seasonal variations of the bird populations as well as the weather conditions you could expect. The following information should help you in both these matters.

The winter period, which I loosely class as being from November to the end of February, can be very changeable as far as the weather is concerned. In each of these months there have been times when the daytime temperatures have been as high as 27°C and the beaches have been crowded with people basking in the sun. At other times the thermometer has struggled to get above 5 or 6°C and bitterly cold winds have been blasting across the region.

However, both of these extremes usually only last for a few days at a time. Although this is the rainy season in this part of Spain, the rains are not reliable and sometimes months pass between wet periods. The wisest choice, if you are coming during this period, is to bring clothing to cover all possibilities.

The birding is good at this time of year and, although the summer visitors have left, they are replaced by the wintering species such as waders and waterfowl. Many of the resident species have their numbers increased by migrant birds escaping the freezing temperatures of the northern European winters. Offshore seabirds such as Great and Arctic Skuas, Razorbill, Red-breasted Merganser, shearwaters, petrels and Puffin can be seen, although the latter is seldom seen except from Gibraltar as it passes through the Strait. Vultures, eagles and other raptorial species have resident populations which can be seen all year, with exceptions. The Short-toed and Booted Eagles, Egyptian Vulture, Black Kite, Hobby and Montagu's Harrier are all summer visitors.

March and April are normally much warmer than the preceding months, with average daytime temperatures of about 18°C. The main problem at this time of year is the strong winds and the occasional rain, so you still require good warm clothing if you are intent on spending time in the country looking for birds.

This is a very busy time in the bird calendar as the main migration is in full swing. Many of the wintering species are returning north and are being replaced by the summer visitors and the passage migrants. Storks, eagles, herons, kites, swallows, swifts, martins and a whole host of other passerine species flood into the area to begin their courtship and breeding rituals and to establish their territories.

From May until the end of October the weather can generally be relied upon to be hot, with very few days of rain. Most of the smaller rivers will dry up, leaving nothing but arid sand and rock on the riverbeds. A few, however, like the Río Padron, the Río Guadalmansa and the Arroyo Vaquero, retain enough water to form lagoons, which are of great benefit to the breeding birds and other wildlife.

During this time, all of the breeding species can be found, along with large numbers of passage migrants. In the area it is possible to see 20 species of warbler, five species of eagle, two species of vulture and 16 other raptor species. In previous years, the first week of May has seen the mass arrival of thousands of Honey Buzzards directly over the area between Marbella and Gibraltar. They are unmissable as they arrive, flying low over the water before reaching the coast and then riding the thermals, in flocks of up to 300, before continuing on their journey northward.

Protected areas

Throughout the area covered by this book there are numerous sites that have been given varying levels of protection by the environmental agency of the Andalusian Government, La Agencia de Medio Ambiente (A.M.A.). The sites in question are usually well marked with cream and green signs every 100 metres or so, indicating the status of the protected area. The four levels of protection you are likely to encounter are:

RESERVA NATURAL. This translates to a nature reserve and four of these, all lagoons, are mentioned in this book. They range in size from the Laguna de la Ratosa (172 hectares) to the vast area of Laguna de Fuente de Piedra (8,663 hectares). Some sites are fenced off to conserve the natural surroundings and wildlife but all offer good opportunities for birdwatching.

PARAJE NATURAL. These are natural areas that again can vary tremendously in size and include estuaries, mountains and beaches. The smallest of these is the estuary of the Río Guadiaro (36 hectares) and the largest is Los Reales (1,215 hectares), which is the mountain directly inland from the town of Estepona. Some may be fenced off and some are open to the public, although certain activities may be restricted or prohibited.

PARQUE NATURAL. These are generally very large nature parks which are open to the public and are mostly mountainous or forested areas. In many cases there are information centres at these sites that offer leaflets and guides to the area. You may also find recreational facilities and many have signposted or colour coded walking trails. Certain activities may be restricted and only selected planning permission for building is granted.

PARQUE NACIONAL. There are only two national parks in Andalucía and only one of these, Doñana, is mentioned in this book. It receives the highest level of protection given by the A.M.A. and entry into the park is strictly controlled and limited to conducted tours with a licensed company. However, the National Park of Doñana is surrounded by the Parque Natural de Doñana, much of which is accessible to the public and produces all of the species of birds that can be seen within the park proper.

Maps

Although most maps of Spain are adequate for touring, it is important that you use the most up-to-date one available because motorways and tollroads are being constructed at an alarming rate. For those who prefer to get right into the countryside, I would strongly recommend the Spanish military maps because they show every road, dirt-track and footpath of a given area (normally about 500 sq kms). These are on the scale of 1:50,000 and are very descriptive in all aspects. They can be ordered from most good bookshops in Britain and Europe. If you are coming from outside of Spain, you should order well in advance (at least eight weeks) of your visit.

Driving in Spain

Although driving in the cities and large towns can be a hair-raising experience for the first-time visitor to Spain, a car really is a necessity if you are on a birding holiday and you can take heart that, away from the heavily built-up areas, driving really can be enjoyable. The roads are mostly in good condition and traffic densities are low, which enables you to take your time and appreciate the wonderful scenery of this part of Spain.

Please remember that drink-driving, speeding and failing to wear a seat belt are all offences here and can, along with any other driving offences, be met by heavy on-the-spot fines. You should ensure that you obey any parking restrictions that are in force as there are some areas where the local police can call the dreaded grua (tow truck) to remove your car from the street. Of course you should never leave anything on display in a parked car, especially if it has a car rental company sticker on it.

Disabled access

I have noticed in most other guide books the subject of disabled/ wheelchair access is generally overlooked, which is a great shame as many people with mobility problems are very keen birdwatchers. Of the sites that I have included in this book there are a few that will not suit people who are not fully mobile. However, most sites have at least some degree of access to part, if not all, of the described area, whilst others can be adequately viewed from a car, road, riverside, or from some other vantage point. I have made notes with reference to wheelchair accessibility under the General Information heading for each site. Hopefully this information will be helpful to anyone who is disabled and will prevent them from travelling long distances to

totally unsuitable sites.

Accommodation

Wherever you go in this part of Spain you will never be far from some form of accommodation, be it hotel, pension (guest house), hostal (small hotel) or camp site. Hotel prices and standards vary greatly and you may be charged anywhere between 40-240 Euros a night for a double room, although the state-run hotels called paradors usually average around 100 Euros per night. These are mostly old buildings such as monasteries, castles and country estates that have been renovated, they are usually in quiet rural locations (ideal for birdwatchers), or in historic towns.

Hostals and pensions are relatively cheap and cheerful places where a double room can start at 18 Euros per night, but may also, in some areas along the coast, cost at least twice that price. Campsites are plentiful, both along the coast and inland and usually have very good facilities, being regularly inspected by officials who may revoke the owner's licence if things do not meet the required standards. Camping fees are normally based on so much per tent/caravan, so much per person and so much per car. Depending on the area and season this can total anywhere between 8-18 Euros a night for two people. Most maps and tourist guides show the locations of any camp sites in the vicinity.

Risks and Hazards

Insects

There are many species of insects (wasps, ants, mosquitos, scorpions, etc.) that are capable of delivering quite painful bites and stings. Insect repellent sprays and creams appear to work adequately during the daytime and I strongly recommend that you invest in one of the many brands that are available. The night time poses the major threat of mosquito bites and to combat this there are various deterrents that all seem effective to some degree.

Anti-mosquito candles give off fumes that are undetectable to humans but will keep your room free of mosquitos and other insects for as long as the candle lasts. This is the best solution if you happen to be camping without an electrical supply. Electrical devices that plug into a wall socket will give off repellent fumes throughout the night. Electrical devices which emit ultra sonic sound waves are very effective and are my preferred method of deterrent. All of these items can be purchased at most supermarkets and pharmacies. The

electrical devices should be bought here in Spain, not in Britain or other countries, as the electrical plugs will not fit Spanish sockets.

Snakes

There are numerous species of snake in this region, but only one, the Lataste's Viper, that is venomous. However, it is not particularly common and its bite should not prove fatal but common sense dictates that any snake bite should receive immediate medical attention.

Cattle

Andalucía is the birthplace of Spanish bullfighting and is, traditionally, the breeding centre of the finest bulls, which have been bred, through many generations, to fight and kill. Even the young, cute-looking bulls will attack you if you give them the chance. Some farms may have signs on a fence stating "Ganado Bravo" (fighting bulls) but even if there is no warning sign the simple rule is to keep out of any field or paddock where cattle are grazing. These animals can be dangerous and the pursuit of no bird, regardless of how rare it may be, is worth the risk.

Wild Animals

Generally there is no threat from wild animals but you may encounter stray or abandoned dogs out in the countryside. Usually these are quite wary of people, having probably been badly abused by humans in the past. However, there are occasional reports of people being bitten. Spain is a rabies-free country but, even so, should you be bitten by a dog, you should seek medical treatment as soon as possible.

Useful Words and Terms

The following is a list of Spanish words and terms that are either used in this book or could be useful on your travels:

Arroyo	Stream
Autopista	Motorway
Bahía	Bay
Cabo	Cape
Cambio de sentido	Turning place / change of direction
Camino	Road / track
Camino Particular	Private road

Privado	Private
Campo	Countryside
Carretera	Road / highway
Carretera cortado	Road closed
Cerro	Hill
Cortijo	Country house
Coto Privado de Caza	Private hunting rights
Desembocadura	Estuary
Desfiladero	Gorge
Desierto	Desert
Entrada Prohibida	No entry
Estuario	Estuary
Finca	Small farm
Ganado Bravo	Fighting bulls
Hostal	Small hotel
Incendio Prohibido	No fires to be lit
Laguna	Lagoon
Loma	Hillock
Mar	Sea
Marismas	Marshes
Mirador	Viewpoint
Montana / Montes	Mountain(s)
No Pasa(r)	Do not pass
Peligro / Peligroso	Danger / Dangerous
Pensión / Pensiónes	Guest house(s)
Playa	Beach
Puente	Bridge
Puerto	Mountain Pass / Port
Rambla	Stream
Río	River
Salinas	Salt pans / marshes
Serranía	Mountainous area
Sierra	Mountain
Venta	Wayside bar / restaurant
Vista	View
Zona Militar	Military land

The use of Bird names

Throughout the Site Descriptions and Bird Calendars in this book I have mainly referred to various birds by their more commonly used British names, sometimes for convenience and sometimes to save time and space. Hence, wherever you see Great Grey Shrike it does, in fact, refer to the Spanish species Southern Grey Shrike (*Larius*

meridionalis) and the Rufous Bush Chat refers to the Rufous-tailed Scrub Robin. These are names that I shall eventually becomed accustomed to using in the future, but I'm afraid I shall probably never get used to the idea of calling such a spectacularly beautiful bird as Purple Gallinule a "Purple Swamp-hen"!

Many of the birds with prefixes, such as "European" Bee-eater, "Eurasian" Wryneck, "Common" Kingfisher, "Northern" Gannet and "Western" Bonelli's Warbler, are referred to without the prefix. I hope that you will accept this as, certainly, the vast majority of the clients on my guided bird tours prefer me to use the more traditional names, as opposed to the official names.

For the purists, and to save any confusion, in the "Birds of the Costa del Sol" list I have used the names officially used by the British Ornithologist's Union. This and a "Rare Birds of the Region" list can be found towards the back of the book.

Author's Note

Whatever time of the year you come to Spain, there is always something that will be of interest to both the keen and casual birdwatcher, if you know where to look. This book can help you find the more elusive birds that you may not normally find without the help of some local knowledge and experience.

Having lived in Spain for over five years and being an avid birdwatcher myself, I have had the opportunity to visit literally hundreds of sites in pursuance of my hobby and my profession as a bird tour guide. Although any site may have something of interest to offer, the sites that I have selected for this book have been chosen because they are, in my opinion, the ones that are the most reliable to produce the widest range of bird species. Each of these locations has been visited by me on many occasions and during each season of the year.

Although a few of my selected sites have been mentioned in other books or guides, most are new and you will not find reference to them elsewhere. Some are large areas which can involve a whole day's visit to fully appreciate, others are small and can be adequately viewed in an hour or so. In all cases, I believe, my local knowledge of these sites enables me to give an accurate and detailed description.

Also in this book I have included a few very important sites such as Doñana. Although it is outside our general area, Doñana is worth visiting, as a full day and even a two day trip.

I hope you will find this book both interesting and helpful in your quest for birds and I would be pleased to receive any views that you may have, favourable or otherwise, as these could be very useful to any revised edition and will, of course, be acknowledged. Please write to:

J.R Butler, Apartado 537,
29680 Estepona
(Málaga),
Spain. (Tel. 637 922 688).

You can also log on to www.zest-leisure.com where you will find my web page giving details of my guided tours and information on the latest birding news from my particular local area from Marbella to Gibraltar. Good birdwatching!

Bee-eater *(Merops apiaster)*

Málaga Province

The Province of Malaga occupies much of the centre and most of the western Costa del Sol and is the principal tourist area in the region. Many important birding sites exist here, including the estuary of the Río Guadalhorce, Laguna de Fuente de Piedra and the Lagunas de Campillos. There is a very wide range of resident species to be found and seasonal visitors are always present. Passage migrants constantly pass through the area and there is significant offshore seabird movement throughout the year.

Our 22 sites offer you the opportunity to see most of the resident and migratory species that are common to the area.

General map of the area and sites of Málaga

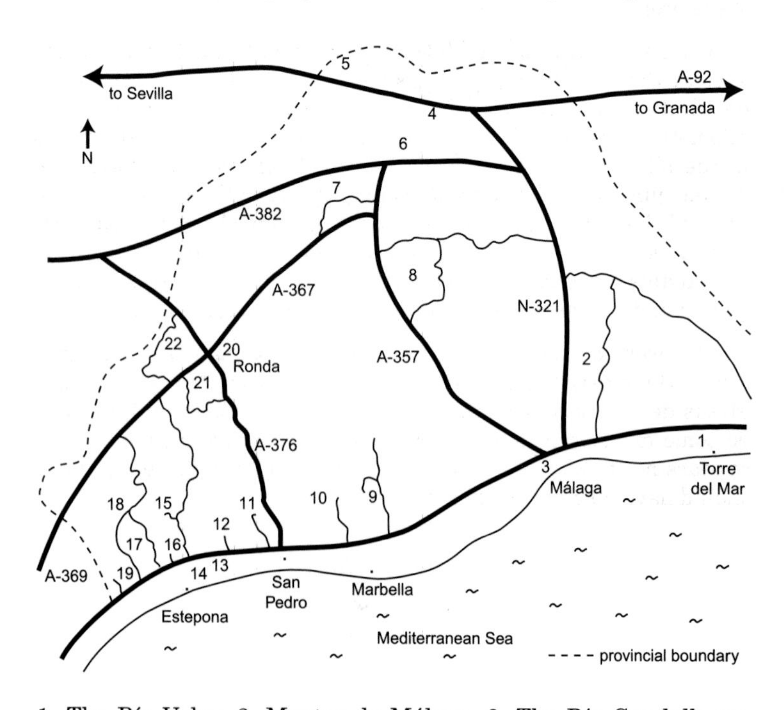

1. The Río Velez. 2. Montes de Málaga. 3. The Río Guadalhorce. 4. Laguna de Fuente de Piedra. 5. Laguna de Ratosa. 6. Lagunas de Campillos. 7. Tajo del Torró / Teba Gorge. 8. Álora / El Chorro / Ardales. 9. Refugio de Juanar. 10. Embalse de Concepción. 11.

Benahavís. 12. Embalse del Taraje. 13. The Río Guadalmansa. 14. The Río Padron. 15. Los Reales. 16. Arroyo Vaquero and Estepona Golf. 17. The Río Manilva, the Roman Baths and the Sierra de Utrera. 18. Casares, the Sierra Crestellina and the Río Genal. 19. Las Mesas de Chullera. 20. Ronda. 21. Serranía de Ronda. Alpandiere-Faraján-Júzcar-Cartajima. 22. Jimera de Libar-Benaoján-Montejaque.

Additional Information

In early 2001, construction work began on the stretch of the N-340 highway between Estepona and Torre Guadiaro to upgrade it from a single carriage road into a dual-carriageway. At the same time, construction work also commenced to extend the A-7 toll-road between these two towns a few kilometres inland. Work on both of these projects is due to be completed sometime in 2002.

Once the work on the N-340 is complete, the entrances to the sites at the Arroyo Vaquero, Casares, the Río Manilva, Las Mesas de Chullera and Sotogrande will change. Although the roadside kilometre markers will remain the same, some of the access points to the sites will either be from slip-roads or roundabouts at the various junctions. If you are travelling from the Estepona direction this will have no significant effect on reaching the site. If you are travelling from the Gibraltar direction you may, if no direct access is available, have to drive to the next roundabout (never more than a few hundred metres) and return back to the access point.

The work on the A-7 toll-road is currently under way and cuts across the sites at the Arroyo Vaquero, the Río Manilva and Las Mesas de Chullera. During the construction of the road there will be some disruption to small areas of each of these sites but there appears not to be any significant effect on the birdlife so far and it should have no adverse effect in the future.

The Río Velez

Although I consider this to be one of the best all-round birding sites on the coast, I do have some reservations about recommending it. The estuary of the river is directly beside a naturist beach and close to a naturist campsite. Although the genuine naturist is no problem whatsoever, the area obviously attracts a few sordid characters and is also becoming notorious as a gay pick-up spot. However, the area concerned is only a small part of a sizeable site and can be avoided.

Both my wife and I have visited the site on dozens of occasions without experiencing any problems, apart from the odd exhibitionist or two who may have thought we had brought our binoculars along to look at them. We were, in fact, looking for something far more interesting such as herons and egrets.

The Río Velez is situated approximately 35 kms east of Málaga, near the town of Torre del Mar. The estuary of the river is surrounded by extensive reedbeds and marshes and attracts a considerable range of waders and other waterbirds throughout the year. On both banks of the river and further upstream there are large expanses of agricultural and open land, with very little development.

When the river is not in flow, the estuary becomes a large lagoon and the remainder of the river dries out and becomes walkable, or driveable, for about 4 kms. A good number of rarities have been recorded here, mainly waders, but this site is probably the best place to find both Avadavats and Black-rumped Waxbills in considerable numbers.

Access

Travelling from the Málaga direction, take the N-340 highway toward Motril and at the exit numbered km 265 turn off and follow the road down to the coast. At the road junction turn left and proceed toward Torre del Mar. Exactly at km 269 there is a crossroads, beside an ancient watch-tower. Turn right here and continue for about 300 metres until you reach an unsurfaced road on the left. Follow this road to the river and then turn right. This will lead you to a parking area on the beach, directly beside the estuary/lagoon.

Travelling from further east you pass through Torre del Mar and after crossing over the Río Velez you turn left at km 269.

The west bank of the river is densely covered by reeds and giant canes which normally hold resident Moorhens, Coots, Little Grebes, Grey Herons and ducks, including Mallards, Shovelers and Red-crested Pochards. In the summer these are normally joined by Squacco, Purple and Night herons, Little Bitterns and Great Crested Grebes.

The central island is marshy and attracts waders, terns and gulls at any time, although the winter and passage periods produce both the maximum numbers and species. To the east of the estuary/lagoon there are more marsh areas and these are favoured by Cattle and Little Egrets, warblers, wagtails and finches.

Further up river, on the western side, there are breaks in the reeds where you can gain access to the river. These areas are predominantly marshy and can generally be relied upon for a good selection of waders, herons and egrets. Greater Flamingos can appear at any time and Spoonbills are fairly common in the winter. If the river is not in flow you can walk, or drive, up to the bridge and beyond.

Most of the surrounding land is agricultural and the main crops are artichokes, tomatoes, cabbages, sweet corn and sugar-cane. The crops in the fields are often rotated and the birds will follow their favourite crops. The Avadavats seem to prefer the artichokes and are more often found in fields where these are growing. The Black-rumped Waxbills, on the other hand, prefer the taller sweet corn and sugar-canes and often flocks of up to 30 birds can be found. Both Rose-ringed and Monk Parakeets inhabit the area and I have also spotted two species of Lovebirds which are obviously escapes, or stem from escaped stock.

Further upstream, beyond the bridge, the riverbed is usually dry (April to October) and can be followed right up to the next bridge and beyond. Below and to the side of the motorway bridge there is an area of water reasonably well vegetated with reeds, tamarisk and oleander that is well worth investigating. This is a good spot for Little-ringed Plovers, Cetti's Warblers, Crested Larks, Hoopoes, Redstarts, Great Grey Shrikes, Woodchat Shrikes, Spotted Flycatchers, Whinchats and Black-eared Wheatears.

Continuing even further upriver you will reach a small stream and a series of small pools that usually hold water throughout the year. This area can also provide good views of waxbills, finches and warblers as they come to the pools to drink and bathe. Night Herons are fairly common here and are often active during the day.

Back at the estuary/lagoon, the east bank should also be explored, either by crossing the riverbed upstream or by walking along the beach. The marshes and reeds here are not so dense and better views can be had of the various warbler species, which have included Reed, Great Reed, Savi's, Sedge, Fan-tailed, Sardinian, Melodious, Willow and Cetti's, along with Iberian Chiffchaffs and Blackcaps.

From the beach you can look out to sea where there are always passing gulls, terns, shearwaters and other seabirds, such as Razorbills and Gannets. Oystercatchers are fairly common in the winter and during passage periods and an occasional Great Skua may appear.

The area is not rich with raptors but there are usually resident Kestrels and Marsh Harriers to be found hunting over the marshes. These can be joined in the summer by Lesser Kestrels and by both Short-toed and Booted Eagles. Ospreys are also a probability in the winter.

When to Visit

The site is of immense interest throughout the year as it always produces a wide variety of species. The breeding season is a good time to visit as the area is drier and you can reach most of the marsh areas on foot. Also the riverbed is driveable for about 4 kms. The winter and passage periods produce the maximum numbers of waders, although a few, such as Little Stint, Curlew Sandpiper, Dunlin and some plovers, may remain all year.

The height of summer is not a good time to visit as it can become unbearably hot in the riverbed and the area around the lagoon becomes very noisy with hordes of beach-goers and campers.

Both early morning and evening visits, although coinciding with peak bird activity times, can be affected by sunshine, either directly, or by reflection off the water. The prime time to visit to enjoy the best light conditions is between 11 in the morning and 4 in the afternoon.

General Information

Although this site is not ideal for disabled or wheelchair birders, much of it can be seen from various roads, tracks or other vantage points. If the riverbed is driveable then you can see most of the area from the car, which serves as an excellent bird hide.

General map of the Río Velez site

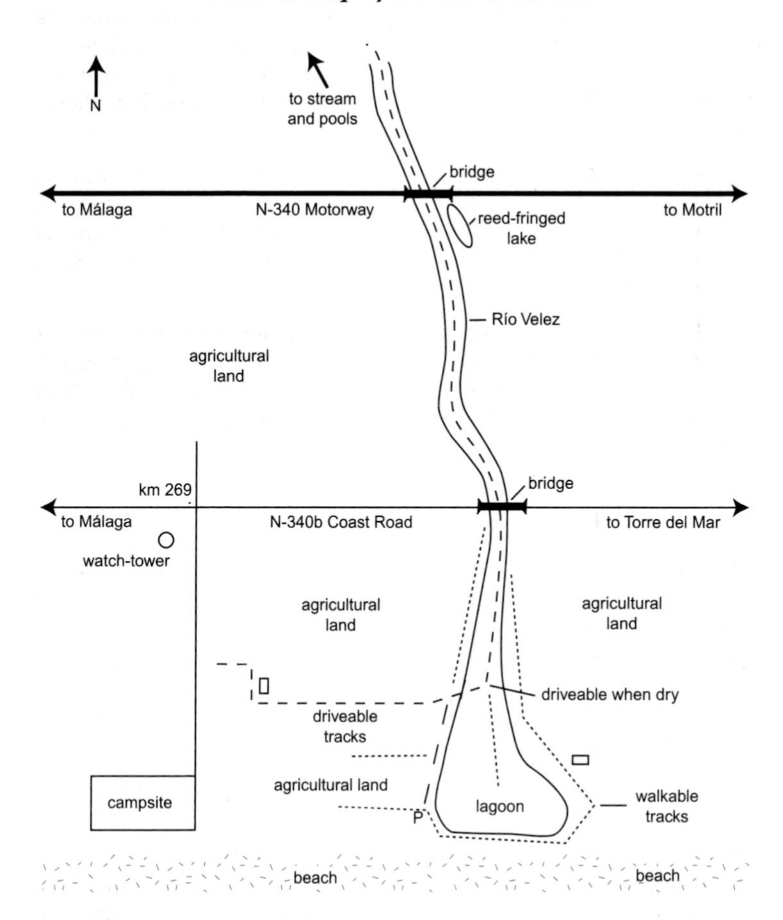

Bird Calendar

Resident

Little Grebe, Mediterranean Shearwater, Grey Heron, Cattle Egret, Little Egret, Mallard, Shoveler, Red-crested Pochard, Marsh Harrier, Kestrel, Red-legged Partridge, Water Rail, Moorhen, Coot, Stone Curlew, Little-ringed Plover, Kentish Plover, Dunlin, Curlew Sandpiper, Little Stint, Redshank, Common Sandpiper, Audouin's Gull, Black-Headed Gull, Yellow-legged Gull, Sandwich Tern, Rock Dove, Wood Pigeon, Collared Dove, Rose-ringed Parakeet, Monk

Parakeet, Little Owl, Barn Owl, Kingfisher, Hoopoe, Great Spotted Woodpecker, Woodlark, Crested Lark, White Wagtail, Grey Wagtail, Robin, Stonechat, Blackbird, Cetti's Warbler, Fan-tailed Warbler, Sardinian Warbler, Dartford Warbler, Long-tailed Tit, Great Tit, Blue Tit, Wren, Great Grey Shrike, Jay, Jackdaw, Spotless Starling, Spanish Sparrow, House Sparrow, Black-rumped Waxbill, Avadavat, Chaffinch, Serin, Linnet, Goldfinch, Greenfinch, Corn Bunting, Cirl Bunting.

Avadavit *(Amandava amandava)*

Summer / Breeding

Little Bittern, Squacco Heron, Night Heron, Purple Heron, Short-toed Eagle, Booted Eagle, Lesser Kestrel, Baillon's Crake, Collared Pratincole, Black-winged Stilt, Common Tern, Little Tern, Whiskered Tern, Turtle Dove, Cuckoo, Scops Owl, Red-necked Nightjar, Common Swift, Pallid Swift, Bee-eater, Sand Martin, House Martin, Red-rumped Swallow, Barn Swallow, Tawny Pipit, Yellow Wagtail, Nightingale, Rufous Bush Chat, Redstart, Black-eared Wheatear, Reed Warbler, Great Reed Warbler, Olivaceous Warbler, Melodious Warbler, Spotted Flycatcher, Woodchat Shrike, Golden Oriole, Ortolan Bunting.

Winter

Great Crested Grebe, Black-necked Grebe, Gannet, Cormorant, Spoonbill, White Stork, Shelduck, Gadwall, Wigeon, Teal, Osprey, Oystercatcher, Avocet, Ringed Plover, Grey Plover, Sanderling,

Ruff, Snipe, Black-tailed Godwit, Bar-tailed Godwit, Whimbrel, Greenshank, Green Sandpiper, Turnstone, Great Skua, Little Gull, Mediterranean Gull, Lesser Black-backed Gull, Razorbill, Crag Martin, Meadow Pipit, Bluethroat, Black Redstart, Song Thrush, Blackcap, Iberian Chiffchaff, Penduline Tit, Siskin, Hawfinch, Reed Bunting.

Passage Migrants

Greater Flamingo, Greylag Goose, Golden Plover, Red Knot, Curlew, Spotted Redshank, Marsh Sandpiper, Wood Sandpiper, Kittiwake, Caspian Tern, Great Spotted Cuckoo, Tree Pipit, Whinchat, Northern Wheatear, Savi's Warbler, Sedge Warbler, Willow Warbler, Pied Flycatcher.

Montes de Málaga

The Montes de Malaga is a vast mountainous region to the north and east of the city of Málaga. This site description deals with the area known as Parque Natural Montes de Málaga which rises to a maximum height of 1,031 metres above sea-level and covers an area of 4,900 hectares.

The park is densely vegetated with a wide range of trees, shrubs and flowers. Typical tree species include Monterey pine, stone pine, poplar, ash, willow, strawberry tree, carob, cork-oak, Holm oak, cypresses and olives. The shrubs, bushes and scrub undergrowth include asparagus, daphne, gum cistus, genista, lavender, yellow retama, oleander, Spanish broom, thorny broom, kermes oak, dwarf fan-palm and gorse.

The whole park is a haven for wildlife and apart from the impressive bird list there are wild boars, foxes, badgers, rabbits, squirrels, genets, polecats, stone martens, bats, snakes, frogs, toads, salamanders and lizards, of which the ocelated lizard and the chameleon are the most spectacular.

Resident bird species such as Azure-winged Magpie, Eagle Owl, Goshawk, Short-toed Treecreeper, Raven, Red-billed Chough, Crested Tit and a whole range of finches, tits and warblers are joined by seasonal visitors which include Booted and Short-toed Eagles, Egyptian Vultures, Golden Orioles, Alpine Swifts, Woodchat Shrikes, Red-necked Nightjars and Siskins.

Inside the park there are many kilometres of dirt roads and tracks that can be driven or walked but there are limited entry points for vehicles. The roads are mostly in good condition and parking anywhere within the park boundaries is never a problem.

Numerous recreation areas (*Areas Recreativas*) have been created with bench seats and tables, water supplies and barbecues that attract day trippers from the city (mainly at weekends) but these and the resulting noise can easily be avoided. Numerous walking trails (*Senderos*) have been created and you will find notice boards advertising these throughout the site. Most points of interest within the park are fairly well signposted and the four main driveable roads have been colour coded.

Access

I know of only four vehicle entry points into the park and these are all from the C-345 which is the old Madrid-Málaga road. From Málaga and the western coastal areas your best route to the site is via the N-340 and then taking the Sevilla-Granada road (N-321) at junction 241. Turn off here at Casabermeja at km 148 and follow the signs for Colmenar. As you approach Colmenar you come to a junction where you turn right where signed for Málaga.

From east of Málaga you can take either the same route from the N340, ie. the N-321 to Sevilla/Granada, or you can turn off the N-340 at km 272 (Velez Málaga) and then follow the new Viñuela-Casabermeja road (A-356) and then turn off where signed for Colmenar. Do not enter the town but follow the signs for Málaga.

Travelling from further inland, ie. Antequera, Campillos, Sevilla, Cordoba, etc., you should approach via the A-92/N-321 and leave at the Casabermeja exit and then continue as per the directions from Málaga.

All three of these routes should bring you to the same location, the junction to the south of Colmenar, where the C-345 leads to Málaga. As stated, this is the old Madrid road and the roadside kilometre markers start at km 532. The distance from Colmenar to the main entry point into the park at Fuente de la Reina is 14 kms, but I will give all distances in accordance with the kilometre markers.

Some 300 metres beyond km 544, there is a small turning to the right with a signpost directing you to a recreation area, a campsite and an ethnological museum at Torrijos. The road is surfaced and leads downhill to a large parking area near the museum. There is a notice board here showing the route of a nature walk (*Sendero de Torrijos*) that leads into the forest.

The length of the walk is only 1.8 kms and is fairly easy going. However, many other little trails invite inspection so that you could find yourself spending hours in this area chasing after birds. Crossbills, Crested Tits, Short-toed Treecreepers, Golden Orioles and a selection of finches are normally to be found here. The car-park and the area around the museum (a preserved 200-year-old farmhouse) can also provide good birdwatching.

Map of the Parque Natural Montes de Málaga

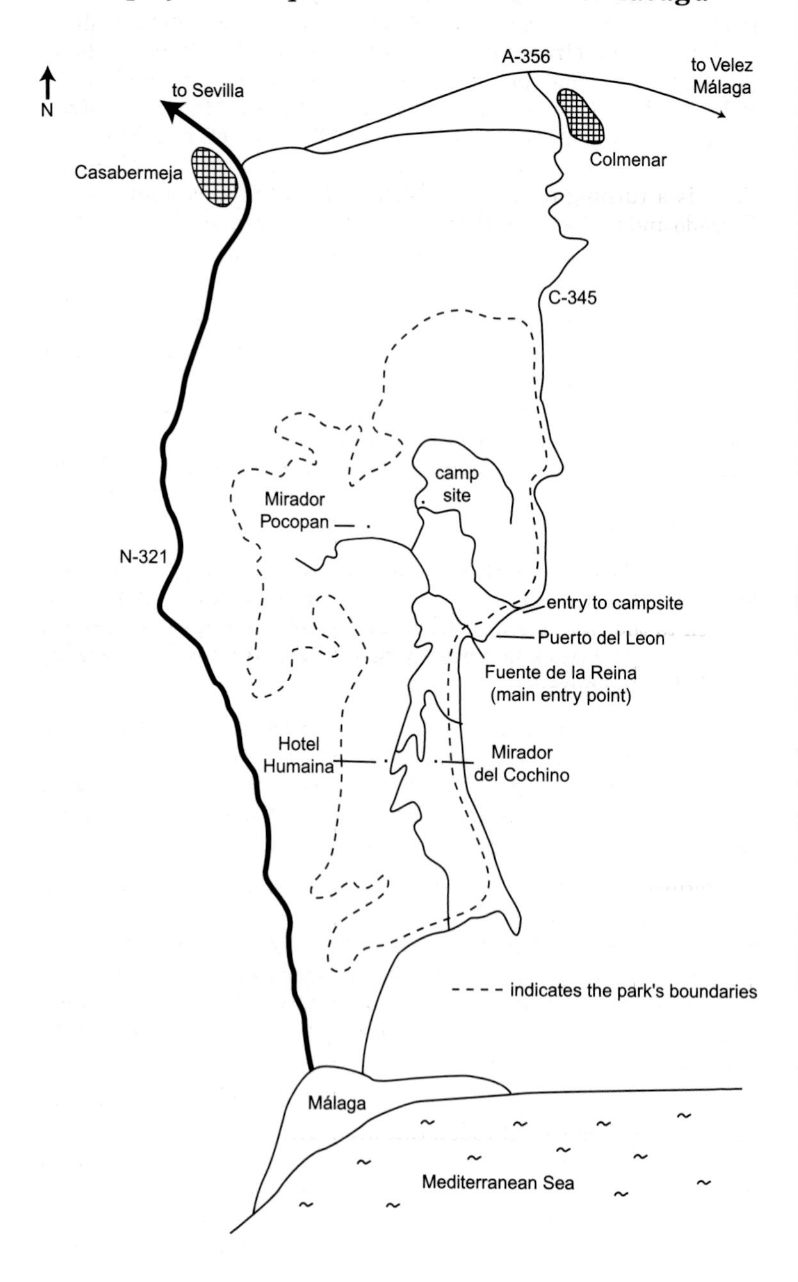

Returning to the main road, turn right and at km 545 you reach Puerto del Leon (the Lion's Pass) which is 900 metres above sea-level. 500 metres further on, you come to Fuente de la Reina (the Queen's Spring) and here, beside a bar, there is a turn-off to the right which is the main entry point into the park. After 100 metres, there is a fork in the road where you keep to the left and follow the unsurfaced track and continue for a further 1.5 kms. At this point, there is a turning to the left which leads to the area known as El Cerrado and to the Hotel Humaina. I personally prefer to go straight ahead at this point, saving the El Cerrado site until later.

After a further 500 metres you come to a wide open space with a circular structure in the middle. It is unmissable as it has a tree growing out of it. Park beside the trees on the left some 15 metres before the structure and you will see a path sloping downhill. This is the start of another forest walk (*Sendero de Cerrado*) which I have taken and found to be very productive for woodland birds that have included Short-toed Treecreeper, Wryneck, Crested Tit, Nuthatch, Golden Oriole, Great Spotted Woodpecker, Jay, Firecrest, Blackcap and Melodious, Olivaceous and Bonelli's Warblers.

The left-hand track directly ahead of your parking place leads to an educational centre, but just before the gates of this there is a track to the right signposted to the mirador "Pocopán" which is 2 kms away. The track is perfectly driveable and there is a parking area below the mirador.

Unfortunately you are now faced with a walk of 300 metres up a very steep hill to actually reach the look-out point. However, should you undertake the trek you will be rewarded with spectacular views of Málaga and the surrounding countryside. This is also an excellent vantage point to watch for vultures, eagles and other birds of prey.

Returning from the mirador, drive past the circular structure and return to the junction that leads to the Hotel Humaina. The hotel is a further 2.3 kms from this point and you can stop anywhere to scan the trees and open ground. The hotel is situated in a valley surrounded on three sides by wooded hillsides but to the south-east there is a large hill which is almost treeless, covered instead by dense shrubs, gorse and scrub.

A nature walk (*Sendero de El Cerrado*) begins from just before the hotel and leads up through this area. The walk is circular and is nearly 2.5 kms in length and can be quite strenuous going in places. However, this particular site is a treasure trove for warblers and even walking only part of the route can produce some very good species. I have, on my visits here, recorded Melodious, Olivaceous, Sardinian,

Subalpine, Willow, Cetti's, Dartford and Fan-tailed Warblers, along with Blackcaps and Iberian Chiffchaffs and, on my latest visit in June 2001, I saw a pair of exceedingly rare Marmora's Warblers that have been reported to the Iberian Rarities Committee.

Also in this area there are Rock Buntings, Blue Rock Thrushes, Red-legged Partridges, Black Redstarts, Great Grey Shrikes and summer visitors that include Woodchat Shrikes, Nightingales, Red-necked Nightjars, Black-eared Wheatears and Bee-eaters.

At the top of the hill the walk reaches the Mirador del Cochino where bench seating makes this a pleasant place to sit and watch the warblers and any other birdlife, including passing Ravens, Jackdaws, Red-billed Choughs and birds of prey. It is also possible to drive to the mirador following a road that leads up from beside the recreation area (*Area Recreativa de El Cerrado*) which is 150 metres above the hotel. This road will eventually lead you out of the park onto the C-345 at km 546.8. This is the third entry/exit point that I know of.

The El Cerrado recreation area that is beside the hotel is also a comfortable place to sit and watch birds when quiet. Finches, warblers, tits, larks, chats, woodpeckers and a whole host of other birds can be seen here. In the very centre of the picnic area there is a single tall eucalyptus tree where Crossbills are often seen feeding. It would appear that the local birds have developed a taste for the seeds of this tree.

Proceeding past the hotel, the road runs for 10 kms, gradually losing altitude as you approach Málaga and eventually joins the C-345 at km 552.9, directly opposite two ventas, the Bodega El Mijeno and the Restaurant El Boticario. This is the fourth and final entry/exit point for the park.

Due to the vast size of the park, you may consider staying and enjoying two, or even more days here. If so, I can strongly recommend the Hotel Humaina. It is set in a very secluded position right in the centre of the park where silence is virtually guaranteed. Not only does it offer excellent birdwatching opportunities from each of the rooms and from the terrace but wild boars, foxes and other nocturnal animals are present each night as the hotel staff put out kitchen scraps near the car parking area to attract them so that the guests may see these creatures at close quarters. The hotel is a three star establishment and the prices in the low season (1st October to 30th June) are very reasonable. The manager and receptionist speak English and all the staff are very friendly.

When to Visit

Although the park is of interest at any time, the maximum number of bird species can be seen in the spring and summer. However, at this time of the year it is best not to visit on a weekend or on a national or local holiday as literally thousands of daytrippers come here for a day in the country. The noise at such times can be horrendous and good birdwatching is impossible.

Being a mountainous region, the temperature is generally a few degrees cooler than on the coast and suitable clothing should be brought with you, especially for the evenings. In the valleys, the temperatures can get very oppressive from May until September when there is very little air movement.

General Information

Due to the very nature of this mountainous site, all of the forest walks are totally unsuitable for wheelchair users and for people with other mobility problems. However, the main tracks leading through the site, although somewhat bumpy in places, do offer the chance to get close to the trees and the scrub areas. Access to the mirador Pocopán is impossible but the Mirador del Cochino can be reached by car and the surrounding area is reasonably level.

The Hotel Humaina can be contacted on telephone number (0034) 952 641025 or you can log-on to their website at www.hotelhumaina.es

Bird Calendar

Resident

Griffon Vulture, Sparrowhawk, Goshawk, Buzzard, Bonelli's Eagle, Peregrine, Kestrel, Red-legged Partridge, Rock Dove, Wood Pigeon, Collared Dove, Little Owl, Eagle Owl, Tawny Owl, Barn Owl, Green Woodpecker, Great Spotted Woodpecker, Woodlark, Crested Lark, Thekla Lark, Grey Wagtail, Robin, Stonechat, Black Redstart, Black Wheatear, Blue Rock Thrush, Blackbird, Mistle Thrush, Cetti's Warbler, Fan-tailed Warbler, Sardinian Warbler, Dartford Warbler, Firecrest, Long-tailed Tit, Crested Tit, Coal Tit, Great Tit, Blue Tit, Nuthatch, Short-toed Treecreeper, Wren, Great Grey Shrike, Jay, Azure-winged Magpie, Red-billed Chough, Jackdaw, Raven, Spotless Starling, Rock Sparrow, House Sparrow, Tree Sparrow, Chaffinch, Serin, Linnet, Goldfinch, Greenfinch, Crossbill, Corn Bunting, Rock

Bunting, Cirl Bunting.

Summer / Breeding

Black Kite, Short-toed Eagle, Egyptian Vulture, Booted Eagle, Turtle Dove, Great Spotted Cuckoo, Scops Owl, Red-necked Nightjar, Alpine Swift, Common Swift, Pallid Swift. Hoopoe, Bee-eater, Crag Martin, House Martin, Red-rumped Swallow, Barn Swallow, Nightingale, Redstart, Black-eared Wheatear, Olivaceous Warbler, Melodious Warbler, Subalpine Warbler, Bonelli's Warbler, Spotted Flycatcher, Woodchat Shrike, Golden Oriole, Ortolan Bunting.

Winter

Wryneck, Meadow Pipit, White Wagtail, Redwing, Song Thrush, Iberian Chiffchaff, Siskin.

Winter

Wryneck, Meadow Pipit, White Wagtail, Redwing, Song Thrush, Iberian Chiffchaff, Siskin.

Passage Migrants

Montagu's Harrier, Honey Buzzard, Whinchat, Northern Wheatear, Willow Warbler, Pied Flycatcher.

Rarity

Marmora's Warbler. A pair in the open scrub area between the Hotel Humaina and the Mirador del Cochina. 17th June 2001

Short-toed Treecreeper *(Certia brachydactyla)*

Paraje Natural del Río Guadalhorce

The estuaries of the Río Guadalhorce are situated just to the southwest of the city of Málaga. The site is currently undergoing major changes and access to the site is not easy due to extensive construction work which is dividing and diverting the course of the river. The site's main attraction is the Paraje Natural which measures some 67 hectares. Within its boundaries are lakes, ponds and marshes. The remainder of the terrain is mainly flat, open scrubland surrounded by water. Recent developments to minimize the risk of the area flooding has resulted in the river being divided into two purpose-built canals which now flow on either side of the site. With the sea as the boundary at the south-eastern end, the site is now virtually an island.

The major wet areas within the site form part of the park and are, in part, fenced off from the public, although good views of most of the lakes and marshes can be had from the official paths or from small hillocks. There are dense growths of tamarisk trees and reeds surrounding these areas. The unprotected area is mainly rough, open scrubland. with scattered trees and shrubs, which supports a good selection of finches, larks, chats and scrub warblers. At the top (north-western) end of the site, where the river has been divided, there are reedbeds, mudflats and marshes where gulls, waders, storks, herons and egrets congregate. The beach is a favourite spot for large flocks of gulls to rest and these often include Lesser Black-backed, Audouin's and Mediterranean gulls. In recent years such rarities as Ring-billed, Franklin's and Laughing gulls have been recorded at this site. The eucalyptus trees, both within the site and outside the boundaries, are the nesting sites of numerous Monk Parakeet colonies.

Apart from gulls and seabirds, other rarities are always a distinct possibility here and Sacred Ibis, Ruddy Shelduck, Black-headed Bunting, Richard's Pipit and Terek Sandpiper have all been recorded in the last 10 years.

Access

At the time of writing, the area surrounding the site is in the final stages of a major re-development. As the open and scrub land, in which the Paraje Natural is situated, has been turned into an island, there are only two current points of entry. The first of these is from the beach and can only be reached by walking along the sand and

only when the two canals of the river cease to flow to the sea.

The second entry point is what appears to be destined as the official entry point and is in the south-western corner of the site. Both points of entry can be reached from the same parking area. It is possible that a third entry point may be opened up once the construction work is complete and this is marked on the map.

Travelling from Málaga or further east on the main N-340 highway, you reach the Río Guadalhorce at km 234. Immediately after crossing over the river you take the first exit signed for San Julián and Guadalmar. At the roundabout at the bottom of the slip-road, pass under the bridge and take the first exit, which leads toward a residential area. After 100 metres, you reach a smaller roundabout where you should turn left (3rd exit). After about 200 metres, the surfaced road bears right but you continue straight ahead along the unsurfaced road. After 700 metres the road again becomes surfaced and leads directly to the beach. As you turn sharply right at the sea front there is a sandy slope that leads to a parking area on the beach.

Travelling from the west, you leave the N-340 where it is signed for San Julián and Guadalmar, just beyond km 232. At the bottom of the slip-road take the first turning right which leads to the small roundabout referred to in the previous directions. Proceed as described. As you drive along the unsurfaced road, you come to a junction on the right where the road again becomes surfaced. The eucalyptus trees at this junction hold several large communal nests of the resident Monk Parakeets, which can always be seen or heard in the trees or flying around the area.

From the parking area, cross over the drainage ditch and climb up a bank. From here most of the site is visible to you on the other side of the river/canal. A causeway some 100 metres to the left offers the easiest access to the area, although you may prefer to walk 200 metres along the beach and enter through a gate. There are many different routes that will take you around the area but I will describe my favourite route as I believe it offers the best chance of seeing the maximum number of birds.

Crossing the causeway, follow the main track which leads directly to a notice board with information and a map of the Paraje Natural. The route around the park is marked in yellow (*ruta amarilla*). At this point, turn left and follow the track which leads alongside the lakes and ponds, the banks of which are heavily vegetated with reeds and tamarisk trees. Greater Flamingos, Spoonbills, herons, egrets, storks, grebes, ducks and waders are usually abundant in the winter

and even in the summer there may still be small numbers of many species present. The surrounding trees and reeds hold finches, tits and warblers, which have included both Melodious and Olivaceous in the spring/summer.

General map of the Río Guadalhorce site

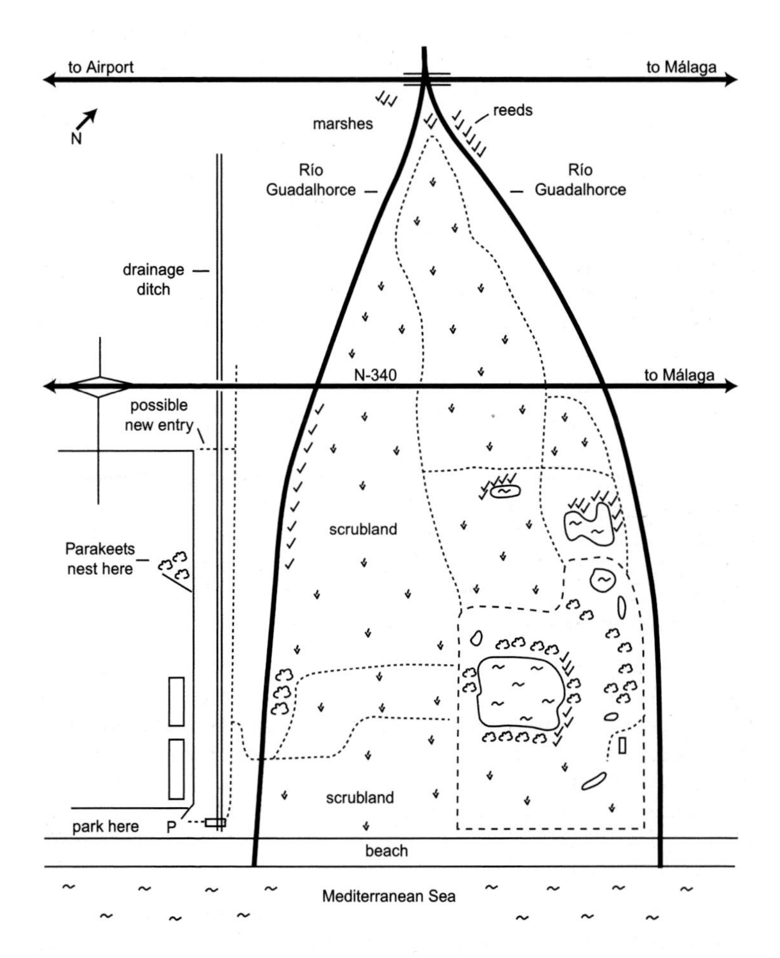

Following the route around the top end of the park, the track leads to another series of smaller ponds. A high earth mound overlooks these and is a good vantage point from which to scan the reeds, trees and water from an elevated position. Until recently a bird hide was situated here but it was burnt down in early 2001. Hopefully this may be replaced in the near future. This particular area has always appeared to be the best spot for seeing White-headed Ducks and grebes, which are normally present throughout the year. Black-winged Stilts and Little Bitterns regularly breed here and, although elusive, Night Herons can also be found amongst the reeds.

Although the yellow route now leads in front of the ponds toward the second canal of the river and back to the beach, there is still a lot more of this site to see. I prefer to follow the track to the left of the earth mound which leads north-westward toward the motorway. About 100 metres along there is another reed-filled lake on the left which is very secluded. This spot also attracts breeding Little Bitterns and Squacco Herons, along with passing Purple Herons.

The track continues through open scrubland where Hoopoes, Bee-eaters, Black Redstarts, larks, pipits and warblers can usually be seen at the appropriate times of the year. The track now passes under the motorway bridge, where Kestrels, Rock Doves, swallows and martins nest, and continues to the end of the site where the river has been divided near to the second motorway bridge. Here there are sizeable reedbeds with mud flats and marsh areas which attract a wide range of species. Flocks of mixed gulls regularly gather on the mud flats and Flamingos, Spoonbills, White Storks, Little Egrets, Grey Herons, Collared Pratincoles and a wide range of ducks and waders can be found at this location. Both Whiskered and Black Terns may be present in the summer and during passage periods. Resident Marsh Harriers are often seen quartering the reedbeds and these are occasionally joined by Hen Harriers in the winter and Montagu's Harriers as they pass through on migration. I have also recorded Tawny Pipit, Redstart, Great Grey Shrike, Woodchat Shrike, Black-eared Wheatear, Nightingale, Whinchat, Reed Warbler, Great Reed Warbler and Dartford Warbler in this area.

On the return trip, pass under the bridge and then climb the bank on the left. This leads to an elevated track which gives good views of the canal and scrubland to the left and an overall view of the open land on the right. Eventually you arrive back at the opposite side of the series of ponds described earlier and after passing these, you rejoin the yellow route which leads to the beach at the south-eastern corner of the park. At one point the track passes an old farm and a walk around this area reveals more lakes, ponds and marshes among the tamarisk trees.

Once you have reached the beach you should look for resting flocks of gulls on the sand. Regular species that can often be found amongst the common Yellow-legged Gulls include Audouin's, Mediterranean, Lesser Black-backed, Black-headed and Little Gulls. Although relatively scarce, I have recorded a pair of Slender-billed Gulls on the beach. Just offshore, especially in the winter, you may see Razorbills, Black-necked Grebes, Red-breasted Mergansers and sea-ducks. Further out to sea there is constant movement of Gannets, shearwaters and skuas. Sandwich Terns can be seen passing along the shore at any time of the year and in the summer and during passage periods you may catch sight of Common, Little and Gull-billed Terns. Although fairly scarce in this area, the Caspian Tern is recorded here with some regularity.

Rather than returning to the parking area via the beach, which can be quite hard going, you can re-enter the park and return back across the causeway. This gives you another chance to scan the scrubland for the more elusive "little brown jobs". Common species to be found in this habitat include Sardinian, Dartford and Fan-tailed Warblers, Corn Buntings, Crested Larks, Serins, Linnets, Hoopoes, Iberian Chiffchaffs, Stonechats, Whinchats and various other finches, pipits and larks.

Various birds of prey can be seen at any point around the site with Kestrel being the most obvious. You may also find Lesser Kestrels, Peregrines, Buzzards, Sparrowhawks, Marsh Harriers, Hen Harriers, Montagu's Harriers, Ospreys and both Booted and Short-toed Eagles.

When to Visit

This site is of great interest at any time of the year and any visit here should produce a good bird list. The winter always provides a wide range of waders, ducks and gulls whilst the breeding season produces the more colourful exotics such as Little Bittern, Squacco Heron, Woodchat Shrike, Black-eared Wheatear and Bee-eater.

Although three years of construction work has gone into the flood prevention scheme that is taking place here, the work is designed primarily to avoid flooding in the nearby residential and industrial areas, and the site itself remains fairly unprotected, especially from the canal nearest the parking area. After particularly heavy periods of rain, this canal may flow over into the site. There is also the danger of extremely high tides breaking over the beach and saturating the lower end of the park and the (at present) rather flimsy crossing over the drainage ditch and the causeway over the canal could be

washed away by the sheer amount of water that flows to the sea following torrential winter rainstorms.

General Information

The site is extremely low-lying with raised banks on both sides. This creates a basin effect where the wind seems to always blow overhead but never at ground level. It can, therefore, become oppressively hot here in the summer months and there are very few shaded spots. I strongly recommend that you carry a good supply of liquids with you if you are visiting at this time of year.

As good as this site is, unfortunately it could not be classed as wheelchair accessible. The beach entry point means a 200 metre trip along loose sand, whilst the entry point over the drainage ditch has a steep slope to negotiate and the causeway has a chain stretched across it to prevent vehicles from entering the site. Although the site is fairly level, the tracks around the area are often very narrow and bumpy and many of the best views can only be obtained by climbing up small hillocks.

Bird Calendar

Resident

Little Grebe, Black-necked Grebe, Cattle Egret, Little Egret, Grey Heron, White Stork, Greater Flamingo, Mallard, Gadwall, Shoveler, Red-crested Pochard, Pochard, White-headed Duck, Marsh Harrier, Sparrowhawk, Buzzard, Peregrine, Kestrel, Lesser Kestrel, Water Rail, Moorhen, Common Coot, Little-ringed Plover, Kentish Plover, Redshank, Common Sandpiper, Audouin's Gull, Black-headed Gull, Mediterranean Gull, Yellow-legged Gull, Sandwich Tern, Rock Dove, Wood Pigeon, Collared Dove, Ring-necked Parakeet, Monk Parakeet, Little Owl, Barn Owl, Kingfisher, Hoopoe, Woodlark, Skylark, Crested Lark, White Wagtail, Grey Wagtail, Robin, Stonechat, Blackbird, Cetti's Warbler, Fan-tailed Warbler, Blackcap, Sardinian Warbler, Dartford Warbler, Long-tailed Tit, Great Tit, Blue Tit, Short-toed Treecreeper, Wren, Great Grey Shrike, Jay, Jackdaw, Spotless Starling, Spanish Sparrow, House Sparrow, Tree Sparrow, Chaffinch, Serin, Linnet, Greenfinch, Goldfinch, Corn Bunting, Cirl Bunting.

Summer / Breeding

Little Bittern, Squacco Heron, Night Heron, Purple Heron, Short-toed Eagle, Booted Eagle, Hobby, Black-winged Stilt, Slender-billed Gull, Common Tern, Little Tern, Black Tern, Whiskered Tern, Turtle Dove, Cuckoo, Common Swift, Pallid Swift, Bee-eater, Sand Martin, House Martin, Barn Swallow, Red-rumped Swallow, Tawny Pipit, Yellow Wagtail, Nightingale, Rufous Bush Chat, Redstart, Black-eared Wheatear, Reed Warbler, Great Reed Warbler, Olivaceous Warbler, Melodious Warbler, Spotted Flycatcher, Woodchat Shrike, Ortolan Bunting.

Collared Pratincole *(Glareola pratincole)*

Winter

Great Crested Grebe, Cormorant, Spoonbill, Shelduck, Wigeon, Teal, Pintail, Marbled Duck, Tufted Duck, Ferruginous Duck, Common Scoter, Red-breasted Merganser, Osprey, Hen Harrier, Merlin, Oystercatcher, Avocet, Ringed Plover, Grey Plover, Golden Plover,

Lapwing, Dunlin, Curlew Sandpiper, Red Knot, Sanderling, Little Stint, Ruff, Common Snipe, Black-tailed Godwit, Bar-tailed Godwit, Whimbrel, Spotted Redshank, Greenshank, Green Sandpiper, Turnstone, Great Skua, Arctic Skua, Little Gull, Lesser Blackbacked Gull, Kittiwake, Razorbill, Wryneck, Meadow Pipit, Water Pipit, Bluethroat, Black Redstart, Song Thrush, Iberian Chiffchaff, Penduline Tit, Reed Bunting.

Passage Migrants

Cory's Shearwater, Mediterranean Shearwater, Gannet, Black Stork, Greylag Goose, Garganey, Black Kite, Montagu's Harrier, Honey Buzzard, Collared Pratincole, Curlew, Wood Sandpiper, Caspian Tern, Gull-billed Tern, Roller, Tree Pipit, Whinchat, Northern Wheatear, Sedge Warbler, Willow Warbler, Pied Flycatcher.

Rarities

There have been many rarities recorded at this site in the last 20 years. You will find reference to these in the rare birds section at the back of the book.

Laguna de Fuente de Piedra

The Laguna de Fuente de Piedra is a vast saline lake almost 7 kms in length and 2.5 kms in width. The lake, together with the areas of scrub, marsh and reedbeds that immediately surround it, has been given the status of Reserva Natural and has been fenced off to prevent human interference. Much of the surrounding countryside has been given over to agriculture with olives, sunflowers and cereal crops predominating the area.

The lagoon, which was once the site of a commercial salt producing concern, is now best known for the large number of Greater Flamingos that live and breed here. In favourable years, up to 10,000 pairs may breed, making this one of the most important Flamingo sites in Europe.

Apart from the Flamingos, there are many other notable breeding species that can easily be seen here. Black-necked Grebe, Gull-billed Tern, Stone Curlew, Black-winged Stilt, Avocet, Bee-eater, Hoopoe and Little Bittern are all regular breeders. Scarcer birds that have bred here in recent years include Purple Gallinule, White-headed Duck, Red-crested Pochard and Slender-billed Gull. It is possible that some, or even all of these may favour the area again in the near future.

Although the lagoon is fed with water from several small streams, it is dependent on adequate rainfall in the winter months if it is not to dry out before spring. At its deepest point the water is only about 1.4 metres (5 feet) and can rapidly evaporate during prolonged periods of sunshine, without any rain. It is possible that after particularly dry winters the water level will be too low for the Flamingos to breed.

The raptorial bird species that you may expect to see here are resident Marsh Harriers, Buzzards, Peregrines and Kestrels. Montagu's Harriers are common in the summer and both Booted and Short-toed Eagles, Black Kites, Sparrowhawks and Lesser Kestrels can also be seen at this time. In the winter months especially, both Hen Harriers and Black-shouldered Kites have been recorded here. During the passage periods and in the winter, the area attracts a great many species of ducks, grebes, geese, herons, egrets, cranes and other waders.

There is a modern visitors' information centre at the site but unfortunately the actual opening times of this do not correspond with the times advertised on the door and very often it is not open

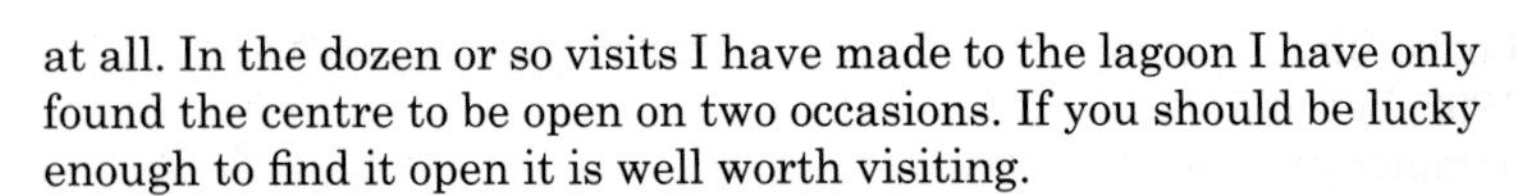

at all. In the dozen or so visits I have made to the lagoon I have only found the centre to be open on two occasions. If you should be lucky enough to find it open it is well worth visiting.

Behind the information centre and the car park there is a large marsh area and several pools that are very attractive to Moorhen, Coot, Purple Gallinule, Little Bittern, ducks, waders and marsh terns. The surrounding scrub and reeds hold good numbers of finches, larks and warblers, including resident Cetti's and summer visiting Reed and Great Reed Warblers. Bee-eaters nest in the bank of a pool beside the information centre and can be observed at close quarters from early April to late September/early October.

The whole of the lagoon, a distance of about 22 kms, can be circled by car. To do so you turn left on leaving the information centre and continue keeping left until you arrive back at the village of Fuente de Piedra. There are numerous places where you can stop and get good views of the lagoon, either from the shelter of your car or by walking a short distance to the perimeter fence.

Access

If you are travelling from a coastal location, you should drive to Málaga and then follow the signs for Sevilla. Once on the main Sevilla highway, the A-92, proceed until you reach the turn-off for the town of Fuente de Piedra at km 132. Once you have left the A-92, drive through the town, following the signs for the lagoon. The entrance to the information centre is on the left-hand side of the road, about 150 metres beyond the railway station and bridge. There is a purpose built carpark just below the centre, which should be used rather than driving down a small track toward the lagoon.

If you are travelling from inland, from areas such as Álora, Ardales, Ronda, Gauçín, etc. consider heading for the main Jerez de la Frontera/Antequera road (the A-382) and then turning left for Fuente de Piedra 10 kms beyond Campillos. This will bring you out at the far end of the lagoon and you can then turn left or right to reach the information centre.

Directly in front of the centre, there is a lookout point complete with a pay-to-view telescope and a notice board with some of the bird species that can be found here. From here you have an elevated view of the whole length of the lagoon. However, distances are such that a decent telescope really is essential. Behind the centre there is a large area of marsh and standing water, whilst to the side there is a series of small ponds. The marsh attracts breeding Moorhens,

Coots, Black-winged Stilts and gulls. Purple Gallinules bred here in 1998, but unfortunately I have not seen any here since then. In the summer you cannot miss the Gull-billed, Whiskered and Black Terns that feed along the marsh. Both Reed and Great Reed Warblers can be found in the reedbeds during the breeding season. Other birds that are commonly seen in this area include Stone Curlew, Hoopoe, Crested Lark, Corn and Cirl Buntings, Sardinian Warbler, Black Redstart, Great Grey Shrike, Woodchat Shrike, swifts, swallows, martins and finches. Bee-eaters usually nest in the steep bank of the small pond nearest the centre.

Below the centre there is a path which leads along the edge of the lagoon and an irrigation channel. This allows you to get good close-up views of some of the wader species. Further along to the left there is a sand spit that sticks out into the water and this is probably the best place to see Kentish, Ringed and Little-ringed Plovers and Little Stints as they feed at the water's edge. Further out there are often small groups of Avocets, Black-tailed Godwits and ducks.

A central track runs left from the information centre and leads between mixed agricultural fields and ends at a railway crossing about a kilometre away. The rough ploughed fields to the left often hold Stone Curlew, Short-toed Lark, Black-eared Wheatear, Hoopoe and shrikes. The fields of cereals can hold Quail, Red-legged Partridge and possibly passing Corncrakes. Both Barn and Little Owls are fairly common in this area throughout the year and Nightjars have been recorded in the vicinity.

Once you have investigated this part of the site you can drive around the rest of the lagoon. It´s best you do this in an anti-clockwise direction. On leaving the centre, turn left onto the road and proceed slowly as there are many marshy areas just beside the road which are the favoured nesting areas of the Avocets. Just after you pass the km 3 mark, there is a large lay-by that was the old road. Park here and view the lagoon from this point. Just inside the fence there are a few small "islands" where waders, gulls and terns sometimes roost. A small track leads down toward the perimeter fence and scattered trees provide some cover, enabling you to get quite close to the water's edge without disturbing the birds.

Continue along the road, keeping left at the junction at km 6. Approximately 2.5 kms from the junction there is an area of seasonally flooded land. This usually consists of two pools and a marshy area where a small stream feeds water into the lagoon. This area is attractive to ducks and gulls in the winter. Beyond the marsh and also to the right is the main breeding area of the Flamingos. The nests are built on the long strips of dry land in the middle of the lagoon. If the Flamingos have bred and the lagoon shows signs of drying out completely, water will be pumped into this part of the lagoon until the young are ready to fly. Apart from the views of the lagoon, the area also holds several interesting bird species in the surrounding trees, scrub and undergrowth. Fan-tailed, Dartford and Melodious Warblers, Woodlarks, Nightingales, Yellow Wagtails, Spotted Flycatchers and Short-toed Treecreepers have all been recorded here.

Map of Laguna de Fuente Piedra

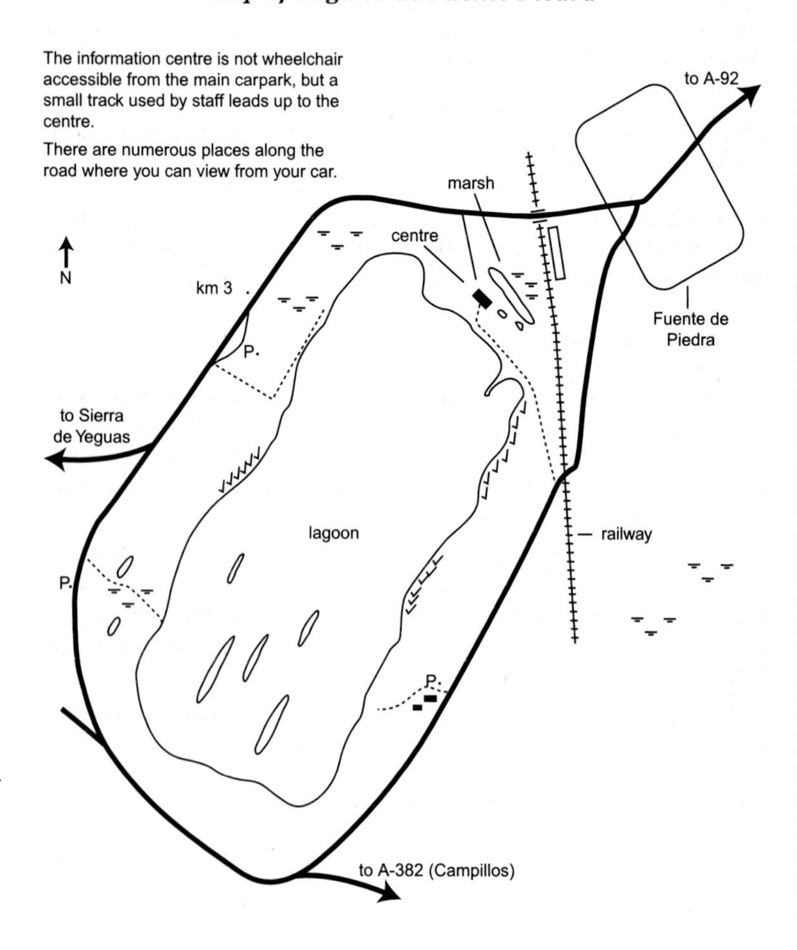

As you continue around the top end of the lagoon you will find other spots that offer good views of the Flamingos. It is in this area that you are most likely to see the wintering Common Cranes. As many as 200 can normally be found here between November and the end of February.

Further around the lagoon you reach another fork in the road. The road to the right leads to the A-382 (Jerez-Antequera road) and is a short cut to Campillos. The left-hand road leads alongside the lagoon back to Fuente de Piedra. At one point you come to a ruined farmhouse on the left of the road. Park here and explore the track that leads through the cereal field to the lagoon. The ruin is a favourite spot for Little Owls, Great Grey Shrikes and Black Redstarts. Quails, larks, pipits, warblers, tits and finches can be found in the fields, trees and reeds that are in the immediate area.

At any point along the route you are likely to see birds of prey. Marsh and Hen Harriers can often be seen over the reeds and marsh areas and Montagu's hunt over the citrus and olive plantations in the summer. Although still fairly scarce, the Black-shouldered Kite is being seen more often in the area, especially in the winter months. During the passage periods and in the summer you can see Black Kites, Booted Eagles, Short-toed Eagles and Lesser Kestrels.

When to Visit

As the lagoon is seasonal, ie. dependent on winter rain, it often dries out before August and can remain dry until October, November and even as late as December as in the winter of 2000/01. At this time the lagoon is not very productive, although there will always be something to interest the keen birder.

In normal conditions the winter and spring is an excellent time for Flamingos., White Storks, Common Cranes, herons, egrets, grebes, ducks and waders. The breeding season produces by far the greatest number of species and the birds are far more visible at this time.

Morning or early afternoon visits are recommended to enjoy the best light conditions. Late afternoon/ evening sunshine is very much a problem if you are viewing from the information centre area. Heat haze can also mar your views during the warmer weather.

Bird Calendar

Resident

Cattle Egret, Little Egret, Mallard, Marsh Harrier, Sparrowhawk, Buzzard, Peregrine, Kestrel, Red-legged Partridge, Water Rail, Moorhen, Coot, Stone Curlew, Little-ringed Plover, Kentish Plover, Black-headed Gull, Yellow-legged Gull, Rock Dove, Wood Pigeon, Collared Dove, Little Owl, Barn Owl, Kingfisher, Hoopoe, Woodlark, Skylark, Crested Lark, White Wagtail, Grey Wagtail, Robin, Stonechat, Black Redstart, Blackbird. Mistle Thrush, Cetti's Warbler, Fan-tailed Warbler, Sardinian Warbler, Dartford Warbler, Firecrest, Long-tailed Tit, Great Tit, Blue Tit, Short-toed Treecreeper, Great Grey Shrike, Jay, Jackdaw, Spotless Starling, House Sparrow, Chaffinch, Serin, Linnet, Goldfinch, Greenfinch, Corn Bunting, Cirl Bunting.

Summer / Breeding

Black-necked Grebe, Little Grebe, Little Bittern, Purple Heron, Greater Flamingo, Red-crested Pochard, White-headed Duck, Black Kite, Short-toed Eagle, Egyptian Vulture, Montagu's Harrier, Booted Eagle, Lesser Kestrel, Purple Gallinule, Black-winged Stilt, Avocet, Collared Pratincole, Common Sandpiper, Slender-billed Gull, Little Tern, Gull-billed Tern, Black Tern, Whiskered Tern, Turtle Dove, Cuckoo, Scops Owl, Nightjar, Common Swift, Pallid Swift, Bee-eater, Sand Martin, House Martin, Red-rumped Swallow, Barn Swallow, Yellow Wagtail, Nightingale, Redstart, Black-eared Wheatear, Reed Warbler, Great Reed Warbler, Olivaceous Warbler, Melodious Warbler, Orphean Warbler, Spotted Flycatcher, Woodchat Shrike, Golden Oriole, Ortolan.

Winter

Great Crested Grebe, Black-necked Grebe, Little Grebe, Grey Heron, Spoonbill, Greater Flamingo, Greylag Goose, Shelduck, Gadwall, Wigeon, Teal, Shoveler, Marbled Teal, Red-crested Pochard, Pochard, White-headed Duck, Hen Harrier, Merlin, Common Crane, Ringed Plover, Lapwing, Dunlin, Little Stint, Snipe, Black-tailed Godwit, Bar-tailed Godwit, Curlew, Whimbrel, Redshank, Greenshank, Green Sandpiper, Common Sandpiper, Lesser Black-backed Gull, Meadow Pipit, Song Thrush, Blackcap, Chiffchaff, Siskin, Reed Bunting.

Passage Migrants

Squacco Heron, White Stork, Black Stork, Garganey, Pintail, Tufted Duck, Honey Buzzard, Corncrake, Ruff, Wood Sandpiper, Roller, Wryneck, Tree Pipit, Whinchat, Northern Wheatear, Willow Warbler, Pied Flycatcher.

Rarities

Surprisingly, for a site of this size and nature, very few rarities have been recorded here. Those that have are listed below.

Lesser Flamingo. There have been several reports but as yet these have not been accepted by the IRC who believe that they are probably escapes.

Fulvous Whistling Duck. A single bird was at the lagoon between 14th of May and 2nd July 1998.

Ring-Billed Gull. A single first winter bird was present on the sand spit to the left of the centre on the 11th of May 2000.

Greater Flamingo *(Phoenicopterus ruber)*

Laguna de la Ratosa

This is a medium sized lagoon encompassed within the 172 hectare Reserva Natural Laguna de la Ratosa and is situated almost on the Málaga/Sevilla border. The lagoon attracts reasonable numbers of Greater Flamingos from the nearby lagoon at Fuente de Piedra and has good resident populations of Moorhens, Coots, Purple Gallinules and Little Grebes, which breed in an extensive reedbed on the south-western edge of the lagoon. During the winter periods, many wader and wildfowl species can be found and Mallard, Shoveler, Teal, Gadwall, Wigeon, Pochard, Redcrested Pochard and White-headed Ducks have all been recorded here.

Summer visitors include Little Bittern, Purple Heron, Black-winged Stilt, Avocet and both Reed and Great Reed Warblers. In fact, most of the species that are to be found at Fuente de Piedra can also be seen here, although in general the numbers are lower. However, this lagoon has not been fenced off and it is possible to get right to the water's edge, thereby facilitating excellent close-up views.

As with the other lagoons in the area, this is seasonal and is therefore liable to lose much, if not all, of its water during the long hot summer periods. The surrounding agricultural land, consisting mainly of olive groves and vegetable crops, attract all the characteristic bird species of the region. These include eagles, kites, harriers, owls and other birds of prey, finches, larks, warblers, tits, pipits, swifts, swallows, martins and buntings.

Access

This site can be easily reached from the main A-92 Granada/Sevilla road by taking exit km 125, signed for La Roda de Andalucía. Once you have left the main road, follow the signs for Alameda (SE-775) and pass through the small village of Los Perez, again following the Alameda signs. When you reach the Sevilla/Málaga border (marked by a large sign), proceed for 1.1 kms and on the right you will see a dirt road. At this point you will also see a large wooden notice board that gives information about the Reserva Natural. The lagoon is 250 metres along the track but it is better to park here and explore the site on foot.

The low lying field beside the notice board often becomes flooded after wet weather and can attract waders and ducks along with other species that may use the shallow water for drinking and bathing.

General map of the Laguna de la Ratosa

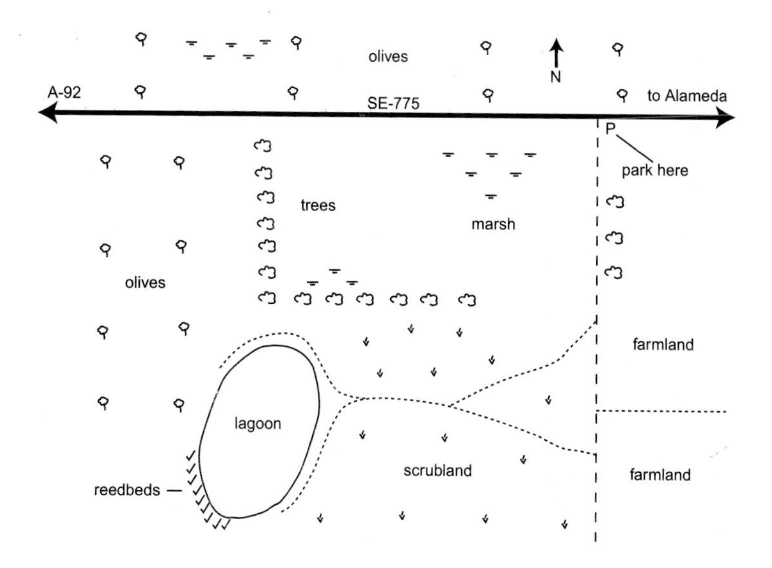

The surrounding olive trees usually hold good numbers of finches and tits throughout the year and these are joined in the summer by Woodchat Shrike, Melodious Warbler and Spotted Flycatcher. All three of the region's Harriers can be seen here at the appropriate time of the year, with Montagu's being especially prominent in the breeding season.

As you approach the lagoon you will notice the reedbeds on the far side. Purple Gallinules, Little Bitterns and other waterfowl breed here as do both Reed and Great Reed Warblers. Resident Cetti's Warblers can always be heard and in the spring the songs of the Nightingales ring out as the males sit prominently in the trees to proclaim their territories.

The surrounding scrub, broom and gorse areas hold resident Fan-tailed, Sardinian and Dartford Warblers and, occasionally, summer visiting Subalpine Warblers. Great Grey Shrikes are common and regularly breed near to the lagoon and can often be seen perched on any fence post or electricity cable.

The cultivated land that is used for vegetable and cereal crops should be checked for Quail, Red-legged Partridge, larks, wagtails, pipits and buntings. Other birds that are regularly seen in the area include Hoopoe, Jay, Short-toed Treecreeper, Black-eared Wheatear and Bee-eater.

When to Visit

As the lagoon is seasonal there is always the possibility of it drying up in the height of summer, so visits here between June and October may prove disappointing. The rest of the year should produce good birdwatching, especially during the spring when the maximum number of species are present.

The close proximity to Laguna de Fuente de Piedra makes it an ideal extension to any trip to that site. As this site is smaller and the distances are much less, it is not affected by heat haze and an ideal time to visit would be during the afternoon/evening when the Fuente site is suffering from the haze problem.

This is a very isolated spot and you are likely to find that, with the exception of one or two farmers, you are the only person in the area. This makes the birdwatching easier and more enjoyable.

General Information

Although most of this site is off-road, it may be possible for a person using a wheelchair to visit the main areas. The main track is rutted in places and can be very muddy after any period of rain. The tracks leading to the lagoon are much narrower but may be navigable with the help of an enabler. If all else fails it is possible to drive down the main track and park about 70 metres from the lagoon.

The birds that can be seen at this site very much correspond with those that can be found at Laguna de Fuente de Piedra and I refer you to that list.

Montagu's Harrier *(Circus pygargus)*

Lagunas de Campillos

This description is of three lakes which are situated near the town of Campillos in the province of Málaga. There are other lakes in the vicinity but they are on private land and therefore not accessible.

The largest, the most interesting and the most easily accessible lake is the Laguna Dulce, which is 2 kms east of Campillos, directly beside the A-382 Antequera-Jerez de la Frontera road. It is rarely much more than a metre deep and is set in an area that has been designated as a Reserva Natural that measures some 80 hectares. Although not fenced off, you should not enter within the signed boundaries of the reserve. Extensive reedbeds surround the lake and support a large variety of both resident and seasonal bird species, many of which breed within the reserve or in the immediate area.

All of the lakes are seasonal and the water levels, which depend on rainfall, can fluctuate greatly. By June or July, or even earlier in dry years, the smaller lakes often dry up completely and even the larger Laguna Dulce has been known to be little more than a dust bowl by late summer. However, most of the breeding species will have reared their young by then.

Greater Flamingos can (depending on water) usually be seen at all of the lakes throughout the year. Purple Gallinules, Avocets, Moorhens, Coots, Little Grebes, Little Bitterns and Cetti's, Reed, Great Reed and Melodious Warblers all breed at the Laguna Dulce and some, if not all of these species, also breed at the other lakes.

During the winter, large numbers of ducks, grebes and waders can usually be guaranteed. Shoveler and Mallard numbers are always high but Wigeon, Teal, Pintail, Gadwall, Pochard, Red-crested Pochard, Tufted Duck and White-headed Duck can also be found. The latter of these has actually bred here in recent years. The waders can include Curlew, Whimbrel, Black and Bar-tailed Godwits, Ruff, Snipe, Dunlin, Little Stint, Redshank, Greenshank and a variety of plovers.

Resident Marsh Harriers are joined by Hen Harriers in the winter and Montagu's in the summer and can often be seen quartering the lakes, reedbeds and nearby plains, farmland and orchards. Other birds of prey include Kestrel, Lesser Kestrel, Sparrowhawk, Peregrine, Buzzard, Black Kite and both Booted and Short-toed Eagles. Resident Great Grey Shrikes are joined by Woodchat Shrikes in the breeding season.

A new bird observation hide (spring 2001) has been erected on the southern bank of the Laguna Dulce that looks out over the site from an elevated position. To each side of the hide there is screen fencing for a distance of about 70 metres. The hide has been designed with disabled people in mind and the entrance is ramped and there is a low window for wheelchair birders. There are also "windows" cut into the screen fencing that offer further views of the site.

Access

The Laguna Dulce is easily reached from the A-382 Antequera-Jerez de la Frontera road, two kilometres east of Campillos, at the km 140 marker. There is ample parking and there is a small information office near to the new bird hide.

If you are travelling from the coast, you can take either the Sevilla road from Málaga before turning onto the A-382 to Campillos, or you can travel up through the Embalses de Guadalhorce and then join the new A-357 road to Campillos. Equally, you can come via Ronda on the A-376/A-367 roads. If travelling from any inland location, you should plan your route to Campillos with the aid of an up-to-date road map.

The Laguna Dulce is situated right beside the A-382 at km 140 and the parking area used to be the old Campillos road. The newly built bird hide has a prominent position that looks out over the lagoon and part of the reedbeds.

During the summer you can find Melodious, Olivaceous, Reed and Great Reed Warblers along with the resident Cetti's, Sardinian and Fan-tailed varieties. The Flamingos, White Storks, herons, egrets and waders are unmissable during the passage periods and in the winter. The ducks and grebes usually prefer the far side of the lagoon, away from human disturbance and traffic noise and because of this a telescope is always a big advantage here.

In November 2000, I saw two Avadavats in the reeds, to the left of where the new bird hide now stands. Other species I have recorded here include Corn and Cirl Buntings, Little Bittern, Squacco Heron, Purple Heron, Black-necked Grebe, Water Rail, Bluethroat and Sedge Warbler.

To reach the next two lagoons, drive into Campillos. On the right-hand side of the road you will see a BP garage and directly opposite this there is a turning to the left. Take this turning and follow the road through the town. As you reach the far side of Campillos you come to a roundabout. Take the third exit from this,

signed for "Colegio San José" and follow the road until you pass under a bridge. Approximately 400 metres beyond the bridge there is a dirt track on the left that leads gently uphill through a field. This track leads directly to the Laguna Salada and you can either drive, or park here and walk the 250 metres to the lagoon.

General map of the Lagunas de Campillos

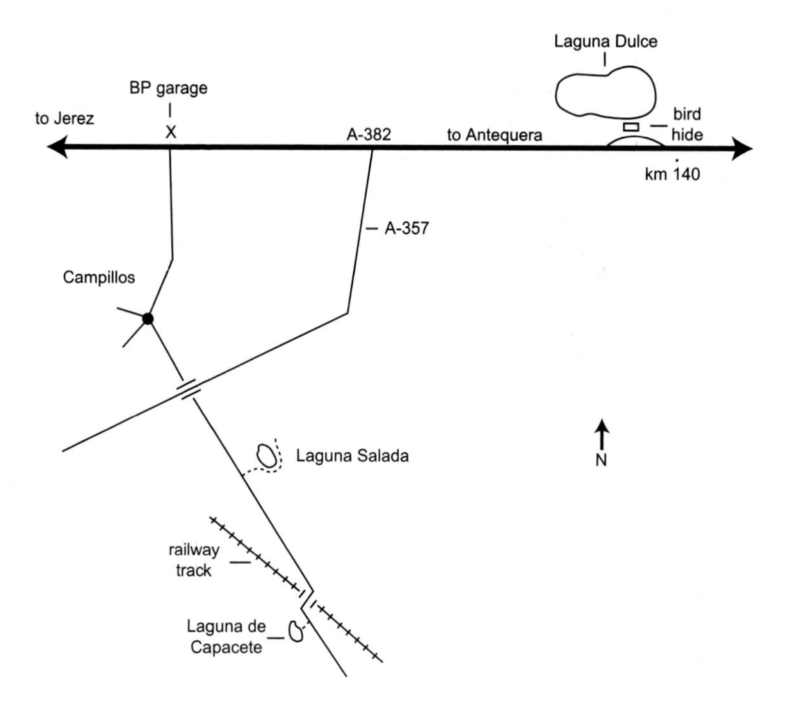

The first impression of this lagoon is that it is quite featureless but there are reedbeds on the far right-hand side and a line of trees that hold the same warbler species as the Laguna Dulce. Both Kentish and Little-ringed Plovers can be found here and there are normally small groups of Greater Flamingos. Other waders include Black-winged Stilts, Avocets, Common Sandpipers, Redshanks, Dunlins and Little Stints.

The track continues around the south-eastern side of the lagoon, passing the trees and reeds to the left and fields of cereal crops to the right. The birds that you can expect to find in these areas include Great Grey and Woodchat Shrikes, Corn, Cirl, Rock and Ortolan

Buntings, Crested Larks, Nightingales, Black-eared Wheatears, wagtails, finches and pipits. Harrier species are as previously stated and Kestrels and Lesser Kestrels are fairly common. Hoopoe, Bee-eater, Quail, Turtle Dove, Cuckoo, European Nightjar and swifts, swallows and martins are always present in the summer.

To reach the final lagoon, the Laguna de Capacete, you should continue along the road for about 1.5 kms and as the road passes over a railway bridge you will see the lagoon directly in front of you (if water is present, of course). After crossing the bridge continue for approximately 250 metres and you will find a small pull-off area and a track on the right-hand side of the road. Park here and walk the short track to the lagoon. This is the smallest and shallowest of the three lagoons and usually dries up before the others. However, if there has been sufficient winter/spring rainfall,, the lagoon may still hold water up to late May or early June. To the right of the track there is a rocky outcrop which can easily be climbed. This gives you the chance to sit down and enjoy an elevated view of the whole site. Once again, the bird species that are to be found here correspond to those at the other lagoons.

When to Visit

The site is of particular interest in the winter when large numbers of waders and waterfowl are present and also in the breeding season, providing of course that water still remains. Once the lagoons dry out completely, the bird numbers decline dramatically. Reflected sunlight is not a major problem at any of the lagoons, although heat haze can sometimes be a factor at the Laguna Dulce.

General Information

The bird hide and the area overlooking the reedbeds at Laguna Dulce are wheelchair accessible and observation holes in the hide are at the appropriate height for wheelchair users. The Laguna Salada is accessible by car and a short part of the track around the lake can be navigated, with care, by wheelchair. It is possible to drive down the short track toward the Laguna de Capacete but this only offers limited views.

Bird Calendar

Due to the close proximity of the Laguna de Fuente de Piedra, many of the birds that are listed for that site can also be seen here. I

therefore refer you to that list. There are, however, two species that I have recorded here that I have not seen at the other site, these being a pair of Avadavats and a single Rufous Bush Chat.

Red-crested Pochard *(Netta rufina)*

Tajo del Torró / Sierra de Teba

The Tajo del Torró is a high-sided gorge through which the Río de la Venta flows on its way to the Embalse del Guadalteba, one of a series of reservoirs to the north-west of Málaga. The sheer walls of the gorge have been eroded by wind and water for millions of years and now rise to over 100 metres above the river. Various caves, ledges, overhangs and many clefts and holes in the cliff walls have turned this particular spot into a favoured nesting site for many bird species.

The old Ronda-Campillos road, the C-341, crosses the river just a few metres to the south of the entrance to the gorge and the bridge is a convenient place to watch from. It is possible, water levels allowing, to walk the whole length of the gorge which is approximately 400 metres long, although this can involve quite a bit of scrambling and rock-hopping. Resident birds to be found here include Black Wheatears, Black Redstarts, Blue Rock Thrushes, Red-billed Choughs, Ravens, Rock Sparrows, Rock Buntings and Wrens. In the breeding season you can find Alpine Swifts, Red-rumped Swallows, Black-eared Wheatears, Nightingales, Bee-eaters and Spotted Flycatchers. Vultures, eagles and owls are also commonly seen in or near the gorge.

Below the bridge there are dense areas of reeds, trees, shrubs and other vegetation. A track leads alongside the river, passing olive plantations and other agricultural land, before reaching the reservoir. Cetti's, Sardinian, Melodious, Olivaceous and Fan-tailed Warblers, Iberian Chiffchaffs, Blackcaps, Nightingales, wagtails, tits and finches can all be found here and Rufous Bush Chats and Woodchat Shrikes are fairly common further downstream in the summer.

To the east of the gorge there is a high sierra where many of the species already mentioned can be seen. The raptor species that are often observed around the sierra include Peregrine, Kestrel, Lesser Kestrel, Buzzard and Bonelli's, Short-toed and Booted Eagles. Griffon Vultures are joined by one or two pairs of smaller Egyptian Vultures in the summer.

Access

The gorge and the sierra are situated about 3 kms east of the town of Teba at a height in excess of 600 metres above sea level. There are various routes to the town and a quick look at a map will show you

your best route.

From Marbella and further west along the coast and also from points to the north, west and south of Ronda, the preferred route would be to drive to Ronda and then take the A-367 road to Campillos. Do not turn off this road at any point as it will, near to Teba, become the C-341 and will lead you directly to the bridge over the Río de la Venta and the gorge.

From Málaga you can either travel up through the Embalses de Málaga on the A-357 or you can leave Málaga via the N-340, turning onto the N-321 Sevilla road at junction 241 and then taking the A-382 Antequera/Jerez de la Frontera road. You then turn left onto the A-357 just before Campillos and finally turn right onto the C-341 to Teba just beyond km 11. From both of these routes you arrive at the sierra first, between kms 11 and 13.

To the south (Teba side) of the bridge there is ample off-road parking. The bridge itself offers reasonable views of the gorge and may, if the river is in full flow, be your only chance of viewing the area. Water levels in the gorge dictate how far up the river you can walk. Access to the gorge is from either side of the bridge with the downstream route being slightly easier. A note of warning: the first 50-75 metres of the riverside track is loose shale and is liable to give way underfoot. Beyond this there are water-smoothed rocks and boulders which are quite slippery and a pair of shoes/boots with a good grip are essential.

Routes to Teba

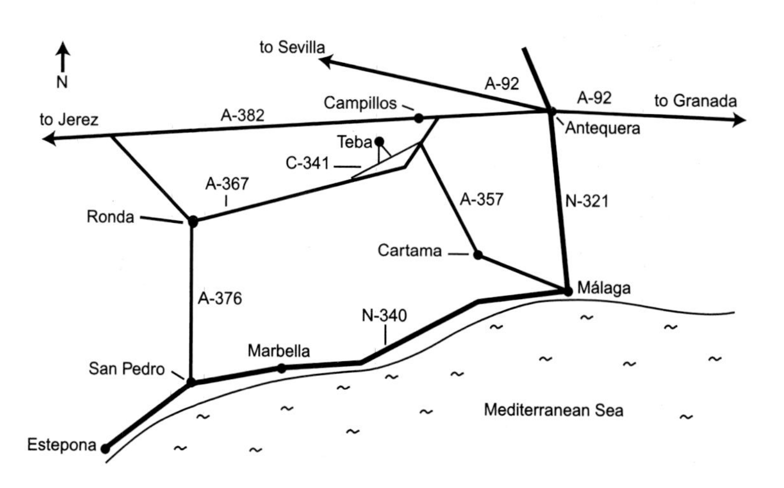

General map of the Tajo de Torró and the Sierra de Teba

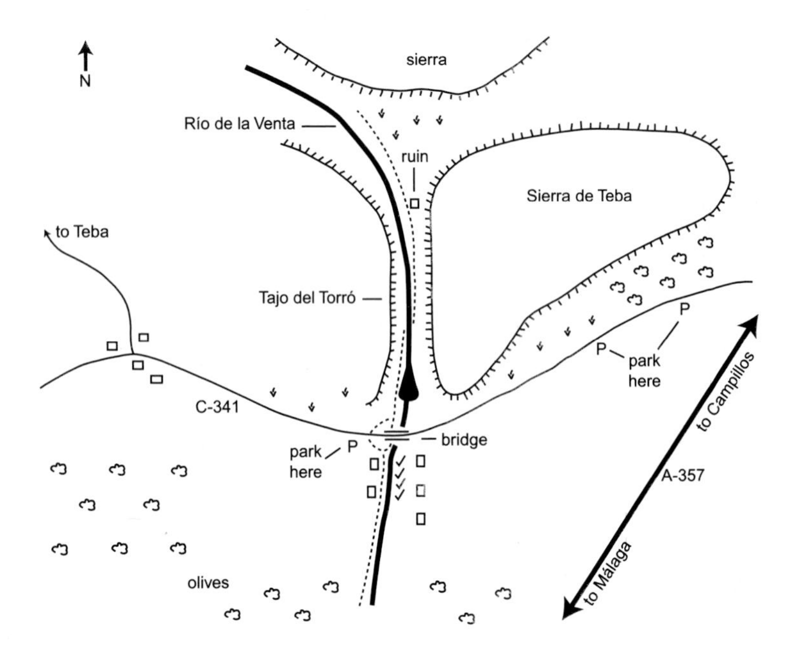

About 25 metres from the bridge there is a small dam with a sluice gate. This tends to hold some water throughout the year. The surrounding rocks are smooth and flat and this is a popular drinking/bathing place for many of the bird species that inhabit the gorge and the immediate area. Further up the river, depending on water levels, you may have to criss-cross the stream if you wish to proceed to the end of the gorge. This can normally be achieved by using the large boulders in the middle of the water's course.

Toward the far end of the gorge there is a ruined mill on the right-hand side. This is an excellent point for viewing nearly all of the site. Just sit here quietly for a while and let the birds come to you. In June 2001, a pair of Egyptian Vultures raised their young in a hole on the eastern rockface just 25 metres from the mill. Swifts, swallows and martins flash through the gorge and good views can be had of Alpine Swifts and Red-rumped Swallows. Jackdaws and Red-billed Choughs can be seen, either on the ledges or riding the air currents, and Peregrines are sometimes seen. Rock Sparrows and Wrens are often seen on the valley floor and the Black Wheatears are unmissable. I have counted six different pairs at this site.

Beyond the mill the area opens up to rocky scrubland where Black-eared Wheatears, Rock Buntings, Great Grey Shrikes, Woodchat Shrikes, warblers and finches are usually present.

Below the bridge the terrain is totally different. Dense reed cover supports Cetti's Warblers and Nightingales, both of which are highly vocal but seldom seen from here. Your best chance of seeing either of these two species is from the bridge above. The trees hold good numbers of finches, warblers and tits. Serins are always present and Spotted Flycatchers and Melodious Warblers are common summer visitors.

The river passes several houses and small farms before reaching olive plantations and fields of sunflowers. Both Rufous Bush Chats and Nightjars can be found in this area along with Hoopoes, Black-eared Wheatears, Woodchat Shrikes and both Corn and Cirl Buntings. Montagu's Harriers occasionally hunt over the fields and olive groves and both Kestrels and Lesser Kestrels can be seen.

The sierra between kms 11 and 13 offers another opportunity to see many of the previously mentioned species. There are several places where you can park off-road to view the area. Bonelli's Eagles, Buzzards, Peregrines, Ravens and Red-billed Choughs can be seen throughout the year and in the breeding season both Short-toed and Booted Eagles are fairly common. Little Owls are often seen on the rocky slopes of the sierra and Rock Sparrows, finches, wheatears and warblers can usually be seen in the olive trees. Eagle Owls have bred here in the past but I am uncertain as to whether any still remain at this time. Although not essential, a telescope is always a major asset here.

The town of Teba has a very long history dating back to and possibly before the Phoenicians, who arrived here some 1,100 years B.C. Evidence of both Roman and Moorish occupation of the town can still be found and many historical sites are scattered around the area. The most spectacular of these is the Castillo de la Estrella (Castle of the Star) which sits on a hill to the south of Teba, overlooking the town. The castle was built by the Moors between the 9th and 12th centuries to defend their territory from the Christians.

The castle is now a tourist attraction and also offers wonderful views of the surrounding countryside. It is also an excellent vantage point from which to watch for passing vultures, eagles, Ravens and Choughs. In the castle grounds you are likely to find Rock Buntings, Blue Rock Thrushes, Woodchat Shrikes, Black-eared Wheatears, Crested Larks, Stonechats, warblers and finches. Directly to the north-west of the castle there is a sierra which is also worth

investigating.

To the north of the town there is agricultural land, another large cliff-face and the Río Almargen. The whole of this area can also produce a wide range of bird species.

When to Visit

The spring and summer offer the far greater numbers of species and access to the gorge is much easier. In the winter, especially after heavy rains, the river may be swollen and viewing may be restricted to the bridge area.

Due to the north-south line of the gorge, you will not be affected by reflected sunlight but temperatures can become pretty oppressive within the gorge on windless days.

General Information

Unfortunately this site is not suitable for wheelchair users. The gorge is fairly hard going, even for people of normal fitness, due to the amount of scrambling involved. The pavement on either side of the bridge is less than a metre wide, allowing very little room for a wheelchai, and the traffic passes over the bridge at high speed. The other parts of the site may partly be observed from a parked car or some other vantage point.

Bird Calendar

Resident

Griffon Vulture, Sparrowhawk, Buzzard, Bonelli's Eagle, Peregrine, Kestrel, Red-legged Partridge, Rock Dove, Wood Pigeon, Collared Dove, Little Owl, Eagle Owl, Barn Owl, Hoopoe, Great Spotted Woodpecker, Woodlark, Crested Lark, Thekla Lark, Crag Martin, Grey Wagtail, Robin, Stonechat, Black Redstart, Black Wheatear, Blue Rock Thrush, Blackbird, Cetti's Warbler, Fan-tailed Warbler, Blackcap, Sardinian Warbler, Long-tailed Tit, Great Tit, Blue Tit, Wren, Short-toed Treecreeper, Great Grey Shrike, Jay, Red-billed Chough, Jackdaw, Raven, Spotless Starling, Rock Sparrow, House Sparrow, Chaffinch, Serin, Linnet, Goldfinch, Greenfinch, Corn Bunting, Rock Bunting, Cirl Bunting.

Summer/Breeding

Short-toed Eagle, Egyptian Vulture, Montagu's Harrier, Booted Eagle, Hobby, Lesser Kestrel, Turtle Dove, Nightjar, Alpine Swift, Common Swift, Pallid Swift, Bee-eater, House Martin, Red-rumped Swallow, Barn Swallow, Nightingale, Rufous Bush Chat, Black-eared Wheatear, Olivaceous Warbler, Melodious Warbler, Spotted Flycatcher, Woodchat Shrike, Ortolan Bunting.

Winter

Cattle Egret, Grey Heron, Stone Curlew, Common Sandpiper, Meadow Pipit, Skylark, White Wagtail, Song Thrush, Iberian Chiffchaff.

Passage Migrants

Greater Flamingo, Black Kite, Honey Buzzard, Yellow Wagtail, Northern Wheatear, Pied Flycatcher. There is also constant movement of gulls, terns and waders as they pass overhead, either on the way to, or from, the lagoons at Campillos and Fuente de la Piedra.

Black-eared Wheatear *(Oenanthe hispanica)*

Álora / El Chorro / Ardales

This is a vast mountainous area to the north-west of Málaga where the city's three main reservoirs are situated. Much of the region is forested with pine and eucalyptus species and other deciduous and evergreen trees. Numerous rivers, including the Río Guadalhorce, flow through the area and agriculture, mainly of citrus crops, takes place in the valleys and on some of the surrounding hillsides. The most spectacular part of this area is the Desfiladero de los Gaitanes (*Chorro Gorge*) where the Río Guadalhorce flows for nearly 3 kms through a narrow 100 metre deep chasm between the Sierra de la Pizarra and the Sierra de Huma.

There is a wide diversity of habitats to be found here and therefore a wide range of both resident and seasonal bird species. As the area is so large, you could easily spend a few days here and still not see half of it. I have, therefore, devised a route that visits what I consider to be the most varied and productive sites where a full day's birdwatching should produce an excellent bird list.

Álora - The Río Guadalhorce

This is a one kilometre stretch of the Río Guadalhorce on the southern outskirts of Álora. It is easily accessible and offers a good selection of waders, waterfowl and passerines throughout the year. The site is bounded by reeds, trees and dense vegetation on one side and by citrus orchards on the opposite side. The main attraction here is the colony of summer visiting Night Herons which are very active and easily seen at any time of the day.

Access

From anywhere along the coast, the easiest way to reach the area is from the N-340 highway, turning off, near to Málaga, where signed for Cártama at junction 231b and then following the A-357 toward Ardales and Campillos. Continue along the A-357 until you reach the second turning for Pizarra/Álora (A-343) at km 40. (Do not take the first turning at km 41). Follow this road for about 6 kms until the Río Guadalhorce runs beside the left-hand side of the road. Approximately 100 metres before the bridge over the river there is a pull-off space and a dirt track down to the river on the left where you can park. This is on the southern outskirts of the town. From spring to autumn, water levels are generally low and it is possible

to walk along the riverbed to the bridge and also upstream, crossing the shallow water by use of stepping-stones. If the river is in heavy flow you should drive across the bridge and turn left at the junction beside the "Los Caballos" bar/restaurant. After about 200 metres you reach a sharp left-hand bend and just beyond this there is a dirt road to the left. Turn here and follow the track, which passes a few houses and then leads between some orchards and the river until it reaches a weir. Park here to explore the whole of the site.

Travelling from inland locations such as Antequera, Campillos, Ronda, etc., you should head for Ardales and then follow the A-357 toward Málaga, turning off onto the A-343 to Pizarra/Álora at km 40.

The river is best visited in the spring/summer when most of the breeding species are present and water levels are much lower. Night Herons are very common here, being fully active and easily seen throughout the summer. Little-ringed Plovers breed on the stony riverbed and Little Bitterns, Little Grebes, Black-winged Stilts, Moorhens and Reed Warblers nest in the reeds upstream from the weir. Amongst the other species regularly seen here are Common and Green Sandpipers, Purple and Grey Herons, Cattle and Little Egrets, White and Grey Wagtails and Kingfishers.

The orchards and trees beside the river often hold some interesting summer visitors such as Golden Orioles, Spotted Flycatchers, Nightingales, Woodchat Shrikes and both Olivaceous and Melodious Warblers. Also to be seen around the site are Bee-eaters, Turtle Doves, House Martins, swifts and swallows, including Red-rumped, all of which breed in the area. During the winter period there are usually Song Thrushes, Blackcaps, Iberian Chiffchaffs, waders, ducks, storks and Hawfinches.

Although the site is of year round interest, it is best viewed once the river has subsided after the winter/spring rains as it is then possible to walk along the riverbed, gaining direct access from the road. When the river is in heavy flow, it is best viewed from the opposite bank where there are orchards and a track about 5 metres above the water level.

The maximum number of breeding and passage species can be seen in the spring (April-June) and in the late summer (September-October). The majority of winter birds are usually present from November and remain until mid-March, although a few may remain for much longer periods.

General map of the Río Guadalhorce at Álora

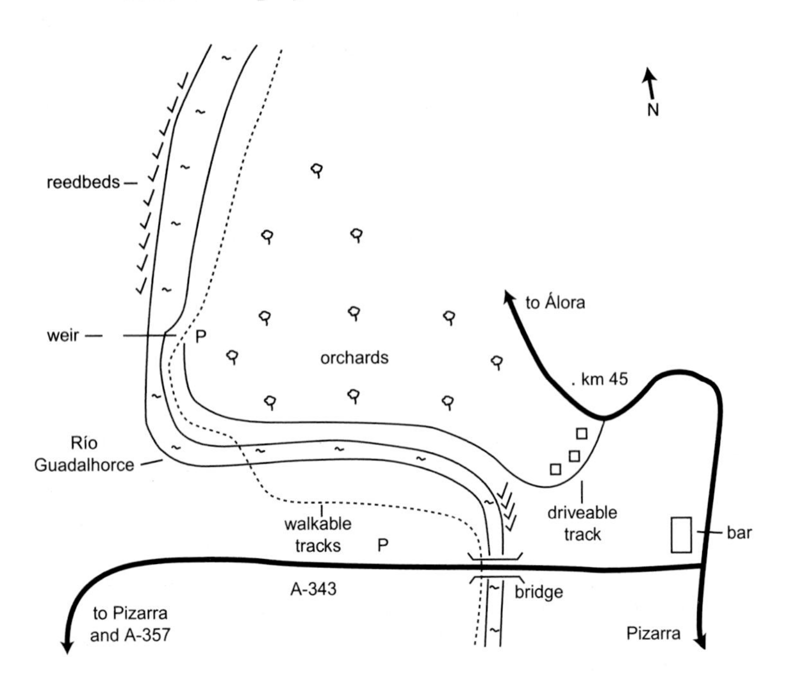

When to Visit

Most of the birds are fairly active and can be seen at any time of the day, though the riverbed can become very hot during the middle of the day and it would be best to visit in the morning or evening.

General Information

The riverbed is very stony and unsuitable for wheelchair users but in the dry season when water levels are low it is possible to drive down to the river and view the nearside of the site from your car. The track on the opposite bank, although somewhat bumpy, is wheelchair accessible and offers elevated views of the river, reedbeds and some of the orchards.

The area downstream from the weir is favoured by the Night Herons, Kingfishers, Little-ringed Plovers and some other waders. The area above the weir, where the water is deeper and more reed-fringed, is preferred by Little Bitterns, Black-winged Stilts,

Little Grebes, herons, egrets and wildfowl.

The orchards and trees along the riverbanks should not be ignored as some very attractive species can be found here. Cirl Buntings, Serins, Sardinian Warblers, Linnets and a selection of other finches, warblers, tits and larks can be seen in addition to those previously mentioned.

Both Marsh and Montagu's Harriers can be seen at the appropriate times of the year and other birds of prey often overfly the site. Hawfinches and Iberian Chiffchaffs are regular winter visitors to the area.

Bird Calendar

Resident

Little Grebe, Little Egret, Mallard, Griffon Vulture, Marsh Harrier, Sparrowhawk, Buzzard, Peregrine, Kestrel, Water Rail, Moorhen, Common Sandpiper, Rock Dove, Collared Dove, Little Owl, Kingfisher, Hoopoe, Great Spotted Woodpecker, Crested Lark, White Wagtail, Grey Wagtail, Robin, Stonechat, Black Redstart, Blackbird, Cetti's Warbler, Fan-tailed Warbler, Sardinian Warbler, Great Tit, Blue Tit, Wren, Great Grey Shrike, Jay, Jackdaw, Raven, Spotless Starling, House Sparrow, Chaffinch, Serin, Linnet, Goldfinch, Greenfinch, Corn Bunting, Cirl Bunting.

Summer/Breeding

Little Bittern, Night Heron, Purple Heron, Short-toed Eagle, Egyptian Vulture, Montagu's Harrier, Booted Eagle, Lesser Kestrel, Black-winged Stilt, Little-ringed Plover, Turtle Dove, Scops Owl, Red-necked Nightjar, Alpine Swift, Common Swift, Pallid Swift, Bee-eater, House Martin, Barn Swallow, Red-rumped Swallow, Nightingale, Black-eared Wheatear, Reed Warbler, Olivaceous Warbler, Melodious Warbler, Spotted Flycatcher, Woodchat Shrike, Golden Oriole.

Winter

Cattle Egret, Grey Heron, Gadwall, Shoveler, Osprey, Common Snipe, Redshank, Green Sandpiper, Meadow Pipit, Song Thrush, Blackcap, Iberian Chiffchaff, Firecrest, Long-tailed Tit, Hawfinch.

Passage Migrants

Squacco Heron, White Stork, Black Stork, Roller, Yellow Wagtail, Whinchat, Redstart, Northern Wheatear, Willow Warbler, Pied Flycatcher, Siskin.

Night Heron *(Nycticorax nycticorax)*

El Chorro Area

Under this heading I have included several sites, ranging from El Chorro itself to a few sites near the reservoirs at the top end of Chorro Gorge. Some of these sites are within the boundaries of the Paraje Natural Desfiladero de los Gaitanes, a natural park covering 2,170 hectares. The area is mainly mountainous with both forested hillsides and barren cliff-faces and holds many of the species that are typical of these types of habitat.

Access

From the previous site, you drive through Álora following the signs for El Chorro. As you approach the village, turn right over the reservoir dam. After a few hundred metres, there is a small junction where you should turn left, following the sign for "Camping El

Chorro". Park opposite the campsite entrance and walk alongside the river/reservoir as far as the large arched railway bridge. The trees along the route hold the common finches, tits and warblers throughout the year but during the summer you can find both Olivaceous and Melodious Warblers. Near to the bridge there is an area of open scrubland surrounded by trees and cacti where Sardinian, Fan-tailed and Dartford Warblers are resident. Looking through the archways of the bridge you can see two rock pinnacles where Black Wheatears, Blue Rock Thrushes and Rock Buntings are commonly found. In the summer these are joined by Woodchat Shrikes and Black-eared Wheatears. Rufous Bush Chats are also a possibility here. House Martins and Red-rumped Swallows nest under the bridge and there is constant overhead movement of Jackdaws, Red-billed Choughs, Ravens, Kestrels, vultures and eagles.

The river/reservoir is normally very unproductive in the summer except for a few Little Grebes and Mallards but, in the winter, you may find Cormorants, egrets, herons and a few other waders and ducks.

After visiting this area, cross back over the dam and turn right. Continue until you reach a pull-off area beside a small bar on the right. From here you have an excellent view of the mouth of the gorge and you also have a reasonable chance of seeing Red-billed Choughs and Peregrines.

Continue along the road until you cross a small bridge where there is a church and a bar. There is room to park off-road and you can check the area around and below the bridge for Cirl and Rock Buntings, Cetti's Warblers, larks, tits and finches. The surrounding rocks and hills can produce views of Black Wheatears, Black Redstarts, Rock Sparrows and Blue Rock Thrushes.

Approximately 800 metres further along the road, there is a turning on the left that leads to Las Ruinas de Bobastro (1,000 year old Moorish Ruins). The area is now mainly pine forest with scrub plants, oleander, broom and fan-palm. A drive along the route to the ruins, with a few stops on the way, can be rewarded with views of Great Spotted Woodpeckers, Short-toed Treecreepers, Crested Tits, Coal Tits, Nuthatches, Jays and Crossbills. Toward the end of the road there is a reservoir but it has very little to offer as it is totally devoid of vegetation and birdlife. The viewpoint at the end of the route looks down into the valley where the Río Guadalhorce flows down from El Chorro towards Álora. This vantage point gives you a chance to watch for passing vultures and birds of prey, especially

Bonelli's Eagles.

As this is the only road up to the Bobastro area, you must turn round and retrace your route to get back to the main road where you turn left. Three kilometres from the turning, you reach a road junction where you turn right. Very soon, you pass a campsite and 1.5 kms beyond this there is a turning to the right, just before the road passes under a tunnel. At this point a nature trail is advertised (*Sendero de Gaitanes*).

This trail leads to the beginning of the Chorro Gorge, which is a spectacular sight after heavy rains as the water crashes through the narrow chasm. You can park here and walk the whole trail (2.5 kms) or you can drive the first 500 metres and park beside a barrier and begin the walk to the gorge from there. This is my preference as this avoids walking past a sometimes noisy bar. Before passing through the barrier, you can visit the two miradors. One is 90 metres away and the second is about 300 metres along the main track. Both offer views of the reservoirs and the surrounding area.

From the barrier, the track leads downhill passing through pine forests where many of the previously mentioned birds can be found. Some distance along the track there is a smaller path to the right which leads around a cliff-face and out into open scrubland. This area is favoured by scrub warblers, wheatears, larks and Blue Rock Thrushes. It is not advisable to walk too far along this track as you have to return back the same way to rejoin the main track. A few hundred metres further on you come to a tunnel and just beyond this there are a few caves in the rock-face where Crag Martins nest.

The track now continues with a forested area to the left and rocky scrubland to the right. This is the best area for Linnets, warblers and larks. As you reach the bottom of the track there is a large building beside a reservoir. On the fence there is a sign informing you that the Caminito del Rey (*The King's Way*) is closed due to it being in a dangerous condition. The King's Way is a narrow suspended footpath that runs the entire length of the gorge (3 kms) from behind the reservoir to El Chorro. In recent years there have been a number of deaths when sections of the path have collapsed and people have plummeted into the chasm below.

You can, however, walk past the building and reservoir as far as the beginning of the Caminito del Rey. The Red-billed Chough is fairly common here and can often be seen riding the wind currents above the gorge. Peregrines are also common as they prey on the hundreds of Rock Doves that live in the gorge. Other birds often found here include Blue Rock Thrushes, Black Redstarts, Black and

Black-eared Wheatears and Rock Buntings.

Between the reservoir and the start of the King's Way there is an expanse of marsh area which is vegetated with tamarisk, oleander and reeds. Many of the local birds use this marsh as a drinking and bathing station whilst others, such as Common and Green Sandpipers, wagtails and warblers, find it to be a rich feeding area.

General map of El Chorro and the Reservoirs

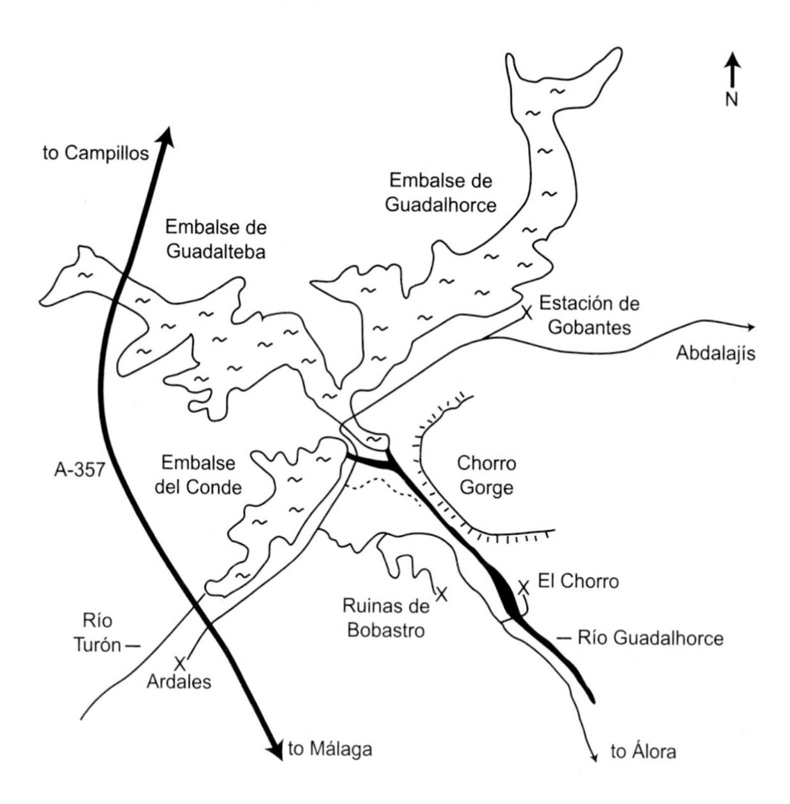

At all times there is likely to be significant overhead activity and you should keep a lookout for Alpine Swifts, Griffon and Egyptian Vultures, Kestrels, Peregrines, and Booted, Short-toed and Bonelli's Eagles. Very occasionally, more so in the winter, Golden Eagles, Monk Vultures and Goshawks are recorded in the area.

On the return trip, you can explore the small path that leads alongside the river/reservoir. This can produce views of Nightingales, Golden Orioles, Reed Warblers, Melodious Warblers and Spotted Flycatchers during the breeding season. Resident species that may be found include Wrens, Sardinian and Cetti's Warblers, Jays, Great Spotted Woodpeckers, Short-toed Treecreepers, Serins and Coal, Great, Blue and Crested Tits. In the winter there may be Iberian Chiffchaffs, Siskins, Bramblings, ducks, herons, egrets and other waders. This path leads for quite a distance and you should decide on a cut-off point somewhere along the route. I usually turn back after about 800 metres, once I have reached a very sheer rockface with overhangs, as by then the path is starting to lead away from the river.

On leaving this site, return to the road and turn right, passing through a tunnel. After about one kilometre you arrive at an area known as Pantano del Chorro where there are a few bars/restaurants and a small hotel. Park opposite the first bar and walk down the road for 100 metres until you reach the dam of the Embalse del Conde. The reservoir does not usually hold much of interest although I have seen Great Crested Grebes, Moorhens, Mallards, Cormorants and a few gulls and waders. To the right, at either end of the dam, there are stepped/sloped paths that lead down into a valley directly below the dam. Here there is always water and the area is particularly well vegetated. At the appropriate times of the year you may find Golden Orioles, Kingfishers, Firecrests, Crossbills, Robins, Nightingales, Wrens, Cetti's Warblers, Reed Warblers, Spotted Flycatchers, finches and tits.

After crossing the main dam you immediately turn left over a smaller dam/sluice-gate. Looking from here you can see hundreds of House Martin nests on the side of the main dam that faces the water.

Return to your car and drive over the dams and 150 metres beyond the Hotel La Posada del Conde you will find a large pull-off area on the right. Here you will find another nature trail advertised (Sendero de los Embalses). This is a short walk, only 750 metres each way, but it is very worthwhile following as it passes through a forest of eucalyptus and mixed pines before reaching the river. Approximately 300 metres along the trail the area on the right opens out to a rock slope where water from the smaller dam/sluice trickles down. I have sat on a low wall beside the trail and watched Blue Rock Thrushes, Rock Buntings and Crossbills, along with other species, drinking at this spot. The cactus growths to the left of the track often attract various warbler species.

Continue down the track for another 150 metres or so and the path divides. The right fork leads to a locked gate in a very lush and shaded area. This is all part of the area below the main dam. The left-hand trail leads alongside the river for 200 metres until it reaches a barrier that marks the end of the walk. Here you can find several duck species along with herons, egrets and a few waders. In the breeding season there are Golden Orioles, Yellow Wagtails, Nightingales and Bonelli's, Reed, Great Reed and Melodious Warblers. The winter birds that can be seen include those previously mentioned.

Returning to your car, you proceed along the road and after one kilometre you pass over the dams of both the Guadalteba and Guadalhorce reservoirs, following the signs for Antequera. At the next junction turn left where signed for V. de Abdalajís. Within one kilometre you reach a fork in the road where you follow the signs for Abdalajís and Estación de Gobantes. Very soon you pass a large disused quarry where Blue Rock Thrushes, Black Wheatears, Black Redstarts, Rock Buntings Kestrels and Peregrines can be found. Some 600 metres further along the road there is a small track to the left that leads down to the water's edge of the Embalse del Guadalhorce. Water birds are few and far between but this spot offers a reasonable chance of finding Lesser Short-toed Larks, Thekla Larks and Black-eared Wheatears.

Continuing along the road you reach an off-road parking area directly opposite the km 6 marker. This gives you the opportunity to scan the rock-face of the Sierra Llana for vultures and eagles and also the dense scrub for Dartford, Fan-tailed, Sardinian and Subalpine Warblers. Beyond this spot the road drops down into a fertile valley where orchards of citrus crops have been planted. This area is frequented by Rock Sparrows, Rock Buntings, Olivaceous Warblers and finches. As you climb out of the valley, there is a junction where you can continue toward Abdalajís or take the road to Estación de Gobantes. The former offers much the same type of terrain as you have already passed through. The latter, on the other hand, is far more vegetated and Great Grey and Woodchat Shrikes, Dartford and Subalpine Warblers and Black-eared Wheatears appear to be more numerous. The wooded area around the small railway station is a fairly reliable spot to see Golden Orioles and Melodious Warblers in the spring and summer.

Although you can continue toward Abdalajís and join the old road from Antequera to Málaga (A-343) at km 25, I prefer to return back through Pantano del Chorro and then proceed to Ardales, where the last site of this route can be found.

When to Visit

The whole of the described area can be profitably visited at any time of the year. However, during the summer the area can become very busy with day visitors and camping holidaymakers. The reservoirs are favourite bathing places and are also often used for various water-sport activities.

General Information

The site at El Chorro, although rather bumpy, is wheelchair accessible. The bridge between El Chorro and the Bobastro turning has no pavement and the road is quite narrow. I would therefore discount this site if you rely on a wheelchair. The Bobastro site is accessible in places but can also be viewed from a car. The Sendero de Gaitanes, although rather hilly, may be accessible to wheelchairs if you can pass through the narrow gap at the barrier. The two walks down from the dam are totally inaccessible as they are both stepped and steeply sloped. The Sendero de los Embalses poses no problems and is also driveable. The remaining parts of this site are mostly wheelchair accessible to some degree and can also be adequately viewed from a car.

As there is so much to do and see in this area, you may consider turning this into a two or three day trip. If this is the case then there are plenty of hotels/hostales in the area that should suit all needs. I can personally recommend the Hotel La Posada del Conde in Pantano del Chorro. The staff speak English and German and are very helpful and most of the rooms look out over forested valleys and you can birdwatch from your room. It is always advisable to book in advance as it is a popular area for sightseers/birders. Call (0034) 952 11 24 11 or 952 11 28 00. You can also log-on to their website at: www.laposadadelconde.com

Bird Calendar

Resident

Mallard, Griffon Vulture, Sparrowhawk, Goshawk, Buzzard, Bonelli's Eagle, Golden Eagle, Peregrine, Kestrel, Red-legged Partridge, Moorhen, Rock Dove, Wood Pigeon, Collared Dove, Little Owl, Eagle Owl, Kingfisher, Great Spotted Woodpecker, Woodlark, Crested Lark, Thekla Lark, Lesser Short-toed Lark, Crag Martin, White Wagtail, Grey Wagtail, Stonechat, Black Redstart, Black Wheatear, Blue Rock Thrush, Blackbird, Mistle Thrush, Cetti's Warbler, Fan-tailed

Booted Eagle *(Hieraaetus pennatus)*

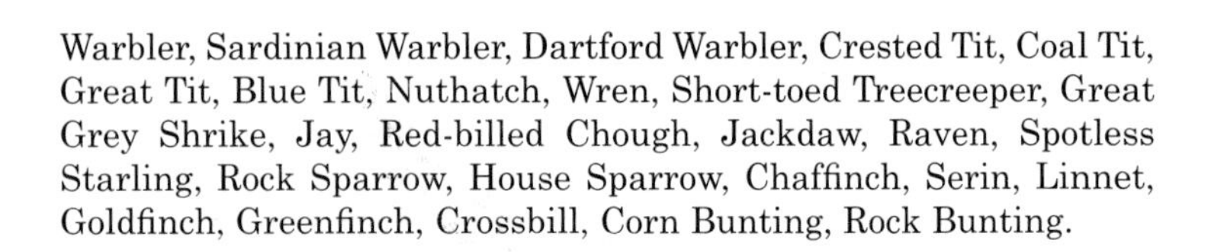

Warbler, Sardinian Warbler, Dartford Warbler, Crested Tit, Coal Tit, Great Tit, Blue Tit, Nuthatch, Wren, Short-toed Treecreeper, Great Grey Shrike, Jay, Red-billed Chough, Jackdaw, Raven, Spotless Starling, Rock Sparrow, House Sparrow, Chaffinch, Serin, Linnet, Goldfinch, Greenfinch, Crossbill, Corn Bunting, Rock Bunting.

Summer / Breeding

Short-toed Eagle, Egyptian Vulture, Booted Eagle, Lesser Kestrel, Turtle Dove, Cuckoo, Scops Owl, Red-necked Nightjar, Alpine Swift, Common Swift, Pallid Swift, Hoopoe, Bee-eater, House Martin, Red-rumped Swallow, Barn Swallow, Yellow Wagtail, Nightingale, Redstart, Black-eared Wheatear, Reed Warbler, Great Reed Warbler, Olivaceous Warbler, Melodious Warbler, Subalpine Warbler, Bonelli's Warbler, Spotted Flycatcher, Woodchat Shrike, Golden Oriole.

Winter

Great Crested Grebe, Cormorant, Cattle Egret, Little Egret, Grey Heron, Shoveler, Osprey, Monk Vulture, Redshank, Green Sandpiper, Common Sandpiper, Wryneck, Skylark, Meadow Pipit, Alpine Accentor, Robin, Ring Ouzel, Redwing, Song Thrush, Blackcap, Iberian Chiffchaff, Firecrest, Brambling, Siskin.

Passage Migrants

Night Heron, Purple Heron, White Stork, Black Kite, Montagu's Harrier, Snipe, Whimbrel, Roller, Whinchat, Northern Wheatear, Willow Warbler, Pied Flycatcher.

Ardales - The Río Turón

This is a one-kilometre stretch of the Río Turón which can be found just to the north-west of the town of Ardales. The riverbed is mostly stony but there are numerous marsh areas and reedbeds along its course. There are also dense growths of oleander beside the river toward the top end of the site. The terrain is fairly flat and is a mixture of agricultural land, rocky outcrops, scrubland and small woods. The river is crossed by an ancient Roman bridge which dates back to the 1st century A.D. This formed part of the old Roman road that linked the towns of Álora and Ronda. The bridge is still in everyday use and serves the many farms and private dwellings in the area. There is a very wide range of bird species to be found at this site and any visit here, regardless of the season, usually produces a good bird list.

Access

From the previous sites near to the reservoirs, you should head for Ardales on the road that runs alongside the Embalse del Conde and continue until you reach the town. As you enter Ardales there is a roundabout, which incorporates a fountain, directly in front of the municipal museum (*Museo Municipal*). Turn right here and at the end of this short road turn left, uphill. At the junction at the top of the hill you need to turn right and after about 70 metres, where the road forks, you keep right. This will lead you downhill to the bridge. Cross over the river here and park. Ardales can also be reached directly via the main A-357 Málaga-Campillos road. Once you have reached the town from the A-357 you should follow the directions above.

After heavy rains the river may be in full flow and much of the site's value is diminished. Normally, however, there is only a gentle flow and the exposed parts of the riverbed hold good numbers of Wagtails, finches and larks. The orchards should be checked for Cirl Buntings and warbler species. Along the route there are a few stone outcrops, around which you can find Black Redstarts, Black and Black-eared Wheatears, Blue Rock Thrushes, Rock Buntings and, occasionally, Rock Sparrows.

The marshy areas of the river attract a few egrets, herons and other waders and Kingfishers are often seen flashing over the surface of the water or sitting on prominent fishing positions above the river.

After about 500 metres, the track turns right, away from the river. A short walk further up this track can be worthwhile as, to the right, just where the track turns left, there is an area of scrubland and a small, sparse orchard. This has proved to be a fairly reliable spot for Lesser Short-toed and Thekla Larks, Great Grey and Woodchat Shrikes and Sardinian, Dartford and Fan-tailed Warblers.

Returning back toward the river you can cross over a ditch and walk further upriver. The banks here are densely covered with oleander but there is an elevated track at the edge of a field that allows you to see most of the river. The reeds and bullrushes should be carefully checked for Cetti's and Willow Warblers, Iberian Chiffchaffs and wintering Penduline Tits.

General map of the Río Turón

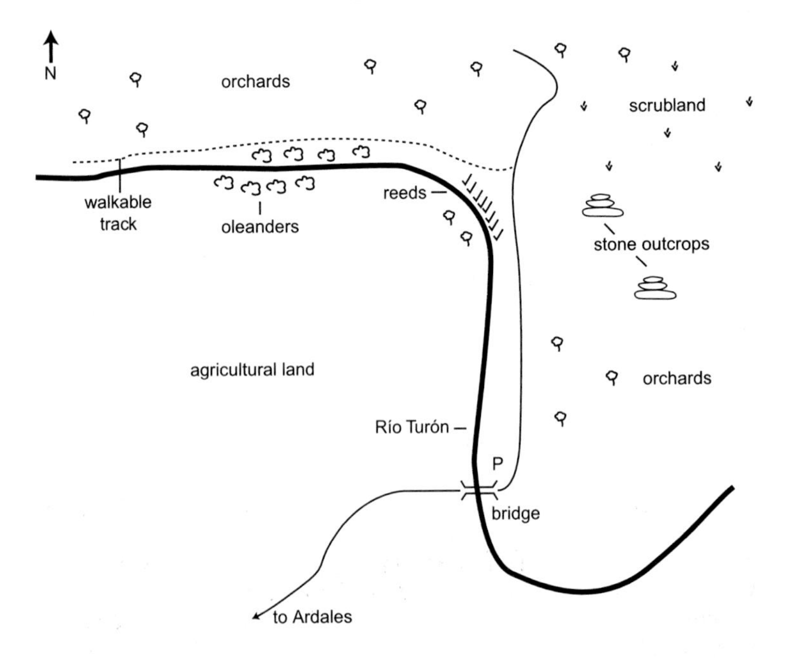

How far up the river you walk is totally up to you but I normally turn back once I have reached the end of the fenced orchard, which should be checked for Cirl Buntings and Melodious Warblers.

The area below the bridge, although not quite so productive as upriver, should not be ignored as I have seen Little-ringed Plovers

in the breeding season and a single Wood Sandpiper here in the autumn.

As the area is reasonably flat, it is quite easy to spot any soaring vultures, eagles and any other passing birds of prey. Also, you can often see Greater Flamingos and other waders/wildfowl on their way to, or coming from, the lagoons at nearby Fuente de la Piedra and Campillos.

When to Visit

The site is of interest at any time of the year, having a good range of resident species and also large numbers of seasonal visitors and passage migrants.

General Information

The main track, both above and below the bridge, is easily accessible for wheelchair birders and it is elevated so that good views are possible. The smaller track that leads beyond the reeds is very narrow and bumpy and should not be attempted by wheelchair users.

The main track can be followed, either by car or on foot, for another 3 kms and leads to the Castillo de Turón, an ancient castle that dates back over 1100 years. Here there are opportunities to stop and scan the surrounding countryside. Toward the end of the track there are some orchards where many species of birds can be found, including Golden Orioles.

Bird Calendar

Resident

Cattle Egret, Mallard, Griffon Vulture, Sparrowhawk, Buzzard, Bonelli's Eagle, Peregrine, Kestrel, Red-legged Partridge, Moorhen, Stone Curlew, Rock Dove, Wood Pigeon, Collared Dove, Little Owl, Barn Owl, Kingfisher, Great Spotted Woodpecker, Woodlark, Crested Lark, Thekla Lark, Lesser Short-toed Lark, White Wagtail, Grey Wagtail, Stonechat, Black Redstart, Black Wheatear, Blue Rock Thrush, Blackbird, Mistle Thrush, Cetti's Warbler, Fan-tailed Warbler, Sardinian Warbler, Dartford Warbler, Great Tit, Blue Tit, Short-toed Treecreeper, Wren, Great Grey Shrike, Jay, Jackdaw, Raven, Spotless Starling, Rock Sparrow, House Sparrow, Chaffinch, Serin, Linnet, Goldfinch, Greenfinch, Corn Bunting, Rock Bunting, Cirl Bunting.

Summer / Breeding

Purple Heron, Short-toed Eagle, Egyptian Vulture, Montagu's Harrier, Booted Eagle, Lesser Kestrel, Little-ringed Plover, Turtle Dove, Cuckoo, Scops Owl, Red-necked Nightjar, Alpine Swift, Common Swift, Pallid Swift, Hoopoe, Bee-eater, House Martin, Red-rumped Swallow, Barn Swallow, Tawny Pipit, Yellow Wagtail, Nightingale, Black-eared Wheatear, Olivaceous Warbler, Melodious Warbler, Subalpine Warbler, Spotted Flycatcher, Woodchat Shrike, Golden Oriole.

Winter

Little Grebe, Little Egret, Grey Heron, White Stork, Shoveler, Common Sandpiper, Green Sandpiper, Wryneck, Skylark, Meadow Pipit, Song Thrush, Blackcap, Iberian Chiffchaff, Long-tailed Tit, Penduline Tit, Siskin.

Passage Migrants

Black Kite, Black-winged Stilt, Redshank, Whinchat, Northern Wheatear, Willow Warbler.

In addition to these species, there is constant overhead movement of birds as they head for, or leave the nearby lagoons at Fuente de la Piedra and Campillos. It is possible that some of these may stop briefly at this site.

Refugio de Juanar

The Refugio de Juanar is a national hotel (Parador) situated 6 kms inland directly north of Marbella. It is set in a mountainous area of the Sierra Blanca at a height of over 700 metres. Beyond the hotel, there are pine and eucalyptus forests and olive plantations. A walkable track leads through these and ends at a mirador (*Mirador de Puerto Rico*) that looks out over the town of Marbella. To the right of the mirador is a mountain peak known as Cruz de Juanar (alt. 1182 metres) that towers over the site.

The differing types of habitat attract a wide variety of bird species as well as other wildlife.

Access

The site can be easily reached from all points along the coast via the main N-340 highway or, if travelling from further inland, by driving to Coín and taking the A-355 Ojén/Marbella road. Travelling eastward toward Málaga, you leave the N-340 at junction 185, which is signed A-355, Ojén. Travelling westward from the Málaga direction, you exit the N-340 at junction 182, also signed for Ojén. Once leaving the main road, the A-355 to Ojén and the Refugio are well signposted and the turn-off to the Refugio is at km 28.

The hotel is 5.2 kms from the A-355 and the connecting road leads through pine forests and rocky hills and valleys. The first 3 kms offer plenty of opportunities to pull off the road and explore the surrounding areas. One of the better spots is on the left, 100 metres beyond the km 1 marker, where you can park and walk into the forest along several tracks. I have always found this to be a very productive spot for Crested Tit, Crossbill, Nuthatch and Short-toed Treecreeper, along with other tits and finches.

Just before the hotel there is an unsurfaced road on the right with a sign directing you to the mirador. Take this road and continue until you reach a parking area in front of a set of gates. From here you have to walk the remaining 1.5 kms to the mirador. Entering through the gate, the road climbs gently upward for about 300 metres, passing through an area of pine trees that can produce a good variety of forest birds. Nuthatch, Jay, Crested Tit and Firecrest are commonly found here and are joined in the summer by Melodious Warbler, Bonelli's Warbler and the occasional Golden Oriole. Winter visitors and passage migrants have included Iberian Chiffchaff and Wryneck.

The scrub and undergrowth in the valley to the right hold resident Sardinian Warblers and summer visiting Nightingales and Spotted Flycatchers. As the road levels out there is a track to the left where de-forestation work has been carried out. A short walk into the forest here can often be rewarded with views of Great Spotted Woodpecker and Short-toed Treecreeper. Wood Pigeons are also very common here.

The main track now passes through olive plantations and broken rocky land. The trees should be checked for finches, tits and warblers at all times and for Hawfinch in the autumn and winter. The ground beneath the trees should be carefully scanned for Thekla Lark, Woodlark, Robin, Black Redstart and Rock Bunting throughout the year and for Hoopoe, Black-eared Wheatear and Woodchat Shrike in the summer. Skylark, Meadow Pipit, Chiffchaff and Linnet are all fairly common in the winter. The more open land often holds Great Grey Shrike, Stonechat and Sardinian and Dartford Warblers, which are resident and during the passage periods you may find Whinchat, Northern Wheatear and Pied Flycatcher.

Beyond the olives there is a ruined building, part of which has been renewed and converted into an office (*Centro de Recuperación*). The ruins are often used as a perch by Little Owls and shrikes and the nearby trees often hold good numbers of Great, Blue, Coal and Crested Tits, Chaffinch, Serin, Goldfinch, Greenfinch, Jay, Great Spotted Woodpecker and Short-toed Treecreeper.

A further 150 metres along the track there is a copse of pine trees that you can walk into and search for Firecrests and Crossbills. The track now leads directly to the mirador, with rocky hillsides to the left and a scrubby valley to the right. The rocks should be scanned for Blue Rock Thrush and Rock Bunting (all year) and for wheatears in the summer. The valley should be checked for Sardinian and Dartford Warblers, which are sometimes joined by Subalpine Warblers in the summer.

The mirador offers the best opportunity to search for raptors. Resident birds include Bonelli's Eagle, Buzzard, Peregrine and Kestrel. In the spring and summer these are often joined by Booted and Short-toed Eagles. Griffon Vultures regularly pass over the area and very occasionally an Egyptian Vulture may appear. Crag Martins are always present near to the mirador and are joined by Alpine Swift, Swallow and House Martin during the breeding season.

General map of the Refugio de Juanar and the Mirador

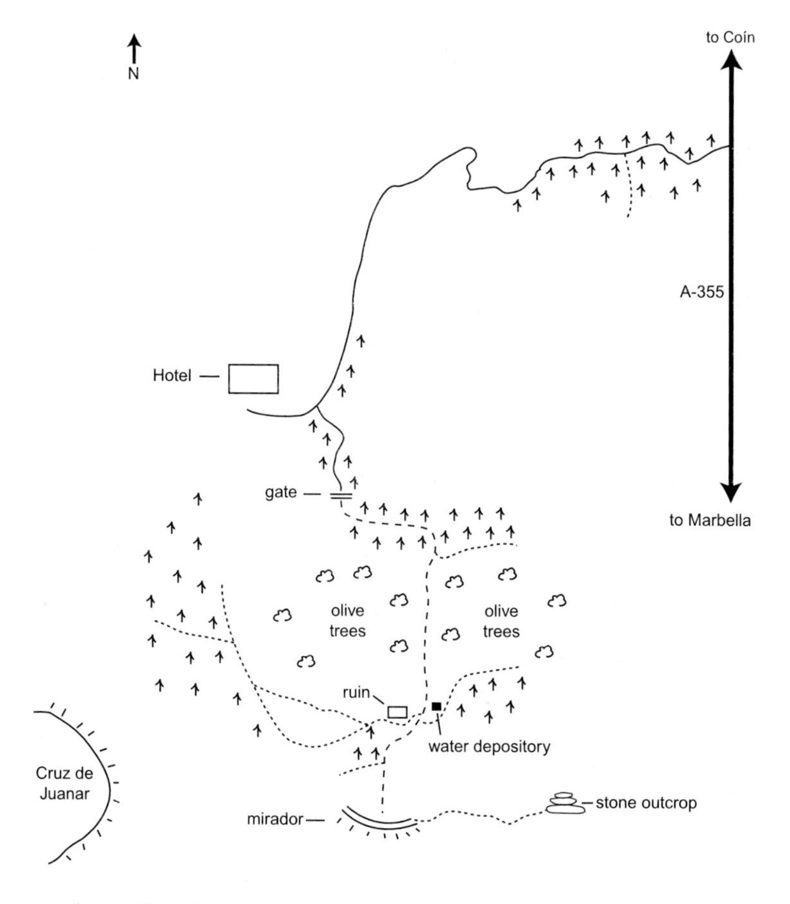

A small rocky track leads from the far end of the mirador to a stone outcrop, about 150 metres away. You may consider taking this track but please take care as a certain amount of scrambling around boulders, as well as walking, is required. The gorse and scrub here offer another chance to find warblers, wheatears and Blue Rock Thrush. Although I have never been lucky enough to see an Eagle Owl here, I have been told by several reliable sources that there are a few living in this area.

On the return trip, there is a track to the right, just before the ruin/office, that leads around between a pine forest and the olive plantation. A short way along there is a concrete water depository that normally has pools of water at the base which often attracts birds to drink and bathe. Regular visitors include Crossbills, warblers, tits and finches. Some large boulders about 50 metres beyond the depository are convenient to sit on and wait for the birds to appear.

Behind the ruin/office, there is a further track that leads downhill through the olives and then runs alongside the forest edge. This track will eventually lead back to the hotel but I prefer to return via the main track because it offers a greater variety of birds.

Once you have returned to the parking area, you can drive or walk to the hotel and explore several tracks in that area. Although the bird species are basically the same as previously mentioned, this seems to be the place where you are most likely to see both Melodious and Orphean Warblers and Blackcaps.

When to Visit

The area is quite popular with Spanish families and tourists alike and can become busy and noisy at weekends and on Spanish national/local holidays and it is not advisable to visit at these times as it is almost certain to prove frustrating. The afternoon/evening sunshine can cause viewing problems on the way up to the mirador but does not affect the return trip.

The highest part of this site is 900 metres above sea-level and therefore the temperatures are always a few degrees lower than they are on the coast. It can also often be more windy, so take some item of warm protective clothing with you, just in case.

General Information

Since the construction of the toll roads (A-7) between Málaga and Estepona, there has been considerable misunderstanding with regard to the roadside kilometre markers where the A-7 and the N-340 join together for about 4 kilometres near to Marbella. For instance, if you are travelling toward Málaga you may see a km marker stating N-340, km 181 and on the same post there is a blue marker stating A-7, km 184. Where this is the case, it is advisable to disregard the distance markers and be guided instead by the large overhead or roadside direction boards.

Gates, barriers and very uneven terrain make the majority of this site unsuitable for people with mobility problems and I certainly would not recommend it for wheelchair users.

Bird Calendar

Resident

Griffon Vulture, Buzzard, Bonelli's Eagle, Peregrine, Kestrel, Red-legged Partridge, Rock Dove, Wood Pigeon, Little Owl, Eagle Owl, Green Woodpecker, Great Spotted Woodpecker, Woodlark, Crested Lark, Thekla Lark, Crag Martin, White Wagtail, Robin, Stonechat, Black Redstart, Blue Rock Thrush, Blackbird, Fan-tailed Warbler, Blackcap, Sardinian Warbler, Dartford Warbler, Firecrest, Coal Tit, Crested Tit, Great Tit, Blue Tit, Nuthatch, Short-toed Treecreeper, Great Grey Shrike, Jay, Red-billed Chough, Jackdaw, Raven, Spotless Starling, House Sparrow, Chaffinch, Serin, Linnet, Goldfinch, Greenfinch, Crossbill, Corn Bunting, Rock Bunting.

Summer/Breeding

Short-toed Eagle, Egyptian Vulture, Booted Eagle, Alpine Swift, Common Swift, Pallid Swift, Red-necked Nightjar, Hoopoe, Bee-eater, House Martin, Red-rumped Swallow, Barn Swallow, Nightingale, Black-eared Wheatear, Olivaceous Warbler, Melodious Warbler, Orphean Warbler, Subalpine Warbler, Bonelli's Warbler, Spotted Flycatcher, Woodchat Shrike, Golden Oriole.

Winter

Wryneck, Skylark, Meadow Pipit, Song Thrush, Iberian Chiffchaff, Brambling, Siskin, Hawfinch.

Passage Migrants

Black Kite, Honey Buzzard, Roller, Whinchat, Northern Wheatear, Pied Flycatcher.

Crested Lark *(Galerida cristata)*

Embalse de la Concepción

The Embalse de la Concepción is a large reservoir situated some six kilometres inland, north-west of Marbella, at a height of 105 metres above sea-level. The reservoir is within the boundaries of the Parque Natural Sierra de las Nieves which covers some 18,500 hectares. The reservoir extends for over five kilometres from the village of Istán to the dam at Balcones del Lago. Although fed by numerous small streams, the main source of water is from the Río Verde, which after passing through the dam continues its course to the sea, west of Marbella.

The road to Istán runs along the eastern side of the reservoir and offers many places where you can stop off-road and enjoy views of the water and the surrounding wooded areas and rocky hillsides. Numerous tracks and dirt roads lead down toward the reservoir which can be either walked or driven, allowing you close access to the water.

Although the reservoir is large, it holds a disappointingly low number of wildfowl and other water birds, due mainly to the lack of reeds and other vegetation at the water's edge. However, in the winter months it is possible to find small numbers of Cormorants, Grey Herons, egrets, gulls, ducks and waders, more so in the many inlets rather than on the open water.

The majority of trees in the area are pine varieties, although there is also a good selection of broadleaved varieties, along with shrubs, gorse and scrub which attract a wide range of birds including finches, tits and warblers. The rocky, sparsely vegetated slopes of the surrounding hills are frequented by Blue Rock Thrushes, Black Wheatears and Rock Buntings.

Vultures, eagles and other resident birds of prey inhabit the area and can often be seen overhead. The owl species that can be found in the general area include Eagle, Tawny, Scops and Little Owls.

During the main passage periods many raptorial and passerine species pass through the region, sometimes stopping for a day or so before continuing their journeys.

Access

The reservoir can be reached from all points via the main N-340 highway, just west of Marbella. Travelling eastward toward Marbella from the Estepona direction you leave the N-340 at junction 174.

Travelling westward from the Málaga direction you turn off at junction 175.

General map of the Urbanización Balcones del Lago

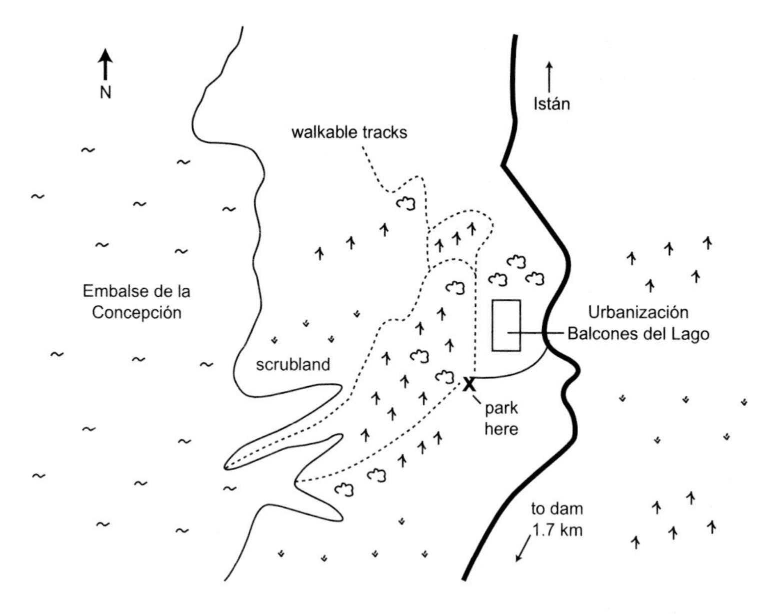

Follow the signs for Istán and after about 1.5 kms the road turns right and passes over the Río Verde. Immediately beyond the bridge there is a track on the left which leads down to the river. Follow this track for 250 metres to a ford across the river. Park here and explore the riverbanks and an area of reeds just upstream. Cattle and Little Egrets can be found here throughout the year and are joined by Grey Herons and waders in the winter and by Black-winged Stilts and Little Bitterns (water permitting) in the spring and summer. After prolonged periods without rain the river may cease to flow but the area above the ford usually remains marshy. Other species that are often found here include Grey Wagtail, Serin, Fan-tailed, Sardinian and Cetti's Warblers (all year), Hoopoe, Bee-eater, Yellow Wagtail, Nightingale, Spotted Flycatcher, Willow Warbler and Melodious Warbler in the breeding season and Iberian Chiffchaff, Meadow Pipit and Black Redstart in the winter.

Return to the main road and proceed toward Istán. As you approach the reservoir there are two small roundabouts in the area known as Balcones del Lago. Park here and scan the valley and the Río Verde on the left for finches, tits and warblers. The hillsides on the right should be checked for Blue Rock Thrushes, Rock Buntings and Crested Larks.

It is not permitted for unauthorized vehicles to take the downhill road that leads across the dam, so please obey the "no entry" sign.

From this point onward there are many places where you can stop off-road and explore the surrounding areas or walk or drive down to the water. One of the better spots is about 1.7 kms from the dam where the Urbanización Balcones del Lago is situated. Turn left into the urbanization and drive downhill to where there are parking bays (see map). Leaving your car here you have the choice of two tracks that you can walk. One leads from the bottom of the parking area but the better walk leads in front of the row of houses before turning left toward the reservoir. This walk is just over a kilometre and although most of it is a fairly gentle descent there is one point that is quite steep, which needs to be considered for the return trip.

To the left of the track there is a wooded valley which holds Blackcap, Chiffchaff, Firecrest, Crested Tit, Wood Pigeon, Collared Dove and an assortment of other tits, finches and warblers. To the right of the track there is rocky scrubland where you are likely to find Redlegged Partridge, Rock Bunting, Blue Rock Thrush and Sardinian, Fan-tailed and Dartford Warblers, all of which are resident birds. These are often joined in the summer by Subalpine Warbler and Black-eared Wheatear. The track ends about 70 metres from the water but there is a very rocky trail that leads quite steeply down to the water's edge if you are feeling really energetic.

On the return trip, you can explore another track that leads off to the left, beside a row of ornamental conifers. This is a semi-circular track and will lead back to the main track after about 300 metres. For those who wish to visit this particular spot but are not good walkers, or are a bit concerned with the gradient, the track is driveable, with care, and there are ample turning points along the route.

Continuing toward Istán, the next site I can recommend is the Ermita de San Miguel on the right-hand side of the road, mid-way between the km 4 and 3 markers. There is a good sized parking area that is marked by a white plinth. The ermita (hermitage) is built into the rocks about 25 metres above the parking area and another 25 metres above this there is a mirador which offers wonderful views out over the reservoir and the surrounding countryside. As you approach the ermita, you see picnic tables and benches scattered around the area. This is a popular spot for Spanish families to visit

at weekends in the warmer months of the year and can become quite crowded and noisy at such times. However, generally the area is quiet and the birdwatching is very good. The pines hold good numbers of Crested Tits and Short-toed Treecreepers along with Nuthatches, Great Spotted Woodpeckers, Jays and a good selection of warblers, finches and tits. During the summer both Melodious and Orphean Warblers are regular visitors and Olivaceous Warblers, although infrequent, are sometimes found.

General map of the Ermita de San Miguel

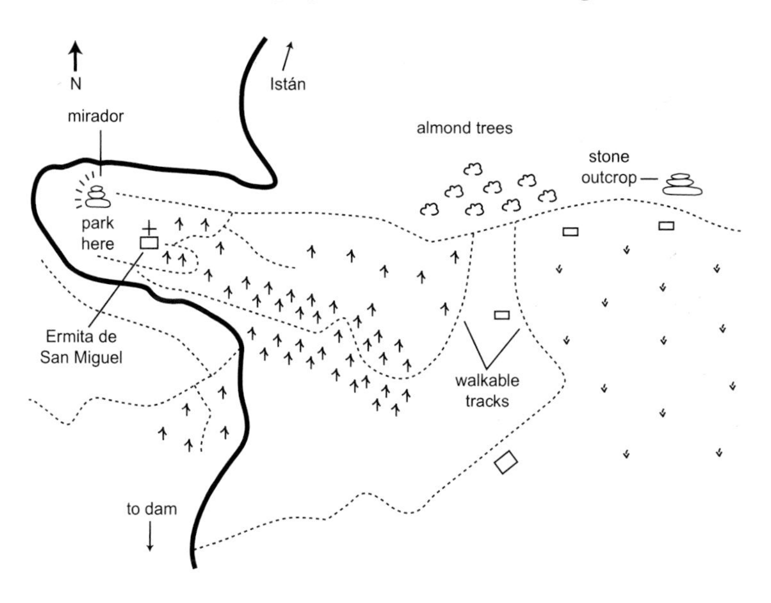

From the mirador a track leads back, passing a small building and then climbs gently upwards toward a stone outcrop. To the left of this track there is a plantation of almond trees which usually attracts sizeable flocks of mixed finches, ie. Chaffinch, Greenfinch, Goldfinch, Serin and an occasional Hawfinch. The rocky hillside to the right often produces Blue Rock Thrush, Rock Bunting, Black Wheatear and Black-eared Wheatear. There are various other tracks in the area which can be followed and will lead you back to the car park. One of these leads directly through a pine forest and offers the best chance of finding Crossbills, especially in the winter.

Approximately 50 metres back from the ermita parking area, on the opposite side of the road, there are others tracks that can be walked which lead downhill toward the water, offering more opportunities to find some of the bird species already mentioned. For the remainder of this site it is really a case of stopping at any suitable spot and looking to see what is about.

When to Visit

The site is of interest at all times but the greater number of species are to be found during the passage periods and in the breeding season.Views of the reservoir can be spoiled by sunlight reflecting off the water in the late afternoons and evenings. Due to the large number of picnickers, day trippers, etc. that visit this area at the weekends, especially during the warmer months of the year, it is advisable to plan your visit for a weekday.

General Information

The sites that I have described mostly involve narrow rocky paths or uneven dirt roads. For this reason I would class the site in general as being unsuitable for wheelchair users and people with other mobility problems.

Bird Calendar

Resident

Cattle Egret, Little Egret, Mallard, Griffon Vulture, Sparrowhawk, Buzzard, Bonelli's Eagle, Peregrine, Kestrel, Red-legged Partridge, Rock Dove, Wood Pigeon, Collared Dove, Little Owl, Eagle Owl, Tawny Owl, Kingfisher, Green Woodpecker, Great Spotted Woodpecker, Woodlark, Crested Lark, Thekla Lark, Crag Martin, White Wagtail, Grey Wagtail, Robin, Stonechat, Black Redstart, Black Wheatear, Blue Rock Thrush, Blackbird, Mistle Thrush, Cetti's Warbler, Fan-tailed Warbler, Blackcap, Sardinian Warbler, Dartford Warbler, Firecrest, Long-tailed Tit, Crested Tit, Coal Tit, Great Tit, Blue Tit, Nuthatch, Short-toed Treecreeper, Great Grey Shrike, Jay, Red-billed Chough, Jackdaw, Raven, Spotless Starling, Rock Sparrow, House Sparrow, Chaffinch, Serin, Linnet, Goldfinch, Greenfinch, Crossbill, Corn Bunting, Rock Bunting, Cirl Bunting.

Summer / Breeding

Little Bittern, Black Kite, Egyptian Vulture, Montagu's Harrier, Booted Eagle, Short-toed Eagle, Turtle Dove, Cuckoo, Scops Owl, European Nightjar, Alpine Swift, Common Swift, Pallid Swift,

Hoopoe, Bee-eater, Sand Martin, House Martin, Red-rumped Swallow, Barn Swallow, Yellow Wagtail, Nightingale, Redstart, Black-eared Wheatear, Olivaceous Warbler, Melodious Warbler, Orphean Warbler, Subalpine Warbler, Bonelli's Warbler, Spotted Flycatcher, Woodchat Shrike, Golden Oriole, Ortolan Bunting.

Winter

Great Crested Grebe, Little Grebe, Cormorant, Grey Heron, Wigeon, Shoveler, Osprey, Coot, Redshank, Green Sandpiper, Common Sandpiper, Wryneck, Skylark, Meadow Pipit, Song Thrush, Iberian Chiffchaff, Starling, Hawfinch,

Passage Migrants

Honey Buzzard, Whimbrel, Great Spotted Cuckoo, Roller, Tree Pipit, Whinchat, Northern Wheatear, Garden Warbler, Willow Warbler, Pied Flycatcher.

Woodchat Shrike *(Lanius senator)*

Benahavís

The village of Benahavís is situated at 184 metres above sea-level in the southern foothills of the Sierra Bermeja mountain range, some five kilometres inland from the coast. Although there is only one road to the village, it can be easily reached from any point along the Costa del Sol from the N-340 highway, just west of San Pedro de Alcántara. The village, proud of its large number of restaurants, is a very popular eating area, especially at weekends when it is flooded with visitors, many of whom drive long distances to enjoy the food and the mountain views.

Although the village itself offers only limited opportunities for birdwatching, it is possible to enjoy a drink on one of the many bar terraces and look out across the valleys and watch eagles, vultures, swifts, swallows and martins passing by. The road leading up to the village and the area surrounding it produce a few very favourable sites which harbour a rich variety of bird species.

The Río Guadalmina passes through a small reservoir to the north of the village and then flows through a rocky wooded valley to the east before following the road down to the sea. At the higher levels, the river passes through narrow gorges and produces some spectacular sights when in full flow.

There are two small reservoirs where herons, egrets, grebes, waterfowl and waders can be found throughout the year. The surrounding forests hold the more common woodland birds that you would expect to find in a typical English or north European wood, such as Nuthatches, Great Spotted Woodpeckers, Spotted and Pied Flycatchers, Jays, finches and warblers, together with Short-toed Treecreepers, Firecrests, Crested Tits and summer visiting Golden Orioles and Melodious and Bonelli's Warblers.

A nearby golf course has two reed-fringed lakes that support good numbers of Moorhens, Coots and Little Grebes and attracts Little Bitterns in the summer and both Squacco and Purple Herons during the spring passage periods. Ducks and Grey Herons are to be found here in the winter time, along with the occasional Great Crested Grebe.

The vegetation that grows alongside the river, ie. trees, bushes, shrubs, gorse and scrub, produces a wide range of finches, warblers, wagtails, tits, larks, chats, redstarts and shrikes. The mountains and rock-faces are the homes of Black Wheatears, Blue Rock Thrushes, Rock Sparrows and Rock Buntings, along with several eagle species and other raptors.

As there are a number of quite separate sites, I shall give directions to, and descriptions of, each of the sub-sites individually.

Access

Benahavís can be easily reached from the main N-340 highway. Travelling from the Gibraltar direction toward Marbella, turn off the N-340 at the signed slip-road between the km 168 and 169 markers and pass under the main road to a roundabout. From here follow the signs for Benahavís. Coming from the Marbella direction, turn off the N-340 where signed at km 169, just beyond San Pedro de Alcántara.

Site One - La Alqueria Golf Course

From the roundabout near the N-340, continue for 2.2 kms until you reach a turning on the left marked by three large banners and a sign for "La Alqueria", which is a golf course. Take this turning and proceed uphill for 1.2 kms until you reach a roundabout at the entrance to the golf club. Take the second exit, marked with a "no through road" sign and follow to the end where there is a turning point. Park here and look down to the golf course where two lakes are obvious, only 50 metres away. These hold Moorhens, Coots and Little Grebes throughout the year and Cattle Egrets and Grey Herons are frequent visitors. During the breeding season there have been Little Bitterns in recent years and both Purple and Squacco Herons have been recorded during the spring migration periods. Wildfowl are attracted to the lakes in winter, with Mallards, Shovelers and Pochards being the most common visitors. The surrounding reeds and scattered trees hold good numbers of finches and warblers, including Cetti's Warbler. The fairways and greens of the course are particularly good for Serins, Meadow Pipits, White and Yellow Wagtails and larks.

The scrubland and rocky areas leading to the course and the surrounding hills often produce Red-legged Partridges, Blue Rock Thrushes and Crested Larks, which are all resident birds. During the spring/summer both Woodchat Shrikes and Black-eared Wheatears are commonly seen. Hoopoes are also plentiful at this time of year but the Great Grey Shrike, although a resident, is more numerous in the winter.

It is not necessary to venture onto the golf course as most of the birds mentioned can be seen from the road. If you should decide that closer inspection of the area is required, please ensure that you keep

to the pathways and do not allow your activities to interfere with the golfers.

General map of the Benahavís road and the sub-sites

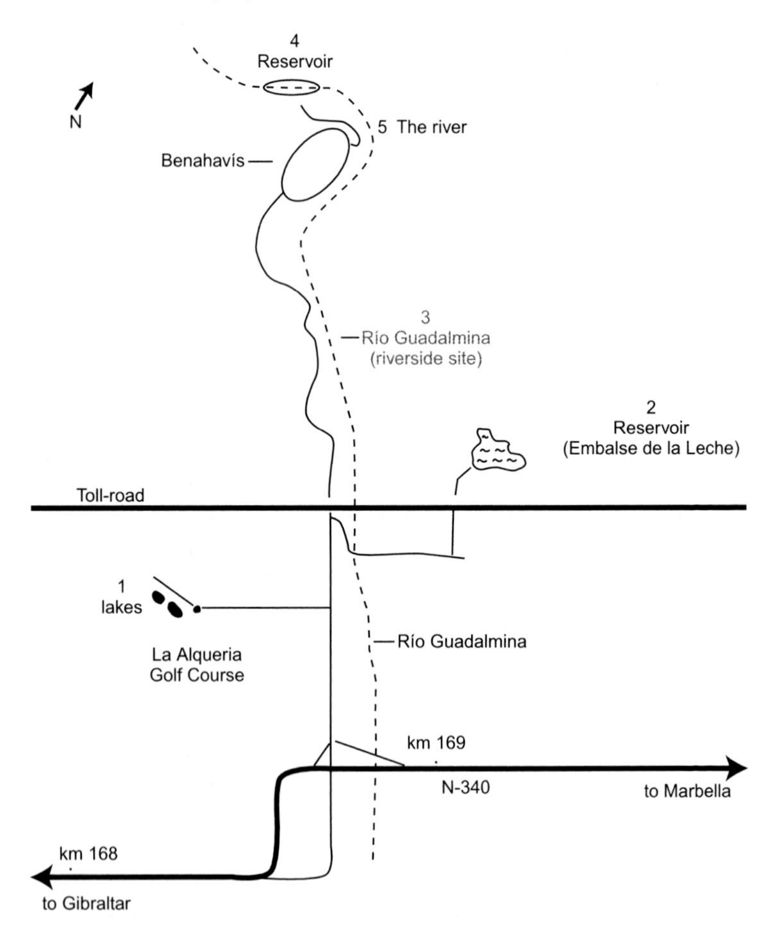

Site Two - Embalse de la Leche - The Reservoir

From La Alqueria, return to the main road and continue for 600 metres. Directly before the tunnel that passes under the toll-road there is a track to the right. Turn here and park 100 metres along the track and search the trees, scrubland and riverbed in this area

as it is a good spot for Blue Rock Thrushes, Black Redstarts, Cirl Buntings, Rock Buntings, Linnets and larks.

Continue by car across the usually dry riverbed and drive up the hill until you reach a dirt-track that leads off to the left. Turn here and proceed for 150 metres and pass under the toll-road. The reservoir is directly ahead. Park overlooking the water and observe the area for a few minutes before leaving your car.

The reservoir has a resident population of feral ducks and geese which includes two Muscovy Ducks. They will be grateful for any scraps of food. Cattle and Little Egrets, Grey Herons, Moorhens and Kingfishers are commomly found here and in the spring/summer you may see Squacco and Purple Herons and Little Bitterns. In the winter the feral ducks act as decoys and help to attract grebes and wildfowl to the water. The wader numbers are never high but you may see Redshanks and Common and Green Sandpipers.

The reservoir is surrounded by trees, mostly eucalyptus, conifers and a few broadleaved varieties. The characteristic bird species here are Chaffinches, Serins, Goldfinches, Greenfinches, Robins, Jays, Wrens, Great Spotted Woodpeckers, Blackcaps, Willow Warblers, Iberian Chiffchaffs, Nuthatches, Short-toed Treecreepers, Firecrests and Great and Blue Tits. The reeds to the right hold Cetti's and Reed Warblers and at least one pair of otters, which can sometimes be seen out in the open.

Follow the path to the right which leads through the trees and across the dam to an area of scattered conifers and scrub. Here there is a small junk-yard with a few rusting pieces of abandoned machinery. This spot is favoured by Hoopoes, Black Redstarts, Crested Larks and Sardinian, Dartford and Fan-tailed Warblers at all times, along with Bee-eaters, Black-eared Wheatears and Woodchat Shrikes in the summer. Unfortunately, the remainder of the track has recently been fenced off, so it is not possible to proceed further and you need to retrace your steps back to the car parking area.

Now walk back toward the tunnel under the toll-road and to the left you will find a track that leads downhill to the bottom of the dam. Here there is a water culvert under the road which has a marsh with reeds and grasses. The birds here are similar to those beside the reservoir but you are more likely to find Grey Wagtails, Song Thrushes, Melodious Warblers, Cirl Buntings, Golden Orioles and Rock Sparrows. The nearby orchards hold Wood Pigeons, Collared and Turtle Doves and a good selection of warblers and finches. Kestrels and Sparrowhawks regularly hunt over the fruit trees and

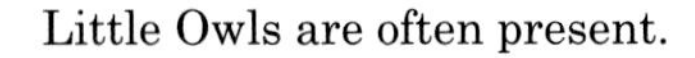

Little Owls are often present.

Other tracks lead through the scrub and waste land to the left of the reservoir that are worth exploring as Dartford Warblers inhabit this area. A further track leads uphill beyond the top of the site, passing through a wooded area before opening up to rocky scrubland with scattered gorse and trees. This is another favourable spot for Great Grey and Woodchat Shrikes, Bee-eaters, warblers and larks. From this position you have clear views of the sky and you should carefully check overhead for Griffon Vultures and Bonelli's Eagles (all year) and for Egyptian Vultures, Booted Eagles and Short-toed Eagles from March to September.

Having visited this area, return to the main road and proceed to the next site.

Map of the Embalse de la Leche

Site Three - The Woods and Río Guadalmina

From the previous site return to the Benahavís road and pass under the toll-road and continue for 1.3 kms. After entering a eucalyptus wood you will see a large pull-off area, where the trees end, on the right. Beside this there is a fence with a chained entrance. Park here and step over the chain and walk diagonally to the left, across the

scrubland, for about 100 metres. This leads to a small cliff edge that looks out over the Río Guadalmina. There is a track down to the river that you may wish to explore. The far bank, which is rocky with scattered trees and shrubs, is a fairly reliable place to see Cetti's Warblers, Black Wheatears, Rock Buntings and Long-tailed Tits. Other regular species include Serins, Great Grey Shrikes and Blue Rock Thrushes.

Walk right, along the clifftop, looking down to the river until you reach the end of the wood. Here there is an area of large rocks surrounded by grass and partly overgrown by stunted trees and shrubs. A small stream trickles down toward the river forming pools that attract many birds which drink and bathe here. During the winter this is a spot usually favoured by Siskins. Numerous paths lead back through the trees toward the parking area.

Map of the Wood and Riverside site

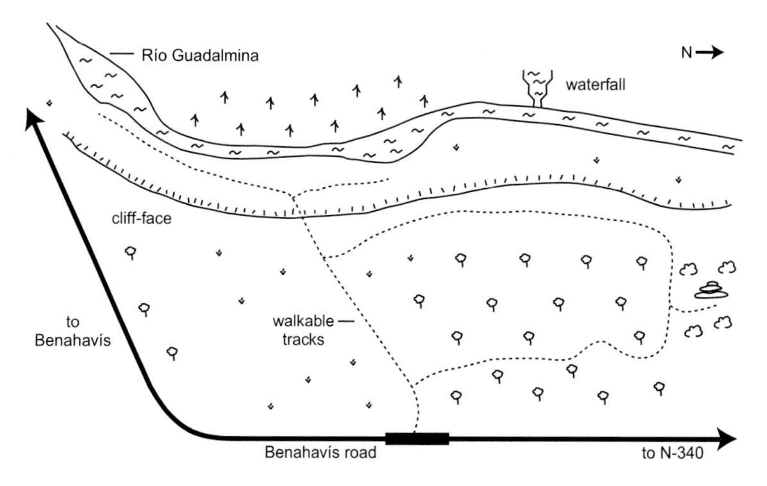

Continue toward Benahavís by car and after one kilometre you reach the first in a series of three miradors (view points) where you can pull off the road and look down to the river in the gorge below. When the river is in full flow the sight is quite spectacular. The miradors also offer good opportunities to watch for Kestrels, Crag Martins, swifts and swallows wheeling overhead and along the rock-face. White and Grey Wagtails are common along the rocky banks of the river and the overhanging vegetation supports Blackcaps, Iberian Chiffchaffs, Fan-tailed and Sardinian Warblers and an assortment of finches and tits.

Site Four - The Reservoir at Benahavís

To reach this site you have to drive to the very end of the village. At this point you have no option other than to turn sharply right, downhill, through very narrow streets. Continue downhill until the road levels and forks. One road leads down toward the football ground and the other turns to the left. At this point take the left-hand fork and follow this road to the reservoir. After 500 metres the surfaced road becomes a dirt-track but remains in good condition. After a further 250 metres there is a small turn-off to the right. There is an old "no entry" sign beside the turning but you can ignore this as you only have to drive in for ten metres and park overlooking the water. Good elevated views of the site are available from this position.

This is a relatively new reservoir (the dam of which was still under construction in August 2001). The vegetation around the water's edge was, at that time, fairly sparse as it had not had time to become fully established. Due to this, the wader numbers are not high but you should expect to see both Cattle and Little Egrets, Grey Herons, Little Grebes, Redshanks and Common Sandpipers. The remainder of this site, however, has a very impressive bird list that more than compensates for the lack of waders and waterfowl.

Return to the main track and drive down to the ford where the river feeds the reservoir. Park close to the ford and view the trees, shrubs and rocks along the riverbank. White and Grey Wagtails, Blackcaps, Willow Warblers, Cetti's Warblers, Cirl Buntings, Song Thrushes, Robins and Kingfishers can normally be seen in this area.

Cross over the ford and turn right, parking beside the water. From here you have reasonable views of most of the reservoir and you can explore the scrubland, small orchard, wooded hillsides and the river below the dam on foot. This area is very productive for Bee-eaters, Great Spotted Woodpeckers, Short-toed Treecreepers, Spotted Flycatchers, Great Grey and Woodchat Shrikes, Cirl, Corn and Rock Buntings, Hoopoes, Black Redstarts, Sparrowhawks, Kestrels and a good selection of warblers, finches, tits, swifts, swallows and martins together with overhead vultures and eagles. An hour or so spent here in the spring or summer can easily produce 40 or 50 different species.

Map of the Reservoir at Benahavís

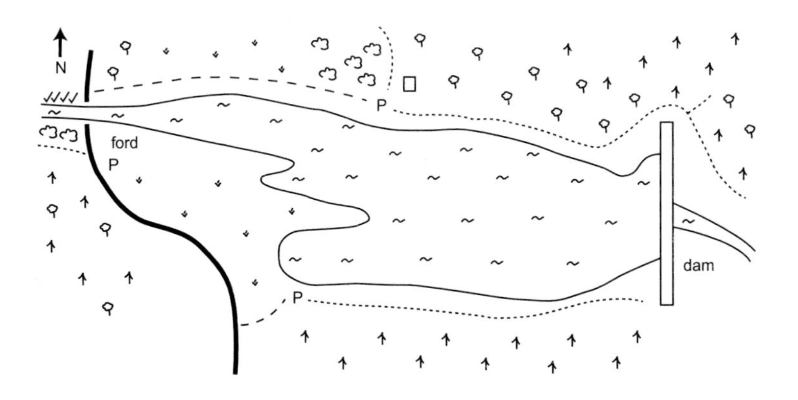

Site Five - The River

Returning toward the village, the road forks after about 650 metres. Take the left-hand fork and at the next junction turn left, downhill, toward the football ground. After 100 metres turn left across the bridge and follow the signs "Piscina, Bar Restaurant, Abierto". Park at the end of the last building and explore the riverside path on foot. Eucalyptus, conifers and broadleaved trees cover both sides of the river's valley and there is a great diversity of shrubs, bushes, heathers, brooms and gorse.

Most of the previously mentioned bird species can also be seen at this location. As with all the other sites, you should keep a watchful eye on the sky for birds of prey. Throughout the year there are Kestrels, Lesser Kestrels, Sparrowhawks, Peregrines, Buzzards, Bonelli's Eagles and Griffon Vultures. In the breeding season you may see Short-toed and Booted Eagles and Egyptian Vultures.

Alpine Swifts and Red-rumped Swallows are always present in the breeding season and there is also the possibility of spotting the much rarer White-rumped Swift.

When to Visit

All of the sites are of interest throughout the year and should produce a good list of birds, with some very interesting species, for a day's outing. Daytrippers and picnickers use most of the sites at weekends or on national/local holidays, especially in the warmer months of the year, so I would recommend that you plan your visit for a weekday to avoid noise disturbance and interference.

General Information

Although most of the sites described are on dirt-tracks, the areas concerned are fairly level and should not pose too much of a problem for wheelchair birders or people with other mobility problems. However, only part of the riverside and eucalyptus wood at site three is accessible to wheelchairs but this should not detract too much from your enjoyment of the area as a whole.

When the river is in flow, access to the Embalse de la Leche will not be possible from the described entry point. The only other access point involves a rather complicated route which I will try to explain.

Travelling from the Gibraltar direction or from the Benahavís road, drive to San Pedro de Alcántara. At the first set of traffic lights (km 170) turn left, where signed for Ronda. Coming from the Marbella direction you should pass through San Pedro and turn right at the traffic lights at km 170.

Proceed along the road for 700 metres and at the first set of traffic lights turn left. Continue for another 700 metres and you reach part of a golf course on the right. About 150 metres further on there is a crossroads where you turn right. Follow this road for just over a kilometre until you reach a small crossroads. There are small signs for "Villa Zazu" (right) and "Casa la Cuesta" (left) which are your landmarks. Take the left turning and then immediately turn right, downhill, next to a small ancient aquaduct. Follow the road until it passes over a small bridge and then climbs uphill. At the top of the hill there is a dirt-track to the right which will lead you under the toll-road and to the reservoir.

The roads from the last set of traffic lights to the site, although quite busy, are in an appalling state and there are many excessively high "speed calming ramps" along the way. These have no markings and are not easily seen, so please be very careful and keep your speed down to avoid damaging the underside of your vehicle.

Bird Calendar

Resident

Little Grebe, Cattle Egret, Little Egret, Grey Heron, Mallard, Griffon Vulture, Sparrowhawk, Buzzard, Bonelli's Eagle, Peregrine, Kestrel, Lesser Kestrel, Red-legged Partridge, Moorhen, Coot, Redshank, Common Sandpiper, Black-headed Gull, Yellow-legged Gull, Rock Dove, Wood Pigeon, Collared Dove, Monk Parakeet, Little Owl, Kingfisher, Hoopoe, Great Spotted Woodpecker, Woodlark, Crested Lark, Thekla Lark, Crag Martin, White Wagtail, Grey Wagtail, Robin, Stonechat, Black Redstart, Black Wheatear, Blue Rock Thrush, Blackbird, Mistle Thrush, Cetti's Warbler, Fan-tailed Warbler, Blackcap, Sardinian Warbler, Dartford Warbler, Great Tit, Blue Tit, Long-tailed Tit, Nuthatch, Short-toed Treecreeper, Wren, Great Grey Shrike, Jay, Jackdaw, Raven, Spotless Starling, Spanish Sparrow, House Sparrow, Tree Sparrow, Chaffinch, Serin, Linnet, Goldfinch, Greenfinch, Common Crossbill, Corn Bunting, Rock Bunting, Cirl Bunting.

Sardinian Warbler *(Sylvia melanocephala)*

Summer / Breeding

Little Bittern, Black Kite, Short-toed Eagle, Egyptian Vulture, Booted Eagle, Quail, Turtle Dove, Cuckoo, Red-necked Nightjar, Alpine Swift, White-rumped Swift, Common Swift, Pallid Swift,

Bee-eater, Sand Martin, House Martin, Red-rumped Swallow, Barn Swallow, Yellow Wagtail, Redstart, Nightingale, Black-eared Wheatear, Reed Warbler, Olivaceous Warbler, Melodious Warbler, Subalpine Warbler, Bonelli's Warbler, Spotted Flycatcher, Woodchat Shrike, Golden Oriole.

Winter

Great Crested Grebe, Shoveler, Pochard, Ringed Plover, Green Sandpiper, Skylark, Meadow Pipit, Song Thrush, Iberian Chiffchaff, Starling, Siskin, Hawfinch.

Passage Migrants

Squacco Heron, Purple Heron, Montagu's Harrier, Honey Buzzard, Roller, Tree Pipit, Whinchat, Northern Wheatear, Willow Warbler, Pied Flycatcher.

Embalse del Taraje

(Cancelada Reservoir)

The reservoir at Cancelada is quite small, probably no more than 30 hectares, but it attracts a wide variety of species throughout the year and has a sizeable population of resident waterfowl, herons and egrets.

Construction work began in early 2000 to develop a golf and country club beside the reservoir which devastated the natural landscape of open scrubland that was a haven for some species of birds. The golf course has now been completed and this has resulted in a drastic reduction in the numbers of larks, wheatears and scrub warblers that once inhabited the area. However, as some species re-located away from the site, the lush greens and fairways of the course have attracted other species such as wagtails and finches.

The south-eastern corner of the site still has a gorse, broom and scrub covered hillside which is an ideal habitat for certain warblers, finches and shrikes. At the southern end of the reservoir there is a large dam, beyond which the land has been cultivated with orange and avocado orchards. There is also an area of mixed trees and giant reeds where leaf warblers, finches and tits are commonly found. Small reedbeds exist both on the eastern and northern edges of the lagoon and it is here that many birds, including Purple Gallinules and Little Bitterns, choose to build their nests. The western side of the site is overlooked by private houses and villas, the gardens and lawns of which reach down to the water's edge.

Access

The Embalse del Taraje is just north-east of the village of Cancelada and is situated mid-way between the towns of Estepona and San Pedro de Alcántara, just under a kilometre inland from the main N-340 highway.

Travelling from the Estepona direction, you leave the N-340 at the exit signed for Cancelada, just beyond km 165. After crossing over the dual carriageway, you see a large set of gates, painted blue, for "Los Flamingos Golf and Country Club".

Travelling from the San Pedro de Alcántara direction you should leave the main road where signed for Cancelada at km 166. At the top of the slip-road the gates to Los Flamingos will be on your right.

Pass through the gates and proceed for 900 metres. Approximately 200 metres before reaching the second gateway to Los Flamingos, there is an expanse of gorse and scrubland on the left and barren ground on the right. A tall red and white telephone mast is clearly seen and this stands beside the track that leads to the reservoir. Park here and follow the track downhill. The dense gorse, broom and scrub to the left is a particularly good area for Sardinian, Dartford and Fan-tailed Warblers, Stonechat and Great Grey Shrike throughout the year. Woodchat Shrikes and Black-eared Wheatears are normally present in the summer and breed in the area. Continuing down the track you reach a larger dirt road which will take you either to the dam (left) or to parts of the golf course. As you approach the reservoir there is an expanse of reeds which holds resident Cetti's Warblers and Iberian Chiffchaffs. These are joined in the spring and summer by Reed, Great Reed and Willow Warblers.

On the water there are usually large numbers of Moorhens, Coots and Little Grebes, all of which breed here. They are often joined in the winter by Great Crested Grebes, Cormorants and a variety of ducks which have included Mallard, Shoveler, Pintail, Teal, Wigeon, Pochard and Red-crested Pochard. Cattle and Little Egrets are usually present in varying numbers throughout the year and in the summer there are Purple and Squacco Herons and Little Bitterns. At least one pair of Purple Gallinules bred here in 2000, in the reeds at the northern end of the reservoir.

It is possible to walk across the dam and this gives you the opportunity to view the whole of the site. Unfortunately, access to the far bank is not possible as it is private land and is fenced off. From the top of the dam you also have good views of the orchards below and an area of giant reeds and marsh. The characteristic birds here are finches, warblers and tits. Blackcaps are abundant in the winter and Siskins have been seen on a few occasions. Spotted Flycatchers, Nightingales and Melodious Warblers are regular breeding species in the summer and Pied Flycatchers are often seen during the passage periods, much more so in the autumn. Kestrels and Sparrowhawks regularly hunt over the orchards and nearby farmland and occasionally a Marsh Harrier may be seen quartering the reeds.

Waders are usually present in the winter and passage periods and I have recorded Grey, Ringed, Little-ringed and Kentish Plovers, Redshank, Greenshank, Dunlin, Black-tailed Godwit, Whimbrel, Snipe, Sanderling and Common, Wood, Green and Curlew Sandpipers. During the summer, Blackwinged Stilts are sometimes present.

Site map of the Embalse del Taraje

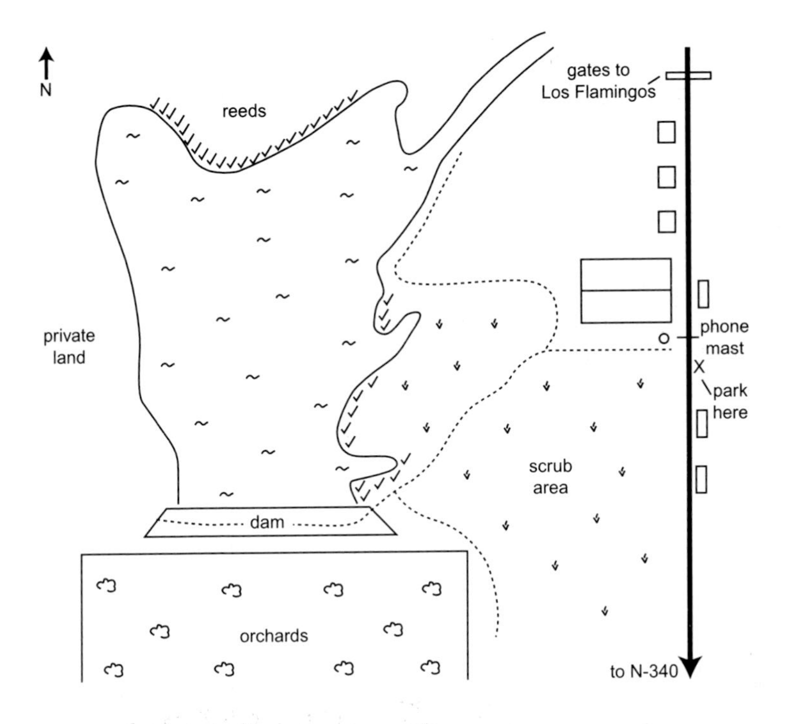

The birds that are regularly seen overhead in the spring and summer include Barn Swallow, Red-rumped Swallow, Common Swift, Pallid Swift and House and Sand Martins. Crag Martins, which are resident birds, are more commonly seen in the winter.

Due to the close proximity of the sierras you are always likely to get good views of passing Griffon Vultures and, if you are lucky, Bonelli's Eagles at any time of the year and in the summer Egyptian Vultures, Booted Eagles and Short-toed Eagles are often seen.

Other birds that can regularly be seen at almost any part of the site, at the appropriate times of the year, are Hoopoes, Bee-eaters, Black Redstarts, Crested Larks, Woodlarks, Skylarks, Thekla Larks, Blue Rock Thrushes, Kingfishers, Northern Wheatears and White, Grey and Yellow Wagtails.

When to Visit

This site is of interest at all times and is generally very quiet except for the occasional dog-walker, golfers or other birdwatchers. Late afternoon sunlight reflecting off the water can be a problem, especially if viewing from the eastern side, and on particularly hot days you may be affected by heat haze.

General Information

Following extremely heavy rains, the amount of water flowing into the reservoir sometimes floods over the dam, completely water-logging the orchards and other farmland. When this happens the local farmers will open the sluice gates in the dam to allow the water to flow down the correct channels. This can completely empty the reservoir and it may take some weeks, until the river's flow abates, before the farmers close the sluice gates and the reservoir begins to refill.

Please note that there is no wheelchair access to this site.

Bird Calendar

Resident

Little Grebe, Cattle Egret, Little Egret, Grey Heron, Mallard, Shoveler, Griffon Vulture, Marsh Harrier, Sparrowhawk, Buzzard, Bonelli's Eagle, Kestrel, Peregrine, Red-legged Partridge, Moorhen, Coot, Purple Gallinule, Kentish Plover, Redshank, Yellow-legged Gull, Collared Dove, Wood Pigeon, Ring-necked Parakeet, Monk Parakeet, Little Owl, Kingfisher, Great Spotted Woodpecker, Hoopoe, Skylark, Woodlark, Crested Lark, Thekla Lark, White Wagtail, Grey Wagtail, Robin, Stonechat, Black Redstart, Blue Rock Thrush, Blackbird, Cetti's Warbler, Fan-tailed Warbler, Sardinian Warbler, Dartford Warbler, Iberian Chiffchaff, Long-tailed Tit, Great Tit, Blue Tit, Great Grey Shrike, Jay, Jackdaw, Raven, Spotless Starling, Spanish Sparrow, House Sparrow, Tree Sparrow, Chaffinch, Serin, Linnet, Goldfinch, Greenfinch, Corn Bunting, Rock Bunting, Cirl Bunting.

Summer / Breeding

Little Bittern, Squacco Heron, Purple Heron, Black Kite, Egyptian Vulture, Short-toed Eagle, Booted Eagle, Black-winged Stilt, Little-ringed Plover, Turtle Dove, Common Swift, Pallid Swift,

Bee-eater, Sand Martin, House Martin, Barn Swallow, Red-rumped Swallow, Tawny Pipit, Yellow Wagtail, Nightingale, Black-eared Wheatear, Reed Warbler, Great Reed Warbler, Olivaceous Warbler, Melodious Warbler, Subalpine Warbler, Willow Warbler, Spotted Flycatcher, Woodchat Shrike, Ortolan Bunting.

Winter

Great Crested Grebe, Cormorant, Wigeon, Teal, Pintail, Pochard, Redcrested Pochard, Grey Plover, Ringed Plover, Dunlin, Curlew Sandpiper, Sanderling, Snipe, Black-tailed Godwit, Whimbrel, Greenshank, Common Sandpiper, Wood Sandpiper, Green Sandpiper, Black-headed Gull, Crag Martin, Meadow Pipit, Song Thrush, Starling, Siskin, Hawfinch, Reed Bunting

Passage Migrants

Collared Pratincole, Roller
Wryneck, Tree Pipit, Whinchat
Northern Wheatear, Sedge Warbler
Pied Flycatcher.

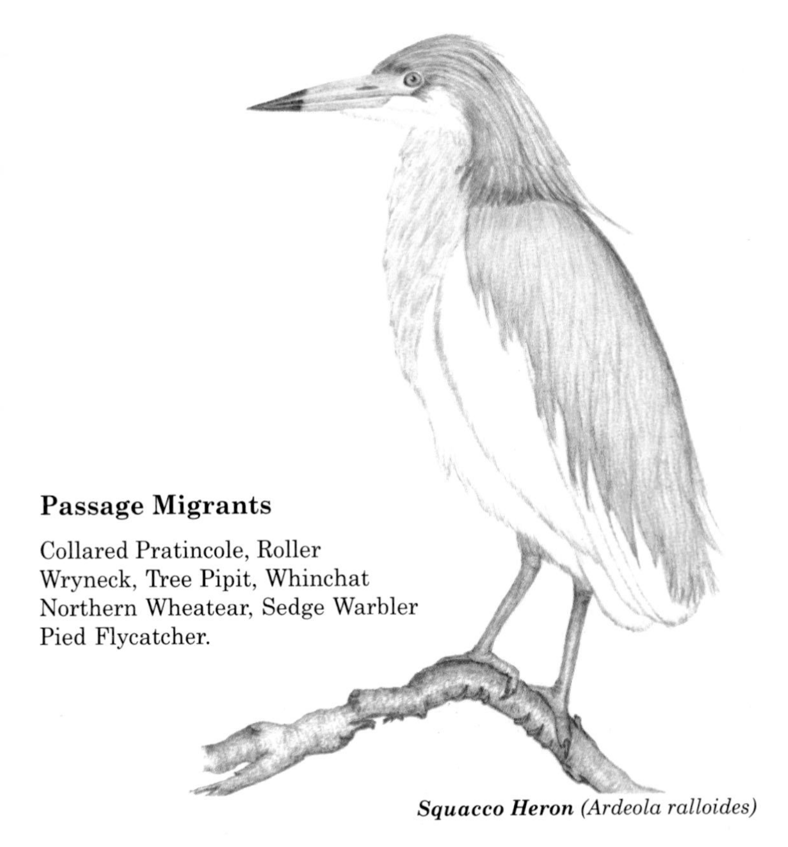

Squacco Heron *(Ardeola ralloides)*

The Río Guadalmansa

This site description covers the last 2.5 kms of the Río Guadalmansa, the estuary and the surrounding areas. There is a very wide variety of habitats and also a great diversity of resident and seasonal bird species that can be found in a relatively small area.

The river, situated between the towns of Estepona and San Pedro de Alcántara, flows from the nearby hills of the Sierra Bermeja mountain range. The main N-340 coastal highway crosses the river at km 164, which is the main entry point to the site. The river is seasonal and dries up after prolonged periods without rain. However, when the flow of water ceases, a lagoon of some 350 metres in length is formed between the roadbridge and the beach. Although the water level in the lagoon may fluctuate, it does not dry out completely as sea water often breaks over the beach and flows into the lagoon during high tides. The lagoon/estuary is bounded on the far bank by mixed trees, shrubs and reedbeds, whilst the near side is mainly scrub land with a few trees. During wet weather the bottom end of this area floods and becomes marshy. Further back there are areas of agricultural land where various vegetable and fruit crops are grown.

Access

Travelling towards Málaga from the Gibraltar direction on the main N-340, you cross over the Río Guadalmansa at km 164. Once across the bridge, take the first exit from the main road and then do a right-handed U-turn back toward the river. Just before the road turns under the bridge, there is a small road on the left, between two electrical pylons. Turn here and follow the road to the end, where there is a beach bar and a water treatment plant. Park here with the river directly beside you.

Travelling from the Málaga direction, there is a turning off the main road 400 metres beyond the km 165 marker, with a small sign for "Sun Beach". Turn off here and then immediately turn left, downhill, running parallel to the N-340. At the bottom of the hill turn left under the bridge and the road to the parking area is on the right, 15 metres beyond the bridge. If you miss this turn-off, you need to drive a further two kilometres to the next junction and return from the opposite direction.

General map of the Río Guadalmansa and the surrounding areas

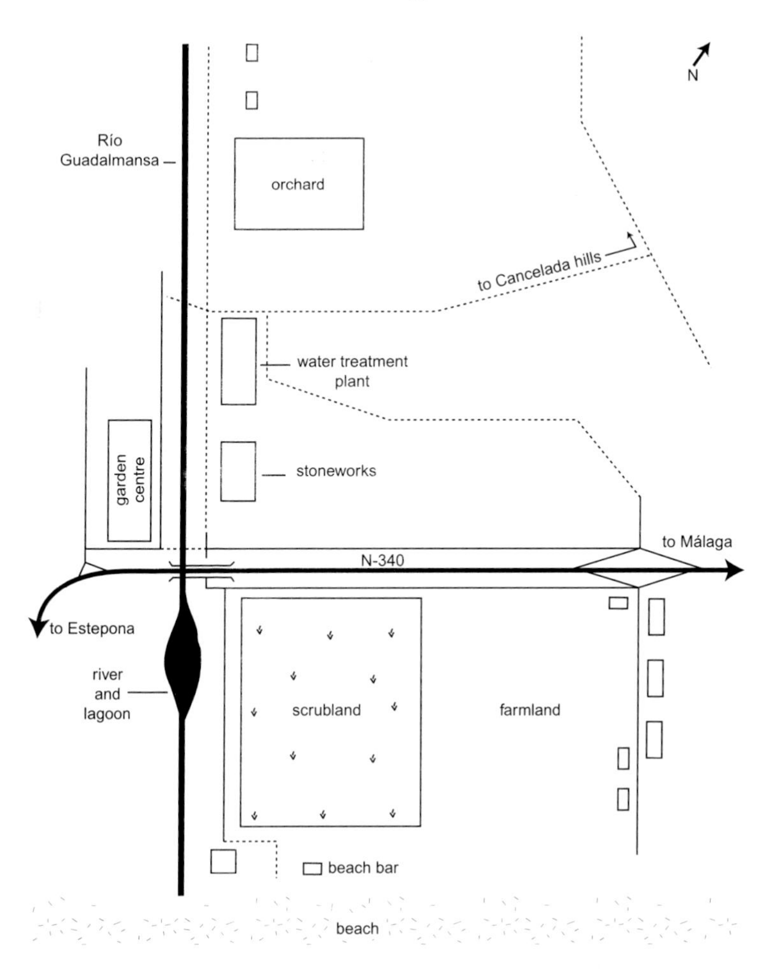

The beach is a good place to start your visit to this site. It offers a variety of waders in the winter that regularly include Ringed and Little-ringed Plovers, Turnstones, Sanderlings and Common Sandpipers. Kentish Plovers are resident and breed on the sandy beach. Offshore you may see passing terns and gulls throughout the year and from autumn to spring there are normally small numbers of Gannets, Great Crested and Black-necked Grebes, Razorbills, Red-breasted Mergansers and shearwaters. Large flocks of mixed gulls frequently form on the beach and careful scanning can produce both Audouin's and Mediterranean Gulls along with the more common Black-headed and Yellow-legged varieties. Kittiwakes and Oystercatchers are scarce in this area but the occasional small group or single bird may be seen passing along the coast.

The river/lagoon holds a good variety of resident birds, including Moorhens, Mallards, Little Grebes, Grey Herons, Cattle Egrets, Little Egrets and a few waders. In the spring and summer the reeds should be carefully checked for Little Bitterns and both Squacco and Purple Herons. The reedbeds also hold Cetti's Warblers (resident), Willow Warblers, Reed Warblers, Iberian Chiffchaffs and Reed Buntings at the appropriate times of the year.

The expanse of scrub land on the east side of the river is home to Sardinian and Fan-tailed Warblers, Stonechats, Crested Larks and a variety of finches. The regular summer visitors to this particular spot are Woodchat Shrikes, Hoopoes, Bee-eaters and Yellow Wagtails. Meadow Pipits, Siskins and Starlings can often be found during the winter months. Wood Pigeons and Collared Doves (all year) and Turtle Doves in the summer can usually be seen, either in the trees or on the overhead electricity cables or pylons.

Cormorants are regular visitors in the winter, usually in the tall trees near the bridge or on the lagoon itself. The bridge area is favoured by swifts, swallows, martins, wagtails, warblers and Kingfishers. Otters are often seen in the marsh area below the bridge and turtles and water snakes inhabit the river. Kestrels, Lesser Kestrels, Buzzards and eagles regularly overfly the site and occasionally Griffon Vultures from the mountains pass overhead as they search for carrion in the nearby farmland.

Beyond the bridge the riverbed is normally dry or marshy, except after heavy rains. A track runs alongside the river, passing a stoneworks and a water treatment plant. Further along there is open waste land and finally orchards and agricultural land. The track is driveable at most times and is wide enough for you to stop and scan the riverbed and the adjacent land without causing problems to other drivers.

The dry riverbed is a nesting site for a few pairs of Little-ringed Plovers and on occasions you may see Collared Pratincoles resting here during the passage periods. I have also recorded both Tree and Spanish Sparrows along this track. The waste land beyond the water treatment plant and the area where the hill has been cut away is a good spot for Rock and Corn Buntings, Little Owls, Crested Larks, chats, warblers and finches. Northern Wheatears can be seen on passage and Black-eared Wheatears breed in the vicinity.

At one point the track passes a fenced avocado orchard and I have seen Redstarts here on numerous occasions during the summer and autumn. The resident Black Redstarts can be found throughout the site at any time of the year, although they are more numerous in the winter. Just beyond the orchard, where the hill has been cut away and terraced to form farmland, a colony of Bee-eaters nest in the cliff face. The birds usually arrive from late March and begin excavating holes in the cliffs for their nests. For six months they are highly visible in this area.

The agricultural land is a favoured site for Hoopoes, Cattle Egrets, Serins, Stonchats, Crested Larks and Woodlarks. These are joined by Skylarks in the winter. The scattered trees hold reasonable numbers of tits, finches and warblers, including Melodious and Olivaceous in the summer. Above the farms, in the rocky hills, it is possible to see Blue Rock Thrushes and Red-legged Partridges.

Bonelli's Eagles, although scarce, do occasionally pass over the area at times, but you are more likely to see the summer visiting Short-toed and Booted Eagles which are regular features at this site. Other birds of prey include Peregrines, Sparrowhawks and Kestrels, which are often seen hunting over the farmland and orchards.

The track ends just beyond the farms and you need to retrace the route back as far as the water treatment plant. At this point you have two choices of which route to take. The first option is to return back along the river, or you can take the track behind the water plant. This leads you back to the N-340, passing a few small farms and private houses. Along this track you can expect to see many of the species previously mentioned.

At the water plant, where the track divides, you will notice a third track which leads uphill. This leads to the hills above the village of Cancelada and the river, an area I will describe later as a subsidiary of the main site.

When to Visit

In the cooler months of the year, the area is generally quiet, with just the occasional dog-walker or fisherman, but in the summer months, especially at weekends, quite a few people are attracted to the beach and a recently opened (2001) beach bar. The resulting noise and activity tends to keep the more secretive birds, such as the Little Bittern and Squacco Heron, well under cover in the reeds.

Although the site is of interest at all times of the year, I would suggest that morning or evening visits be made to the lagoon/estuary area to minimize the effect of human interference. The remainder of the site is usually quiet except for occasional lorries going to and leaving the stoneworks.

Visits during the spring migration period (March to May) can be very rewarding.

General Information

The scrubland near the lagoon is fenced with a single strand of wire. This is more of a boundary marker than an attempt to keep people out. There are numerous tracks that you can walk, but with a pair of binoculars you can view the whole area from the road, causing less disturbance to the birds.

At the top end of the lagoon, near the bridge, there is a white pylon set on a grassy bank. Using the pylon as cover, you can climb the bank and look down to the marshy areas beside the lagoon. There are a few tracks that will take you down to the water's edge. It is in this area that most of the waterfowl, waders, egrets and herons can be seen.

For most of the year the riverbed above the bridge is dry, enabling you to cross from one bank to the other, either on foot or by car. One area on the far bank that can be productive is the garden centre. The assortment of flowers, shrubs and trees attracts a lot of insects, which attract many insect eating birds and small rodents and lizards. These, in turn, attract the raptors, especially Sparrowhawks and Kestrels.

As the area is generally quiet and is completely flat, this site, or at least most of it, is wheelchair accessible when dry. It may prove problematical in wet weather but most of the site can also be viewed from a car.

Bird Calendar

Resident

Little Grebe, Gannet, Cattle Egret, Little Egret, Grey Heron, Mallard, Griffon Vulture, Sparrowkawk, Buzzard, Bonelli's Eagle, Peregrine, Kestrel, Red-legged Partridge, Moorhen, Coot, Little-ringed Plover, Kentish Plover, Redshank, Black-headed Gull, Yellow-legged Gull, Sandwich Tern, Rock Dove, Wood Pigeon, Collared Dove, Monk

Parakeet, Little Owl, Kingfisher, Hoopoe, Great Spotted Woodpecker, Woodlark, Crested Lark, Crag Martin, White Wagtail, Grey Wagtail, Robin, Stonechat, Black Redstart, Blue Rock Thrush, Blackbird, Cetti's Warbler, Fan-tailed Warbler, Sardinian Warbler, Long-tailed Tit, Great Tit, Blue Tit, Great Grey Shrike, Jackdaw, Spotless Starling, Spanish Sparrow, House Sparrow, Tree Sparrow, Chaffinch, Serin, Goldfinch, Greenfinch, Linnet, Corn Bunting, Rock Bunting, Cirl Bunting.

Summer / Breeding

Little Bittern, Squacco Heron, Purple Heron, Short-toed Eagle, Egyptian Vulture, Montagu's Harrier, Booted Eagle, Lesser Kestrel, Black-winged Stilt, Common Tern, Little Tern, Whiskered Tern, Turtle Dove, Common Swift, Pallid Swift, Bee-eater, Sand Martin, House Martin, Barn Swallow, Red-rumped Swallow, Yellow Wagtail, Nightingale, Redstart, Black-eared Wheatear, Reed Warbler, Olivaceous Warbler, Melodious Warbler, Willow Warbler, Spotted Flycatcher, Woodchat Shrike, Ortolan Bunting.

Winter

Great Crested Grebe, Black-necked Grebe, Cormorant, Wigeon, Shoveler, Pintail, Osprey, Oystercatcher, Ringed Plover, Dunlin, Sanderling, Blacktailed Godwit, Common Sandpiper, Turnstone, Audouin's Gull, Little Gull, Mediterranean Gull, Lesser Black-backed Gull, Kittiwake, Red-breasted Merganser, Razorbill, Skylark, Meadow Pipit, Song Thrush, Starling, Iberian Chiffchaff, Siskin.

Passage Migrants

Mediterranean Shearwater, Black Kite, Honey Buzzard, Collared Pratincole, Little Stint, Green Sandpiper, Wood Sandpiper, Tree Pipit, Whinchat, Northern Wheatear, Roller, Sedge Warbler, Pied Flycatcher.

Cancelada Hills and the Monte Mayor Golf
(Subsidiary site to the Río Guadalmansa)

The subject areas of this sub-site are the foothills of the Sierra Bermeja mountain range that overlook the village of Cancelada and the Monte Mayor Golf Club. They can be reached by taking the third track that I referred to in the description of the Río Guadalmansa. It is clearly indicated on the map and leads uphill from behind the water treatment plant. After following this track for 500 metres you reach a junction with a larger dirt-road where you should turn left.

A short distance further on the road becomes surfaced, passing between some private houses and fincas. Once beyond these houses the road begins to climb uphill.Follow the road and as it turns round to the right you will see a private house, above the road level, on the right-hand side. About 70 metres beyond this, as the road turns to the left, there is an open area on the right where you can pull off the road and park.

The rocky scrubland around this area and the slope down toward the river hold reasonable numbers of Sardinian, Fan-tailed and Dartford Warblers, Red-legged Partridges, Great Grey Shrikes and Blue Rock Thrushes throughout the year. These are joined in the summer by Woodchat Shrikes, Subalpine Warblers and Hoopoes. From this location you can also look down into a valley and see part of the Cancelada reservoir (*Embalse del Taraje*).

There are tracks that lead down through the scrubland toward the water but, at the present time (August 2001), construction work is currently underway to build a golf and country club (Los Flamingos) around the top end of the reservoir so access to it is not possible from here at this time.

However, access may be possible once the building work has been completed. The reservoir and the easy access to it, is the subject of a separate site description.

Continuing from this point follow the road and signposts to Monte Mayor Golf Club, a distance of about 4.5 kms. It may be worth stopping every now and then to scan the surrounding countryside and rock-faces.

Yet another golfing complex is being developed in these hills, the Marbella Club Golf Resort. Shortly after the entrance to this you reach a forested area which is worth stopping at as the trees here hold Crested Tits, Jays, Great Spotted Woodpeckers and Short-toed Treecreepers. Bonelli's Warblers are also present in the spring and summer. Where the road makes a sharp left-handed U-turn there is a path leading into the forest that can be explored on foot.

Monte Mayor Golf Club is set in a valley surrounded by forests and has a small stream running through the course. You can park in the club car-park and take a walk around the area, obviously making sure that you keep to the footpaths so as not to interfere with the golfers. Rock Buntings, Hoopoes and Black-eared Wheatears are quite prominent here. Also to be found are the same species that are

in the previously mentioned forest area, which, in fact, forms the lower boundary of the golf course. Other birds that are commonly found here include a good selection of warblers, finches, tits, larks, wagtails and pipits. Eagles, vultures and numerous other birds of prey are regularly seen overhead.

Care should be taken when identifying larks along this route as the Thekla and Crested Larks tend to overlap. Remember, the Crested Lark's crest is always erect and the Thekla Lark has much bolder breast spots.

To return to the main N-340 highway you need to drive back the same way and pass through the village of Cancelada.

Little Bitern *(Ixobrychus mintus)*

The Río del Padron

The Río del Padron flows some 12 kms from the nearby Sierra Bermeja mountain range and reaches the sea at the Playa del Padron, located just a few kilometres east of the town of Estepona, and can be easily reached via the main N-340 highway.

The driveable/walkable stretch of the river, which this site account describes, is 6.5 kms in length and a car is desirable. For most of the year, especially in the summer, the river above the roadbridge is usually dry for about 3 kms because numerous farms further upriver drain off water to irrigate their crops. When the flow ceases, a lagoon is formed between the bridge and the beach. This lagoon is approximately 100 metres long and 25 metres wide and is bounded on both sides by trees, shrubs and reedbeds. This creates a haven for herons, egrets, waders and waterfowl. Although the level of the water may fluctuate I have never known it to dry up completely.

Heading inland, the habitat changes from dry, rocky wasteland, which holds Red-legged Partridges, Black Redstarts, Hoopoes, larks, chats, warblers and wheatears, to agricultural land, and then on to pine forests as the track climbs some 200 metres above sea-level. The forests are home to the usual array of finches and warblers along with Jays, Great Spotted Woodpeckers, Short-toed Treecreepers, Nuthatches and Crested Tits. As the track descends into a valley, more agricultural land, mainly orchards of avocados and citrus fruit, becomes prominent. From this point onward the river usually holds water and good elevated views of the river and its valley are possible. Beyond the farmland, the track again rises up through forests of pine and both deciduous and evergreen broadleaved trees before finally dropping down to end beside the river in a secluded wooded valley.

As the distance of this site is so great, I will concentrate my notes on what I consider to be the better spots to find the best variety of bird species. Highlighting these particular locations does not mean the other areas along the route are not worth stopping at.

All along the route, with the exception of the lagoon, you should keep a watchful eye on the sky as vultures very often pass by, and eagles and other birds of prey regularly hunt over the agricultural land.

Access

Travelling from the Gibraltar direction toward Málaga on the main N-340 highway, you pass the Kempinski Resort Hotel at km 159. Immediately beyond this, the road crosses the Río del Padron. Turn off the main road after the bridge and, at the roundabout, turn back along the beach toward the river.

Travelling from the Málaga direction toward Gibraltar, you leave the N-340 just after km 160 and pass under the roadbridge and take the second right from the roundabout to reach the river.

After passing a beach bar, the road turns right beside the river/lagoon. Here a stand of eucalyptus trees offers a good shaded parking area. Alternatively, and this is my preference, you can pass under the bridge and turn round and then park directly beneath the bridge, facing the lagoon. This enables you to view most of the area without getting out of your car and perhaps disturbing birds that may take flight once you actually do leave your car to walk around the lagoon. Obviously, if the river is in flow you will not be able to fully circle the site.

The river/lagoon has mixed trees, shrubs and reeds on both sides, and looking from the bridge area the left-hand side has extensive reedbeds toward the bottom end. The right bank has fewer reeds but there is a marshy area midway along that is attractive to waders.

The trees and reeds harbour a good variety of warblers, with Sardinian, Cetti's, Melodious, Reed and Willow Warblers all being present at the appropriate times of the year. In the winter months Iberian Chiffchaffs, Blackcaps and Siskins are usually to be found around the lagoon.

Waders can normally be seen from October to April or May and these regularly include Redshanks, Common and Green Sandpipers, Sanderlings, Dunlins and Ringed, Little-ringed and Kentish Plovers. Occasionally a few Turnstones may appear and I have also recorded Wood Sandpipers here. Black-winged Stilts are frequent summer visitors to the area and may be seen at any point along the course of the river. Grey Herons, Cattle and Little Egrets, Moorhens, Coots and Little Grebes can be found at any time of the year and Purple and Squacco Herons and Little Bitterns are sometimes present in the summer, or during the passage periods. Wildfowl are not common here, with the exception of Mallards, but on occasions a few ducks will appear in the winter months.

Other species that are regularly seen here, either resident or seasonal visitors, include White, Grey and Yellow Wagtails, Wood

Pigeons, Collared Doves, Turtle Doves, Black Redstarts, Kingfishers, Bee-eaters, Crested Larks, Meadow Pipits, Nightingales, Woodchat Shrikes and Hoopoes, along with swallows, martins and swifts. Birds of prey are not common here, with Kestrel and Lesser Kestrel being the only regular visitors.

General map of the Río Padron site

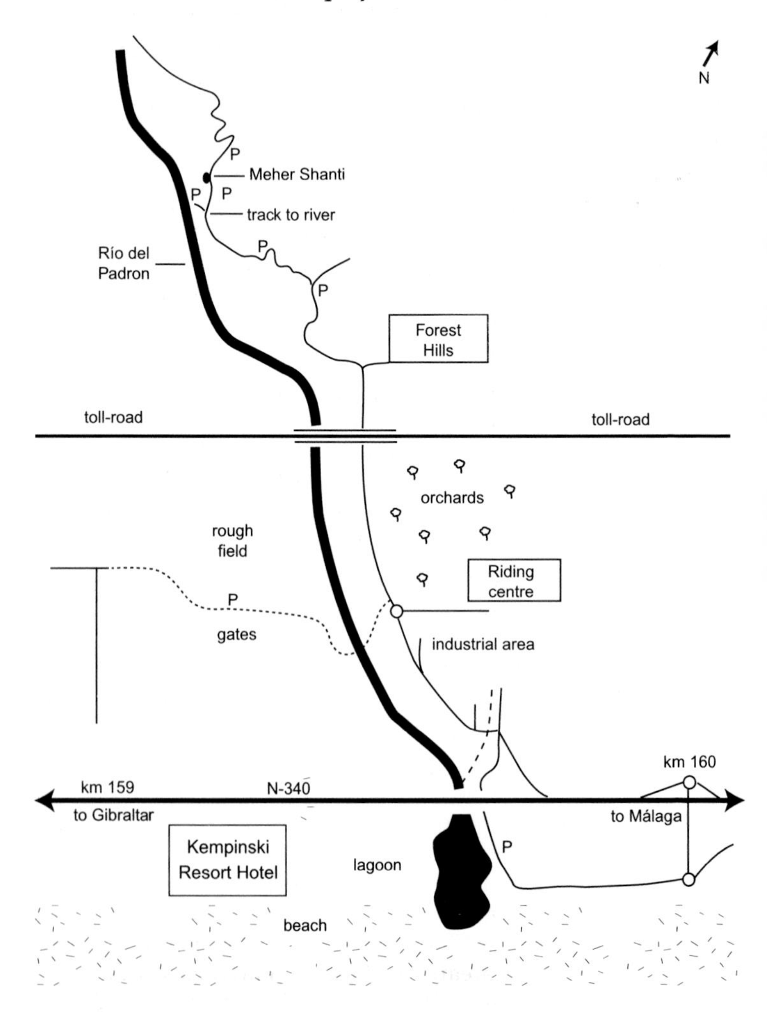

Whilst in the area of the lagoon, you should check the beach and the sea. Mixed flocks of gulls often form on the sand and many use the lagoon to bathe. Black-headed and Yellow-legged are always present and careful scanning of the flocks may produce Audouin's, Slender-billed, Little, Mediterranean and Lesser Black-backed Gulls.

Sandwich Terns are fairly regular, passing along the coast throughout the year and in the summer both Common and Little Terns can also be seen. The only marsh tern I have recorded at this location was a single Whiskered Tern, feeding at the lagoon.

Offshore, especially from late September to May, Great Crested and Black-necked Grebes, Gannets, Razorbills, Red-breasted Mergansers and Common Scoters can turn up and at most times of the year shearwaters are passing by.

The area immediately above the bridge sometimes holds an inch or two of water for a few weeks after the rest of the riverbed has dried up and this is a favourite feeding spot for Red-rumped and Barn Swallows, Common and Pallid Swifts and House Martins from February/March through to October. Crag Martins are regular in the winter and Sand Martins, although more commonly seen in the summer, may also be seen occasionally at other times.

About 100 metres above the bridge, to the right of the river, there is a copse of eucalyptus and other trees and the course of a usually dry stream. This area is also a good spot for many of the species I have already mentioned and I have seen Monk Parakeets here on numerous occasions. I suspect these birds are from a small breeding colony at the nearby Torre del Velerín.

Once you have finished viewing this area, you should drive upriver, following the route on the map. The first kilometre of this part of the river, up to the riding centre (*Escuela de Arte Ecuestre*), is best avoided due to the fact that it is mainly an industrial area with a marble factory and a cement producing plant and the air here is usually full of dust from these industries.

From the roundabout, near to the riding centre, up to the toll road flyover (1.5 kms), there are many orchards that are worth scanning for Cirl Buntings, finches and warblers. Sparrowhawks, in the winter, and Montagu's Harriers, in the summer, can sometimes be seen hunting over the fruit trees. The scrubland on both banks of the river can produce Fan-tailed, Sardinian and Dartford Warblers, Corn and Rock Buntings, Crested Larks, Black Redstarts, Northern and Black-eared Wheatears, Red-legged Partridges, Stonechats, Whinchats, Hoopoes, Great Grey and Woodchat Shrikes, Rednecked Nightjars and Little Owls.

From this point onwards, keep an eye out for eagles and other birds of prey overhead. Resident Griffon Vultures from the nearby mountains can be seen all year, as can Buzzards, Kestrels and Peregrines. During the summer, both Booted and Short-toed Eagles, Black Kites and Montagu's Harriers are fairly common and occasionally an Egyptian Vulture may be seen passing over the area in search of food. Honey Buzzards pass through the area in great numbers in early May but it is rare for any to remain as they prefer to move further north.

After passing under the toll-road flyover you reach the entrance to the Forest Hills complex. Do not enter through the gates but instead, turn left onto an unsurfaced track which leads between some private houses and villas. After 250 metres there is a large set of white gates with the name "La Oropendola" (the Golden Oriole). This is very aptly named as orioles can often be seen around the area during the summer. A further 250 metres brings you to a fork in the road where you should take the left-hand track, which leads downhill, following the course of the river. However, I would suggest that you park just before the fork and scan the valleys on both sides before proceeding. Finches and warblers are usually prominent and in the summer it is a fairly reliable spot to see Woodchat Shrikes, Nightingales, Golden Orioles and also Subalpine Warblers.

Continue along the track, stopping occasionally to view the river and the surrounding forest, until you reach a sharp U-bend which passes over a small water course (usually dry). The gully on the left has been productive in the past for Melodious Warblers, Blackcaps and Nightingales. The trees hold a reasonable assortment of finches, warblers and tits, along with Nuthatches, Great Spotted Woodpeckers, Short-toed Treecreepers and Jays. Blue Rock Thrushes can sometimes be spotted on the rocky hilltops to the right of the road.

A further 500 metres brings you to a few farmhouses and a smaller track that leads down to a ford crossing the river. You should ignore this turning and follow the main track to the right, keeping the river on your left-hand side. Continue for another 600 metres, passing more farms, until you reach another track leading down toward the river. Take this track and park at the bottom of the hill by a growth of giant reeds. There is a walkable track beside the reeds and there is also a rather rickety foot bridge crossing the river. This area is particularly good for Long-tailed Tits (*subspecies irbii*), Nightingales, Cetti's Warblers and Robins. Woodchat Shrikes are fairly common and Hawfinches can be found in the winter, usually in the scattered fruit trees nearby. During the summer, especially around the large growths of prickly pear cactus, you may find Rufous Bush Chats.

Return up the hill and turn left onto the original track and proceed for about 250 metres and you will notice a house named "Rivendell". Drive beyond this house for a further 150 metres to another house named "Meher Shanti". This is unmissable as it is painted a pinkish colour and has a blue domed roof. Park here and walk back down the track as far as Rivendell. This area of mixed trees and shrubs usually produces Crested Tits, Nuthatches, Short-toed Treecreepers, Melodious Warblers, Golden Orioles and, occasionally, Firecrests.

Continue for another 300 metres along the track and you will find a large scraped area of land, on the right, which is an ideal parking place. You are now just one kilometre from the end of the route and you now have the choice of walking or driving the remaining part. If you decide to walk, I must point out that the first 300 metres is quite a strenuous uphill climb. If you decide to drive you should be aware that the track can be very rutted and broken in places, but it is driveable if you take care. I personally prefer to walk as the forest and undergrowth becomes much denser and the birds more numerous, so the chances of seeing certain species is enhanced. Also, the views of the river and surrounding hills and valleys can be better appreciated. This part of the site is very good for many of the woodland and forest birds previously mentioned.

The track finally ends in a clearing in a valley, right beside the river. Large rocks and scattered trees for shade make this a comfortable place to sit and let the birds come to you whilst enjoying the silence, away from the noise of the coast. I have recorded Wrens, Mistle Thrushes and Ring Ouzels at this particular spot.

On the return trip, look for a small track leading off from the right-hand side of the road about 15 metres before the roundabout near the riding centre. If the riverbed is dry, you can turn here and cross to the opposite bank. You will find the exit track 50 metres downriver. This track leads uphill and after 200 metres there is a white gateway on the left. Park directly opposite the gates and scan the roughly ploughed field beside the track. Stone Curlews have nested in this area in 1998, 1999, 2000 and 2001. Also in this area you can find Cirl, Corn and Rock Buntings, Olivaceous Warblers, Great Grey Shrikes, Red-necked Nightjars and Little Owls. To return to the N-340, continue along the track for 200 metres and as soon as you reach the surfaced road turn left. This will lead you downhill to a roundabout beside the N-340, just outside Estepona. Obviously, if the river is in flow this final part of the site will not be an option.

When to Visit

The site is of interest at all times and usually produces a good bird list. The whole length of the site is generally quiet but the area around the lagoon can sometimes be frustratingly noisy, especially in the summer when the beach is busy.

Please note that apart from the beach bar there is no other source of refreshment anywhere along the route and you should take an adequate supply of water or other liquids with you.

General Information

Planning permission has been granted by the Estepona Town Council for a recreation centre to be built beside the river/lagoon and I feel it will not be too long before construction is started. Whilst the construction work is taking place, there may be disruption and the value of the lagoon part of the site may be diminished. However, the experience of the building of the Kempinski resort shows that the site can very quickly get back to normal once construction work has been completed.

Most of this site, although rather uneven, is wheelchair accessible or can be viewed from a car or some other vantage point, and I would class this area as being a reasonable site for people with mobility problems.

Bird Calendar

Resident

Little Grebe, Cattle Egret, Little Egret, Grey Heron, Mallard, Griffon Vulture, Buzzard, Bonelli's Eagle, Peregrine, Kestrel, Lesser Kestrel, Red-legged Partridge, Moorhen, Coot, Stone Curlew, Little-ringed Plover, Kentish Plover, Redshank, Common Sandpiper, Black-headed Gull, Yellow-legged Gull, Sandwich Tern, Rock Dove, Wood Pigeon, Collared Dove, Monk Parakeet, Little Owl, Kingfisher, Hoopoe, Great Spotted Woodpecker, Woodlark, Crested Lark, White Wagtail, Grey Wagtail, Robin, Stonechat, Black Redstart, Blue Rock Thrush, Blackbird, Mistle Thrush, Cetti's Warbler, Fan-tailed Warbler, Sardinian Warbler, Dartford Warbler, Blackcap, Firecrest, Long-tailed Tit, Crested Tit, Coal Tit, Great Tit, Blue Tit, Nuthatch, Wren, Short-toed Treecreeper, Great Grey Shrike, Jay, Jackdaw, Raven, Spotless Starling, House Sparrow, Tree Sparrow, Chaffinch, Serin, Linnet, Goldfinch, Greenfinch, Corn Bunting, Rock Bunting, Cirl Bunting.

Summer / Breeding

Little Bittern, Purple Heron, Black Kite, Short-toed Eagle, Egyptian Vulture, Montagu's Harrier, Booted Eagle, Black-winged Stilt, Common Tern, Little Tern, Whiskered Tern, Turtle Dove, Red-necked Nightjar, Common Swift, Pallid Swift, Bee-eater, Sand Martin, House Martin, Barn Swallow, Red-rumped Swallow, Tawny Pipit, Yellow Wagtail, Nightingale, Rufous Bush Chat, Redstart, Black-eared Wheatear, Reed Warbler, Olivaceous Warbler, Melodious Warbler, Subalpine Warbler, Bonelli's Warbler, Spotted Flycatcher, Woodchat Shrike, Golden Oriole.

Winter

Great Crested Grebe, Black-necked Grebe, Wigeon, Shoveler, Common Scoter, Red-breasted Merganser, Sparrowhawk, Ringed Plover, Grey Plover, Dunlin, Sanderling, Black-tailed Godwit, Green Sandpiper, Turnstone, Audouin's Gull, Little Gull, Mediterranean Gull, Lesser Black-backed Gull, Kittiwake, Razorbill, Crag Martin,Skylark, Meadow Pipit, Ring Ouzel, Song Thrush, Iberian Chiffchaff, Starling, Siskin, Hawfinch.

***Hoopoe** (Upupa epops)*

Passage Migrants

Mediterranean Shearwater, Gannet, Squacco Heron, Osprey, Honey Buzzard, Oystercatcher, Wood Sandpiper, Roller, Wryneck, Tree Pipit, Whinchat, Northern Wheatear, Willow Warbler, Pied Flycatcher.

Los Reales

Los Reales is the highest peak of the Sierra Bermeja mountain range which stretches from Casares to San Pedro de Alcántara. It is immediately inland of the town of Estepona and at its highest point is 1449 metres above sea-level. The higher slopes are dominated by pine forests and it is one of the few remaining areas in Spain where the Spanish Fir (*Pinsapo*) can be found. The road leading up the mountain, although full of twists and turns, is in very good condition and passes through a succession of varying habitats which attract different bird species.

The views from the summit are astounding and on clear days you can see the snow covered peaks of the Sierra Nevada mountains almost 100 miles away to the east, as well as Gibraltar and the coast and mountains of the African continent to the south and south-west.

The area has been designated as the Paraje Natural Los Reales de Sierra Bermeja, covering 1,215 hectares and is a haven for a wide variety of wildlife. Unlike many areas, it is not fenced off to the public and is accessible at almost any point.

Access

The entry point to Los Reales from the coast is from the town of Estepona. It can also be reached from the north via the A-369 Ronda-Jimena de la Frontera road, turning off at Algatocín and passing through Jubrique.

Travelling from the Gibraltar direction, on the N-340, you take the third exit for Estepona, midway between the km 154 and 155 markers. Follow the road through a set of traffic lights and at the first roundabout turn left. Continue through two more sets of traffic lights and at the third set, next to the Mercadona Supermarket, turn left onto the road signed for Peña Blanca and Jubrique.

Travelling from the Málaga direction on the N-340, you take the first exit for Estepona, just before km 158. Follow the road through a series of roundabouts and at the first set of traffic lights, just before entering the town, turn right. Continue through two more sets of lights and at the third set, on the brow of a hill, turn right, where signed for Genalguacil.

Although approached from different directions and signposted to different towns, this is the same road (MA-557) to Los Reales.

Unfortunately, at the time of writing, there are no roadside kilometre markers on this road and any distances given are taken from my own vehicle's kilometre counter and from maps. If you take the traffic lights as being km 0, you should be able to follow my distances to the various sub-sites that are described along the route.

Approximately 3.8 kms along the road, there is a dirt track that turns off to the right, just before the spot where overhead electricity cables pass over the road. The track leads to a small copse of about 20 pine trees on a hill overlooking scrubby valleys on both sides.

This area has been productive in the past for Dartford, Sardinian, Subalpine, Olivaceous and Fan-tailed Warblers, Crested Lark, Woodlark, Hoopoe, Bee-eater, Great Spotted Woodpecker, Black-eared Wheatear, Turtle Dove, Stonechat, Woodchat Shrike and a variety of finches. Both Booted and Short-toed Eagles are commonly seen here in the spring and summer, whilst Bonelli's Eagles and Griffon Vultures may be seen overhead at any time. During the summer, European Nightjars (*C. europaeus*) can sometimes be seen at dusk.

Further along the road, there is a white concrete block on the righthand side with "K6" painted on it, and 250 metres beyond this there is a track to the left on a very sharp bend. Pull in here and scan the scrub, gullies and rocky hillside for Great Grey Shrike, Blue Rock Thrush, Hoopoe, Little Owl, Black Redstart, Red-legged Partridge, Nightingale, Blackcap and other warblers and finches.

Within a further 2 km, you come to a series of pull-off spots on the left where small streams (usually bone dry in the summer) pass under the road. Stopping at any of these and venturing a short way into the forest can produce sightings of Crested, Coal, Great and Blue Tits, Nuthatch, Jay, Short-toed Treecreeper and Great Spotted Woodpecker throughout the year. Seasonal visitors include Golden Oriole, Spotted Flycatcher, Melodious Warbler and Bonelli's Warbler in the summer and Iberian Chiffchaff and Brambling in the winter.

After 15 kms, you reach a crossroads at an area known as Puerto de la Peña Blanca. You can park here and explore the surrounding area. The pines hold the usual finches and warblers along with Short-toed Treecreeper and Nuthatch. Here there are good views over the Genal Valley where several white villages can be seen in the distance. Vultures, eagles and other raptors are often present and may be seen hunting over the valley and the pine forests.

General map of the Estepona-Los Reales road

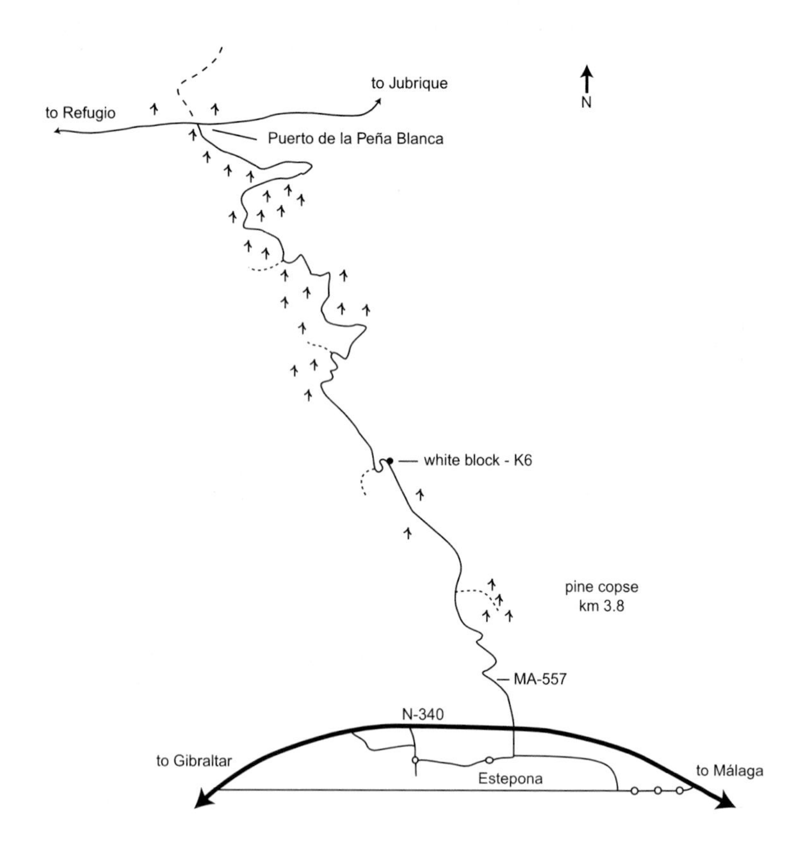

From here you take the road to the left signed "Paseo de Los Pinsapos, 3.2 km" and "Refugio, 4.5 km", which leads uphill. After 2.9 kms, there is a very sharp right-hand bend and on the left there is a flat rock formation. Park here and explore the rocks and scrub for Blue Rock Thrush, Black-eared Wheatear and Rock Bunting. Thekla Larks are also to be found here and should not be confused with the Crested Larks which prefer much lower altitudes.

The Paseo de Los Pinsapos (the Pinsapo trail) is on the next hairpin bend and is marked with a wooden sign. There is room to park and explore the trail which leads through the pines. The birds at this location are not particularly numerous but the Pinsapos appear to be the trees most favoured by Firecrests.

The road now leads directly to the area known as El Refugio, where there is a venta (bar/restaurant) and a picnic area amongst the trees, complete with tables and barbecues. Just before the venta there is a car parking area with views down to Estepona and further east towards Fuengirola. The valley in front of the car park is a fairly reliable place to find Rock Bunting, Crested Tit and Nuthatch. I have, on one occasion, seen a pair of Black Wheatears at this location.

Leaving your car parked here walk along the road, passing the bar, until you reach another parking area, the "Plazoleta de Salvador Guerrero". At the far end of this area there is a narrow path that follows the contours of the mountain and leads to a mirador, about 375 metres away. Walking along this path you may see Thekla Lark, Sardinian Warbler, Blue Rock Thrush, Crag Martin and Black Wheatear, which are all resident species. In the summer these are joined by Black-eared Wheatear, Common Swift, Pallid Swift, Alpine Swift, House Martin, Barn Swallow and, occasionally, White-rumped Swift. The views here include Gibraltar, Algeciras Bay and the Moroccan coast to the south and Casares to the west.

Returning to your car, take the road that leads uphill to the summit of the mountain. The road is steep and is in a very bad state but it is driveable with care. I recommend you drive directly to the top, leaving any stops for the downhill trip. The road ends at a fenced compound containing radio and television masts and aerials and there is room to park. To the left of the compound there is an electricity pylon and beside this there are a few rough steps leading to a path that will take you to the mountain's peak. This vantage point gives you excellent all-round views which include, on clear days, Africa and Gibraltar. The snow covered peaks of the Sierra Nevada mountains in Granada can also be seen, 100 miles to the east. The trees that are mostly found at the summit are Pinsapos, stunted by the wind and growing close to the ground. This is the best place to find the Firecrests, although Chaffinches and Nuthatches are also fairly common here.

Good views can be had of Griffon Vultures, Bonelli's Eagles, Buzzards, Ravens and Red-billed Choughs as they pass both above and below your position. Although not common, Golden and Spanish Imperial Eagles do sometimes venture into the area, especially in the winter when food may be scarcer in their own territories. In the summer there are always Booted Eagles in the vicinity and there is also the possibility of seeing one or two Egyptian Vultures. Eagle Owls breed in the general area but these are more commonly seen hunting at dawn and dusk.

On the trip downhill, stop near to a white building and explore the forest here. Crested Tits, Firecrests and Crossbills can often be found amongst the mixed pines. Make several other stops at any convenient place on the way back to the Refugio.

If you should wish to explore further areas, you can return to the Puerto de la Peña and take either the road to Jubrique or the unsurfaced road to Genalguacil. I am not very familiar with either of these routes so any exploration of these areas on your part would have to be on a "stop and see" basis.

When to Visit

The area around the Refugio is very popular with local families at weekends and on national/local holidays in the warmer months of the year when they spend the day here having picnics and barbecues. The resulting noise and human activity is not conducive to good birdwatching and I would recommend a weekday visit to this site.

Visits here at any time of the year should produce a good bird list but obviously the summer/breeding season will offer the most species.

There can be great temperature differences between the coast and the mountain and there is often much more wind, so take a few items of warm protective clothing in the car. Do not rely on the bar being open, as it often isn't. Instead, take a packed lunch and an adequate drink supply with you.

If you can see beforehand that the mountain top is covered by cloud, I would suggest you delay your visit to this site until a clearer day because the visibility at the top can be reduced to little more than a few metres in such conditions and good birdwatching is almost impossible.

General Information

With the exception of the areas at the Puerto de la Peña Blanca and the Refugio, this site is not really wheelchair accessible, although various aspects can be viewed from a car.

The main part of this site is well over 1000 metres above sea-level. If you suffer from any form of heart problems, or any other complaint that can be aggravated by rarified air, you should think carefully before visiting the site as the nearest medical assistance is a half hour's drive away.

General map of the Refugio and the summit of Los Reales

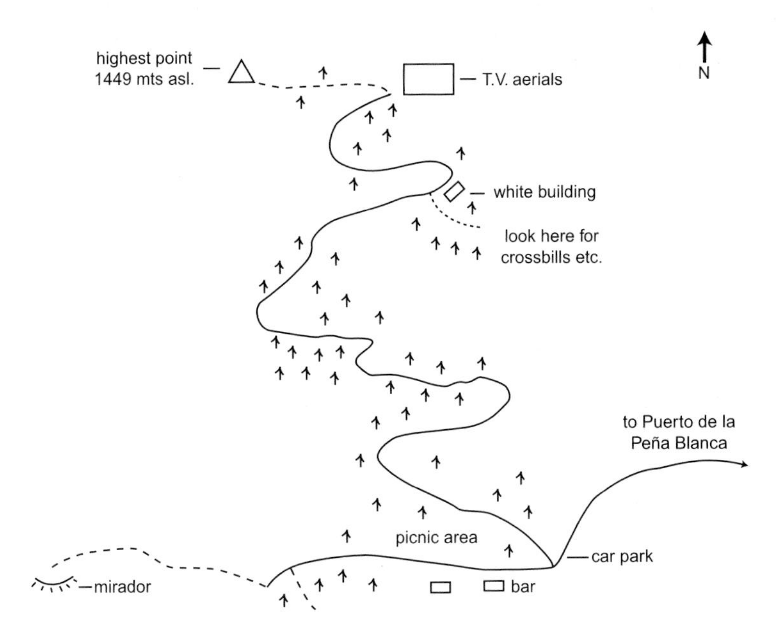

Bird Calendar

Resident

Griffon Vulture, Sparrowhawk, Buzzard, Bonelli's Eagle, Golden Eagle, Spanish Imperial Eagle, Peregrine, Kestrel, Lesser Kestrel, Red-legged Partridge, Rock Dove, Wood Pigeon, Collared Dove, Little Owl, Tawny Owl, Eagle Owl, Green Woodpecker, Great Spotted Woodpecker, Woodlark, Crested Lark, Thekla Lark, Crag Martin, White Wagtail, Robin, Stonechat, Black Redstart, Black Wheatear, Blue Rock Thrush, Blackbird, Mistle Thrush, Fan-tailed Warbler, Blackcap, Sardinian Warbler, Dartford Warbler, Firecrest, Crested Tit, Coal Tit, Great Tit, Blue Tit, Nuthatch, Wren, Short-toed Treecreeper, Great Grey Shrike, Jay, Red-billed Chough, Jackdaw, Raven, Spotless Starling, Rock Sparrow, Tree Sparrow, Chaffinch, Serin, Linnet, Goldfinch, Greenfinch, Common Crossbill, Corn Bunting, Rock Bunting.

Summer / Breeding

Black Kite, Short-toed Eagle, Egyptian Vulture, Booted Eagle, Turtle

Dove, Cuckoo, Nightjar, White-rumped Swift, Alpine Swift, Common Swift, Pallid Swift, Hoopoe, Bee-eater, House Martin, Barn Swallow, Nightingale, Black-eared Wheatear, Olivaceous Warbler, Melodious Warbler, Subalpine Warbler, Bonelli's Warbler, Spotted Flycatcher, Woodchat Shrike, Golden Oriole, Ortolan Bunting.

Winter

Red Kite, Merlin, Meadow Pipit, Song Thrush, Chiffchaff, Starling, Brambling, Siskin.

Passage Migrants

Honey Buzzard, Roller, Tree Pipit, Whinchat, Northern Wheatear, Pied Flycatcher.

Crested Tit *(Parus cristatus)*

The Arroyo Vaquero and Estepona Golf

The Arroyo Vaquero flows from the southern slopes of the Sierra Bermeja mountain range and enters the sea at the Playa del Moral, some three kilometres south-west of the town of Estepona. The main N-340 highway crosses over the river at km 150 and access to both the seaward and inland parts of this site can be found there.

After prolonged dry spells, especially in the summer, the river ceases to flow at the lower end as various farms upstream draw off water to irrigate their land. However, when this happens, a lagoon normally forms from just below the roadbridge, to the beach, which usually holds waders and waterfowl along with a number of farm ducks and geese. The trees, reeds and shrubs that surround the river/lagoon attract good numbers of finches, tits and warblers.

Above the bridge, the road to Estepona Golf runs parallel with the river as it passes through areas of agricultural land for the first 600 metres before opening up, on the left, to common land and then to an area of scattered trees and dense gorse, broom and scrub. Both banks of the river are vegetated by trees, reeds, shrubs and cane.

The road and river then run alongside the fourth fairway and the fifth green of the golf course. Beside the fifth green, the surfaced road turns sharply left, uphill, towards the golf clubhouse and a residential area, which are of little interest as far as birding is concerned. The site route continues directly ahead, passing alongside the sixth and seventh holes of the golf course. Beyond this, the land again becomes agricultural for about 500 metres and then rises up gently through wooded and shrub areas beside the river, on the right, with open rocky ground with sparse scrub cover on the left of the track. Small trails lead down to the river and they are always worth exploring.

Unfortunately, a recent forest fire in this area (August 2000) has destroyed some of the undergrowth and a few of the trees but the vegetation has already begun to regenerate itself. A bigger threat to the area at the moment is the construction of a massive flyover for the new toll-road that will connect Estepona and Torre Guadiaro. Work is progressing at a steady rate and hopefully the flyover will be completed before this book is published.

Beyond the construction site there is a steep rock-face of a sandstone ridge known as Lomo Redondo, where Blue Rock Thrush, wheatears and raptors are commonly found. At this point the track divides. The uphill track leads to arid scrubland, a haven for warblers, before ending at a gateway to private land on the crest of another hill. The downhill track leads to a private estate known as "Cortijo Blanco". The lush growth of trees, shrubs, reeds and undergrowth near to the cortijo attracts many finches and warblers throughout the year.

At all times of the year, but more so in the spring and summer, vultures, eagles and other raptors overfly the area and good views are possible. During the northern passage, many migrating birds can be seen riding the thermals to regain height before continuing their journey.

The length of this site is approximately 6 kms and can be walked or driven in its entirety. I prefer to drive the first two kilometres to the golf course, stopping at a couple of selected areas en route and then walking the rest of the site.

Access

Travelling from the Málaga direction toward Gibraltar on the main N-340 highway, you reach the bridge over the Arroyo Vaquero at km 150. Immediately after crossing the bridge you turn right where it is signed for Estepona Golf and explore the inland parts of the site first.

Travelling from the Gibraltar direction, you turn right at km 150 immediately after crossing the bridge and explore the lagoon first. By following these guidelines you will only have to cross a very fast and dangerous stretch of road once instead of three times.

To simplify things, I will describe the site as I visit it, for instance, coming from and returning to Estepona.

After turning off the main road, stop near the bridge and walk down to the river. From autumn to spring, waders can usually be found here and have included Ringed, Little-ringed and Kentish Plovers, Redshank, Dunlin, Wood Sandpiper and Common Sandpiper. In the spring and summer Black-winged Stilts and Purple Herons can be seen. Both Cattle and Little Egrets are common and may be seen at any time. Larks, pipits and wagtails frequent the stony riverbeds and the trees that grow profusely on both banks hold resident Goldfinch, Greenfinch and Serin. Cetti's Warblers are common residents in the reeds. During the summer the migrant visitors include swallows, swifts, martins, Bee-eater, Nightingale and Reed, Willow, Olivaceous and Melodious Warblers. Amongst the wintering species there are Iberian Chiffchaff, Siskin and Black Redstart. Most of these species can be seen at any point along the site route.

General map of the Arroyo Vaquero and Estepona Golf

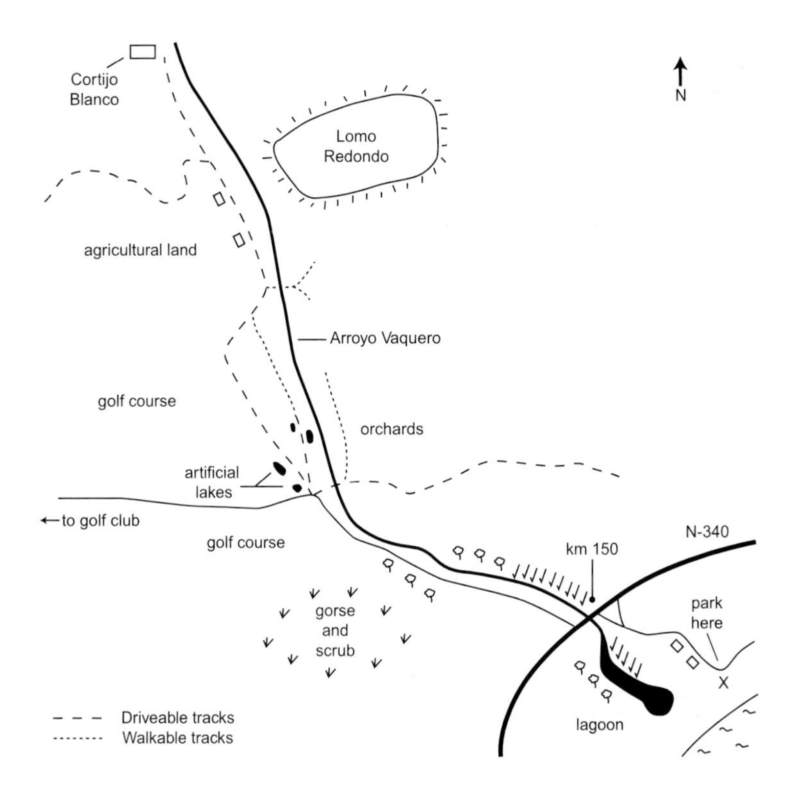

The farm on the opposite side of the road is also a productive area for many species, including Wood Pigeon, Collared Dove, Hoopoe, Little Owl, Kestrel and Turtle Dove.

Although you can stop anywhere along the route, the next real point of interest is one kilometre from the bridge. Here there is a large area of open land on the left and then an expanse of dense gorse, broom and scattered trees. The trees hold the usual array of finches and leaf warblers, whilst the gorse is particularly good for Sardinian, Fan-tailed and Dartford Warblers. Great Grey Shrike (all year) and Woodchat Shrike in the breeding season are fairly common, as are Stonechat, Kestrel, Corn Bunting, Crested Lark and Buzzard. In the summer both Short-toed and Booted Eagles, Black kite and Egyptian Vulture can be seen overhead. European Nightjars also frequent this area but are usually only seen at dusk.

Continue until you pass the 5th green of the golf course. At this point the road turns left and leads uphill towards the golf clubhouse. Directly opposite is a dirt track leading to the 6th Tee and another signed for "Cortijo Blanco". Park here and explore the four artificial lakes that form part of the golf course (see map). Various pinnioned species of ducks and swans have been introduced to the lakes and these include Tufted Duck, Red-crested Pochard, Mandarin Duck and Carolina Woodduck. Although nice to see, they can hardly justify a tick in your book. However, they do act as decoys and can attract genuine wildfowl and waders in the winter and during the passage periods. I have recorded Greylag Goose, Mallard, Shoveler, Wigeon, Moorhen, Coot and Little Grebe here.

Directly opposite the 5th green, there is a river crossing that can be driven or walked across if the water is not in full flow. A track to the left runs alongside the river with orange orchards on the right. This is a good spot for Hoopoe, often to be seen feeding on the track itself, and for Robin, Nightingale and Melodious Warbler.

The other track leads right from the river crossing and passes a few scattered farms before reaching open, broken ground with scattered trees, shrubs and cacti. This area can usually be relied on for Bee-eater, Woodchat Shrike, Black-eared Wheatear, Nightjar and Rufous Bush Chat in the summer.

The area around the 6th Tee is particularly well vegetated and the fairways of the 6th and 7th holes can produce large winter flocks of Meadow Pipits, Cattle Egrets, White Wagtails, Siskins and other finches. During the summer months, Yellow Wagtails and Spotted Flycatchers are prominent and passage periods regularly produce good numbers of Whinchat, Pied Flycatcher, Roller and Northern Wheatear. Throughout the year there are Blue, Great and Long-tailed Tits, Great Spotted Woodpecker, Short-toed Treecreeper and Jay.

From this point, you have the choice of driving or walking the rest of the route. In the winter I normally leave my car here and walk up the right-hand track beside the golf course, returning later along the other track. If you decide to drive further, you need to take the left-hand track for 700 metres and then turn right, uphill, before dropping down into a valley beside the river. In the summer, I usually park here and cover the remainder of the route (2.3 kms) on foot.

From here the first 500 metres is mainly farmland with vegetable fields and orchards of avocado and citrus fruit. Both Corn and Cirl Buntings can be found around the farmland, along with Skylark,

Crested Lark, Bee-eater, Cattle Egret and a selection of finches and warblers. Buzzards and Kestrels are often seen and Sparrowhawks regularly hunt over the orchards. In the summer, Montagu's Harrier, Black Kite, Egyptian Vulture and eagles can be found.

As the track leads uphill, the terrain changes to rock and scrub on the left and trees and shrubs on the right, beside the river. A recent fire in this area has damaged or destroyed some of the vegetation but appears not to have had a significantly adverse effect on the birdlife. Small paths and trails lead down to the river and are well worth exploring. Long-tailed Tits and Blackcaps inhabit the trees beside the river and Chaffinches are common here. Grey Wagtails and Wrens are sometimes seen on the riverbed and the stony banks.

Just beyond the fire-damaged area, a new toll-road flyover is being constructed, causing some disturbance to the birdlife, but this may be completed by the end of 2001 and the area should return to normal very quickly.

Further along the track, you reach the brow of the hill where the track divides. The main track drops downhill towards the Cortijo Blanco whilst the other track, to the left, climbs rather steeply uphill. The sheer rock-face of the Lomo Redondo is directly opposite this point on the far side of the river. This is a very reliable spot for Blue Rock Thrush and Rock Bunting. Crag Martins are regularly spotted flying overhead, as are Griffon Vultures, eagles and other raptors. It is possible to see Black Wheatears here but they are quite elusive and may take patience to find, but the summer-visiting Black-eared variety are much more accommodating and are easily spotted.

The short track down to the cortijo is surprisingly well vegetated and usually produces good numbers of finches, warblers, tits and both House and Tree Sparrows. Golden Orioles can be seen in the summer. The cortijo marks the northern limits of the site.

The uphill track opposite the Lomo Redondo passes through an area of arid scrubland and a small wooded area before ending at a set of gates to private land. Thekla Larks are common here and the warbler population includes resident Sardinian, Fan-tailed and Dartfords. Subalpine Warblers are sometimes present in small numbers in the summer and Whinchats often remain in the area for a short time during the passage periods, especially during September.

The Lagoon

To visit the lagoon, return along the route to the junction with the N-340 and turn left, over the bridge, toward Estepona and then immediately turn off the main road onto a track directly beside the km 150 marker. After about 30 metres, you join a surfaced road which runs for 200 metres toward the sea, passing through a residential area. As the sea comes into view, the road turns sharply to the left. At this point there is a parking area almost on the beach. The river/lagoon is 70 metres to the right and can be reached by walking across the sand.

The far side of the lagoon is bounded by trees, reeds and dense undergrowth and is overlooked by a housing development. The near side has sparse tamarisk scrub and a few scattered trees and reeds. The resident birds that can be found around the lagoon include the same finches, warblers, tits, larks and wagtails that I have previously mentioned. Seasonal visitors include Sand Martins, Red-rumped Swallows, Whiskered Terns, Willow Warblers and Black-eared Wheatears during the spring and summer. In the winter you can expect to see Iberian Chiffchaff, Siskin, Black Redstart and Kingfisher.

The waders seen here correspond with those that can be seen near the bridge, the exceptions being Green Sandpiper, which I have recorded here on two occasions, and Greater Flamingo, which can appear at any time of the year, although these are usually juvenile birds.

Living on the lagoon are a number of farm ducks and geese, Moorhens, Coots, Mallards and Little Grebes. These can be joined in the winter by passing Wigeon and Shovelers.

The most exceptional bird to be seen here was an Egyptian Goose. It arrived at the lagoon on the 6th June 2000 and remained in the area until it was found dead in November 2000. This was only the fifth such goose to be recorded in Spain and reported to the Iberian Rarities Committee, and only the second ever recorded and reported in Andalucía. I am rather proud of the fact that both the Andalusian birds were found by myself and reports, supported by photographic evidence, were submitted by me to the IRC regarding this bird and one I recorded nearby in January 1999.

Whilst in the vicinity of the lagoon, you should check the beach and the sea for other birds. Flocks of mixed gulls regularly form on the beach near to the lagoon and, although these are mainly Yellow-legged and Black-headed varieties, I have also recorded Audouin's

and Mediterranean Gulls here. It is not uncommon to see terns passing along the coast and I have recorded Sandwich Terns (all year) and both Common and Little Terns in the summer. Gannets and shearwaters can normally be seen offshore throughout the year although they are far more numerous and prominent in February-April and August-November. Other birds that may be seen offshore are Razorbills, Red-breasted Mergansers, Common Scoters and both Great Crested and Black-necked Grebes. Mostly these are seen in the autumn and winter although single birds or small groups can appear at any time.

When to Visit

The site is of interest throughout the year and any visit here should produce a good bird list. There is always the possibility that the lagoon may dry up completely in the height of summer and visits here may prove useless at this time. Also in the summer it can become oppressively hot and I recommend you carry an adequate supply of water with you.

General Information

Part of this site runs alongside a golf course and although it is never particularly busy you should keep to the footpaths and not allow your birdwatching activities to interfere with the golfers.

With the exception of the lagoon, this site is suitable for people with mobility problems. Much of the area is wheelchair accessible. Those areas that are not directly accessible can be viewed from a car or from some other vantage point.

Bird Calendar

Resident

Little Grebe, Mediterranean Shearwater, Gannet, Cattle Egret, Little Egret, Greater Flamingo, Mallard, Griffon Vulture, Sparrowhawk, Buzzard, Bonelli's Eagle, Kestrel, Red-legged Partridge, Moorhen, Coot, Little-ringed Plover, Kentish Plover, Redshank, Common Sandpiper, Black-headed Gull, Yellow-legged Gull, Sandwich Tern, Rock Dove, Wood Pigeon, Collared Dove, Monk Parakeet, Little Owl, Barn Owl, Kingfisher, Hoopoe, Great Spotted Woodpecker, Woodlark, Skylark, Crested Lark, Thekla Lark, Crag Martin, White Wagtail, Grey Wagtail, Robin, Stonechat, Black Redstart, Black Wheatear, Blue Rock Thrush, Blackbird, Mistle Thrush, Cetti's Warbler, Fan-tailed Warbler, Sardinian Warbler, Dartford

Warbler, Long-tailed Tit, Great Tit, Blue Tit, Short-toed Treecreeper, Wren, Great Grey Shrike, Jay, Jackdaw, Raven, Spotless Starling, House Sparrow, Tree Sparrow, Chaffinch, Serin, Linnet, Goldfinch, Greenfinch, Corn Bunting, Cirl Bunting, Rock Bunting.

Summer / Breeding

Black Kite, Short-toed Eagle, Egyptian Vulture, Montagu's Harrier, Booted Eagle, Lesser Kestrel, Common Tern, Little Tern, Whiskered Tern, Turtle Dove, Cuckoo, Black-winged Stilt, Nightjar, Alpine Swift, Common Swift, Pallid Swift, Bee-eater, Sand Martin, House Martin, Red-rumped Swallow, Barn Swallow, Tawny Pipit, Yellow Wagtail, Nightingale, Rufous Bush Chat, Redstart, Black-eared Wheatear, Reed Warbler, Olivaceous Warbler, Melodious Warbler, Subalpine Warbler, Willow Warbler, Spotted Flycatcher, Woodchat Shrike, Golden Oriole, Ortolan.

Winter

Great Crested Grebe, Black-necked Grebe, Cormorant, Grey Heron, Greylag Goose, Shelduck, Wigeon, Teal, Shoveler, Pochard, Common Scoter, Red-breasted Merganser, Osprey, Oystercatcher, Ringed Plover, Dunlin, Sanderling, Green Sandpiper, Turnstone, Audouin's Gull, Little Gull, Mediterranean Gull, Lesser Black-backed Gull, Kittiwake, Razorbill, Meadow Pipit, Song Thrush, Blackcap, Iberian Chiffchaff, Siskin, Hawfinch.

Passage Migrants

Squacco Heron, Purple Heron, Whimbrel, Wood Sandpiper,Roller, Wryneck, Tree Pipit, Whinchat, NorthernWheatear, Pied Flycatcher.

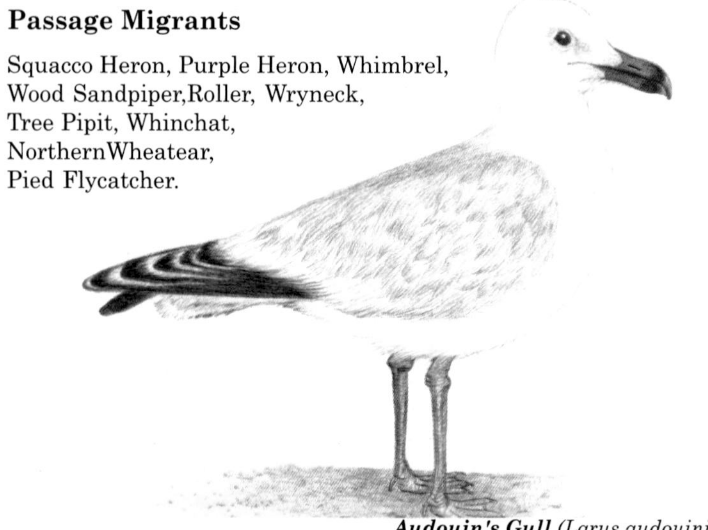

Audouin's Gull *(Larus audouinii)*

The Río de Manilva / The Roman Baths / The Sierra de Utrera

The Río de Manilva flows from the hills near the village of Casares and runs some eight kilometres to the sea on the northern outskirts of Sabinillas. At the midway point of its course, the river passes the Roman baths in the area of La Hedionda (*Baños Romanos de La Hedionda*) and follows the contours of the Sierra de Utrera, a large limestone ridge with strange rock formations.

After prolonged dry periods and especially during the summer months, the river ceases to flow for the first and last 3 kms of its course, but the middle section, fed by underground springs in the area of the baths, flows throughout the year. This is the most attractive part of the river and also the most productive for birdlife. This, therefore, is the area which this site description will concentrate upon.

The area known as La Hedionda was obviously named in recognition of the sulphurous water that flows from the underground springs and the baths. The water is a very distinct greyish blue colour and has a rather strong smell. It is hardly surprising that the literal translation of the name La Hedionda is "the stinking place". In spite of this, the area was once a very popular spot with the Spanish, who would come to holiday here and enjoy the peace and tranquility that the secluded, shaded valley offers and also to bathe in the baths, believing in the supposed health giving and curative properties of the water.

Although long abandoned and neglected, the buildings and gardens that were once associated with this resort are still obvious and now offer good nesting sites to many species of birds. The area, however, is still popular with campers and day visitors in the warmer months of the year, especially at weekends and during the school holidays. Unfortunately, many of these people appear to have no respect for nature or the environment and cause damage, create noise and leave a depressing amount of rubbish strewn about the area.

The Sierra de Utrera is a limestone ridge which runs for some 3 kms in a north-south direction. At its highest point it is 349 metres above sea-level and it forms the western side of the valley at La Hedionda. Balancing rocks and layered formations of the limestone make it worth a visit just for the sights alone. A small track, following the course of a usually dry stream (*Canuto de la*

Utrera), leads in through a gorge which then opens out in a secluded valley that passes through a cleft in the ridge. Sheer rock faces and a dense floor covering of gorse, shrubs and scrub has turned this spot into a haven for some species of birds, such as Blue Rock Thrush and Great Grey Shrike.

Due to the varying types of habitats that are to be found in the general area, the diversity of species ranges from waders, forest birds, scrub dwellers and mountain species, together with a good variety of raptors, which are usually evident overhead and includes eagles and vultures.

Access

Travelling toward Gibraltar from the Málaga direction on the main N-340 highway, you turn off to the right after crossing the Río de Manilva. The actual turning is just before km 145, directly before the "Gran Bar" which is well signed.

Travelling in the opposite direction, you turn left immediately beyond the Gran Bar, after passing km 145.

If you are travelling from inland, ie. Casares, Gaucín or further, you take the road to Manilva and just before reaching the town you turn left, beside a large quarry. There is an advertising sign for the Roman Oasis Restaurant which should guide you to the site. To simplify matters, the rest of the description will be given as if you were coming inland from the N-340.

The road leads between agricultural land on the right and a small industrial area on the left. After 700 metres, the road runs parallel with the river, passing through more farmland. The fields, orchards and the river hold a good selection of birds throughout the year and includes pigeons, doves, finches, wagtails, warblers, larks and tits. Cattle Egrets are particularly obvious in the fields and during the summer Hoopoes, Bee-eaters, Nightingales, Melodious Warblers and Golden Orioles can also be found along the route.

Although you can stop at any point along the road to view the area (I suggest you make at least two stops), my description of the site begins at an old Roman aquaduct, which can be seen on the right of the river some 3 kms from the main road. The aquaduct has a resident family of Little Owls which regularly breed here and can often be seen on top of the structure or around the nearby farm buildings. Jackdaws, Kestrels and Woodchat Shrikes also nest in and around the aquaduct.

General map of the overall site

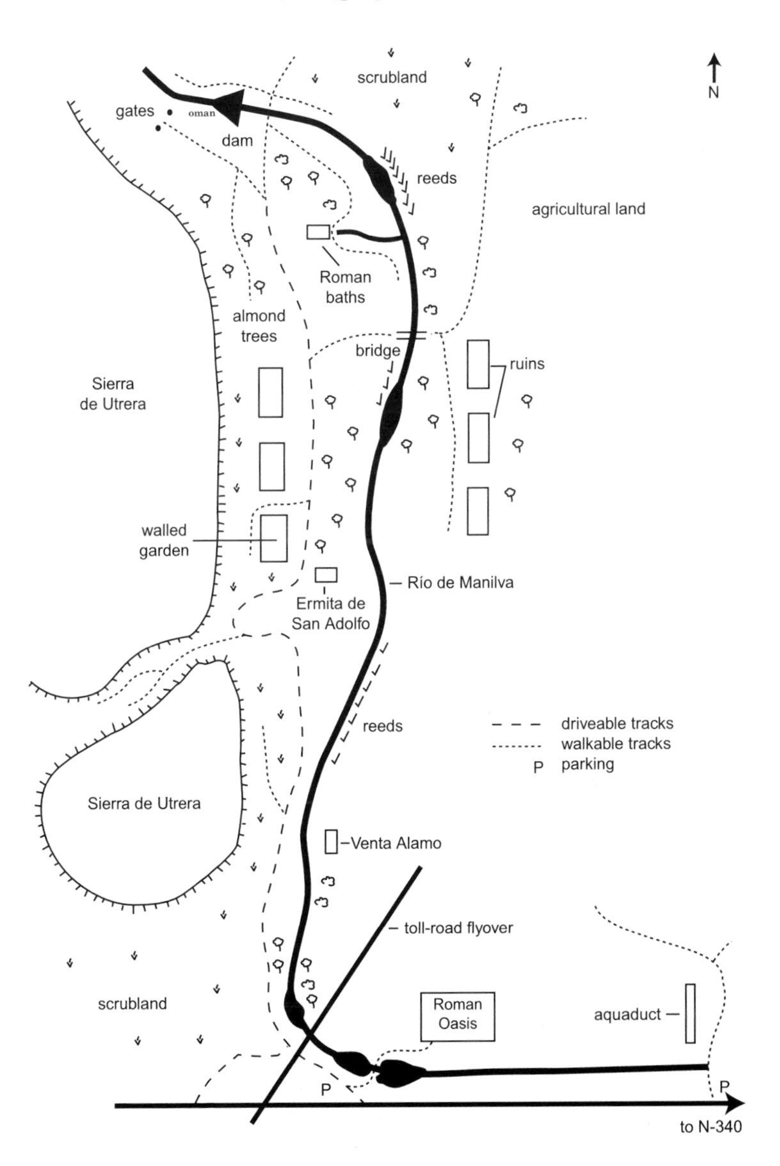

To view this area, you park 100 metres before the aquaduct, beside a few tall trees and a clump of giant reeds. At this point there is a track which crosses the river (not passable if the river is in full flow) that enables you to climb up a hill and view the aquaduct and the surrounding farmland from an elevated position. Stone Curlews can sometimes be found in the vineyards at the top of the hill and Red-necked Nightjars are often present in the summer.

A further 500 metres along the road, you see the Roman Oasis Restaurant on the right-hand side. Directly beside this there is a track to the right with room to park. Pull off here and explore the rest of the site on foot. On either side of the Roman Oasis's entrance there are small pools (sometimes used by bathers) which regularly attract wagtails, finches, warblers and a few waders. The track now leads upstream, alongside the river, and passes under a new toll-road flyover. In this area there are some mixed trees, shrubs and scrub. Small shaded pools offer ideal drinking and bathing stations for many bird species and the surrounding vegetation provides cover, enabling you to get good close-up views without disturbing the birds.

After 250 metres, you reach the Venta de la Alamo, a seasonal bar that is not normally open in the winter. The river from this point onward is bound by reeds and should be checked for Cetti's, Reed and Willow Warblers at the appropriate times of the year. During the spring, Nightingales are highly visible and audible as the males sing to declare their territories and to attract a mate.

Opposite the bar there is a parking area where a small track leads off to the left of the main track. This leads to an area of broken, rocky ground beneath a cliff face. The scrub usually holds Sardinian and Fan-tailed Warblers and during the passage periods (March-May and August-October) you may find both Northern and Black-eared Wheatears and Whinchats. The breeding season usually produces Bee-eaters, Woodchat Shrikes and very occasionally, Subalpine Warblers. Regular winter visitors are Black Redstarts, Meadow Pipits and Rock Buntings.

Returning to the main track, continue until it turns sharply to the left and then right. Here you will find a track on the left that leads into the valley that passes through the Sierra de Utrera. Approximately 100 metres along the track, the rock face comes into view and the valley opens out. To both sides of the valley, there are cacti, trees, shrubs and scrub, whilst the floor of the valley is densely covered with gorse, shrubs and spiny broom. Great Grey Shrikes can normally be found here and Woodchat Shrikes are common in the spring and summer. Crag Martins nest in the sheer rock face and Blue Rock Thrushes can be seen at any point.

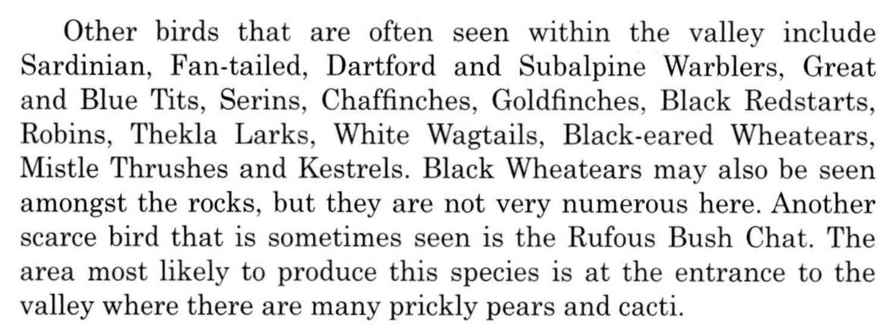

Other birds that are often seen within the valley include Sardinian, Fan-tailed, Dartford and Subalpine Warblers, Great and Blue Tits, Serins, Chaffinches, Goldfinches, Black Redstarts, Robins, Thekla Larks, White Wagtails, Black-eared Wheatears, Mistle Thrushes and Kestrels. Black Wheatears may also be seen amongst the rocks, but they are not very numerous here. Another scarce bird that is sometimes seen is the Rufous Bush Chat. The area most likely to produce this species is at the entrance to the valley where there are many prickly pears and cacti.

After leaving the valley, continue along the track, passing the Ermita de San Adolfo (church), toward the Roman baths. The mixed trees here hold the usual array of finches along with Siskin in the winter. The walled garden, beside the abandoned buildings on the left, can produce both Melodious and Garden Warblers in the summer and Iberian Chiffchaffs and Blackcaps in the winter. The garden is best viewed from a path behind the buildings.

Ignoring the first track that leads down to the river, continue along the main track until it forks. Take the left fork which leads uphill and explore the trees and shrubs as far as the white gates marked "HNOS OCAÑA". Returning back downhill you will notice another path leading uphill to the right. This leads to a neglected plantation of almond trees, an area also quite good for finches and warblers throughout the year and for Black-eared Wheatears and Black Redstarts during the summer and winter respectively. Behind the almonds there are mixed conifers and broadleaved trees which can produce Jays, Golden Orioles, Nuthatches and tits.

Return down to the original fork in the track and turn left, downhill, toward the river. When not in full flow it is possible to cross the river here. To the left there is a small concreted dam which is a reliable spot to see both White and Grey Wagtails and Cetti's Warblers. Various paths lead uphill and along the river to the right that are worth exploring. The hill is inhabited by Red-legged Partridges, Red-necked Nightjars, Great Grey and Woodchat Shrikes, Stonechats and Rock Buntings. The hill also offers an excellent opportunity to watch for birds of prey. Kestrels are regularly seen hunting along the eastern cliffs of the Sierra Utrera and Griffon Vultures from the nearby Sierra Crestellina can often be seen overhead. The Bonelli's Eagle is a resident species seen at any time of the year, but you are most likely to see the more common summer visitors, the Booted and Short-toed Eagles. Sparrowhawks, Buzzards and Peregrines complete the list of raptors that are to be found around this site.

Crossing back over the river at the same point, follow its course until you reach the flow of water from the Roman baths, which are contained within a rather plain white-walled building. You can cross the water at the baths and then continue along the riverbank. The far side of the river is bounded by dense reeds, trees and shrubs and is an ideal habitat for warblers, finches and tits, including Long-tailed Tits. Redstarts can sometimes be found in this area during the summer and passage periods.

Much of the area on the baths' side of the river used to be gardens and the trees here are mainly apple, orange, lemon, lime, olive, fig and pomegranate. Also in the area are tamarisk, oleander, eucalyptus, cork-oak and cistus scrub along with other mixed trees and shrubs. The selection of fruit and berries attracts many species of birds to the area, particularly in the later part of the year (September -November), when the harvest is most plentiful. The insect-eating birds that are fairly common here include Great Spotted Woodpeckers, Short-toed Treecreepers, Spotted Flycatchers and Hoopoes.

Although not numerous at this site, waders can usually be found at some point along the river, the more common species being Little-ringed Plovers, Redshanks, Snipe and Common, Green and Wood Sandpipers during the winter and passage periods. Summer visitors have, in the past, included Black-winged Stilts, Little Bitterns and very occasionally, Squacco Herons. Both Cattle and Little Egrets may be seen at any time of the year along with Grey Herons.

Just down from the baths there is an ancient Roman bridge which gives access to the far side of the river. The ruined buildings here are favoured nesting sites for Barn Swallows, House Martins, House Sparrows and Spotless Starlings. Red-rumped Swallows and Sand Martins are also to be found in the area during the breeding season.

To the left of the ruins, there is a track that leads uphill offering good elevated views of the river and reeds and is worth exploring. The area to the right of the track is agricultural land and I have, in the past, seen Stone Curlews and Corn Buntings here together with Skylarks and Crested Larks.

The trees on the far side and top end of the farmland have produced two good summer visitors in the shape of both Orphean and Olivaceous Warblers. Other species that appear with some regularity include Wood Pigeons, Rock Doves, Collared Doves and Kingfishers (all year), Turtle Doves and Pallid Swifts (summer), Starlings and

Song Thrushes (winter), Whinchats and Pied Flycatchers (passage periods).

Irregular birds, ie. those I have only seen here once, include Egyptian Vulture, Black Kite, Tawny Pipit and Hawfinch.

To return to your car, you cross back over the bridge and follow the main track.

When to Visit

This site is of interest at all times of the year and any visit here normally produces a good bird list. Due to the north-south aspect of the site, there is never a problem with sunlight affecting your views.

During autumn and winter, the area is very quiet, but in the spring and summer you may find that campers and picnickers are present, especially at weekends and national/local holidays. July and August should be avoided as this is the time of the school holidays and any visit to this site during this time will prove very disappointing as there will almost certainly be hundreds of other people in the area whose sole intention, so it would appear, is to make as much noise and cause as much disruption as possible.

If you should decide to visit during this period then you should plan a morning visit to hopefully avoid most of the noise.

General Information

The main track that runs alongside the river is wheelchair accessible, but the valley and all other tracks are not.

Bird Calendar

Resident

Cattle Egret, Little Egret, Grey Heron, Mallard, Griffon Vulture, Sparrowhawk, Buzzard, Bonelli's Eagle, Peregrine, Kestrel, Red-legged Partridge, Moorhen, Stone Curlew, Rock Dove, Wood Pigeon, Collared Dove, Little Owl, Kingfisher, Hoopoe, Great Spotted Woodpecker, Skylark, Crested Lark, Thekla Lark, Crag Martin, White Wagtail, Grey Wagtail, Robin, Stonechat, Black Redstart, Black Wheatear, Blue Rock Thrush, Blackbird, Mistle Thrush, Cetti's Warbler, Fan-tailed Warbler, Sardinian Warbler, Dartford Warbler, Long-tailed Tit, Great Tit, Blue Tit, Nuthatch, Wren, Short-toed

Treecreeper, Great Grey Shrike, Jay, Jackdaw, Spotless Starling, House Sparrow, Tree Sparrow, Chaffinch, Serin, Linnet, Goldfinch, Greenfinch, Corn Bunting, Rock Bunting.

Summer / Breeding

Little Bittern, Squacco Heron, Black Kite, Short-toed Eagle, Egyptian Vulture, Booted Eagle, Turtle Dove, Nightjar, Swift, Pallid Swift, Bee-eater, Sand Martin, House Martin, Red-rumped Swallow, Swallow, Nightingale, Rufous Bush Chat, Redstart, Black-eared Wheatear, Reed Warbler, Olivaceous Warbler, Melodious Warbler, Garden Warbler, Orphean Warbler, Subalpine Warbler, Willow Warbler, Spotted Flycatcher, Woodchat Shrike, Golden Oriole.

Winter

Little-ringed Plover, Snipe, Redshank, Green Sandpiper, Common Sandpiper, Meadow Pipit, Song Thrush, Blackcap, Chiffchaff, Starling, Siskin, Hawfinch.

Great Grey Shrike *(Lanius excubitor)*

Passage Migrants

Wood Sandpiper, Tawny Pipit, Whinchat, Northern Wheatear.

Casares / The Sierra Crestellina / The Río Genal

The white mountain village of Casares, situated 10 kilometres inland at the southern end of the Sierra Crestellina, is one of the most photographed villages in the whole of Andalucía and attracts tourists in great numbers throughout the year, but this appears to have little effect on the birdlife in and around the village.

The village has been built on the side of a hill. Its western side is a sheer rock face and some of the houses have been built right to the edge of a 200 metre vertical drop. Winding roads and alleys lead up through the village to a 500-year-old church and to an ancient Moorish castle dating back almost 1300 years. The church is the nesting site of a colony of Lesser Kestrels and this is as good a place as any to get good close-up views of this species.

During the spring and summer, there is always a good selection of swallows, swifts and martins overflying the area. These include White-rumped and Alpine Swifts and Red-rumped Swallows. The castle is an excellent vantage point from which to observe these species and it also offers magnificent views toward Gibraltar and across the Genal valley, although to the south-west the countryside has been blighted somewhat by the recent erection of large electricity-generating windmills. Vultures, eagles and other raptors are regularly seen overhead as are Red-billed Choughs and Ravens from the nearby mountains.

The Sierra Crestellina, to the north-west of Casares, is a limestone ridge that runs for about four kilometres in a northerly direction. At its highest point it is 906 metres above sea-level and towers some 480 metres over the village. The sierra is within the boundaries of a natural park and access is not easy, although the Manilva to Gaucín road runs parallel to the ridge and offers numerous opportunities to stop and scan the peaks, rock-faces and the surrounding countryside. Griffon Vultures, Bonelli's Eagles, Sparrowhawks, Peregrines, Black Wheatears, Crag Martins and at least one pair of Eagle Owls are resident here. Summer visitors include both Short-toed and Booted Eagles, Egyptian Vultures, Bee-eaters and Woodchat Shrikes.

The surrounding area is a mixture of agricultural land, shrubs and trees and supports a large number of warblers, finches, buntings, larks, pipits and chats. Great Grey Shrikes and Blue Rock Thrushes are fairly common here, as are Black Redstarts.

The Río Genal, where the Manilva-Gaucín road crosses over

the river at km 21, flows through the Genal valley and is usually sheltered from the strong winds that can affect the rest of the area. It can become very hot and humid here, even in the cooler months of the year. The river and its banks usually hold good numbers of wagtails, finches, larks, tits and warblers, along with Moorhens, egrets, herons and plovers. In the summer you can find Golden Orioles, Bee-eaters and Melodious Warblers. Wintering species include Iberian Chiffchaffs, Siskins and Blackcaps.

The area of pasture land beside the river is also quite productive for many of the previously mentioned species, with Woodchat Shrikes and Black Redstarts being particularly common. The wooded hillside can produce Jays and Great Spotted Woodpeckers and the cork-oaks and eucalyptus trees on the opposite bank are favoured by Short-toed Treecreepers.

Access

Travelling from the Málaga direction toward Gibraltar on the main N-340 highway, turn right to Casares after km 147. Travelling from the Gibraltar direction, turn left after km 146. The turning is well signed. The distance from the main road to the village of Casares is 14 kilometres and there are numerous opportunities to stop along the route to view the different habitats.

The first point of interest is after 2.5 kms where there is an electrical sub-station on the right-hand side of the road. Very often eagles and other raptors can be seen on the pylons, keeping an eye out for their next meal. On the opposite side of the road there is a valley which holds a small lake. This is best viewed from a track some 50 metres before the sub-station. Although there is no clearly defined path to the lake, you can walk down through the scrubland to reach it. Care needs to be taken, especially in the summer, due to the many thorny plants in the area. The lake regularly holds Moorhens, Little Grebes, herons, egrets, warblers, finches, larks and chats. Little Owls and Red-legged Partridges can also be found and Corn Buntings are particularly common.

Continuing along the road for a further 6.5 kms, you come to a large pull-off area on the right, approximately 700 metres after passing the Venta Victoria (a good place for tapas). A large green and white sign with the wording "Andalucía por si, para España y la humanidad" is your landmark. A track leads from the parking area and passes through scattered cork-oaks before reaching a set of gates marked with a double M. This track and the area around the gate is a good spot for Jays, Great Spotted Woodpeckers, Short-toed

Treecreepers, Nuthatches and finches, tits and warblers. Although there is a sign saying the track beyond the gates is private, you would not be challenged if you were to explore the first 100 metres or so of the track.

General map of the road to Casares

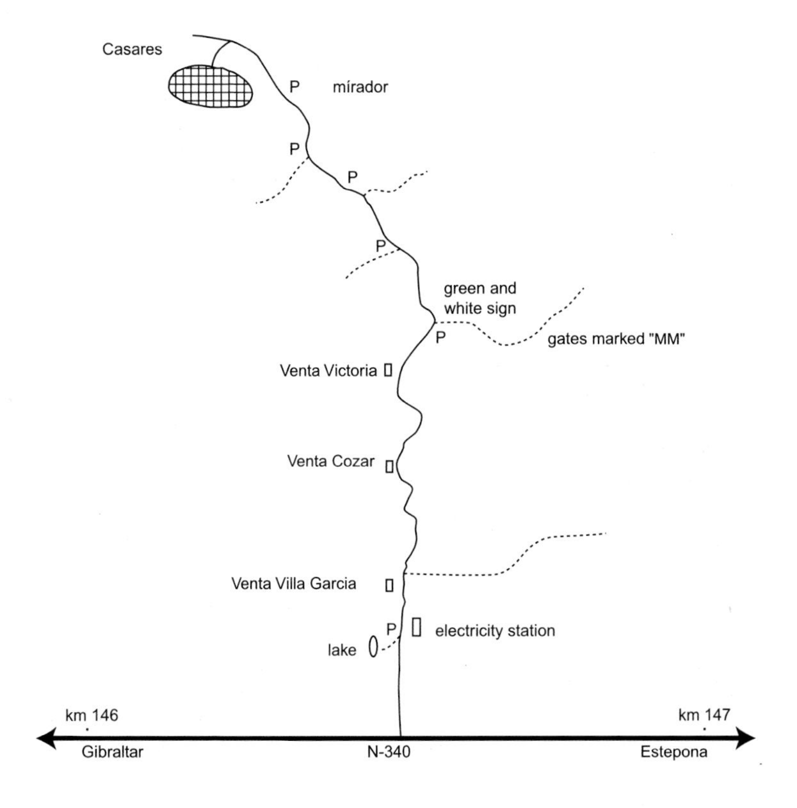

Further along the road to Casares, the cork-oaks merge with pines and other trees and it is worth stopping a few times at any suitable parking place to look for Firecrests, Crested Tits and Jays, which tend to inhabit the higher pine forests. In the summer, you could be lucky enough to find a few Golden Orioles.

As you arrive at the outskirts of Casares there is a mirador with parking spaces on the right. It is worth stopping here and looking across to the village itself. As well as offering good photographic views, you can often get close-up sightings of vultures and eagles as they pass overhead.

Continue along the road until you reach the turning that leads into the village. If you wish to visit the church and castle, which offer the best views of the swallows, swifts and Lesser Kestrels, you have to find a parking space and walk. The roads and alleyways that lead upward can be quite steep in places but the views and the birds are worth the effort. During the breeding season, White-rumped, Alpine, Pallid and Common Swifts can all be found, together with Barn and Red-rumped Swallows and House Martins. The Crag Martins are resident and can be seen throughout the year.

On leaving the village, turn left and follow the road until you reach the junction of the Manilva-Gaucín road. Turn right toward Gaucín and proceed for 650 metres. On the right you see the Venta la Laguna and about 50 metres beyond this, on the left-hand side of the road, there is a pull-off area. A track leads downhill from here, through rocky and scrub areas, to a few small plots of agricultural land. Walking down the track for 500 metres or so can be very rewarding. At one point there is a small stream on the left, which attracts many birds but it tends to dry up in the summer. Corn, Rock and Cirl Buntings can all be found here along with Thekla, Wood and Skylarks. Blue Rock Thrushes are often found near to the large outcrop of rocks to the left of the track whilst Great Grey Shrikes prefer the fence posts surrounding the agricultural plots. Dartford, Sardinian and Fan-tailed Warblers are resident here and the summer visiting warblers include Subalpine and occasionally Spectacled Warblers. Woodchat Shrikes, Hoopoes and Bee-eaters are all common breeding species.

As you drive along the road beside the Sierra Crestellina, you will find suitable places to stop and view the ridge, rock-faces and the valley on the opposite side of the road. Resident species here include Griffon Vultures, Bonelli's Eagles, Peregrines, Sparrowhawks, Lesser Kestrels, Ravens, Red-billed Choughs, Crag Martins, Little Owls and Eagle Owls. In the breeding season you can expect to find Short-toed and Booted Eagles, Egyptian Vultures and both Northern and Black-eared Wheatears. The Black Wheatears, although resident, are quite elusive and careful scanning of the rock-face may be required to find them.

After passing the sierra, continue along the road, now dropping down into the Genal valley, until you reach the bridge that crosses the Río Genal near to the km 21 marker. About 100 metres before the bridge, there is a pull-off point and a set of gates. Park here and enjoy the views of the river from an elevated position. The

surrounding trees and shrubs normally hold a fair assortment of finches, including Serins all year and Siskins in the winter. Warblers are also well represented, with many of the previously mentioned species being present as well as Melodious and Willow Warblers in the summer and Iberian Chiffchaffs and Blackcaps during the winter. The cork-oaks to the right of the parking area usually produce Short-toed Treecreepers and Nuthatches.

Continue across the river, either on foot or by car, and about 40 metres beyond the bridge there is a small track, almost hidden when driving in this direction, which cuts back sharply to the right. This leads first to the gates of a private estate and then turns toward the river and then alongside it. About 70 metres from the bridge, there is a small area where you can park and gain access to the water's edge. When not in full flow (most of the year) the riverbed of stone and shingle is exposed. Both White and Grey Wagtails are usually present all year and Yellow Wagtails can normally be seen in the spring and autumn. Little-ringed Plovers nest along the shingle banks in the breeding season.

Walk upstream along the track until you can go no further due to the collapse of the riverbank. The exposed mudbank on the left has, in the past, been a nesting site for a small colony of summer visiting Bee-eaters that burrow into the banks to make their nests. Kingfishers have also been known to nest in this spot. The trees, reeds and giant canes between the path and the river hold the usual array of finches and warblers, along with Long-tailed and other tit species.

Spotted Flycatchers are regular summer visitors and also nest locally, but the Pied Flycatcher is usually only seen during the passage periods, more so in the autumn. Nightingales are fairly common from mid-April onwards and although renowned for being rather shy birds you can normally get good views of them here, especially in April/May when the males are singing loudly from prominent positions to claim their territories and to attract a mate.

Both Cattle and Little Egrets are reasonably common at the river, as are Moorhens and Grey Herons. Kingfishers are often seen darting along the river or perched on a branch of a dead tree, ready to dive for the next meal.

The rough pasture land that is beside the path is very productive for a wide range of species throughout the year. The residents that may be present in varying numbers all year are Crested, Thekla and Woodlarks, Cirl Buntings, Black Redstarts and Stonechats. The Meadow Pipits and Linnets are far more common in the winter, whilst Whinchats and Black-eared Wheatears are summer visitors.

The mixed woodland at the far side of the pasture is a fairly reliable place to see Jays and Great Spotted Woodpeckers (all year) and Golden Orioles in the summer months.

Swallows, swifts and martins can usually be seen around the bridge and this area, together with the stretch of river beyond the bridge, should also be explored, although you can only proceed for a short distance.

All of the birds of prey mentioned earlier can also be seen in this area and it is good practice to keep checking the sky as eagles and vultures very often pass by quite low overhead.

When to Visit

The whole of the described area is of interest at any time of the year and should produce a good bird list. Weekdays are preferable to weekends, especially in the summer, as the riverside site is also a popular spot for family picnics and barbecues.

Visits during the migration periods can prove to be particularly rewarding, especially the spring passage.

General map of the Sierra Crestellina

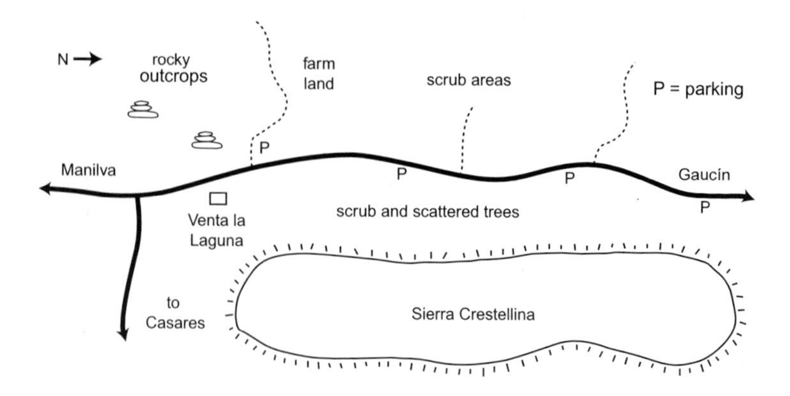

General Information

Many parts of this site are reasonably accessible to wheelchair birders, especially where off-road parking is an option. This includes

most of the forest tracks on the way to Casares. The church and castle in the village are a problem as the roads and alleys leading up to them are quite steep and can sometimes be very slippery. Vehicle access to this area is possible although quite difficult. The track near to the Venta la Laguna is not suitable for wheelchairs as it is very steep and uneven in places. A few off-road parking spaces allow you to view the Sierra Crestellina without too many problems and viewing from within a car is also an option. The riverside site, although a little bumpy in places, is mainly accessible.

Bird Calendar

Resident

Little Grebe, Cattle Egret, Little Egret, Grey Heron, Griffon Vulture, Sparrowhawk, Buzzard, Bonelli's Eagle, Peregrine, Kestrel, Lesser Kestrel, Red-legged Partridge, Moorhen, Rock Dove, Wood Pigeon, Collared Dove, Little Owl, Eagle Owl, Barn Owl, Kingfisher, Great Spotted Woodpecker, Woodlark, Crested Lark, Thekla Lark, Crag Martin, White Wagtail, Grey Wagtail, Robin, Stonechat, Black Redstart, Black Wheatear, Blue Rock Thrush, Blackbird, Mistle Thrush, Cetti's Warbler, Fan-tailed Warbler, Sardinian Warbler, Dartford Warbler, Firecrest, Long-tailed Tit, Crested Tit, Coal Tit, Great Tit, Blue Tit, Nuthatch, Short-toed Treecreeper, Wren, Great Grey Shrike, Jay, Jackdaw, Red-billed Chough, Raven, Spotless Starling, Rock Sparrow, House Sparrow, Tree Sparrow, Chaffinch, Serin, Linnet, Goldfinch, Greenfinch, Common Crossbill, Corn Bunting, Rock Bunting, Cirl Bunting.

Summer / Breeding

Black Kite, Short-toed Eagle, Egyptian Vulture, Booted Eagle, Little-ringed Plover, Common Sandpiper, Turtle Dove, Cuckoo, Red-necked Nightjar, Alpine Swift, White-rumped Swift, Common Swift, Pallid Swift, Hoopoe, Bee-eater, Short-toed Lark, House Martin, Barn Swallow, Red-rumped Swallow, Tawny Pipit, Yellow Wagtail, Nightingale, Black-eared Wheatear, Olivaceous Warbler, Melodious Warbler, Spectacled Warbler, Subalpine Warbler, Bonelli's Warbler, Willow Warbler, Spotted Flycatcher, Woodchat Shrike, Golden Oriole, Ortolan Bunting.

Winter

Whimbrel, Green Sandpiper, Common Sandpiper, Wryneck, Skylark, Meadow Pipit, Dunnock, Song Thrush, Blackcap, Iberian Chiffchaff,

Starling, Brambling, Siskin.

Passage Migrants

White Stork, Black Stork, Red Kite, Montagu's Harrier, Honey Buzzard, Golden Eagle, Roller, Whinchat, Northern Wheatear, Pied Flycatcher.

Griffon Vulture *(Gyps fulvus)*

Las Mesas de Chullera

The Mesas de Chullera is a large expanse of open heathland some two kilometres inland from the coast at a height of approximately 100 metres above sea-level. It is fairly flat and is densely covered by low-growing shrubs, heathers, brooms, wild flowers, herbs, grasses, gorse and other scrub vegetation.

This is classic warbler country and the resident Sardinian, Fan-tailed and Dartfords are usually joined in the breeding season by Olivaceous, Orphean, Melodious, Subalpine and Spectacled Warblers. Winter visitors regularly include Firecrests, Iberian Chiffchaffs and Blackcaps.

The soil is light and sandy and numerous sandbanks provide ideal nesting sites for colonies of Bee-eaters. Scattered trees, mainly stone pine, holm oak and eucalyptus, attract and sustain a good variety of bird species throughout the year.

Birds of prey are often present and vultures regularly pass overhead in search of carrion in the nearby farmland. The area is very close to the Strait of Gibraltar and therefore benefits from many passing birds during the migration periods.

Access

Access to the site is easiest from the main N-340 highway between Puerto de Duquesa and Torre Guadiaro, near to km 141. Travelling from the Málaga direction, turn right 200 metres beyond the km 141 marker. At this point there are two parallel roads, the first a dirt-road that leads uphill to the site. The second road leads to the "Aldea Hills" urbanization, which should be ignored. Coming from the Gibraltar direction, turn left at km 140.8, directly beyond the Aldea Hills development.

At the time of writing, construction work was underway to convert the N-340 highway into a dual-carriageway. This may result in some minor change to the access point, such as a slip-road or roundabout being situated at the turn-off.

The dirt-road, which is in quite a bad condition, but passable with care, leads up towards the Mesas de Chullera, passing a few private houses on the left and a ruined building on the right. The fence posts and telegraph wires should be checked for Bee-eaters, Monk Parakeets, Spotted Flycatchers, Stonechats and shrikes.

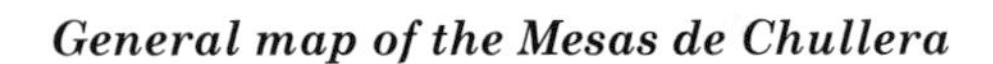

General map of the Mesas de Chullera

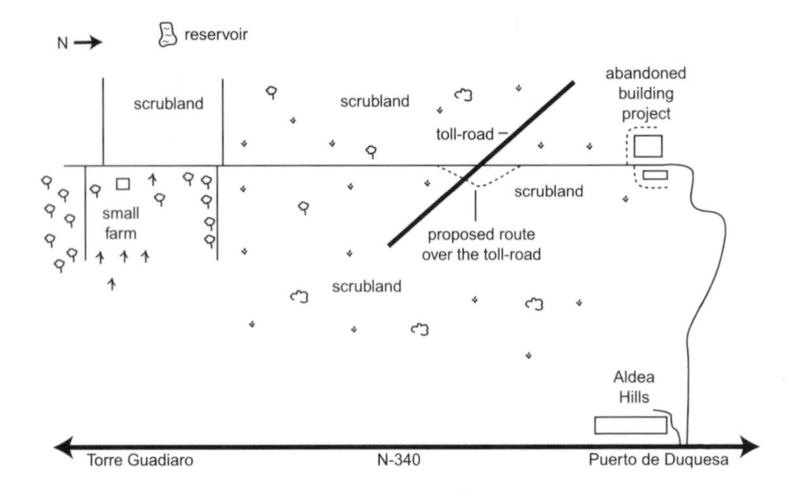

After 1.7 kms, you reach an abandoned building project where it is common to find Little Owls, Black Redstarts and Blue Rock Thrushes. A short time spent walking around this location will usually be rewarded with a few interesting species. Crested Larks are abundant and in the summer you may also find Black-eared Wheatears.

Follow the road for a further kilometre and you come to an area where a toll-road is currently being constucted. This is due to be opened sometime in 2003. At the present time (August 2001) the road leads directly through the construction site, but once the toll-road is completed there will be a bridge to carry traffic over it.

Once beyond the toll-road, you are in the heart of the site and can park anywhere to check the surrounding spiny brooms, kermes oaks, fan-palms, shrubs, gorses and scrub. The warblers, which often perch prominently on top of the vegetation, include resident Dartford and Sardinian and summer visiting Subalpine and Spectacled Warblers.

Further along the road, you reach a staggered crossroads with a copse of stone pine on the left. The trees here can prove productive for Melodious Warblers in the summer and for Firecrests and Iberian Chiffchaffs in the winter. Hoopoes, Woodlarks, Skylarks, Serins, Linnets and other finches are all fairly common at this spot.

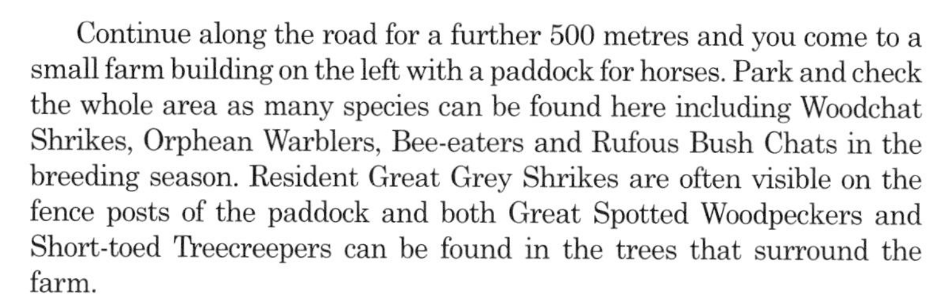

Continue along the road for a further 500 metres and you come to a small farm building on the left with a paddock for horses. Park and check the whole area as many species can be found here including Woodchat Shrikes, Orphean Warblers, Bee-eaters and Rufous Bush Chats in the breeding season. Resident Great Grey Shrikes are often visible on the fence posts of the paddock and both Great Spotted Woodpeckers and Short-toed Treecreepers can be found in the trees that surround the farm.

Walk beyond the farm and take the left-hand track which leads between a eucalyptus forest on the right and a small orchard and scattered stone pines on the left. This is a particularly good location for finding Olivaceous Warblers, Blackcaps, Corn and Rock Buntings, tits and finches.

Monk Parakeets from a very large breeding colony two kilometres away are often to be found in the eucalyptus trees and they are occasionally joined by one or two Black-hooded Parakeets. Bee-eaters can be found nesting in any sandy bank, sometimes just a few feet above the ground. Lesser Kestrels from two nearby colonies can regularly be seen hunting in numbers over most of the site and are sometimes joined by Common Kestrels. Amongst the other birds of prey there are Buzzards, Black Kites, Booted Eagles and Short-toed Eagles. Griffon Vultures are a common sight throughout the year and in the summer Egyptian Vultures can sometimes be seen overhead.

Honey Buzzards pass through the area in great numbers from late April to the end of May and can be spotted riding thermals, often in flocks of up to 300, to gain height before continuing their journeys north.

There are numerous other tracks around the site that invite exploration. One of these leads to an area that overlooks a distant small reservoir. Unfortunately, access to the reservoir is not possible as it is on private land, but views of Grey Herons, gulls and several duck species can be had.

During the breeding season the whole of the site is constantly overflown by swifts, swallows and martins, whilst in amongst the scrub you may be lucky enough to catch a glimpse of Quails and Red-legged Partridges.

To leave the site, I strongly recommend you return the same way that you came. It is possible to continue straight ahead and find tracks to either San Enrique or San Martín del Tesorillo but both of these are in an appalling state and you risk serious damage to your vehicle.

When to Visit

This site is of year-round interest but obviously the spring/summer will produce the greater number of species. The area is fairly flat and exposed and can suffer from strong winds in the cooler months of the year. It would, therefore, be wise to take some item of warm protective clothing with you. After heavy rains, the road and tracks are sometimes flooded with large pools of water. These are never as deep as they may look and can be negotiated by driving as close to the edge of the road as possible.

During the summer, there are always Red-necked Nightjars present and if you wish to see this species you should plan your visit for the late evening as they only appear after dusk, unless accidentally flushed.

General Information

During dry weather most of this site is accessible to wheelchair birders as the sandy roads become compacted by passing traffic. However, after rain the roads flood and the wet sand makes the use of wheelchairs very difficult. This should still not stop you from visiting the site as much of it can actually be viewed almost as well from a car.

Bird Calendar

Resident

Cattle Egret, Griffon Vulture, Buzzard, Kestrel, Lesser Kestrel, Red-legged Partridge, Rock Dove, Wood Pigeon, Collared Dove, Black-hooded Parakeet, Monk Parakeet, Little Owl, Barn Owl, Hoopoe, Great Spotted Woodpecker, Woodlark, Crested Lark, White Wagtail, Stonechat, Black Redstart, Blue Rock Thrush, Blackbird, Fan-tailed Warbler, Sardinian Warbler, Dartford Warbler, Great Tit, Blue Tit, Short-toed Treecreeper, Wren, Great Grey Shrike, Jay, Jackdaw, Raven, Spotless Starling, House Sparrow, Chaffinch, Serin, Linnet, Goldfinch, Greenfinch, Corn Bunting, Rock Bunting.

Summer / Breeding

Black Kite, Short-toed Eagle, Egyptian Vulture, Booted Eagle, Quail, Turtle Dove, Red-necked Nightjar, Common Swift, Pallid Swift, Bee-eater, House Martin, Barn Swallow, Red-rumped Swallow, Tawny Pipit, Nightingale, Rufous Bush Chat, Redstart, Black-eared

Wheatear, Olivaceous Warbler, Melodious Warbler, Orphean Warbler, Spectacled Warbler, Subalpine Warbler, Spotted Flycatcher, Woodchat Shrike.

Winter

Sparrowhawk, Wryneck, Skylark, Crag Martin, Meadow Pipit, Robin, Song Thrush, Blackcap, Iberian Chiffchaff, Firecrest, Long-tailed Tit, Siskin.

Passage Migrants

Montagu's Harrier, Honey Buzzard, Roller, Tree Pipit, Yellow Wagtail, Whinchat, Northern Wheatear, Garden Warbler, Pied Flycatcher.

Spectacled Warbler *(Sylvia conspicillata)*

Ronda

The ancient town of Ronda stands 744 metres above sea-level about an hour's drive inland from the coast and can be easily reached from all parts of the region. The history of the town is well documented in countless guide books and tourist leaflets, so I will concentrate on the birding aspect of the town and the surrounding areas.

Due to the huge tourist industry that has built up in Ronda, there will always be large crowds of people present and parking can sometimes be difficult. However, the hordes of people do not seem to have an adverse effect on the bird population which has learnt to co-exist with the constant noise of traffic and visitors and this is, without doubt, the prime site to see Red-billed Choughs at very close quarters.

A street guide of the town will be helpful and this can be bought from any shop or you can get a free guide, complete with potted history, from the Tourist Information Office in the town.

Access

Ronda can be reached by road from any direction and a quick look at a map will show you your most direct route. The town can also be reached by train from any station on the Algeciras-Bobadilla line. The journey from Los Barrios, San Roque, Castellar de la Frontera or Jimena de la Frontera stations offers a relaxing trip through spectacularly scenic countryside for a very reasonable fare.

Once in Ronda, I suggest you first make your way to El Puente Nuevo (the new bridge, 18th century) which joins new Ronda, to the north-west, with the old town to the south-east. Directly beside the bridge there is a mirador. The bridge spans the Tajo gorge, a 100 metre deep chasm, through which flows the Río Guadalevín.

The sheer cliff-faces of the gorge are the roosting and nesting sites of the resident Red-billed Choughs which are always easily seen, sometimes from just a few metres away, as they pass both over and through the bridge as well as riding the wind current as it whistles through the Tajo.

Other resident birds that can be seen here with some regularity include Blue Rock Thrush, Black Wheatear, Black Redstart, Rock Sparrow, Rock Bunting, Crag Martin, Peregrine, Kestrel and Serin, along with other finches and various warblers. These are often joined in the spring and summer by Lesser Kestrel, Spotted Flycatcher, Barn Swallow, Red-rumped Swallow, House Martin and Common, Pallid and Alpine Swifts and if you are lucky you may see the scarce White-rumped Swift that is occasionally recorded here.

Although the gorge is full of interest, you should regularly scan the sky as Ravens, Black Kites, vultures and eagles often pass by overhead.

After viewing the gorge from above, walk to the Puente Viejo (old bridge, 17th century) about 250 metres to the east (refer to your street map). Here the river passes just a few metres below you and the walls of the Tajo tower overhead. Good views can be had of most of the birds already mentioned but here you are more likely to see both White and Grey Wagtails, Black-eared Wheatears, Nightingales, Blackcaps, Iberian Chiffchaffs and Sardinian, Willow and Melodious Warblers.

By again consulting your street guide, you can find ways down to the valley floor where Cattle Egrets, Cetti's Warblers and waders may be found. Getting down to the river is relatively easy but climbing back up again is another matter entirely. The street guide will also indicate a route along the old town walls (murallas) to the east which give excellent views over the surrounding farmland and open pastures.

When to Visit

A visit here at any time of the year will normally produce some very interesting species but to see the widest variety you should visit between April and September.

General information

Due to its exposed mountainous position, it is very often quite windy in Ronda and you should go prepared with some warm protective clothing. The volume of people, the narrow pavements and the steep hills inhibit the use of wheelchairs and there are no parking facilities that allow you to view the various parts of this site from a car.

Perhaps the only point that is accessible is the new bridge, where seating bays have been incorporated into the side walls that may allow a wheelchair user to sit and view parts of the gorge without blocking the pavement.

Bird Calendar

Resident

Cattle Egret, Griffon Vulture, Sparrowhawk, Buzzard, Bonelli's Eagle, Peregrine, Kestrel, Rock Dove, Little Owl, Skylark, Thekla Lark, White Wagtail, Grey Wagtail, Stonechat, Black Redstart, Black Wheatear, Blue Rock Thrush, Blackbird, Cetti's Warbler, Fan-tailed Warbler, Sardinian Warbler, Great Tit, Blue Tit, Wren, Great Grey Shrike, Red-billed Chough, Jackdaw, Raven, Spotless Starling, House Sparrow, Rock Sparrow, Serin, Linnet, Goldfinch, Greenfinch, Corn Bunting, Rock Bunting.

Summer / Breeding

Black Kite, Short-toed Eagle, Egyptian Vulture, Booted Eagle, Lesser Kestrel, Turtle Dove, Cuckoo, Scops Owl, White-rumped Swift, Alpine Swift, Common Swift, Pallid Swift, Bee-eater, House Martin, Red-rumped Swallow, Barn Swallow, Nightingale, Redstart, Black-eared Wheatear, Melodious Warbler, Spotted Flycatcher, Woodchat Shrike, Ortolan Bunting.

Winter

Grey Heron, Green Sandpiper, Common Sandpiper, Meadow Pipit, Blackcap, Iberian Chiffchaff.

Passage Migrants

Honey Buzzard, Whimbrel, Wryneck, Whinchat, Northern Wheatear, Pied Flycatcher.

Alpine Swift *(Apus melba)*

Serranía de Ronda

Alpendeire / Faraján / Júzcar / Cartajima

This is a circular route of about 50 kms passing through, or beside, four white mountain villages in the hills to the south of the town of Ronda. The highest parts of the route are mountainous with only a sparse covering of broom, cistus and other scrub plants along with scattered, stunted trees. The valleys are well vegetated with cork-oak, pines, Holm oak and other broadleaved tree varieties. A certain amount of agriculture occurs in the region with olives and sweet chestnuts being the principal crops. The diversity of habitats produces a wide range of different bird species of both resident and seasonal visitors.

Access

There are only two entry points into the region by car, both of which are very easy to find. The first is from the main Ronda-San Pedro de Alcántara road (A-376) at the turn-off for Parauta and Cartajima at km 133.6. The second is from the main Algeciras-Ronda road (A-369) at km 9.7, signed for Alpendeire,Faraján and Júzcar. As I have always visited the site from the second entry point, I will describe it from there.

On turning off the A-369 onto the MA-515, drive through fenced open land with stony slopes and a rock face to the left where Blue Rock Thrushes, Black Wheatears, Thekla Larks, Black Redstarts and scrub warblers can be found. Beyond this, the road starts to descend toward Alpendeire. At km 4.1, there is a track to the left, directly opposite an almond plantation. A short walk here may produce good views of any of the aforementioned birds and also of vultures, eagles and other raptors overhead. The almond trees should be checked for Rock Buntings and warbler species.

At km 7.2, a bridge crosses a seasonal mountain stream, beside which there is a large pull-off area. The rocky gorge and the olive grove below the bridge should be checked for wheatears, larks, finches, tits and warblers. Rock Sparrows are sometimes present in the olive grove.

As you reach Alpendeire, take the left-hand fork signed for Faraján, on the MA-516. About 200 metres beyond the village, there is a rather scruffy pull-off area on a sharp bend. Stop here and view the valley below. Just above this point, on the opposite side of the road, there is a statue and 25 metres further along the road there are steps and a slope leading up to it. This is, in fact, a small memorial garden to Fray Leopoldo de Alpendeire, who was a local monk, born in 1864. The garden serves as an excellent viewpoint and there are bench seats where you can sit and watch for smaller birds as well as passing raptors.

General map of the Alpendeire-Cartajima route

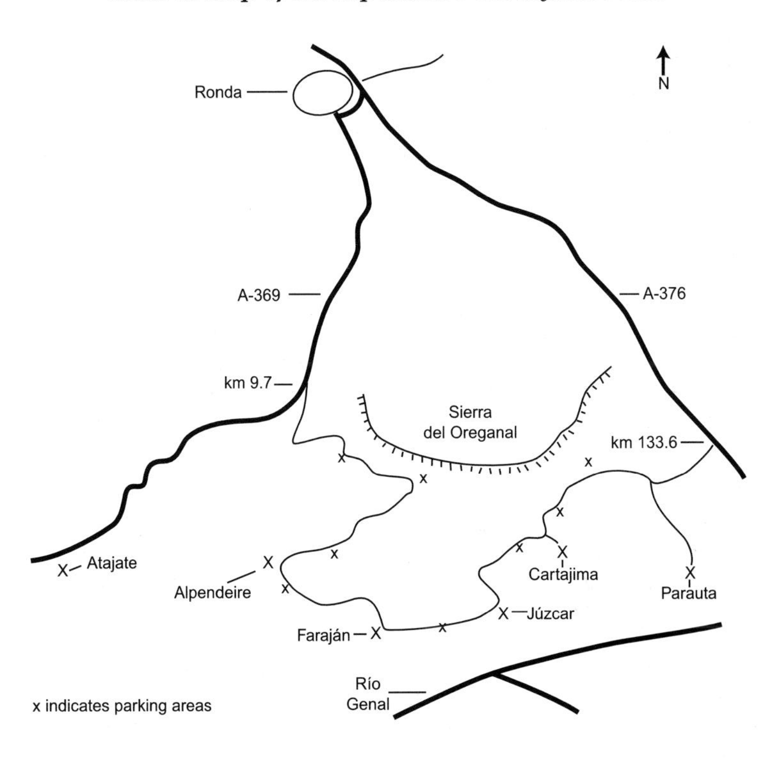

From the village the road passes through much more vegetated areas with cork-oak, Holm oak, almonds, olives and pines. Stopping anywhere along the road can produce a wide variety of woodland birds such as Short-toed Treecreepers, Nuthatches, Golden Orioles, Jays, tits, finches, warblers and woodpeckers.

Arriving at Faraján, turn immediately left onto the MA-517 which is signed for Júzcar. Once again, there are numerous pull-off areas along the road which will provide opportunities to search for those species already mentioned. Cork-oaks, pines, oleanders and brooms form much of the vegetation.

At Júzcar, continue through the village where the road now becomes the MA-518 to Cartajima, which for the first kilometre or so passes through large plantations of sweet chestnuts and olives. This is a very good area for Hoopoes, Great Grey Shrikes, Jays, Short-toed Treecreepers, tits, warblers and finches. Beyond the orchards, the road runs alongside a very sheer cliff face. Stopping places are very limited but there are one or two spots where you can get off the road. The rocks and cliffs often produce good views of Kestrels, Peregrines, Crag Martins, Black Wheatears, Black Redstarts and Blue Rock Thrushes. In the breeding season both Booted and Short-toed Eagles are present and you may catch sight of Egyptian Vultures.

Nearer to Cartajima, there are a few convenient parking areas from where you can inspect the cliffs and also the cultivated valley to the right where Redstarts, Woodchat Shrikes, Golden Orioles and Melodious Warblers are regularly seen. The scrubby hillside has resident populations of both Sardinian and Dartford Warblers.

As you approach Cartajima, take the left-hand road toward Parauta on the MA-519. Half a kilometre along this road, there are olive trees on the left. Stop anywhere here and search the olive groves for Rock Sparrows, which are very common here. Also you may find Black-eared Wheatears, shrikes and Cirl, Corn and Rock Buntings. Further along the road there is a pull-off area where a seasonal stream passes under the road. Here there is another large rock face where Black Wheatears and Blue Rock Thrushes are common.

Continuing along the road, you pass through open hill country until you reach a junction with signs for either Parauta or Ronda. Parauta is a very small village and is of little interest as far as birds are concerned. However, this road, which is the only one in and out of the village, presents some good opportunities to park and watch out over the area. If you do not wish to go into the village you should continue along the MA-519 leading to the Ronda-San Pedro road, the A-376 at km 133.6, the other entry point.

When to Visit

This route is of interest at all times and the varying habitats should enable you to produce a good bird list. Visits during the main passage periods will normally be rewarded with views of migrating eagles, kites and other raptors, including large numbers of Honey Buzzards.

The main breeding season is between April and June and it is at this time when you are likely to see the maximum number of species.

General Information

Although there are a few walking opportunities along the route, the area can also be adequately viewed from a car or from numerous vantage points. This is of great benefit to any wheelchair birders and people with other mobility problems, as you do not have to keep getting out of the car to be able to see most of the species.

Please note that there are no petrol stations along the described route, so make sure you have plenty of fuel before starting your tour.

Bird Calendar

Resident

Cattle Egret, Griffon Vulture, Sparrowhawk, Goshawk, Buzzard, Bonelli's Eagle, Peregrine, Kestrel, Lesser Kestrel, Red-legged Partridge, Rock Dove, Wood Pigeon, Collared Dove, Little Owl, Tawny Owl, Barn Owl, Green Woodpecker, Great Spotted Woodpecker, Woodlark, Crested Lark, Thekla Lark, Crag Martin, Robin, Stonechat, Black Redstart, Black Wheatear, Blue Rock Thrush, Blackbird, Mistle Thrush, Blackcap, Sardinian Warbler, Dartford Warbler, Firecrest, Long-tailed Tit, Coal Tit, Great Tit, Blue Tit, Nuthatch, Short-toed Treecreeper, Wren, Great Grey Shrike, Jay, Red-billed Chough, Jackdaw, Raven, Spotless Starling, House Sparrow, Rock Sparrow, Chaffinch, Serin, Linnet, Goldfinch, Greenfinch, Crossbill, Corn Bunting, Rock Bunting, Cirl Bunting.

Summer / Breeding

Black Kite, Short-toed Eagle, Egyptian Vulture, Booted Eagle, Turtle Dove, Cuckoo, Scops Owl, Red-necked Nightjar, Alpine Swift, White-rumped Swift, Common Swift, Pallid Swift, Hoopoe, Bee-eater, House Martin, Barn Swallow, Red-rumped Swallow, Nightingale, Redstart, Black-eared Wheatear, Melodious Warbler, Subalpine Warbler, Bonelli's Warbler, Spotted Flycatcher, Woodchat Shrike, Golden Oriole, Ortolan Bunting.

Winter

Red Kite, Merlin, Wryneck, Skylark, Meadow Pipit, White Wagtail, Dunnock, Ring Ouzel, Fieldfare, Redwing, Song Thrush, Iberian Chiffchaff, Brambling, Siskin, Hawfinch.

Passage Migrants

Montagu's Harrier, Honey Buzzard, Roller, Yellow Wagtail, Whinchat, Northern Wheatear, Pied Flycatcher.

Rock Bunting *(Emberiza cia)*

Jimera de Libar / Montejaque / Benaoján

Serranía de Ronda / Parque Natural Sierra de Grazalema

This is a circular route of about 70 kilometres taking in three villages in the upper valley of the Río Guadiaro to the south-west of Ronda. Part of the area is located within the boundaries of the Parque Natural Sierra de Grazalema, an area rich in wildlife and scenic beauty.

The region is mostly mountainous and there are stark contrasts between barren rock formations and well forested hillsides. The river valley is particularly fertile and a certain amount of agriculture takes place, with oranges, lemons, olives and almonds being grown. Habitats change quickly along the route and this leads to a wide diversity of bird species and other wildlife. The mountain tops are the domain of Ravens, Red-billed Choughs, vultures and eagles, whilst the rocky slopes and cliff faces are preferred by Rock Buntings, Blue Rock Thrushes, Black Wheatears and shrikes. In the riverine woodlands you can find Golden Orioles, finches, tits and warblers, and in the forested areas there are Jays, Short-toed Treecreepers and woodpeckers. The river itself attracts a wide range of herons, egrets, storks, waders, ducks and other waterfowl.

Access

Coming from the north, east or south, head for Ronda and pass through the town to find the A-369 Ronda-Algeciras road. The turning that leads into the route is at km 19.5, immediately after passing through the village of Atajate, and is signed for Jimera de Libar and Cortes de la Frontera. Coming from the west, ie. Gaucín, Estepona, Sotogrande, Gibraltar, take the A-369 to Ronda before taking the turn-off described above.

This is a narrow, winding road which passes through plantations of almonds, oranges and olives, and there are many opportunities to stop and search the immediate areas. Beside the road, there are numerous wooden electricity poles and many of these have been used as nest sites by Great Spotted Woodpeckers. At 4.1 kms from the main road, there is a pull-off area on the left with good views down into the valley and across to a sheer rock-face. This is a fairly reliable place to see Blue Rock Thrushes and Kestrels. The olive grove on the other side of the road produces finches, shrikes, warblers, larks and woodpeckers.

One kilometre further along the road you reach the village of Jimera de Libar. Do not enter the village as it is of little interest birdwise, but carry on along the road which leads to the railway station. As you reach Libar, there is a notice board with details of three walks (*senderos*) you can take. This gives the directions, the degree of difficulty, the type of route and the normal time required to complete the walk. I have not taken any of these routes myself so I cannot comment on any birds that may be found along them.

Continuing downhill toward the station, you reach a road junction where you turn left. This leads to a bridge across the Río Guadiaro. At the next junction, turn right where signed for Benaoján. After about 3 kms you come to a very barren rock formation which is part of the Sierra del Palo, and just beyond this there are a few small farms where it is possible to pull off the road and scan the rocks and the trees and scrub area toward the river.

One kilometre further on, there is a turning to the Cueva de la Pileta (caves) where there are paintings dating from the Neolithic and Palaeolithic periods. A further 800 metres along the road brings you to a viewpoint (*vista panoramica*) where you can pull off the road and enjoy the view down into the Guadiaro valley and check the rocks that tower overhead. Again, this is classic scrub warbler and Black Wheatear country and I have seen Dartford, Sardinian and Subalpine Warblers here.

At the junction at Benaoján, turn left toward Montejaque and 100 metres after entering the village turn very sharply right onto the road signposted for Sevilla and Algodonales (MA-505). This road passes first through agricultural land and then a large seasonal reservoir, the Embalse de Montejaque, which is not shown on many maps as it is very often dry. You now drive through the Puerto de Tabizna, which is a very rugged mountain pass where, unfortunately, it is almost impossible to stop.

At the other side of the pass, midway between kms 4 and 3, there is a large pull-off area on the left where there is a notice board showing the route of a walk that can be taken (*Sendero de El Hundidero*). The walk is one kilometre long and leads down the dirt road to the left. The first few hundred metres passes through open scrubland where Hoopoes, larks, finches and warblers are common and where Black-eared Wheatears breed in the summer.

Further along the track, you pass an old ruined building and reach a circular knoll with a copse of trees. Both Great Grey and Woodchat Shrikes breed in this area. The right-hand track around the knoll ends after about 100 metres but it offers magnificent

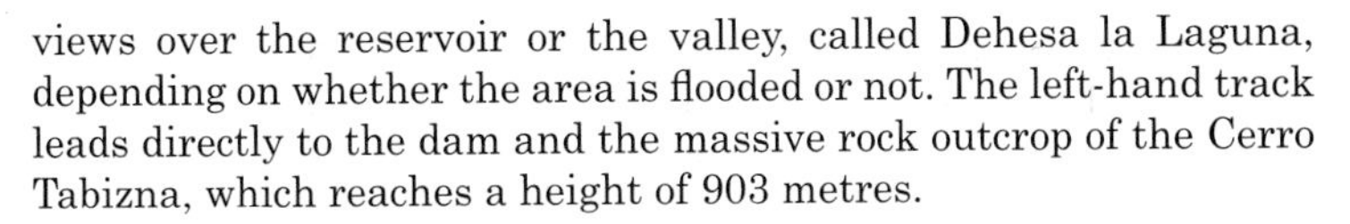

views over the reservoir or the valley, called Dehesa la Laguna, depending on whether the area is flooded or not. The left-hand track leads directly to the dam and the massive rock outcrop of the Cerro Tabizna, which reaches a height of 903 metres.

It is not possible to cross the dam but, if you are feeling energetic, there is a zig-zag trail that leads down behind the dam to a very secluded valley where Blue Rock Thrushes, Rock Buntings, Black Wheatears and Black Redstarts are always present. This is an excellent spot from which to look for overhead raptors, which include Griffon Vultures, Bonelli's Eagles, Peregrines, Kestrels and, occasionally, Golden Eagles. In the spring and summer you should have no difficulty in finding Egyptian Vultures and both Booted and Short-toed Eagles, all of which breed locally. Red-billed Choughs are often seen here and martins, swallows and swifts are highly visible in the summer, including good numbers of Alpine Swifts and one or two pairs of White-rumped Swifts.

It is possible to reach the Cerro de Tabizna via the route that leads uphill from the car-park but toward the end of this track the going becomes very steep and quite hazardous and I do not recommend it.

After visiting this site, return along the road to Montejaque and then proceed to Benaoján. Pass through the village and then follow directions to Ronda along the MA-507 road. After 1.5 kms, there is a turning to the right, signed for Estación de Benaoján (railway station). Follow this road and park near to the station. Now follow the road to the right that will lead you to a level-crossing over the rail tracks and directly down to the Río Guadiaro. Once across the bridge you will find information on two walks that can be followed. The first route, to the left, leads to the Cueva del Gato (the cave of the cat) and beyond. Although the walk is given as 4.2 kms long, the actual caves are less than two kilometres away and you should not plan to walk beyond that point.

The second route, Sendero del Río Guadiaro, is the one that I prefer as I find it far more interesting as far as birding is concerned. This takes you out into the country with forests to the left and the river and its bordering vegetation to the right. After about two kilometres, the railway track on the opposite side of the river enters a tunnel and near here you will come to a large abandoned farmhouse, which is as far along the route that I have personally walked. There is a great diversity of birds to be seen along this trail, including Golden Orioles, Jays, Bee-eaters, Short-toed Treecreepers, Wrens, larks, finches, tits, woodpeckers, redstarts, wagtails, swifts, swallows, martins, flycatchers, herons, egrets, storks, ducks and waders. Once again you will see birds of prey as they pass by overhead.

General map of the Jimera de Libar to Benaoján to Montejaque route

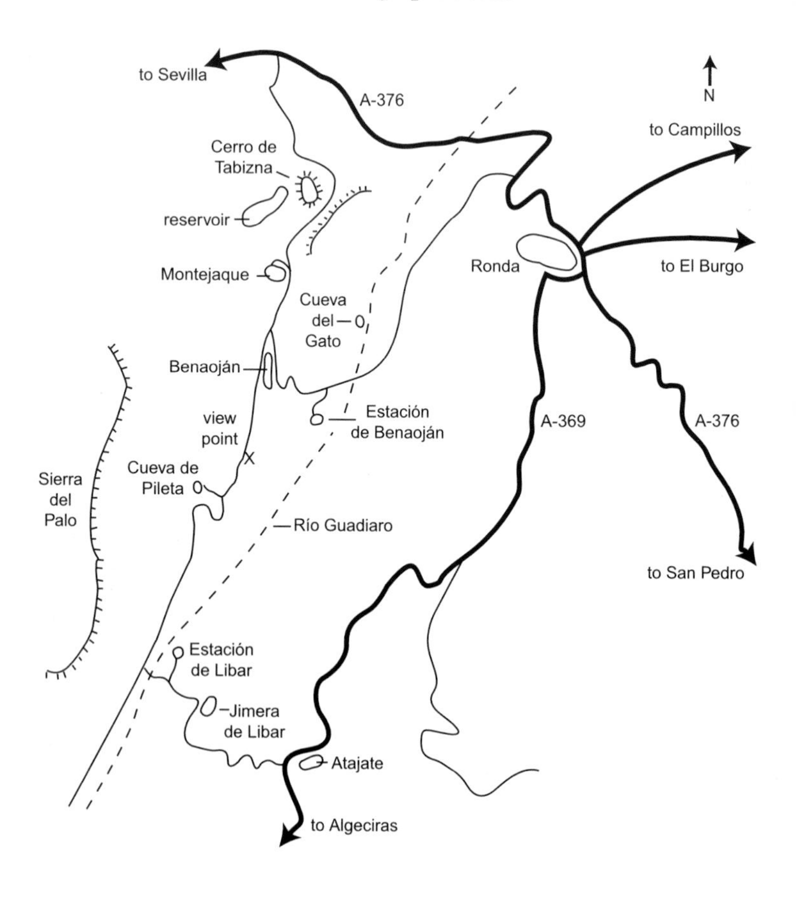

On leaving Estación de Benaoján, turn right toward Ronda to get back to the A-376 or return back through Benaoján if you are returning home via the A-369.

When to Visit

Although this route has plenty to offer throughout the year, the time to see the maximum number of species is between mid-March and June. This will include most of the breeding species and passage migrants.

General Information

Although much of this site is unsuitable for wheelchair birders, there are parts, such as the first section of the Cueva del Gato walk, that are wheelchair accessible. However, most of the area and a lot of birding can be done from a car or from certain vantage points along the route.

Bird Calendar

Resident

Cattle Egret, Grey Heron, White Stork, Mallard, Griffon Vulture, Buzzard, Sparrowhawk. Goshawk, Bonelli's Eagle, Peregrine, Kestrel, Lesser Kestrel, Red-legged Partridge, Water Rail, Moorhen, Common Sandpiper, Rock Dove, Wood Pigeon, Collared Dove, Little Owl, Eagle Owl, Tawny Owl, Barn Owl, Kingfisher, Green Woodpecker, Great Spotted Woodpecker, Woodlark, Crested Lark, Thekla Lark, Crag Martin, White Wagtail, Grey Wagtail, Robin, Stonechat, Black Redstart, Black Wheatear, Blue Rock Thrush, Blackbird, Mistle Thrush, Cetti's Warbler, Blackcap, Sardinian Warbler, Dartford Warbler, Firecrest, Long-tailed Tit, Coal Tit, Great Tit, Blue Tit, Nuthatch, Short-toed Treecreeper, Wren, Great Grey Shrike, Jay, Red-billed Chough, Jackdaw, Raven, Spotless Starling, Rock Sparrow, House Sparrow, Tree Sparrow, Chaffinch, Serin, Linnet, Goldfinch, Greenfinch, Crossbill, Corn Bunting, Rock Bunting, Cirl Bunting.

Summer / Breeding

Black Kite, Short-toed Eagle, Egyptian Vulture, Booted Eagle, Black-winged Stilt, Turtle Dove, Cuckoo, Scops Owl, Red-necked Nightjar, Alpine Swift, White-rumped Swift, Common Swift, Pallid Swift, Hoopoe, Bee-eater, House Martin, Red-rumped Swallow, Barn Swallow, Nightingale, Rufous Bush Chat, Redstart, Black-eared Wheatear, Melodious Warbler, Subalpine Warbler, Bonelli's Warbler, Spotted Flycatcher, Woodchat Shrike, Golden Oriole, Ortolan Bunting.

Winter

Little Egret, Red Kite, Merlin, Redshank, Green Sandpiper, Wryneck, Skylark, Meadow Pipit, Dunnock, Ring Ouzel, Fieldfare, Redwing, Song Thrush, Iberian Chiffchaff, Starling, Brambling, Siskin, Hawfinch.

Passage Migrants

Squacco Heron, Purple Heron, Black Stork, Montagu's Harrier, Honey Buzzard, Wood Sandpiper, Roller, Yellow Wagtail, Whinchat, Northern Wheatear, Pied Flycatcher.

Egyptian Vulture *(Neophron percnopterus)*

Cádiz Province

The province of Cádiz has a short stretch of Mediterranean coastline but its Atlantic coastline (*Costa de la Luz*) beyond Gibraltar has some of the finest beaches and birdwatching sites in the region. Practically all of the Cádiz coastline is directly below the main migration routes to and from the African continent and is, without doubt, the prime area in Europe to watch migrating storks and raptors during the spring and autumn passage periods. There are several very important lagoons and wetlands where both resident and wintering wildfowl and waders, including Common Cranes and Great Egrets, can be found with some regularity.

I have chosen nine sites in the province, but as most of these are large areas with numerous sub-sites, the actual number of sites is nearer to 30.

General map of Cádiz and the sites

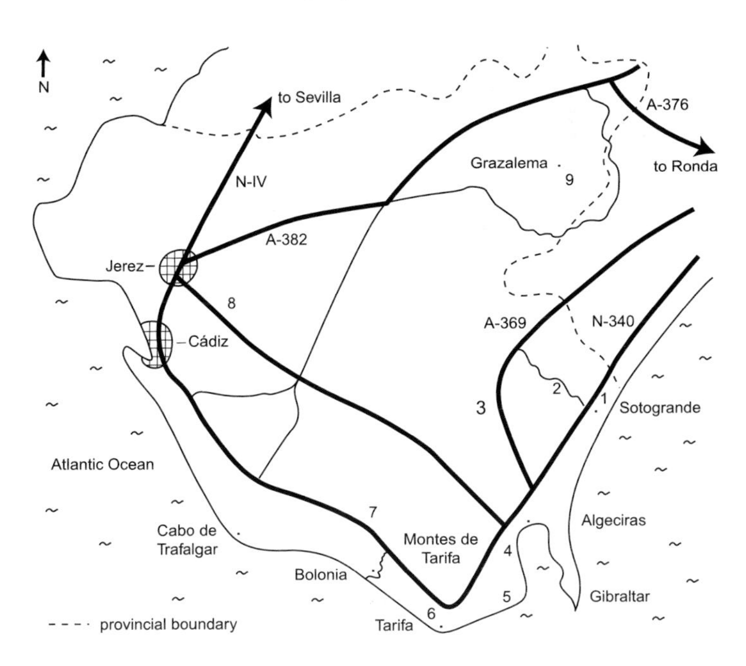

1. Sotogrande. 2. San Enrique wood. 3. Castellar de la Frontera. 4. The Río Palmones. 5. Punta Carnero and Punta Secreta. 6. Tarifa. 7. La Janda. 8. Laguna de Medina. 9. Parque Natural Sierra de Grazalema.

Sotogrande

Sotogrande is an exclusive residential and holiday development towards the western end of the Costa del Sol, midway between the town of Estepona and Gibraltar. It has been built surrounding the estuary of the Río Guadiaro and on the north-eastern bank there is a large residential area and a marina (*Puerto Sotogrande*), along with many businesses, bars and restaurants. To the south-west of the river, luxury villas predominate the area, along with a golf course, tennis club, beach club and polo fields.

Apart from all of the construction that has taken place, the area has many permanent and seasonally wet sites which are. of vital importance to many species of birds. Unfortunately, building is still in progress and some favourable sites could be threatened in the future, though I feel confident the sites I have selected will not be affected.

The main map gives an overall picture of the Sotogrande area, whilst each of the sub-site descriptions will have a more detailed map to accompany the text.

Although the calendar for the birds will be for the site as a whole, it is obvious that some species will be seen at one location and not at another. Where this is the case, I will make special reference to a particular species in the relevant sub-site description so that you do not spend time looking for a particular bird that will only be seen elsewhere.

Being so close to the main migration routes to and from Africa, the area benefits from many passing species during the main passage periods. Many scarcities and an increasing number of both Spanish and European rarities are now being recorded here and, with the recent improvements to the Paraje Natural and to the estuary, I feel the area will become even more attractive to a greater number of species that could use this location for breeding or as an overwintering site.

Access

There are only two main access roads into the Sotogrande area, both from the main N-340 highway. Both of these roads have security posts with barriers manned by uniformed guards. Most normal traffic is allowed to enter without check, but camper-vans and caravans are usually refused entry unless you can convince the guards that you have no intention of camping overnight.

Map of Sotogrande area

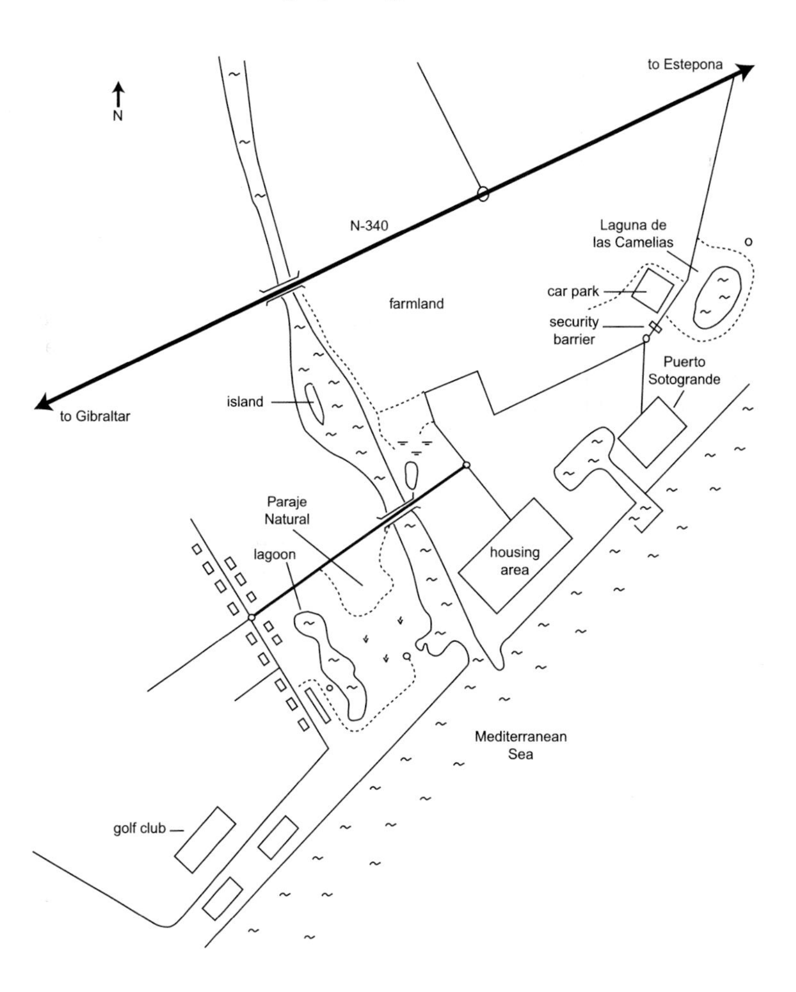

Travelling from the Estepona direction, take the turn-off to Puerto Sotogrande at km 135 and then turn left under the roadbridge. This leads directly to the entry point and the first site.

Travelling from the Gibraltar direction, I would advise you to ignore the first turn-off for Sotogrande, just before km 130, and instead continue along the N-340, crossing over the Río Guadiaro and then taking the Puerto Sotogrande exit just before km 135. This allows you to view the sites in the order that they are presented.

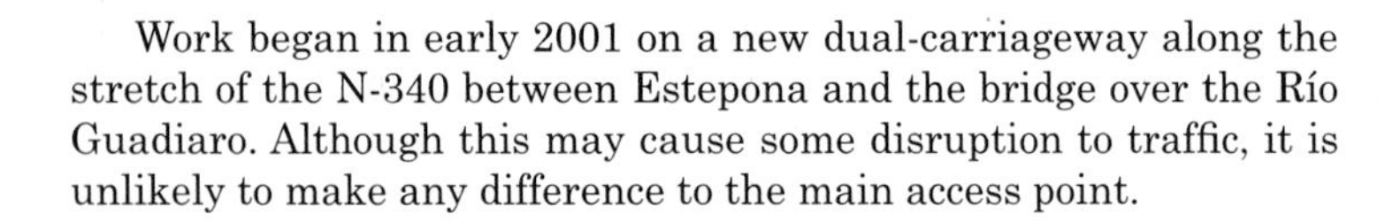

Work began in early 2001 on a new dual-carriageway along the stretch of the N-340 between Estepona and the bridge over the Río Guadiaro. Although this may cause some disruption to traffic, it is unlikely to make any difference to the main access point.

Laguna de Las Camelias

Although not large (250x60m), the lagoon is surrounded by extensive reedbeds and supports a variety of birds and other wildlife. Resident species include Purple Gallinules, Moorhens, Little Grebes, Kingfishers, Cetti's Warblers, Reed Buntings and Water Rails. During the summer, you can expect to see Little Bitterns, Squacco and Purple Herons, Whiskered Terns, Hoopoes, Sand Martins, Nightingales and Reed, Melodious and Willow Warblers. Common wintering species often include Great Crested Grebes, Cormorants, Pochards, Shovelers, Wigeon, Little Gulls, Crag Martins and Meadow Pipits.

One side of the lagoon adjoins a sandy beach and offers the opportunity to look for seabirds and waders. The top end has a seasonal marshy area which is attractive to ducks and waders, and further back there is a small wood and scrubland. These areas should not be overlooked as they are also attractive to several species.

Access

On the immediate approach to the Sotogrande complex, you come to a road barrier which is manned by security guards. Just before the barrier, there is a car-park on the right. Park here and cross the road to view the lagoon from an elevated position. Most of the lagoon is visible from this vantage point. Two resident families of Purple Gallinules are to be found here, both seeming to have their own territories. The first group is often seen at this end of the lagoon, usually in the reeds to the left. The second group appears to favour the top right-hand corner of the lagoon.

Directly opposite the road barrier, there is an entrance through the hedge which gives access to the beach, lagoon and surrounding areas. There are numerous tracks which lead through the reeds taking you almost to the water's edge. Scan the reeds on the opposite bank for gallinules and Water Rails (all year) and for Purple and Squacco Herons and Little Bitterns in the summer. The reeds also hold various warblers, Reed Buntings and occasionally, wintering Penduline Tits. As evening approaches, up to 200 Cattle Egrets fly in to roost in the reedbeds and are often joined by a few Little Egrets.

At this point it may be beneficial to view the beach. Large flocks of gulls regularly form close-by and careful scanning may reveal Audouin's and Mediterranean Gulls amongst the more common species. Wader numbers are never very high here, usually only Kentish and Little-ringed Plovers, Common Sandpipers and Redshanks. Sandwich, Common and Little Terns often pass along the coast, whilst off-shore there may be Gannets and shearwaters. During the winter, there are usually a few Razorbills, Red-breasted Mergansers, Common Scoters and both Black-necked and Great Crested Grebes to be seen in the bay.

Continue to the top end of the lagoon until you reach a dirt-road near to a private house and a ruined watchtower. The tower plays host to Rock Doves, Jackdaws and Kestrels. Black Redstarts, Hoopoes and Woodchat Shrikes prefer the more barren land here and both the shrikes and the Kestrels can often be seen hunting for the lizards and insects that abound at this particular location.

The dirt-road will lead you around the top of the lagoon, passing a seasonal marsh and a wooded area. This is a good spot for Sardinian, Fan-tailed and Cetti's Warblers, Crested Larks, Black-eared Wheatears, Blackcaps, tits and finches. During the summer, both Melodious Warblers and Nightingales are fairly common here.

Map of the Laguna de las Camelias

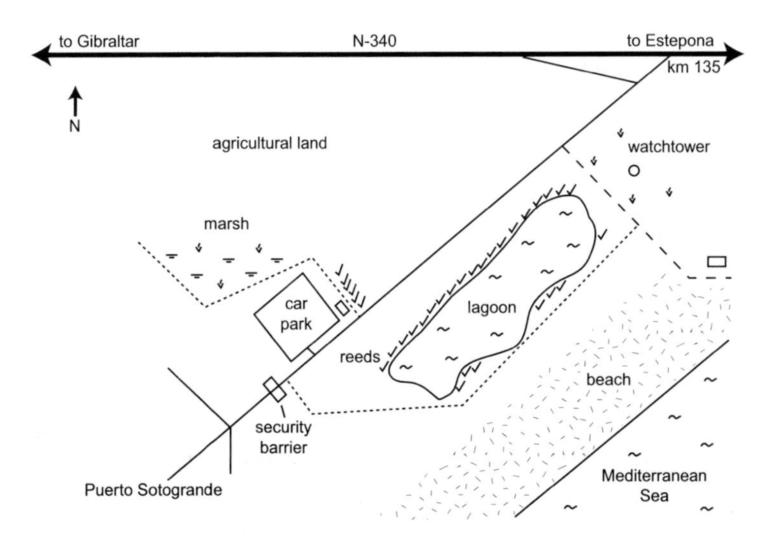

Once you have reached the road, walk along the grass verge using suitable places to view the lagoon and reedbeds. Arriving back at the car-park, you will notice a path which leads between a building and a hedge of tall canes. This passes beside a seasonally flooded marshland and then on to agricultural land. The path is only a few hundred metres long but it is worth exploring before leaving this particular location. The birds that are commonly seen here are tits, finches, larks, warblers, doves and pigeons. Kestrels and Buzzards regularly hunt over the cultivated fields and occasionally a Peregrine may be seen. The fence posts beyond the fields should be checked as raptors often perch on these.

The East Bank of the Río Guadiaro

The site comprises a 1.5 km stretch of the east bank of the Río Guadiaro, situated between two bridges. The varying habitats make this a very attractive area for a wide variety of bird species. At the southern end, there is a small lagoon and a marsh which are surrounded by a stand of eucalyptus trees, tamarisks, oleanders, reeds and other shrubs and scrub plants. It is very secluded and holds reasonable numbers of waders in the winter and during passage periods. These regularly include Snipe and both Green and Wood Sandpipers. Little Grebes, Coots and Moorhens are common here and an assortment of ducks are usually present.

Along the river there are woods and dense vegetation which hold a good selection of finches, tits, warblers and other passerines. Redstarts and Golden Orioles are regular summer visitors. In the middle of the river there is a long, narrow island which is the roosting site for a sizeable colony of Cormorants and many Grey Herons and egrets. Toward the northern end of the site there are wide expanses of agricultural land where Hoopoes, Black Redstarts, Black-eared Wheatears, Crested Larks and Meadow Pipits can be found at the appropriate times of the year.

The roadbridge which carries the N-340 highway over the river marks the northern end of the site. The river is tidal and at low tide you can look upriver to exposed mudflats where waders, waterfowl and gulls often congregate to feed.

The site in general is regularly overflown by Buzzards, Kestrels, Griffon Vultures and eagles. Sparrowhawks can sometimes be seen flying low over the nearby orchards and Ospreys often hunt along the river.

In the winter and during passage periods, Snipe, Avocets, Redshanks, Common and Green Sandpipers, godwits and plovers

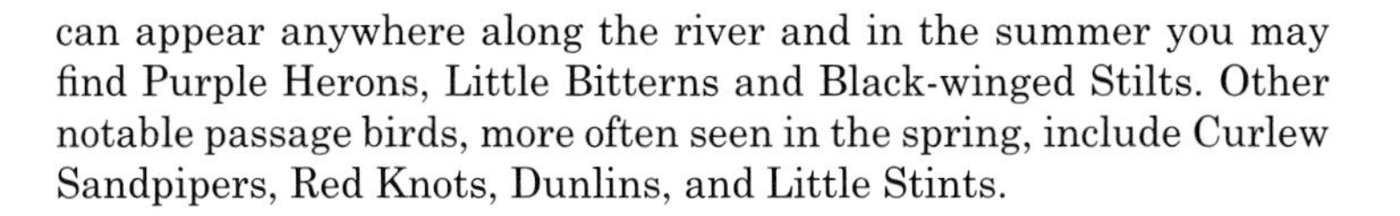

can appear anywhere along the river and in the summer you may find Purple Herons, Little Bitterns and Black-winged Stilts. Other notable passage birds, more often seen in the spring, include Curlew Sandpipers, Red Knots, Dunlins, and Little Stints.

Access

From the previous site at the Laguna de las Camelias, pass through the security barrier and take the first exit from the roundabout. Proceed for just over one kilometre and the road passes a field on the left which is being excavated to form a lake. Drive right around the field and at the bottom right-hand corner, almost level with a line of trees, there is an area where you can park off-road. This is right beside the small lagoon and marsh.

General map of the Riverside site

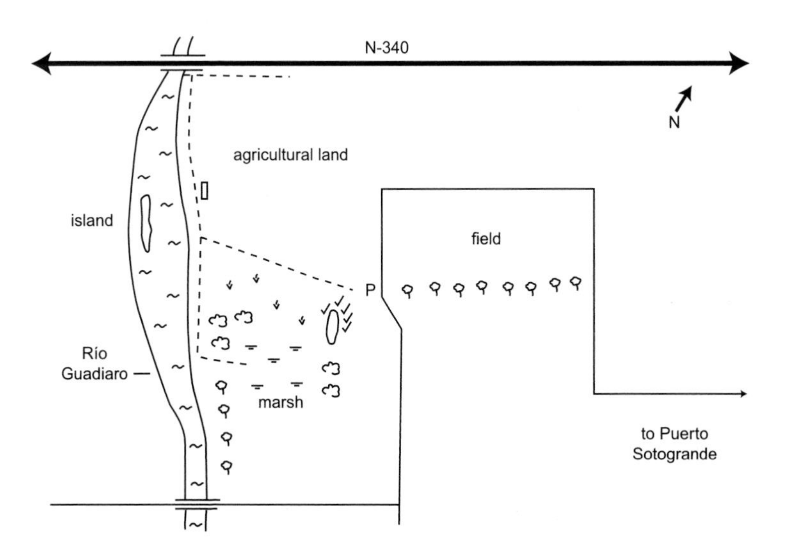

After viewing the immediate area, take the diagonal track (see map) that leads toward the river. At the present time (August 2001), construction of a block of apartments is under way but access to the river is not affected. The track which runs alongside the river is permanent and clearly defined but sometimes the vegetation obscures your view of the water. However, numerous small trails lead toward the riverbank affording good clear views.

Beyond the bridge, there is a plantation of orange trees where both Cirl and Corn Buntings are often seen along with wagtails, tits, warblers and finches. Sparrowhawks and Kestrels are regular visitors to this spot, hunting for small birds and rodents that feed in the orchards. On a few occasions, I have seen Ospreys hunting near the bridge in the winter months and in the summer both Booted and Short-toed Eagles are fairly common.

The return trip to the roadbridge is about three kilometres and the time taken is totally dependent on how often and for how long you stop. I usually manage to cover the trip in about one and a half hours.

The Estuary and the Parque Natural

Although I have included this area as a single site it is, in fact, three distinctly separate areas within the Parque Natural. To simplify matters, I will treat each part individually under different headings.

The Paraje Natural is an expanse of land, measuring some 27 hectares, that lies beside the estuary and the west bank of the Río Guadiaro. Within the boundaries of the park, there is a lagoon with extensive reedbeds and a few marsh areas that are all attractive to birds and other wildlife.

In the past, the area was open and local families used it for picnics and barbecues, whilst young motorcyclists utilized it to practice their off-road riding skills, totally disrupting the whole of the site. Fortunately, in 1999 the Andalusian Government spent 213 million pesetas on the park and the estuary, erecting fences, gates, boardwalks and a bird observation hide. At the same time a large scale re-vegetation programme was undertaken to cover the areas of ravaged and barren land. Access within the park is now restricted to elevated boardwalks and has had the desired effect of reducing human disturbance. The birds and other wildlife are now thriving in this new environment.

(a) The Boardwalk

On leaving the previous site, continue along the road and take the first exit from the roundabout. The road now crosses over the river and approximately 150 metres beyond the bridge you find a wooden gateway and a notice board on the left-hand side. This is the entrance to the northern end of the park. You can park off-road beside the gate and wander along the boardwalk which gives good elevated views of the surrounding scrub and shrub areas and the edge of the reedbeds. At one point you pass over a small river and a marsh, before arriving at the end of the walk beneath the bridge. From this point you have reasonable views upriver and also down toward the estuary. Egrets, herons, grebes, Cormorants, Coots, Moorhens and ducks can normally be seen here.

To return to your car, you can either retrace your steps along the boardwalk or climb a slope at the other side of the bridge which leads to the road. I personally prefer the former route.

Buzzards and the resident population of at least twenty Monk Parakeets often perch on the railings of the boardwalk and Marsh Harriers regularly hunt over the park. The scrubland is particularly good for Sardinian, Fan-tailed and Cetti's Warblers, whilst the trees in the park hold good numbers of finches, tits and leaf warblers.

During the migration periods, many bird species pass directly overhead and good views of Black Kites, Honey Buzzards and other birds of prey are possible. In summer, the sky above the park is full of swifts, swallows, martins and Bee-eaters.

(b) The Paraje Natural, the Lagoon and Beach

On leaving the boardwalk site, drive a few hundred metres to a roundabout and turn left. After 500 metres, there is a large wooden gate and a notice board on the left-hand side of the road. This is the entry point to the southern end of the park. Directly beside the gate there are a number of parking bays.

On entering the park, you very soon come to a bird observation hide that looks out over the lagoon, marshland and extensive reedbeds. The hide offers the best chance of viewing Purple Gallinules and wintering Penduline Tits at close quarters. At least ten gallinules are resident here and are often clearly visible in the reeds directly in front of the hide and on the marsh at the far side of the lagoon. The best time to see them is in the winter months, before the reeds and other vegetation grow too high. In the spring and summer, when they are breeding, they become more secretive. In the winter months, the Penduline Tits often feed on the bullrushes in front of the hide and Bluethroats may also be present, normally on the marshy area at the far side of the water.

Other birds that are more commonly found in the winter include Wrynecks and both Reed and Cirl Buntings. Greater Flamingos are liable to appear at any time, either here or at the estuary, but only singularly or in small groups.

This is a good spot for summer visitors and you can expect to see Whiskered Terns, Purple and Squacco Herons, Little Bitterns, Sand Martins, Black-winged Stilts, Melodious Warblers, Woodchat Shrikes and Nightingales.

During the spring passage period and, to a lesser extent in the summer, both Sedge and Willow Warblers are often present. Other regular birds seen at the lagoon include White, Grey and Yellow Wagtails, Grey Herons, Little Grebes, Stonechats, Whinchats, finches, larks, pipits, tits, warblers and ducks.

Notable birds of prey that can be seen with some regularity are Marsh Harriers, Ospreys, Buzzards, Black Kites, Kestrels, Lesser Kestrels, Sparrowhawks, Peregrines, Short-toed and Booted Eagles and Griffon Vultures. Passage periods can produce Red Kites, Montagu's Harriers and Honey Buzzards.

General map of the Estuary and the Paraje Natural

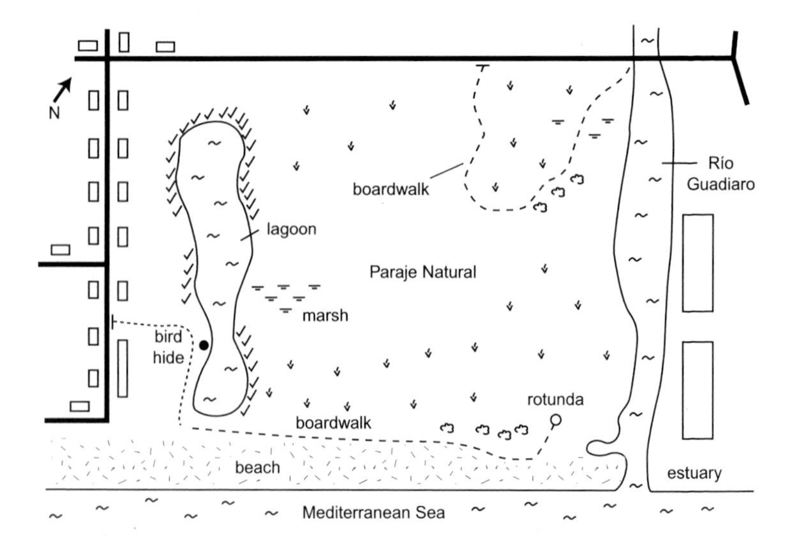

A minute's walk from the hide will bring you to the beach and the second boardwalk, which skirts the southern end of the park. The elevated position enables you to see more of the lagoon, the surrounding reedbeds and the scrubland.

Good offshore views can be had from here and the birds to be seen include Mediterranean Shearwaters, Gannets and Sandwich Terns throughout the year. In the winter small numbers of Razorbills, Black-necked Grebes and Common Scoters are normally visible.

Along the sandy beach and the re-vegetated sand-bar, Kentish Plovers, Crested Larks, Serins and other finches can always be seen. In the summer, Black-eared Wheatears and Woodchat Shrikes are fairly common, as are Hoopoes and Bee-eaters.

(c) The Estuary

Following the boardwalk to the end, you come to a covered rotunda with bench seating. From this vantage point you have further good views across the park but, more importantly, clear views of the estuary. Directly in front of the rotunda there is a tidal marsh and a small, shallow lagoon which is regularly visited by a wide variety of species. Although many of the birds from the other sites can also be found here, I will concentrate my list for this area mainly on waders, waterfowl and seabirds.

The greatest concentration of birds occurs during passage periods and in the winter but it is not uncommon to find small numbers of waders here throughout the year.

The river, estuary and the tidal mudflats are only about 75 metres away from the rotunda and, although good views are possible, a telescope is always a great advantage to help identify the smaller waders, etc.

Large flocks of mixed gulls are usually present, either on the water, mudflats or sand-bar. Careful scanning of these flocks may reveal Audouin's, Slender-billed, Mediterranean, Black-headed, Lesser Black-backed and Little Gulls, along with Kittiwakes, amongst the hundreds of Yellow-legged Gulls.

Wildfowl are represented by Mallards, Shovelers, Gadwalls, Wigeon and Teal. Occasionally, small numbers of Greylags may stop to feed during passage periods and Shelducks may also be present.

I have recorded an impressive wader list at this location which includes Avocets, Black-winged Stilts, Golden Plovers, Little Stints, Ruffs, Snipe, Spotted Redshanks and Green, Wood, Marsh and Curlew Sandpipers. All the waders mentioned in the bird calendar have been seen at the estuary. Other regular visitors here are Great Crested, Black-necked and Little Grebes, Grey and Purple Herons, Cattle and Little Egrets, Cormorants, Sandwich, Common, Little and Whiskered Terns, Ospreys, Spoonbills and Greater Flamingos, all of which may be found at the appropriate times of the year.

Kingfishers regularly use the tidal lagoon and in the winter it is possible to see Bluethroats, usually in the area to the left where the tamarisks overhang the water. However, silence and a degree of patience is required to see this species.

When to Visit

These sites are of interest at all times to the keen birdwatcher. The winter period is exceptionally good for waders and wildfowl and also for Penduline Tits, Bluethroats and both Reed and Cirl Buntings. The Marsh Harriers, Ospreys and Purple Gallinules are highly visible at this time of year and the offshore seabirds are much more numerous.

During the northward passage period, good numbers of eagles, kites and other raptorial species can be seen overhead, together with swifts, swallows, martins and many other migrating passerines.

The summer visitors bring a bit of colour to the area, with Hoopoe, Bee-eater, Golden Oriole, Woodchat Shrike and Black-eared Wheatear usually present.

The sites can be visited at any time of the day, although times of low-tide are preferable at the estuary and along the river as the mudflats are then exposed and feeding waders are more abundant. Early morning sunlight reflecting off the water can affect vision at the estuary and afternoon sun can be a problem at the riverside site. Human disturbance is usually minimal at all times except in the height of summer when the beaches can become busy.

Due to the exposed nature of the estuary, it is often quite windy at this location. In the summer this is not a real problem but at other times of the year I recommend you take with you an item of protective clothing, such as a windcheater or jumper.

General Information

Unfortunately, as good as this area is, there is no reasonable access to any of the sites for wheelchair birders. The Laguna de las Camelias is bounded by 1.5 metre high hedges on one side and by a soft sandy beach on the other. The riverside track is very uneven and often quite muddy. The boardwalks at the Paraje Natural have been erected using anti-motorcycle barriers which also have the effect of stopping wheelchair users from enjoying the park.

Bird Calendar

Resident

Little Grebe, Mediterranean Shearwater, Gannet, Cattle Egret, Little Egret, Grey Heron, Greater Flamingo, Mallard, Shoveler, Osprey, Griffon Vulture, Sparrowhawk, Buzzard, Peregrine, Kestrel, Lesser Kestrel, Water Rail, Moorhen, Purple Gallinule, Coot, Little-ringed Plover, Kentish Plover, Redshank, Common Sandpiper, Audouin's Gull, Black-headed Gull, Yellow-Legged Gull, Sandwich Tern, Rock Dove, Wood Pigeon, Collared Dove, Monk Parakeet, Little Owl, Kingfisher, Hoopoe, Great Spotted Woodpecker, Crested Lark, Woodlark, White Wagtail, Grey Wagtail, Robin, Stonechat, Black Redstart, Blackbird, Cetti's Warbler, Fan-tailed Warbler, Sardinian Warbler, Blackcap, Long-tailed Tit, Great Tit, Blue Tit, Nuthatch, Wren, Short-toed Treecreeper, Great Grey Shrike, Jay, Jackdaw, Spotless Starling, Spanish Sparrow, House Sparrow, Tree -Sparrow, Chaffinch, Serin, Linnet, Goldfinch, Greenfinch, Corn Bunting, Cirl Bunting, Reed Bunting.

Summer / Breeding

Little Bittern, Squacco Heron, Purple Heron, Short-toed Eagle, Booted Eagle, Black-winged Stilt, Little Tern, Whiskered Tern, Turtle Dove, Cuckoo, Red-necked Nightjar, Common Swift, Pallid Swift, Bee-eater, Sand Martin, House Martin, Red-rumped Swallow, Barn Swallow, Tawny Pipit, Yellow Wagtail, Nightingale, Rufous Bush Chat, Redstart, Black-eared Wheatear, Reed Warbler, Olivaceous Warbler, Melodious Warbler, Willow Warbler, Spotted Flycatcher, Woodchat Shrike, Golden Oriole.

Winter

Great Crested Grebe, Black-necked Grebe, Cormorant, Spoonbill, White Stork, Wigeon, Teal, Red-crested Pochard, Pochard, Red-breasted Merganser, Common Scoter, Marsh Harrier, Oystercatcher, Avocet, Ringed Plover, Grey Plover, Golden Plover, Lapwing, Dunlin, Sanderling, Little Stint, Ruff, Snipe, Black-tailed Godwit, Bar-tailed Godwit, Curlew, Whimbrel, Spotted Redshank, Greenshank, Green Sandpiper, Turnstone, Little Gull, Mediterranean Gull, Lesser Black-backed Gull, Kittiwake, Razorbill, Wryneck, Skylark, Crag Martin, Meadow Pipit, Bluethroat, Song Thrush, Iberian Chiffchaff, Starling, Penduline Tit, Siskin.

Passage Migrants

Black Kite, Red Kite, Egyptian Vulture, Montagu's Harrier, Honey Buzzard, Collared Pratincole, Curlew Sandpiper, Red Knot, Marsh Sandpiper, Wood Sandpiper, Caspian Tern, Common Tern, Gull-billed Tern, Roller, Great Spotted Cuckoo, Tree Pipit, Whinchat, Northern Wheatear, Sedge Warbler, Garden Warbler, Pied Flycatcher, Ortolan Bunting.

Purple Gallinule *(Porphyrio porphyrio)*

San Enrique wood

The wood at San Enrique is one of the few broadleaved woodlands in the area. It consists of a mixture of deciduous and evergreen trees and shrubs and holds an excellent variety of woodland birds at any time of the year. Although the greater number of species are present during the summer/breeding season, some interesting wintering birds can also be found here.

The wood itself is not large, probably measuring no more than 300 metres in length and 75 metres in width. However, the entry to this site and the surrounding areas of farmland offer a good selection of differing habitats and, therefore, a much wider variety of bird species.

The approach track leads between large plantations of oranges, lemons and avocados, many of which are bordered by large coniferous hedges, before opening up to an area of wild meadowland which runs for almost the entire length of the nearside of the wood. The far side is bounded by the Río Guadiaro, a tidal river. At low tide, exposed mudflats and shingle banks offer good feeding opportunities for a variety of waders.

At the top end of the wood, partial damming of the river has created a marshy area with small lagoons, mudflats and gravel inlets. This area attracts herons, egrets, waders and wildfowl.

The whole of this site is regularly overflown by eagles and other raptors and occasionally Ospreys may be seen hunting along the river. Griffon Vultures from the nearby mountains are common as they pass over the farmland searching for carrion.

Access

Travelling from the Málaga direction toward Gibraltar on the main N-340 highway, you pass through the village of Torre Guadiaro and at the roundabout, just after km 134, you turn right towards Pueblo Nuevo de Guadiaro. Coming from the Gibraltar direction, you cross the Río Guadiaro at km 133 and at the end of the dual-carriageway take the second exit from the roundabout.

Exactly one kilometre from the roundabout, there is a sign for San Enrique and 50 metres beyond this there is a turn-off to the left, directly opposite a large white sign with the words "ATENCIÓN, TRAVESÍA PELIGROSO". Turn here and after 50 metres the surfaced road ends and becomes a dirt track. Proceed for a further 150 metres and at this point there is a crossroads. The route to the site is directly ahead but the track is often closed to traffic with a chain. I strongly suggest that you park here and walk down the track, even if the chain is not across the track, as it may well be on your return and you could find yourself locked in, with no other route out.

Map of the San Enrique wood and approach area

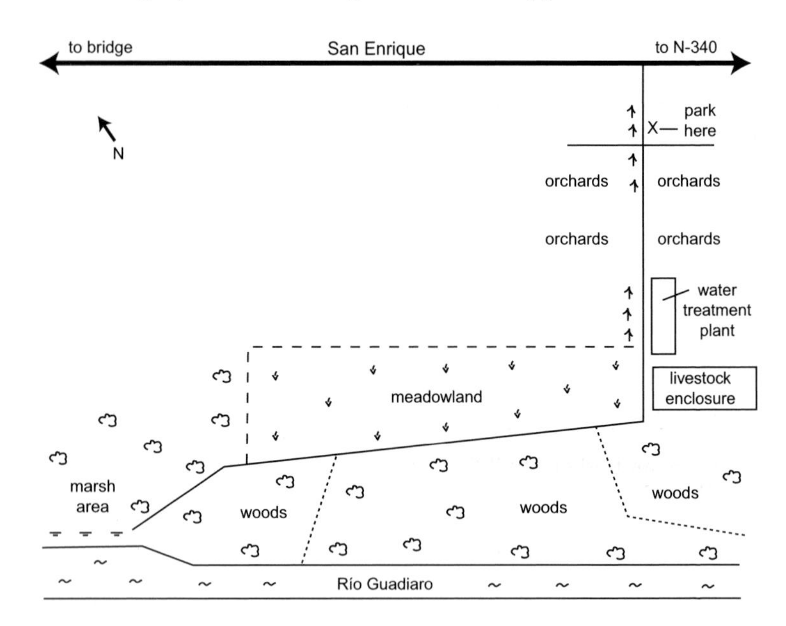

Before starting down the track, scan the open land between your position and the main road. Cattle Egrets are regularly seen here, as are Crested Larks, Meadow Pipits, Serins and other finches. Check the electricity poles and cables for raptors, doves and other birds.

Walking down the track, you pass between large orchards of citrus fruit and avocado. These orchards should be checked for Cirl Buntings, larks, finches and warblers. Montagu's Harriers (summer) and Sparrowhawks can sometimes be seen hunting here and at any point along the route you are likely to see Hoopoes. At the bottom of the track, just before it turns to the right, there is a water treatment plant and a livestock enclosure. This is a fairly reliable spot for Tree Sparrows and White Wagtails, along with numerous finches and tits.

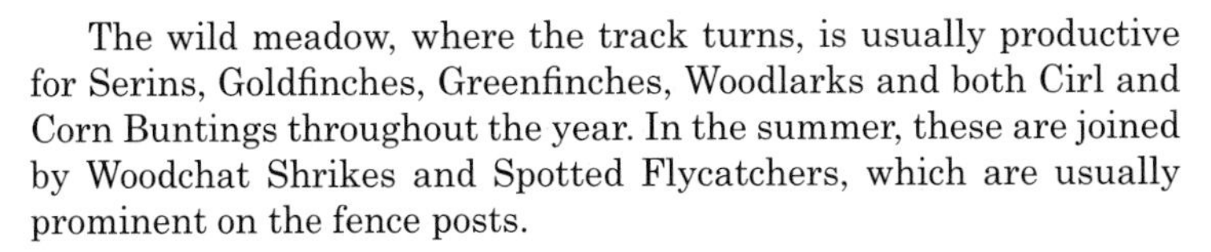

The wild meadow, where the track turns, is usually productive for Serins, Goldfinches, Greenfinches, Woodlarks and both Cirl and Corn Buntings throughout the year. In the summer, these are joined by Woodchat Shrikes and Spotted Flycatchers, which are usually prominent on the fence posts.

The small track to the left (indicated on map) leads into the lower end of the wood and to the river. The trees here are rather dense and therefore the birds are not too easy to see, but patience should bring its reward. A fallen tree just inside the wood offers the chance to sit and wait for the birds to appear. After visiting this part of the wood, return to the main track and continue alongside the meadow until you reach the top end of the wood. Here, some of the trees have been cut down and the views of the birds are much better. The resident species include Great Spotted Woodpeckers, Long-tailed, Great and Blue Tits, Jays, Short-toed Treecreepers, Nuthatches, Cetti's Warblers, Sardinian Warblers, Fan-tailed Warblers and finches. The summer migrants include Golden Orioles, Redstarts, Cuckoos, Nightingales, Melodious Warblers, Willow Warblers and Scops Owls. In the winter, Siskins, Iberian Chiffchaffs and Blackcaps are regular visitors.

The main track continues through the wood and ends at a marshy area beside the Río Guadiaro. Partial damming of the river in 1998 has resulted in a very barren area being transformed into a haven for birds and other wildlife. The marsh that has been created has small pools and lagoons where reeds and other vegetation have become established. In the middle of the river, gravelbanks have formed and become the nesting sites for Little-ringed Plovers.

Egrets, herons and Kingfishers are commonly seen and in the summer Barn Swallows, Red-rumped Swallows, swifts, martins and Bee-eaters are always present. During the winter month, waders are attracted to this spot and you may find Redshank, Ringed Plover, Dunlin, Snipe and Common and Green Sandpipers. Crag Martins replace the other hirundines at this time of the year.

Along the whole length of this site, keep an eye on the sky as the entire area is regularly overflown by Buzzards, Kestrels, and Griffon Vultures throughout the year. In the summer, these are joined by Booted and Short-toed Eagles and occasionally Egyptian Vultures.

Subsidiary site

On the opposite side of the river, there is a sub-site to the wood that is well worth exploring whilst you are in the vicinity. This site includes a one-kilometre stretch of the river, a wooded area, polo fields, orchards, meadows, rocky outcrops and the river bridge. The bottom end of this site is directly opposite the marsh area of the previous site and gives differing aspects of the river.

To reach this site, return to the road and turn left, passing through San Enrique. After 1.2 kms, turn left and cross the bridge over the river and continue for a further 500 metres. At the second left-handed bend, there is a track on the left which leads back toward the bridge. Follow the track and park underneath the bridge and explore the site on foot.

The track to the right runs alongside the river for almost a kilometre. Due to the partial damming of the river at the top end of the previous site, much of the low-lying land beside the riverbank has become flooded or marshy, creating a haven for some birds. Moorhens, Mallards and Little Grebes can usually be seen throughout the year, along with Purple Herons and Little Bitterns in the summer and Grey Herons, Cormorants, Gadwalls and a few waders in the winter.

At the dam, where the track turns up towards the road, you have the option to either return alongside the river or to walk along the road until you reach the track you first drove down. I have taken both routes on many occasions and find the riverside track preferable, although the road offers elevated views across the orchards and also good views of the rocky hillside on the left. It is here that you are most likely to see Black Redstarts, Great Grey Shrikes, Sardinian and Fan-tailed Warblers, Red-legged Partridges and possibly, Blue Rock Thrushes. Regardless of which route you choose, first check the small field on the left between the dam and the road, part of which has been planted with orange trees but much of it has been left as wild meadow and attracts Cirl Buntings and mixed finches.

As at the previous site, Hoopoes can be seen anywhere along the route at most times of the year and Bee-eaters and Woodchat Shrikes are very obvious from late March until mid-September. The views of the eagles and other raptors are generally better on this side of the river as there are fewer trees to obscure your vision.

In the summer, there is always plenty of swift and swallow activity near the bridge and the polo fields are also worth scanning, as practically anything can turn up here at any time. Certainly you should expect to see pipits, larks, wagtails, buntings, sparrows and mixed finches.

The trees in this area are mostly eucalyptus and conifers and do not hold the same variety as the broadleaved woodland. However, Jays, Great Spotted Woodpeckers, Robins, Short-toed Treecreepers and a mixture of warblers and finches are always to be found.

The riverbank beyond the bridge is easily accessible and consists mainly of stones, rocks and gravel. A walk along here will usually produce reasonable views of Kingfishers, herons, egrets, wagtails, plovers and other waders.

Unfortunately it is only possible to walk a short distance along this bank as the vegetation has now crept down to the water's edge. Any area of reeds should be checked for Cetti's Warblers (all year), Reed Warblers (summer) and Sedge Warblers during the passage periods. Melodious Warblers are fairly common in the breeding season and Olivaceous Warblers, although nowhere near as numerous, can be found in the summer.

Map of the Subsidiary site

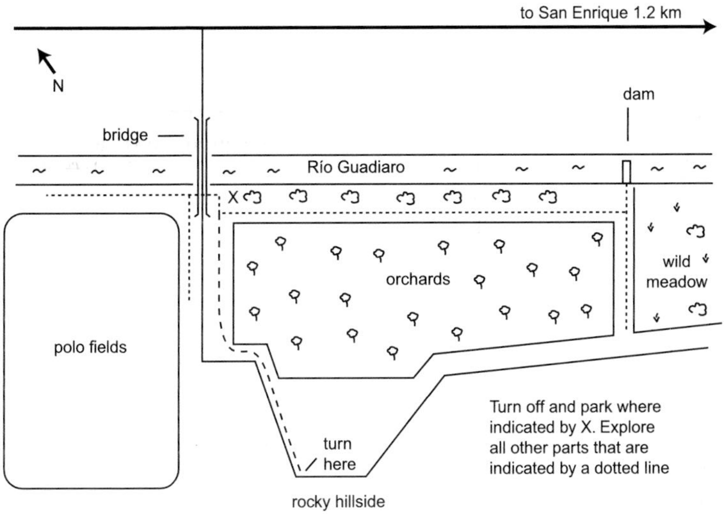

When to Visit

I have always found this to be a very rewarding site at any time of the year, not only for the large variety of birds but also for the few hours of peace and quiet that it offers. However, during the summer, especially at weekends, you may find that a few local families descend upon the area for a day out by the river, complete with barbecues and loud music. Obviously this is not conducive to good birdwatching. Also in the summer I would suggest that you visit in the morning or evening as the mid-afternoon temperatures can become very oppressive at this site.

General Information

The first part of this site is completely flat and involves a round trip of approximately 2 kms. It is, therefore, a very gentle walk and, with the possible exception of the marsh area, fully wheelchair accessible to any disabled birdwatcher. The sub-site, although being slightly harder going, should not prove too difficult for wheelchair birders with, perhaps, the exception of the river bank beyond the bridge.

Bird Calendar

Resident

Little Grebe, Cattle Egret, Little Egret, Grey Heron, Mallard, Osprey, Griffon Vulture, Sparrowhawk, Buzzard, Bonelli's Eagle, Kestrel, Red-legged Partridge, Moorhen, Little-ringed Plover, Black-headed Gull, Yellow-legged Gull, Rock Dove, Wood Pigeon, Collared Dove, Little Owl, Kingfisher, Hoopoe, Great Spotted Woodpecker, Skylark, Crested Lark, White Wagtail, Grey Wagtail, Robin, Stonechat, Blackbird, Mistle Thrush, Cetti's Warbler, Fan-tailed Warbler, Sardinian Warbler, Long-tailed Tit, Great Tit, Blue Tit, Nuthatch, Short-toed Treecreeper, Great Grey Shrike, Jay, Jackdaw, Raven, Spotless Starling, House Sparrow, Tree Sparrow, Chaffinch, Serin, Linnet, Goldfinch, Greenfinch, Corn Bunting, Rock Bunting, Cirl Bunting.

Summer / Breeding

Little Bittern, Purple Heron, Black Kite, Short-toed Eagle, Booted Eagle, Egyptian Vulture, Montagu's Harrier, Turtle Dove, Cuckoo, Scops Owl, Swift, Pallid Swift, Bee-eater, Woodlark, Short-toed Lark, Sand Martin, House Martin, Red-rumped Swallow, Swallow, Tree Pipit, Yellow Wagtail, Nightingale, Redstart, Black-eared Wheatear, Reed Warbler, Olivaceous Warbler, Melodious Warbler, Willow Warbler, Spotted Flycatcher, Woodchat Shrike, Golden Oriole, Ortolan.

Winter

Cormorant, Wigeon, Teal, Shoveler, Marsh Harrier, Ringed Plover, Dunlin, Snipe, Redshank, Green Sandpiper, Common Sandpiper, Crag Martin, Black Redstart, Song Thrush, Blackcap, Chiffchaff, Starling, Siskin.

Passage Migrants

Honey Buzzard, Wood Sandpiper, Whinchat, Northern Wheatear, Sedge Warbler, Garden Warbler, Pied Flycatcher.

Golden Oriole *(Oriolus oriolus)*

Castillo de Castellar
(Castellar de la Frontera)

Castillo de Castellar is an early 13th century Moorish castle some 15 kms inland from the Bay of Algeciras. It is within the boundaries of the Parque Natural de los Alcornocales and sits on a hill overlooking the Embalse de Guadarranque (reservoir) and offers 360 degree views of the surrounding areas.

The old town of Castellar de la Frontera, which includes the castle, became almost deserted in the 1970's when the new town (*Nuevo Castellar de la Frontera*) was built some 5 kms away, but has since been re-populated by mostly central and northern Europeans who have moved here to adopt an alternative life-style and to live in the abandoned castle.

The area is quite hilly and rocky but seldom are there peaks that rise above 350 metres. The lower levels are densely vegetated, mostly by cork-oak, pine and eucalyptus. A certain amount of agriculture takes place in the valleys and on the gentler slopes. The differing types of habitat attract a wide variety of bird species and other wildlife. During the migration periods, particularly in the spring, it is an ideal location to watch for passing raptors and storks.

Access

Travelling from the Algeciras direction toward Málaga on the main N-340 highway, turn off where signed for Castellar at km 115 and then follow the A-369.

Travelling from the Málaga direction on the N-340, you can turn off at km 115 but there is a much more interesting route which leads inland from junction km 130, near Sotogrande, and takes you directly to Nuevo Castellar, passing through open countryside and hills that offer good opportunities to stop and search for eagles and other raptors.

If you are coming from further inland, drive to Jimena de la Frontera and then take the A-369 Algeciras road.

Apart from the Castillo, there are a few other interesting sites within the area that I have discovered and found to hold good bird populations. I will describe these as sub-sites to the Castillo and, depending on the direction of your approach, you can decide in which order you wish to view them.

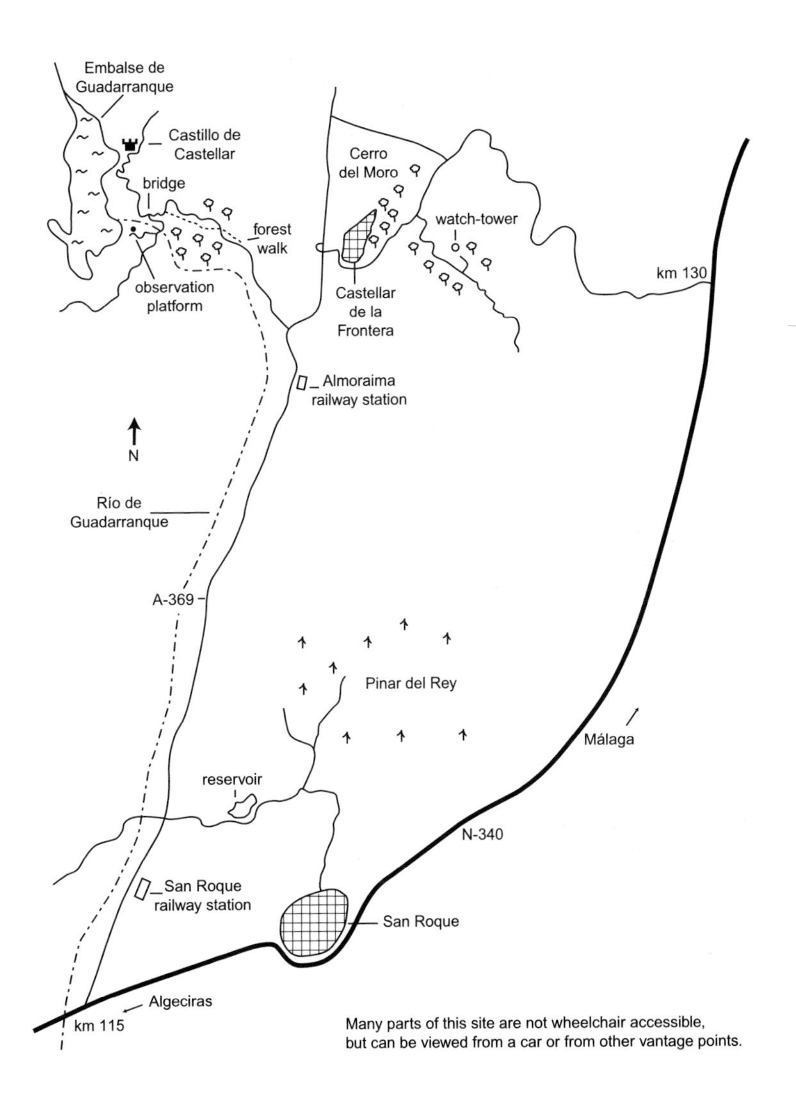

The Castle

The turn-off for Castillo de Castellar is midway between kms 80 and 81 on the A-369. The road passes three of the sub-sites on the way to the castle and I will mention these in the order you reach them. The first of these is what I call the forest walk. Approximately 2.5 kms from the main road, there is a small pull-off area on the right, just as the road turns quite sharply to the left. Directly in front of the pull-off area, there is a track leading downhill that is the old road, now disused and overgrown but still driveable. You can leave your car here and walk along the track (1.5 km) or you can drive part way down and park. The mature trees and undergrowth hold a good variety of woodland birds including resident Crested Tit, Nuthatch, Great Spotted Woodpecker, Green Woodpecker, Short-toed Treecreeper, Firecrest and Hawfinch. In the summer you can also find Golden Oriole, Hoopoe, Nightingale and both Orphean and Melodious Warblers. In the winter, Chiffchaff, Blackcap and Meadow Pipits are always present.

Continuing along the road for a further 2 kms, you reach a bridge over the Río Guadarranque, just before the Venta Jarandilla. Park here and explore the area surrounding the bridge. The birds found here correspond with those previously mentioned, but you are also likely to find White and Grey Wagtails, Wren and Moorhen throughout the year and occasional Green Sandpipers during the passage periods and in the winter.

Drive across the bridge and after 250 metres, take the right-hand fork where the road divides. This is signed with a "no entry" symbol but you can disregard this as this part of the road is public. The no entry sign refers to an area near to the dam some two kms further on. Proceed for about 1.5 kms and you will reach a parking area on the right.

Here there is a stone outcrop with steps leading up to an observation platform over-looking the reservoir and across to the castle. This is an ideal spot to watch the local Griffon Vultures, Bonelli's Eagles and other raptors. It is also an excellent vantage point during the passage periods. In this area you can also find Blue Rock Thrush, Black Redstart and Rock Bunting. During the summer, Black-eared Wheatears are common and Northern Wheatears are often seen in the spring as they pass through the area.

Return to the bridge and proceed up toward the castle 3.5 kms further on. Once passed the km 6 marker, you can find places to pull off the road. The rocky hillsides, stunted trees, gorse, cacti and scrub hold Blue Rock Thrush, Dartford, Sardinian and Fan-tailed Warblers, Cirl Bunting and an assortment of finches and tits. In summer, you may also find Rufous Bush Chat, Subalpine Warbler and Hoopoe.

Once inside the castle you can wander around the narrow streets and find numerous "look-out" points. These offer good close-up views of the resident Crag Martins as they pass by the outside walls. These are joined in the summer by Swallow, Red-rumped Swallow, Pallid

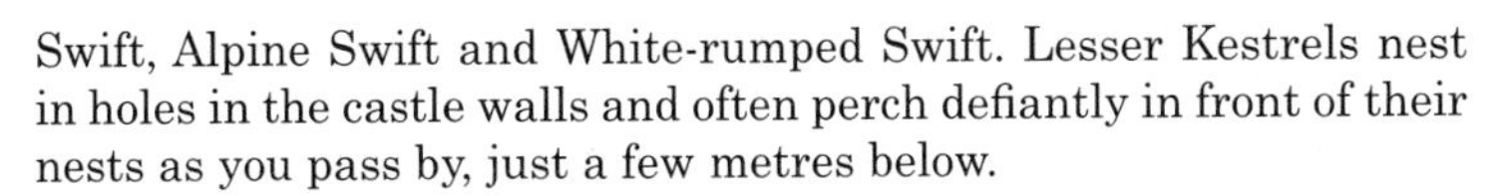

Swift, Alpine Swift and White-rumped Swift. Lesser Kestrels nest in holes in the castle walls and often perch defiantly in front of their nests as you pass by, just a few metres below.

The views of the vultures, eagles and other raptors are much enhanced from the castle as you can often see them passing below you, as well as overhead. During the spring and summer, a visit here could produce Griffon and Egyptian Vultures, Bonelli's, Booted and Short-toed Eagles, Black and Red Kites, Peregrine, Sparrowhawk and both Kestrel and Lesser Kestrels.

There are three other sites I can recommend you visit whilst in the area. The first of these is the municipal park (*Area Recreativa Cerro del Moro*) on the outskirts of Nuevo Castellar. To reach this site, return to the A-369 and turn left. After 1 km, you pass under a bridge and 200 metres further on you turn left where signed for the town. Follow the signs for Málaga and Estepona and pass through to the far end of the town. As you pass the last buildings on the left, there is a grassy area with decorative stones. This is the entrance to Cerro del Moro. Park here and explore the various paths through the park which holds a good selection of woodland birds including Nuthatch, Jay, Great Spotted Woodpecker, Short-toed Treecreeper, tits and finches. In the summer, these are joined by Woodchat Shrike, Golden Oriole and Spotted Flycatcher.

Much of the surrounding area is agricultural and a mirador and various other view points allow you to look out over these cultivations where Montagu's Harriers are often seen in the breeding season as they quarter their hunting territories.

To reach the next site, proceed along the road (CA 534) for just over 1.5 kms and turn right. This road leads uphill for 1.3 kms where the surfaced road turns into a dirt track. Park anywhere around here to explore the various aspects of this site. A road to the left leads upwards toward a watch tower where good views of eagles and raptors can often be had and is well worth the few minutes walk to reach it.

The surrounding trees and undergrowth should also be checked for resident finches, warblers, tits and summer visitors that can include Orphean, Melodious and Olivaceous Warblers. The spring passage often produces a few Rollers and during the autumn passage Pied Flycatchers are regularly present for short periods before continuing their journey. Winter visitors have included Siskin, Blackcap, Song Thrush and Chiffchaff.

Proceeding along the dirt road, you pass over a cattle grid

into open scrubland on the right and farmland on the left. This area normally holds resident Great Grey Shrike, Crested Lark, Corn Bunting, Black Redstart, Stonechat and Dartford, Sardinian and Fan-tailed Warblers. Seasonal species include Woodchat Shrike, Spotted Flycatcher, Spectacled Warbler, Tawny Pipit and Ortolan Bunting. During the passage periods, you may find Whinchat and Northern Wheatear. Nightjars are also present in the summer but these are only seen at dusk unless you happen to disturb a resting bird.

The last site in the area I can recommend is the pine forest at Pinar del Rey. To reach this site you need to travel toward Algeciras on the A-369 and turn off to the left, at a crossroads, between kms 87 and 88. This side road will lead you beside a small reservoir, exactly at the km 2 marker. You can park near to a set of gates and view the water over a wall or through gaps in the vegetation.

Although the area does not hold a lot of species, it is possible to find small numbers of Moorhen, Little Grebe, egrets, waders and wildfowl. Further along the road, at the km 4 marker, turn left into the Pinar del Rey and park at any convenient spot. You can wander through the woods and explore the numerous trails. Although the bird species are similar to those that can be found at the previous sites, I think that the Crested Tits and Short-toed Treecreepers are more easily seen here.

When to Visit

Each of the sites described here are of interest throughout the year but the breeding season produces the maximum number of species. The northward migration period (late february to May) normally produces large falls of raptors in the evenings and any elevated position near to woods and forests can give excellent views as the birds circle the areas looking for roosting sites.

Both the Cerro del Moro and the Pinar del Rey are very popular with local families at the weekends, especially during the warmer months of the year, and they often spend the day at these sites, either picnicking or having barbecues. The resulting noise and disturbance obviously has a detrimental effect on most birds. I would, therefore, suggest you plan a weekday visit to this area.

General Information

Due to the number of sites that are in the area it would require an all day visit to see them all and I suggest that you bring a packed lunch

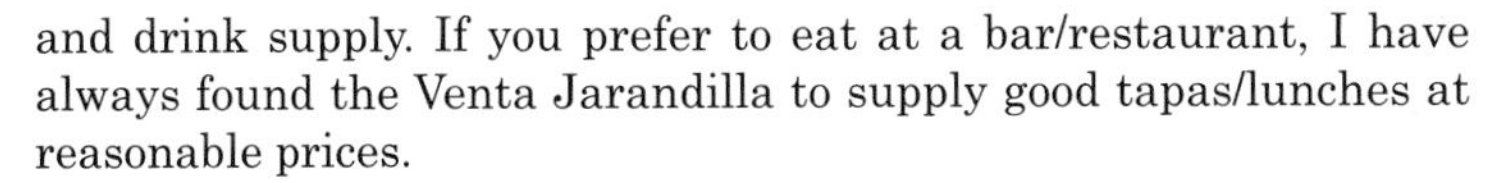

and drink supply. If you prefer to eat at a bar/restaurant, I have always found the Venta Jarandilla to supply good tapas/lunches at reasonable prices.

Although the Embalse de Guadarranque (reservoir) may look an attractive prospect for birds, I have often found my treks down to the water to be disappointing and I would suggest you save the time and effort involved in reaching the water by enjoying the sites that I have described.

Finally, on arriving at the castle you may be asked for a parking fee by a parking tout. Parking is free and it is up to you to decide whether pay or not. If the tout insists, then a firm "No" is usually enough to deter him. However, some people who have refused to pay have returned later to discover minor damage to their cars. Although it may seem like a protection racket, a small outlay of one euro could save you added expenses on repairs later.

Bird Calendar

Resident

Little Grebe, Cattle Egret, Little Egret, Grey Heron, White Stork, Red Kite, Griffon Vulture, Sparrowhawk, Buzzard, Bonelli's Eagle, Peregrine, Lesser Kestrel, Kestrel, Red-legged Partridge, Moorhen, Stone Curlew, Rock Dove, Wood Pigeon, Collared Dove, Little Owl, Tawny Owl, Kingfisher, Green Woodpecker, Great Spotted Woodpecker, Woodlark, Crested Lark, Thekla Lark, Crag Martin, White Wagtail, Grey Wagtail, Robin, Stonechat, Black Redstart, Blue Rock Thrush, Blackbird, Cetti's Warbler, Fan-tailed Warbler, Sardinian Warbler, Dartford Warbler, Firecrest, Long-tailed Tit, Crested Tit, Coal Tit, Great Tit, Blue Tit, Nuthatch, Short-toed Treecreeper, Wren, Great Grey Shrike, Jay, Jackdaw, Raven, Spotless Starling, House Sparrow, Tree Sparrow, Chaffinch, Serin, Linnet, Goldfinch, Greenfinch, Hawfinch, Crossbill, Corn Bunting, Rock Bunting, Cirl Bunting.

Summer / Breeding

Black Kite, Short-toed Eagle, Egyptian Vulture, Montagu's Harrier, Booted Eagle, Black-winged Stilt, Little-ringed Plover, Common Sandpiper, Turtle Dove, Cuckoo, Scops Owl, Nightjar, White-rumped Swift, Alpine Swift, Common Swift, Pallid Swift, Hoopoe, Bee-eater, Short-toed Lark, Sand Martin, House Martin, Red-rumped Swallow, Swallow, Tawny Pipit, Yellow Wagtail, Nightingale, Rufous Bush Chat, Redstart, Black-eared Wheatear, Olivaceous Warbler,

Melodious Warbler, Orphean Warbler, Spectacled Warbler, Bonelli's Warbler, Spotted Flycatcher, Woodchat Shrike, Golden Oriole, Ortolan Bunting, Subalpine Warbler.

Winter

Great Crested Grebe, Mallard, Wigeon, Shoveler, Merlin, Coot, Lapwing, Redshank, Green Sandpiper, Wryneck, Skylark, Meadow Pipit, Song Thrush, Blackcap, Chiffchaff, Starling, Brambling, Siskin.

Lesser Kestrel *(Falco naumanni)*

Passage Migrants

Purple Heron, Black Stork, Hen Harrier, Honey Buzzard, Common Crane, Great Spotted Cuckoo, Roller, Tree Pipit, Whinchat, Northern Wheatear, Ring Ouzel, Garden Warbler, Willow Warbler, Pied Flycatcher.

The Río Palmones

(The village, river, estuary and marshes)

The village of Palmones is situated beside the Río Palmones, on the outskirts of Algeciras, in the province of Cádiz. It is approximately 130 kms from Málaga and can be easily reached from all points along the coast via the main N-340 highway.

The river, with its estuary and surrounding salt marshes and flood plains, is an important feeding area for a very wide range of migrating birds, as well as resident and wintering species.

The close proximity to Gibraltar, only 7 kms away across the Bay of Algeciras, means that it is practically below the main migration routes to and from the African continent. It is therefore ideally placed to attract passing birds throughout the year. The site itself is in two very separate parts, each having its own access point. I will describe each part individually in the order which you should visit them, taking into account the effect that sunlight reflecting from the water can have on your views here.

The Village and Estuary

Access

Travelling west from the Málaga direction, the village can be reached by turning off the N-340 dual-carriageway at the exit at km 112. A massive advertising sign for Carrefour Supermarket, which can be seen well in advance, is directly opposite the turn-off.

Travelling eastward from the Algeciras direction, leave the N-340 at km 111. The road to Palmones is well signposted and you should have no problem finding the village.

Palmones has been built along the east side of the river and offers excellent views of the estuary, sand dunes and part of the salt marsh area on the far bank of the river. Parking is relatively easy and there is an attractive promenade running directly beside the river, almost to the estuary itself. Bench seats are spaced out along the promenade, enabling you to sit and observe the area in a degree of comfort.

The river, which flows into the Bay of Algeciras, is tidal and at low tide mixed flocks of gulls regularly settle on the exposed sand-bars to rest. Although these are mainly Yellow-legged and Black-headed Gulls, a careful scan can produce Audouin's, Slender-billed, Mediterranean, Lesser Black-backed and Little Gulls. A good selection of waders can usually be seen feeding on the mudflats and in the tidal creeks during the passage periods and in the winter. Both sea and marsh terns are frequent visitors and I have recorded Sandwich, Common, Little and Caspian Terns here, along with Whiskered and Black Terns. The resident birds of prey include Buzzard, Kestrel, Marsh Harrier, Sparrowhawk, Peregrine and Osprey and during the migration and summer there are always vultures, eagles and kites present. The herons, Cormorants, White Storks and egrets are unmissable as they often congregate in large flocks on the salt marshes. Spoonbills and Greater Flamingos are often present in small numbers throughout the year, more so in winter, and the local fishermen take pride in pointing these out to any birdwatcher.

General map of the village and river

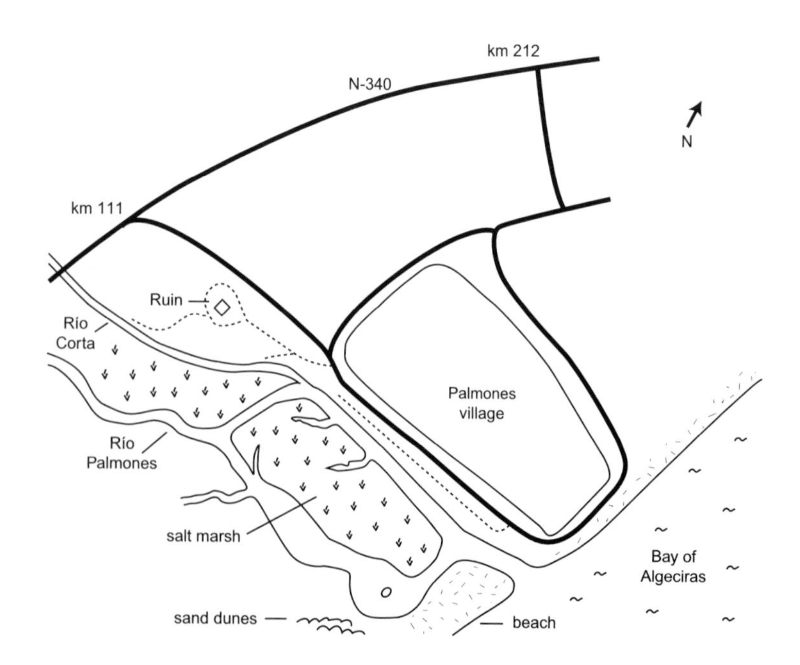

The beach, which is easily accessible, should also be visited, especially in the winter, as Razorbill, Red-breasted Merganser, grebes and sea ducks are often visible on the water.

At the top end of the village, opposite the industrial area, there is an expanse of open grassland well worth exploring. Various trails lead around the area and beside a smaller river (*Río Corta*) where Little Grebes, egrets and ducks are commonly found. The open land holds Sardinian and Fan-tailed Warblers, Corn Buntings, Linnets, Serins and other finches. The ruined and abandoned buildings are nesting sites for Spotless Starlings, sparrows, swallows and martins. Looking westward toward the main road, you can see the nests of the resident White Storks on top of specially erected posts.

Once you have visited the village, river and estuary, proceed to the second part of the site in the area of El Rinconcillo, on the western bank of the Río Palmones. To reach this area, return to the N-340 and follow the signs for Algeciras.

The Río Palmones - The municipal park, river, flood plains and salt marsh

The municipal park at El Rinconcillo gives a much wider view of the areas around the river. There is a bird observation hide with a roof terrace which allows you to view the marshes from an elevated position. Access to the marshes and flood plains can be gained here and there are agricultural areas which are also of interest.

Access

Having rejoined the N-340, heading toward Algeciras, you pass over the Río Palmones at km 109. After 700 metres, there is a set of traffic lights. You need to be in the nearside lane as you have to turn right at the lights and then swing round to the left, around the traffic island, as you have to cross both carriageways of the N-340. Once across the light-controlled junction, choose the middle lane and continue along the road for about 250 metres until you reach a roundabout. Turn right here and proceed down the road for 650 metres. On the right-hand side there is an orange painted pub/cafeteria with the word "Burguer" painted on the wall. Turn left directly opposite this building and follow the road for one kilometre. At this point the surfaced road ends and becomes a dirt road. Continue and follow the track and after you have turned right you will see a set of gates in the hedge. This is the entrance to the park and you should leave your car here and explore the site on foot.

There have been instances recently where people have arrived and found the park gates locked for some reason. If this is the case then an alternative route into the park will need to be taken. You should notice a centre for abandoned animals 50 metres from the park entrance. By following around the walls of this centre, you will come into the bottom corner of the park (see map).

Once inside the park, you will notice a walled water-treatment plant on the right, surrounded by conifers. Fifty metres further on there are three large trees on the right of the path. Leave the path here and, using the trees as cover, look down over the bank to the tidal creek below. Moorhens, Kingfishers, egrets, herons, ducks and waders, including Green Sandpipers, use this area to feed. As you walk through the park you are likely to see both Fan-tailed and Sardinian Warblers, Stonechats, Corn Buntings, Woodchat Shrikes, Crested Larks, Meadow Pipits and a selection of finches.

General map of the municipal park, marshes and flood plains

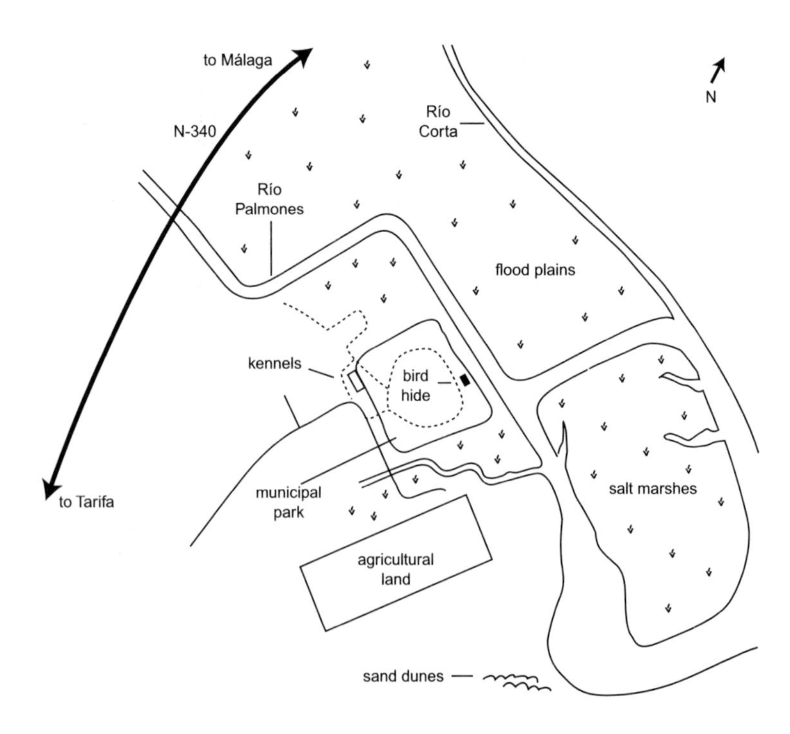

At the far side of the park, there is a bird observatory, the inside of which has been badly vandalized. However, it does offer shelter from wind and rain. Steps lead up to an open-air viewing gallery

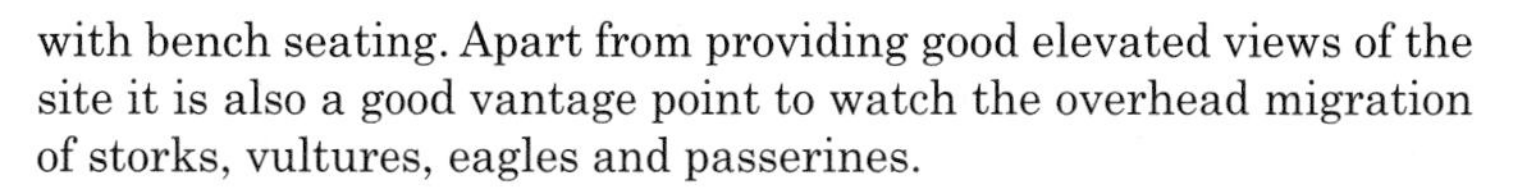

with bench seating. Apart from providing good elevated views of the site it is also a good vantage point to watch the overhead migration of storks, vultures, eagles and passerines.

From the observatory, looking left across the river and marsh toward the main road, you can see the nesting White Storks. Tall poles with platforms have been erected and the storks have now colonized this area. Many are resident but summer visitors increase the numbers. It is always worth scanning the telegraph poles, pylons and overhead cables, as they are favourite perches for Ospreys, Buzzards and Kestrels.

The tidal marsh and flood plains to the left are very productive areas for Spoonbills, Curlews, Whimbrels, herons, egrets, ducks, including Marbled Teal and a variety of waders. At low tide the mudflats to the left and those directly in front of the observatory regularly produce Redshanks, Greenshanks, Common Sandpipers, Black-winged Stilts, plovers and godwits.

The scrub and marshland that make up the central island can, at times, hold hundreds of Grey Herons and the area around the creek, where the river widens, is a reliable spot for Mallards, Shovelers, Teal, Wigeon, Little Grebes, Cormorants, waders and gulls. Further down the river, where it turns toward the estuary, there is a small island. It is in this area that the Greater Flamingos are most often seen. It is also another good spot for Spoonbills and waders, although the distance is such that a telescope is required to make positive identification of the smaller species. This area can be reached via the sand dunes and I will give directions to this area later in this site account.

The whole of the site is regularly overflown by both Marsh and Hen Harriers, Buzzards, Peregrines, Ospreys and Kestrels. Marsh terns, sea terns, Kittiwakes and other gulls often fly past the observatory. Once you have viewed the river and marsh, continue around the park to the bottom corner. Here there are two old portacabins that have been abandoned. To the right of these is an area of dense gorse. A trail leads in amongst the gorse, passing a dumping ground of old lamp posts and pylons. Here you can see Fan-tailed, Sardinian, Dartford and Cetti's Warblers, Black Redstarts and both Great Grey and Woodchat Shrikes.

Returning to the portacabins, pass between them and follow an overgrown track that runs alongside the wall of the kennels. At the end of the track you can look out over another part of the marsh and an expanse of reedbeds. Shrubs and trees provide good cover and you can scan the area without disturbing any birds that may be present.

A smaller track leads down a little bank and then turns right beside the gorse. After about thirty metres, the path reaches a slightly raised track which leads out into the marsh and then toward giant reeds and meadowland before ending near to a few houses. The birds that can be seen here include shrikes, larks, finches, pipits, Reed Buntings, Penduline Tits, Stone Curlews and waders, including Common, Green, Wood and Marsh Sandpipers.

To avoid walking through the built up area, retrace your steps back to the park. On leaving the park walk along the dirt road past the water treatment plant. There is a bridge over a creek, which is a good spot to see Moorhen, Common and Green Sandpipers, Grey Wagtails and egrets. Beyond the bridge, as the road turns left, there is a gateway to agricultural land. Just beside the gate there is usually a pile of rotting vegetation which attracts many insect eating birds. Behind this, against the fence, there is a small wet area which I have found, over the years, to be a very reliable place to see Cetti's Warblers and wintering Bluethroats. However, my best views of the Bluethroats have been when I have parked my car here and waited patiently. The remainder of the marsh here holds the usual array of warblers, wagtails and finches.

The final part of this site you may wish to visit is the lower part of the river beside the sand dunes. To reach this location, drive to the surfaced road and after 300 metres take the first turning left. Follow the road to the next junction and again turn left. Continue to the end of this road, where the surface turns to sand and turn right. This will bring you to the beach and a parking area beside a beach bar. From here you have the choice of taking straight to the dunes or walking along the beach for about 200 metres before crossing diagonally across the dunes. The tracks through the dunes can be quite hard going and I personally prefer the beach walk as this gives you the opportunity to look for sea birds such as gulls, terns, scoters, mergansers, grebes and Razorbills. The near side of the river is reasonably well-vegetated with shrubs and bushes and by using these as cover it is possible to get almost to the water's edge without causing disturbance to the birds.

The species that are commonly found here include Ringed, Little-ringed, Kentish, Golden and Grey Plovers, Sanderling, Turnstone, Oystercatcher, Dunlin, Little Stint, Knot, Curlew Sandpiper and both Black and Bartailed Godwits. The gull and tern species are similar to those already mentioned. The other noticeable birds are Spoonbill and Greater Flamingo. Avocets and Shelduck are sometimes present but are much scarcer and are usually only seen on passage or in the winter.

When to Visit

The site is of interest at all times, with many resident species. Wader and waterfowl numbers are highest in the winter and both Spoonbill and Greater Flamingo are more commonly seen at this time. Scarcer wintering species include Penduline Tit, Bluethroat and Marsh Sandpiper. Some waders, such as Redshank, Common Sandpiper and Ringed, Little-ringed and Kentish Plovers can be found throughout the year. During the northward passage period, between February and May, storks, vultures, eagles, kites and other raptors are highly visible overhead. The summer/breeding season attracts many passerines along with increased numbers of White Storks.

Weekday visits are preferable to weekends as both the village and the municipal park are much quieter then. Morning visits to the village and afternoon visits to the park are recommended.

General Information

Although the first part of this site is easily accessible to wheelchair users, the second part would be very hard going and should not be visited without the help of an enabler. Even then, some parts of the site will be inaccessible.

Bird Calendar

Resident

Little Grebe, Cattle Egret, Little Egret, Grey Heron, Spoonbill, White Stork, Greater Flamingo, Mallard, Osprey, Griffon Vulture, Marsh Harrier, Sparrowhawk, Buzzard, Peregrine, Kestrel, Moorhen, Stone Curlew, Ringed Plover, Little-ringed Plover, Kentish Plover, Redshank, Common Sandpiper, Audouin's Gull, Black-headed Gull, Yellow-legged Gull, Common Tern, Sandwich Tern, Whiskered Tern, Rock Dove, Wood Pigeon, Collared Dove, Little Owl, Kingfisher, Skylark, Crested Lark, White Wagtail, Grey Wagtail, Robin, Stonechat, Blackbird, Cetti's Warbler, Fan-tailed Warbler, Sardinian Warbler, Dartford Warbler, Long-tailed Tit, Great Tit, Blue Tit, Great Grey Shrike, Jay, Jackdaw, Spotless Starling, House Sparrow, Chaffinch, Serin, Linnet, Goldfinch, Greenfinch, Corn Bunting, Reed Bunting.

Summer / Breeding

Purple Heron, Black Kite, Short-toed Eagle, Booted Eagle, Eleonora's Falcon, Lesser Kestrel, Black-winged Stilt, Little Tern, Black Tern,

Turtle Dove, Cuckoo, Nightjar, Swift, Pallid Swift, Hoopoe, Bee-eater, Sand Martin, House Martin, Red-rumped Swallow, Swallow, Tawny Pipit, Yellow Wagtail, Nightingale, Black-eared Wheatear, Reed Warbler, Melodious Warbler, Spotted Flycatcher, Woodchat Shrike.

Winter

Great Crested Grebe, Black-necked Grebe, Cormorant, Greylag, Shelduck, Gadwall, Wigeon, Teal, Shoveler, Marbled Teal, Red-crested Pochard, Common Scoter, Red-breasted Merganser, Hen Harrier, Merlin, Coot, Oystercatcher, Avocet, Grey Plover, Golden Plover, Lapwing, Dunlin, Curlew Sandpiper, Knot, Sanderling, Little Stint, Ruff, Snipe, Black-tailed Godwit, Bar-tailed Godwit, Curlew, Whimbrel, Marsh Sandpiper, Greenshank, Wood Sandpiper, Green Sandpiper, Turnstone, Slender-billed Gull, Little Gull, Mediterranean Gull, Lesser Blackback, Kittiwake, Razorbill, Crag Martin, Water Pipit, Bluethroat, Black Redstart, Song Thrush, Blackcap, Chiffchaff, Willow Warbler, Penduline Tit, Starling.

Passage Migrants

Little Bittern, Squacco Heron, Red Kite, Egyptian Vulture, Montagu's Harrier, Honey Buzzard, Bonelli's Eagle, Collared Pratincole, Caspian Tern, Alpine Swift, Roller, Tree Pipit, Whinchat, Northern Wheatear, Pied Flycatcher.

***White Stork** (Ciconia ciconia)*

Rarity

A Common Rosefinch, (*Carpodacus erythrinus*) which is a Spanish rarity, was recorded at Palmones in November 1986. This record was accepted by the IRC.

Punta Carnero and Punta Secreta

These two points form part of the rocky headland on the south-eastern end of the Bay of Algeciras in the province of Cádiz and offer excellent views of the Strait of Gibraltar and the Moroccan coastline which is only about 20 kilometres away.

At Punta Carnero you can look directly down to the stony beach below where numerous lines of rocks reach out like fingers into the sea. At Punta Secreta there is a curved rock formation that sweeps around the sandy beach and is easily accessible from the development of houses and villas that have been built in the valley and along the sea-shore. The surrounding hillsides are vegetated with gorse, cistus, broom, oleander and scattered pine trees and hold a good selection of warblers, finches, larks and chats. Roadside parking is limited but the lighthouse at Punta Carnero offers easy off-road parking and good views out to sea.

The main interest at these two sites, only 1.5 kms apart, are seabirds, waders and scrub dwellers and during the migration periods, especially the northward passage, it is one of the best sites to watch the movement of storks, vultures, eagles, kites and other raptors. It can also produce good views of migrating Rollers, Bee-eaters, Golden Orioles, warblers, finches, wagtails, flycatchers and larks.

Access

The sites can be easily reached from the main N-340 highway, just south of the town of Algeciras. Travelling from the Málaga direction, you reach the end of the dual-carriageway once you have passed Algeciras. Approximately 150 metres further on there is a set of traffic lights where you turn left towards the village of Getares. Do not turn directly left from the main road as that is illegal. Instead, filter right around the traffic lights and then cross both lanes of the road when signalled to do so. The Guardia Civil are often in this area and fines for illegal turning can be very high. Travelling from the Tarifa direction, things are much simpler as you turn right at the lights immediately after passing the km 102 marker.

Follow this road for about 1 kilometre and then take the first exit from the roundabout. After a further kilometre, the road runs briefly beside the Río Picaro before it swings away to its estuary on the Playa de Getares. You can park here and check the river, reeds and marshes. During the winter, herons, egrets, ducks and waders are usually evident and in the spring and summer you may find Little Bitterns and Black-winged Stilts.

Both Squacco and Purple Herons pass through the area on passage and can sometimes be found at this location. The surrounding open countryside should be scanned for warblers, finches, larks, shrikes, raptors and both Corn and Cirl Buntings.

A kilometre or so further along, the road runs directly beside the sea for a few hundred metres and gulls regularly gather on the shore. Any gull flocks should be carefully checked as quite often you can find Audouin's and Mediterranean Gulls amongst the ubiquitous Yellow-legged.

The road now leads uphill toward Punta Carnero and there are a few parking spaces on the way up. At the brow of the hill there is room for 3 or 4 cars to park off-road. This spot looks out directly above lines of rocks where waders can normally be found. These can include Redshank, Greenshank, Dunlin, Sanderling, Turnstone, Whimbrel, Common Sandpiper and plovers. Purple Sandpipers are very scarce winter visitors to the region but single birds are regularly recorded and in January 2000 an unprecedented sighting of a group of six birds was recorded at the nearby beach at Punta Secreta.

Just offshore there is a small group of rocks which are officially classified as an island (*Isla Cabrita*) where gulls, terns, Cormorants and waders often congregate to feed and rest. During the northward migration period (February-May), this is probably as good a place as any to watch for incoming vultures, eagles, kites and other raptors. On clear days they can be seen coming from many kilometres away and sometimes they arrive at the Spanish coast flapping so low over the water that they have to climb sharply to clear the cliffs. At times like this they sometimes pass just a few metres overhead and wonderful views are possible.

The most spectacular sight of the year is when the annual movement of Honey Buzzards takes place. This usually occurs from late April into May, when many thousands of the birds cross from Africa. They usually arrive in waves, sometimes several hundred strong, milling around until they find a thermal that will help them regain lost height before continuing their northward journeys.

In the scrubby hillsides you can find resident Sardinian and Fan-tailed Warblers, finches, larks, and chats and in the breeding season there are Nightingales, Black-eared Wheatears, Spotted Flycatchers, Woodchat Shrikes, Melodious and Spectacled Warblers, Lesser Kestrels, Bee-eaters and a host of swallows, swifts and martins.

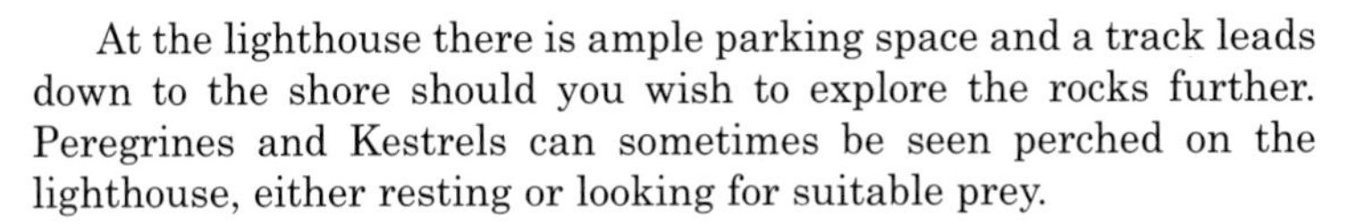

At the lighthouse there is ample parking space and a track leads down to the shore should you wish to explore the rocks further. Peregrines and Kestrels can sometimes be seen perched on the lighthouse, either resting or looking for suitable prey.

Less than a kilometre along the road you reach Punta Secreta and you can park and look down on the area from above before driving down to the beach. To the right of the point there are more offshore rocks that are known as Isla de las Palomas although they are so far off that even with a telescope you will have difficulty making any positive identification of the smaller birds that are often seen on the island.

Once you have arrived at the built-up area, there are numerous paths that will lead you to the beach and the rocks. Once again waders, gulls and terns are the most obvious birds although Crested Larks, Linnets and Serins are often seen on the landward edge of the beach.

Offshore, in the strait, there is constant seabird movement between the Atlantic Ocean and the Mediterranean Sea. Shearwaters, petrels, skuas, terns, grebes, Razorbills, Red-breasted Mergansers and sea ducks can be seen at the appropriate times of the year.

When to Visit

These sites are of interest at all times but without doubt the main attraction here are the winter waders, the passing seabirds and the migrating storks, eagles, kites and other raptors although a good selection of other species can always be found.

In the warmer months of the year the beach at Punta Secreta is extremely popular and birdwatching at this time is virtually impossible here.

General Information

Due to its exposed coastal location, the area can suffer from the strong easterly or westerly winds that are associated with the Strait of Gibraltar and it is always prudent to take some form of suitable protective clothing with you.

Alongside the road leading to and from the site, there are a number of ruined and abandoned buildings that are worth checking for Kestrels, Little Owls, Hoopoes, Black Redstarts, Black-eared Wheatears and shrikes.

Although the area is not particularly wheelchair friendly, many of the bird species mentioned can be viewed from the car-park in front of the lighthouse and from various other vantage points along the route.

Although not essential, a telescope is always a great advantage here, especially to help identify the waders on the rocks and offshore islands.

General map of Punta Carnero and Punta Secreta

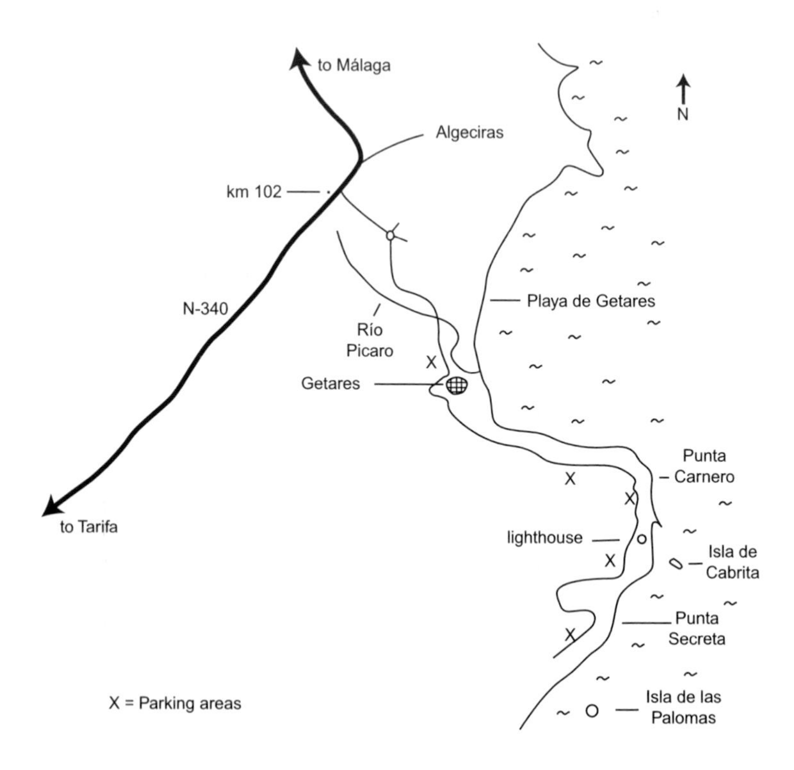

Bird Calendar

Resident

Cory's Shearwater, Mediterranean Shearwater, Gannet, Cattle Egret, Little Egret, White Stork, Greater Flamingo, Mallard, Griffon Vulture, Marsh Harrier, Sparrowhawk, Buzzard, Peregrine, Kestrel, Red-legged Partridge, Moorhen, Kentish Plover, Redshank,

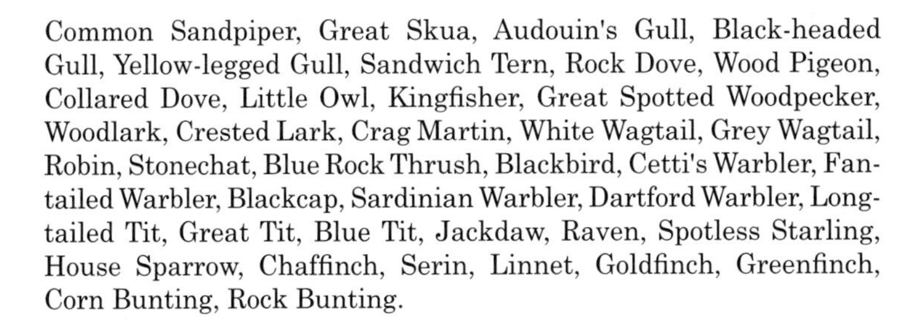

Common Sandpiper, Great Skua, Audouin's Gull, Black-headed Gull, Yellow-legged Gull, Sandwich Tern, Rock Dove, Wood Pigeon, Collared Dove, Little Owl, Kingfisher, Great Spotted Woodpecker, Woodlark, Crested Lark, Crag Martin, White Wagtail, Grey Wagtail, Robin, Stonechat, Blue Rock Thrush, Blackbird, Cetti's Warbler, Fan-tailed Warbler, Blackcap, Sardinian Warbler, Dartford Warbler, Long-tailed Tit, Great Tit, Blue Tit, Jackdaw, Raven, Spotless Starling, House Sparrow, Chaffinch, Serin, Linnet, Goldfinch, Greenfinch, Corn Bunting, Rock Bunting.

Summer / Breeding

Storm Petrel, Little Bittern, Squacco Heron, Purple Heron, Black Kite, Short-toed Eagle, Egyptian Vulture, Booted Eagle, Lesser Kestrel, Black-winged Stilt, Little-ringed Plover, Common Tern, Little Tern, Turtle Dove, Cuckoo, Scops Owl, Nightjar, Common Swift, Pallid Swift, Hoopoe, Bee-eater, Sand Martin, House Martin, Red-rumped Swallow, Barn Swallow, Tawny Pipit, Yellow Wagtail, Nightingale, Black-eared Wheatear, Reed Warbler, Melodious Warbler, Orphean Warbler, Spectacled Warbler, Spotted Flycatcher, Woodchat Shrike, Ortolan Bunting.

Winter

Little Grebe, Great Crested Grebe, Black-necked Grebe, Cormorant, Grey Heron, Gadwall, Wigeon, Common Scoter, Osprey, Coot, Oystercatcher, Avocet, Ringed Plover, Grey Plover, Golden Plover, Dunlin, Sanderling, Little Stint, Purple Sandpiper, Snipe, Black-tailed Godwit, Whimbrel, Greenshank, Green Sandpiper, Turnstone, Arctic Skua, Little Gull, Mediterranean Gull, Lesser Black-backed Gull, Kittiwake, Razorbill, Meadow Pipit, Black Redstart, Song Thrush, Iberian Chiffchaff, Great Grey Shrike, Siskin, Cirl Bunting.

Passage Migrants

Black Stork, Red Kite, Hen Harrier, Montagu's Harrier, Honey Buzzard, Eleonora's Falcon, Merlin, Collared Pratincole, Curlew Sandpiper, Curlew, Wood Sandpiper, Caspian Tern, Lesser Crested Tern, Gull-billed Tern, Great Spotted Cuckoo, Alpine Swift, Roller, Wryneck, Tree Pipit, Rufous Bush Chat, Whinchat, Redstart, Northern Wheatear, Olivaceous Warbler, Garden Warbler, Bonelli's Warbler, Willow Warbler, Pied Flycatcher, Golden Oriole.

Honey Buzzard *(Pernis apivorus)*

Tarifa

The town of Tarifa is situated on the Atlantic shore (*Costa de la Luz*) at the western end of the Strait of Gibraltar in the province of Cádiz and can be easily reached via the main N-340 highway. The close proximity to the African continent, only 16 kilometres away, makes this an area of great importance during the migration periods when spectacular movements of storks, vultures, eagles, kites and other raptors, along with seabirds, cross and pass through the strait. An estimated half a billion birds will pass through the area during these times.

To facilitate the watching and recording of bird movement, a network of observatories has been built in strategic positions, some coastal and some further inland in the sierras.

To the north-east of the town are the Montes de Tarifa, a series of hills that include Sierra del Bujeo, Sierra del Cabrito, Sierra del Algarrobo and Sierra de Ojén. To the north-west of Tarifa there is the Playa de los Lances, a wide sandy beach that stretches for about 5 kms. A few kilometres further along the coast, near to Punta Paloma, the Río del Valle flows to the sea at the Playa de Valdevaqueros and forms a lagoon and marsh area beside giant sand dunes.

Still further on, there is the coastal town of Bolonia, famous for the Roman ruins (*Ruinas Romanos de Baelo Claudia, 1st century B.C.*). Here the Arroyo de Alpariate forms a lagoon at the back of the beach which attracts waders and gulls. This area is overlooked by the Sierra de la Plata, where the scarce White-rumped Swifts regularly breed in the summer, and the Loma de San Bartolomé, the home of a colony of Griffon Vultures. A few kilometres north of Tarifa there are other impressive sierras and the Embalse de Almodóvar situated within the boundaries of the Parque Natural de los Alcornocales.

All of these sites are within a 15 kms radius of Tarifa and most will be described in this chapter.

Playa de los Lances

This beach to the north-west of Tarifa is about 5 kms in length and in places is almost 400 metres wide. The beach has an unusual effect in that the landward part is about 2 metres lower than at the shoreline. Two sizeable rivers, The Río Jara and the Río de la

Vega, along with a smaller stream, the Arroyo del Salado, flow onto the beach and merge to create a lagoon between the shoreline and the sand dunes. On occasions, at high tide, the sea breaks over the shoreline and the water flows down to the back of the beach and combines with the river water. When this occurs, vast wet areas are created on the beach.

The area attracts large flocks of mixed gulls in the winter and also large concentrations of waders. Regular visitors here include Black-headed, Audouin's and Mediterranean Gulls, Greater Flamingos, Spoonbills, herons, egrets and terns. Even during the summer, you can normally find small numbers of Dunlin, Sanderling, Redshank, Ringed Plover and Grey Plover. Kentish Plovers breed on the beach and in the dunes and Little-ringed Plovers also breed nearby in dried stony riverbeds.

The expanse of dunes, pastures and fallow land between the beach and the N-340 is designated as a Paraje Natural and various sectors of this have been fenced off to create ornithological reserves. A causeway from the Río Jara campsite gives access to the Paraje Natural.

Beyond the Río Jara there is a forested area of stone pine and scrubland which harbours finches, larks, pipits, shrikes, warblers, doves and chats, amongst other species.

Access

There are two very convenient parking areas that give easy access to the site. The first of these can be reached by turning off the main N-340 where it is signed for Tarifa at km 83.4. After approximately 300 metres, take the first turning right and follow the road to a parking area just above the beach, beside the local football ground. This gives direct access to the beach and the Paraje Natural, although I have always found this part of the site to be less interesting than the far end. I will, therefore, describe the site from my preferred point of access which can be reached by turning off the N-340 at km 80.5, some 300 metres beyond the bridge over the Río Jara. Here there is a small road that leads through the stone pines and ends at a large parking area beside the beach.

Coming from the Tarifa direction, you cannot turn directly left here. Instead you filter right and then cross both lanes of the road to enter the forest. Turning directly left can result in a hefty fine if you are caught. You may, depending on the time of year, be charged a small parking fee at this site.

General map of the Playa de los Lances area

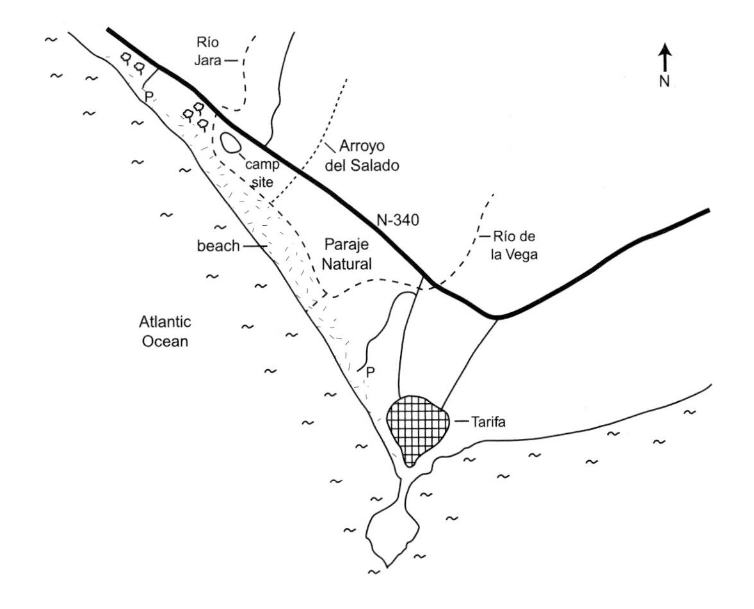

Various trails lead through the pine forest which are always worth exploring. The pines hold Short-toed Treecreepers, Jays, Nightingales, finches, tits, warblers and flycatchers. The scrub areas between the pines and the beach can produce larks, pipits, wagtails, redstarts and chats.

A track leads through the low dunes towards the Río Jara. At the river you will normally find a fair selection of waders, herons and egrets. Both Kingfisher and Osprey can sometimes be found fishing along the river where Moorhen, ducks and warblers are also evident. From this point onwards you either have to walk along the beach or cross the causeway at the campsite to enter the Paraje Natural.

The latter route offers the greater chance of seeing passerines but you can only walk as far as the Arroyo del Salado before having to retrace your steps back to the beach. The river follows the contours of the sand dunes, sometimes creating small islands. It is here that you are likely to find resting and feeding waders which, in the winter, regularly include Whimbrel, Curlew, Snipe, Turnstone, Oystercatcher, Common Sandpiper, Ruff, Golden Plover, Lapwing and both Black and Bar-tailed Godwits along with those previously mentioned.

During the passage periods and in the summer you may see Purple Heron, Avocet, Black Stork, Collared Pratincole and Black-winged Stilt along with great numbers of passerines. Wintering seabirds that can often be seen off-shore include Gannet, Razorbill, Common Scoter, Red-breasted Merganser, Great and Arctic Skuas, gulls, terns, shearwaters and occasional Black-necked Grebes.

Although there is bird movement across and through the strait throughout the year, the quietest months are November-January, when only White Storks, Gannets, shearwaters and skuas may be on the move.

The beach also offers the opportunity to observe the main migration of storks and raptors but there are numerous other sites nearby that are better suited for this and they will be described separately.

Santuario de Nuestra Señora de la Luz
(Sanctuary of Our Lady of the Light)

The sanctuary is set in a large walled garden about four and a half kilometres from the Playa de los Lances. The garden contains a mixture of broadleaved, pine, eucalyptus, palm and olive trees which attract a wide variety of bird species. Various viewpoints look out over both sides of the valley in which the sanctuary is set. Most of the characteristic resident passerines can be found here along with summer visitors such as Nightingale, Rufous Bush-chat, Redstart, Black-eared Wheatear and both Melodious and Olivaceous Warblers. Griffon Vultures from the nearby sierras are often seen overhead and during both the migration periods you are likely to see many species of raptors.

Access

From the main N-340, turn off at km 81.3, just 100 metres from the entrance to the campsite. The road passes through a pair of curved white pillars which should be your landmark. After 1 kilometre, the road (CA-P2214) forks left and runs beside a dense hedge of prickly pear and other cacti and then passes over a small stream (Arroyo de Ramos). Park here and check the surrounding open pastures for finch flocks, larks and pipits. Waders, notably Little-ringed Plovers, may be seen in the riverbed and Hoopoes and Rufous Bush Chats can be found near the cacti. The road now passes the Sierra de Enmedio on the left where vultures, eagles and other raptors are usually visible. Blue Rock Thrushes and Crag Martins are resident here and there is always the chance of seeing both White-rumped and Little Swifts in the area, although the latter is extremely rare.

Two kilometres further on, the road enters the Parque Natural de los Alcornocales before arriving at a small village and the sanctuary. You can drive up to the sanctuary and park inside the gardens, which are open to the public.

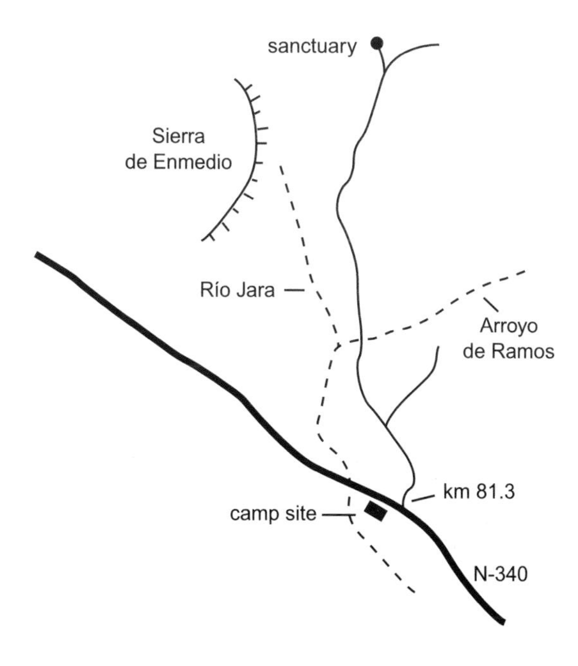

When to Visit

The whole of this area is of interest throughout the year, depending on your preference of birds. The winter is the prime time to see waders, waterfowl and seabirds, whilst the summer can produce most of the characteristic breeding species. For those whose interest is in the raptors, a visit in March or April will be most rewarding.

General Information

Tarifa is known as the "windsurf" capital of Europe due to the very high winds caused by the vortex effect created by the two land masses on either side of the Strait of Gibraltar. It is therefore a good idea to come well-prepared with good protective clothing so that your day will not be ruined by uncomfortable winds that can easily reach 50-60 kph.

As there is so much to see in the area, you may wish to spend more than one day here. There are plenty of suitable hotels/hostales in Tarifa. My personal preference is to stay at the Río Jara Campsite as it gives good views of the river and direct access to the beach.

For those who prefer a little more comfort, I can recommend the rural tourism centre of Huerta Grande on the outskirts of Pelayo at km 96.2, where there are country houses offering rooms and log cabins that can be rented for longer periods. The birdwatching here is very good as the centre is set in the Alcornocales Natural Park, surrounded by cork-oaks with magnificent views down to the coast. It is also only a few minutes drive away from Tarifa and most of the other sites included in this chapter. You can telephone the centre (0034) 956 679 700 or you can log on to their web site at http://www.cherrytel.com/hugra The information centre at Huerta Grande has a wide range of useful guides and leaflets, some in English.

Bird Calendar

Resident

Little Grebe, Cory's Shearwater, Mediterranean. Shearwater, Gannet, Grey Heron, Cattle Egret, Little Egret, White Stork, Greater Flamingo, Mallard, Griffon Vulture, Marsh Harrier, Sparrowhawk, Buzzard, Kestrel, Moorhen, Stone Curlew, Ringed Plover, Kentish Plover, Grey Plover, Dunlin, Redshank, Sanderling, Common Sandpiper, Great Skua, Arctic Skua, Audouin's Gull, Black-headed Gull, Yellow-legged Gull, Sandwich Tern, Rock Dove, Wood Pigeon, Collared Dove, Little Owl, Kingfisher, Hoopoe, Great Spotted Woodpecker, Woodlark, Skylark, Crested Lark, White Wagtail, Grey Wagtail, Robin, Stonechat, Blackbird, Cetti's Warbler, Fan-tailed Warbler, Blackcap, Sardinian Warbler, Iberian Chiffchaff, Firecrest, Great Tit, Blue Tit, Short-toed Treecreeper, Great Grey Shrike, Jay, Jackdaw, Raven, Spotless Starling, House Sparrow, Chaffinch, Serin, Linnet, Goldfinch, Greenfinch, Corn Bunting, Cirl Bunting.

Summer / Breeding

Little Bittern, Purple Heron, Black Kite, Short-toed Eagle, Egyptian Vulture, Lesser Kestrel, Black-winged Stilt, Collared Pratincole, Little-ringed Plover, Little Tern, Turtle Dove, Cuckoo, Common Swift, Pallid Swift, Bee-eater, Short-toed Lark, Sand Martin, House

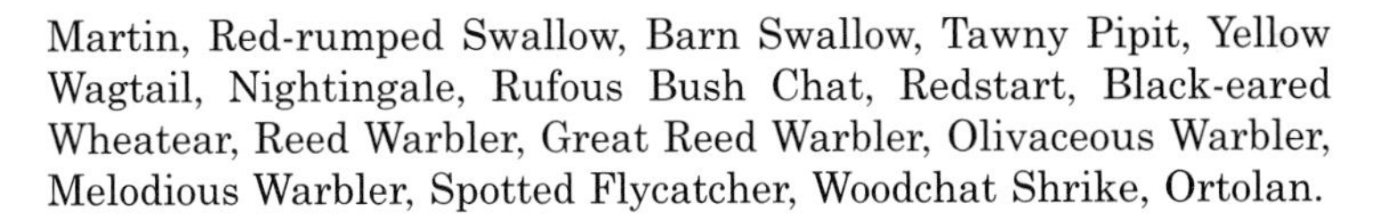

Martin, Red-rumped Swallow, Barn Swallow, Tawny Pipit, Yellow Wagtail, Nightingale, Rufous Bush Chat, Redstart, Black-eared Wheatear, Reed Warbler, Great Reed Warbler, Olivaceous Warbler, Melodious Warbler, Spotted Flycatcher, Woodchat Shrike, Ortolan.

Winter

Great Crested Grebe, Black-necked Grebe, Cormorant, Spoonbill, Greylag Goose, Shelduck, Gadwall, Wigeon, Teal, Shoveler, Red-crested Pochard, Common Scoter, Red-breasted Merganser, Osprey, Oystercatcher, Avocet, Lapwing, Golden Plover, Knot, Little Stint, Ruff, Snipe, Black-tailed Godwit, Bar-tailed Godwit, Curlew, Whimbrel, Spotted Redshank, Greenshank, Green Sandpiper, Turnstone, Grey Phalarope, Mediterranean Gull, Little Gull, Lesser Black-backed Gull, Kittiwake, Caspian Tern, Common Tern, Razorbill, Calandra Lark, Crag Martin, Meadow Pipit, Bluethroat, Black Redstart, Song Thrush, Penduline Tit, Starling, Reed Bunting.

Passage Migrants

Squacco Heron, Black Stork, Red Kite, Hen Harrier, Montagu's Harrier, Honey Buzzard, Hobby, Quail, Common Crane, Curlew Sandpiper, Marsh Sandpiper, Wood Sandpiper, Spotted Redshank, Pomarine Skua, Lesser Crested Tern, Gull-billed Tern, Black Tern, Whiskered Tern, Great Spotted Cuckoo, Alpine Swift, Roller, Wryneck, Tree Pipit, Whinchat, Northern Wheatear, Sedge Warbler, Spectacled Warbler, Willow Warbler, Pied Flycatcher, Golden Oriole.

Rarities

White Pelican. One recorded near Tarifa in August 1996 and three others recorded during the autumn migration in 1999.

Lammergeier. One recorded in the strait in August/September 1998 and another at Punto Cabrito on the 14th September 1999.

Rüppell's Vulture. One recorded close to Tarifa during the autumn migration in 1999.

Long-Legged Buzzard. One recorded in the area in 1986 and three birds recorded in the Montes de Tarifa during the autumn migration in 1999.

Spotted Eagle. One recorded in the Montes de Tarifa in autumn 1999.

Lesser Spotted Eagle. Two recorded in the Montes de Tarifa in autumn 1999.

Red-footed Falcon. One recorded in the Montes de Tarifa in spring 1999.

Lanner. Three recorded in the Montes de Tarifa in autumn 1999.

Dotterel. There are several records from the Playa de los Lances.

Short-billed Dowitcher. One record from the beach in August 1988.

Buff-breasted Sandpiper. One recorded on the beach in October 1998.

Terek Sandpiper. One recorded on the beach in May 1995.

Royal Tern. One recorded on the beach September 1996.

Little Swift. At least six sightings have been made in the area between 1985 and 1999.

Purple Heron *(Ardea pupurea)*

Embalse de Almodóvar

This is a rather large reservoir fed by numerous small rivers and streams to the north of Tarifa. Unfortunately, it is rather sterile in that it has very little in the way of reeds or other vegetation at the water's edge. However, during the winter and spring it attracts various herons, egrets, waterfowl and waders and the surrounding open countryside holds a good variety of passerine species. The nearby sierras can produce Blue Rock Thrush, Black Redstart and Black Wheatear throughout the year and the summer visitors regularly include Nightingale, Black-eared Wheatear and Ortolan Bunting. Vultures, eagles and other raptors are often seen hunting over the area or passing along the sierras.

A causeway passes alongside the northern edge of the water where you can park without causing obstruction to other traffic.

Access

To visit this site, turn left on leaving the sanctuary and follow the road (CA-P2213) for 11.5 kms until you reach the old Facinas to Los Barrios road. Turn right here and continue for 4.5 kms to reach the reservoir.

Whilst travelling on the CA-P2213 you pass through a particularly rocky area with scattered trees and scrub between kms 8 and 9. I have found this to be a very productive spot for Little Owl, Hoopoe, Woodlark, Crested Lark, Tree Pipit, Tawny Pipit, Rufous Bush Chat, Black Redstart, Black-eared Wheatear, Great Grey Shrike, Woodchat Shrike, Rock Bunting, Linnet and warblers, which can include both Spectacled and Subalpine.

Further along the road there are areas of cork-oak and olive groves where it is possible to find Cirl and Corn Buntings and Rock Sparrows.

After turning right towards Los Barrios, you reach a few scattered houses on the right and a recreation/picnic area on the left, which is planted with mainly cork-oak. A few minutes walking through the park can produce Great Spotted Woodpecker, Short-toed Treecreeper, Jay, Serin and other finches and tits. However, during local/national holidays and at weekends during the summer, the park is likely to be full of marauding humans and serious birdwatching is impossible.

The next 4 kilometres between the park and the reservoir is probably the worst stretch of tarmac road I have ever driven along and particular care needs to be taken here to avoid large ruts, holes and bumps.

General map of the route to the Embalse de Almodóvar

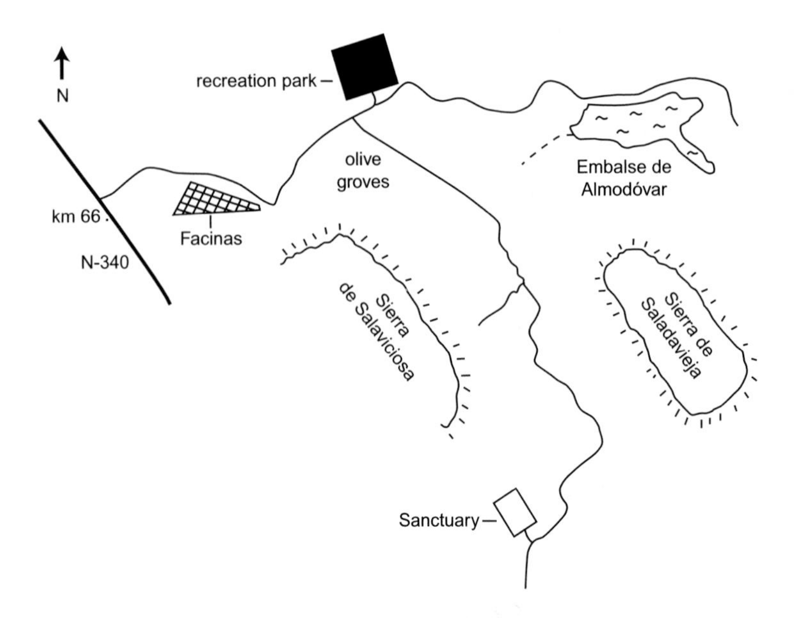

At the reservoir you can park anywhere along the causeway or off-road once you have passed over it. The waders that are commonly seen here include Redshank, Common Sandpiper, Green Sandpiper, Black-winged Stilt and occasional Dunlin.

Both Cattle and Little Egrets can be found at any time and Grey Herons are common in winter. Waterfowl are also attracted to the water and Mallards, Wigeon and Shovelers have been seen here along with Moorhens and Little Grebes.

Most of the passerine species mentioned earlier can also be seen around the reservoir and birds of prey are often evident, the most common being Kestrel, Booted Eagle and Short-toed Eagle. Ospreys can also be seen occasionally during the winter and spring.

General Information

Although this is a particularly rocky area and the drive may be somewhat bumpy, much of this site can be viewed from a car and both the recreation park and the causeway at the reservoir are wheelchair accessible. I would, therefore, class this site as suitable

for people with mobility problems.

Bird Calendar

Most of the birds that can be seen at this site are the same as those in my list of birds for the Playa de los Lances, with the exception of the seabirds, of course.

Short-toed Eagle *(Circaetus gallicus)*

Río de Valle - Punta Paloma

The Río de Valle flows to the sea at the north-western end of the Playa de Valdevaqueros, some 10 kms from Tarifa. The river winds through open grassy areas and there are small reedbeds and marshes just before the beach. When the river ceases to flow a lagoon forms at the back of the beach and this can attract waders and gulls, similar to those seen at Tarifa beach, in the winter and passage periods.

Giant sand dunes form the western end of the beach and a small road leads uphill beyond the dunes to the Punta Paloma where there are forests of stone pine and good views out to sea. The elevated position here is a useful vantage point for watching passing seabirds and also incoming raptors. Part of this land is the property of the military and is, therefore, out of bounds to the public. These dunes are often used by naturists who use this quiet area to sunbathe in the nude.

Map of the Rio de Valle and the Punta Paloma.

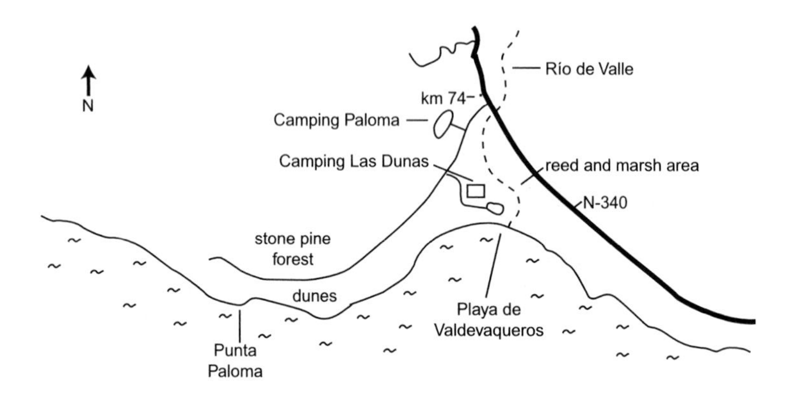

Access

The site can be easily reached from the N-340 by turning off where it is signed for Punta Paloma at km 74.1. This road leads uphill through an avenue of eucalyptus trees and passes beside Camping Paloma. Approximately half a kilometre further on, there is a turning to the left with directions to Playa de Valdevaqueros and Camping Las Dunas. Follow this road to the end where there is a large circular parking area and then take the track at the far end that leads towards the river. Marshy areas and reeds to the left provide cover for waders where Snipe, Ruffs and godwits can sometimes be found in the winter months along with numerous other species.

Once the spring rains have ended, the river ceases to flow to the sea and a lagoon often forms at the back of the beach, sometimes as far as the giant dunes. This also attracts waders and gulls in the quieter months. Warblers, larks, finches and other passerines are always present and in the summer the Nightingales and Cetti's Warblers have competitions to see which can sing the loudest.

After visiting this area, return to the road and turn left, uphill, towards the Punta Paloma. The stone pine forest here holds the usual array of birds that you would expect to find in such a habitat. The main attractions here are the good views offered of the Atlantic Ocean and the elevated position from which to watch seabirds as they head for and arrive from the strait. Shearwaters, Gannets and skuas are often visible throughout the year and these can be joined in the winter and during passage periods by Razorbills, Red-breasted Mergansers, Common Scoters and Audouin's, Little and Mediterranean Gulls and a variety of terns which can include Caspian, Lesser Crested, Common, Arctic, Sandwich, Little, Black and Gull-billed.

General Information

The beach and campsites are very popular in the summer and the area gets particularly crowded at weekends and during holiday periods which is not conducive to good birdwatching. Even in the winter you may find that a group of intrepid windsurfers have invaded the beach but they are generally too involved with their sport to be of nuisance near to the river and the lagoon. The main parts of this site are not particularly suited to persons with mobility problems.

Bolonia

The village of Bolonia was built beside the old Roman settlement of Baelo Claudia which dates from 102 B.C. It is on the coast and has a typical Atlantic beach consisting of fine white sand with large dunes to the western end. A small river, the Arroyo de Alpariate, flows past the village creating areas of dense reed and shrub cover along its course before entering the sea midway along the beach. As with many of the other rivers in the area, when it is not in full flow a lagoon normally forms at the back of the beach. A convenient parking area directly overlooks this spot. In the winter, the river/ lagoon is very attractive to a wide range of waders, waterfowl, gulls and terns. The vegetated river banks provide cover for many passerine species, notably warblers, wagtails and finches.

Most of the immediate surrounding area is arid scrubland and rough broken ground. Further to the north-west there is the range of hills known as the Sierra de la Plata where the very scarce White-rumped Swift has bred regularly in recent years. To the east there is the impressive Loma de San Bartolomé, a 442 metres high outcrop that is the home of a colony of Griffon Vultures. Various watercourses carry rainwater down to the sea and it is along these that you are most likely to find Rufous Bush Chats in the breeding season.

Access

The site can be easily reached from the main N-340 by turning off where signed for Bolonia at km 70.2 (It is also signed for Ruinas Romanos de Baelo Claudia). This road, the CA-P2216, climbs quite steeply to the Puerto de Bolonia, 2.8 kms from the main road. At this point there is a small crossroads and a wayside bar/cafe. The dirt road to the right leads to a bird observation post and then on through open pastures where Black-eared Wheatears, Woodchat Shrikes and Bee-eaters are common in the summer and finches, buntings, larks, pipits and warblers can be found all year. The observatory looks out toward the Loma de San Bartolomé and also faces the direction from which the migrating storks, eagles and other raptors arrive during the spring migration.

As you reach Bolonia, there are two left-hand turns. The first of these roads leads past the village along the coast for about one kilometre. At the end of the built-up area there is open scrubland on the left and sand dunes on the right. These areas should be searched for Corn and Cirl Buntings, warblers, wheatears, larks, pipits and finch flocks. As with other dry open land in the vicinity, you stand a good chance of finding Rufous Bush Chats in the summer.

The second left turning referred to takes you across the bridge over the Arroyo de Alpariate to a parking area just above the beach. The river/lagoon is only 15 metres away and in the winter, when the maximum numbers of waders are present, it may not be necessary to leave your car to see Whimbrel, Redshank, Common Sandpiper, Dunlin, Sanderling and Ringed, Grey and Kentish Plovers. Gulls and sometimes terns can also be seen at the lagoon or on the beach.

The dense vegetation near the bridge provides good cover for many birds and should be carefully checked for warblers and other species. I have seen Fan-tailed, Sardinian, Melodious, Cetti's, Olivaceous, Sedge and Willow Warblers here at the appropriate times of the year, together with Iberian Chiffchaffs and Blackcaps. Kingfishers and Nightingales are fairly common here and Grey Wagtails are quite often seen.

This location is not ideal for passing seabirds with the exception of gulls and terns, although you may be lucky and see the odd shearwater or skua. The Roman ruins which are about 200 metres from the bridge are worth visiting, not only for the historical aspect of the site but also because the guided tour may produce views of Little Owls, Black Redstarts, Black-eared Wheatears, Blue Rock Thrushes and both Great Grey and Woodchat Shrikes, all of which like to perch on the ruins whilst looking for suitable prey such as insects and lizards.

General map of the Bolonia area

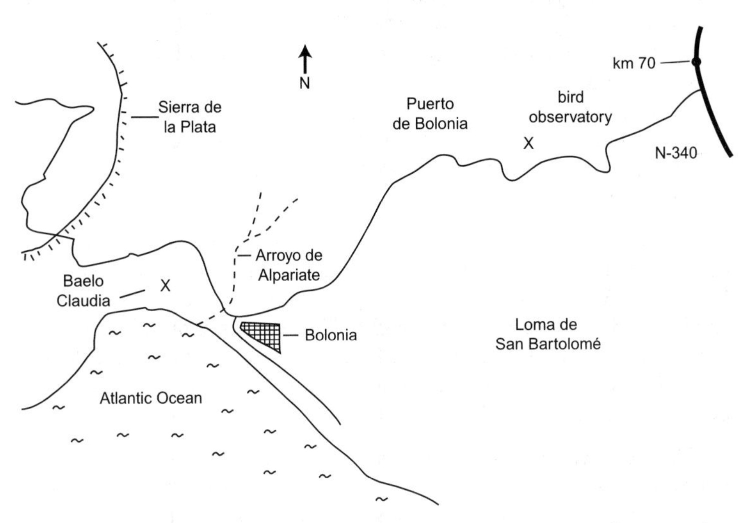

Just beyond the ruins, there is a large plantation of stone pine where most of the usual pine forest birds can be found. These include Great Spotted Woodpecker, Short-toed Treecreeper, Jay, Spotted Flycatcher, finches, tits and warblers.

After visiting this area, cross back over the bridge and turn left. This road leads through open scrubland before climbing up towards the Sierra de la Plata. After a couple of kilometres, the road forks to the left with a sign that reads "No pasar. Zona militar". This is military land and you should not enter. Continuing along the main road, you reach another sign that reads "Carretera cortada, zona militar". You can ignore this sign as it is only a warning that the road becomes closed to the public further along the route. You can proceed for another 3 kms or so before you reach the military road barrier with a "No pasar" sign.

As you climb up through the sierra you will come to a sheer cliff face. Park here and scan the rocks for Blue Rock Thrushes and for Red-rumped Swallows and the scarce White-rumped Swifts that breed in the general area. The swift population, although growing slowly, is not large and there is no guarantee that you will see one no matter how patient you are. As with most aspects of birdwatching, it really is a case of being in the right place at the right time.

When to Visit

Being a coastal town, the area attracts large numbers of beach-goers in the summer and this disrupts all aspects of birdwatching at the lagoon. However, most of the other parts of the site remain quiet and generally undisturbed and visits here at any time of the year can prove fruitful.

The observation post at Puerto de Bolonia will provide the best results during easterly winds in March and April for most of the raptor species, although the first two weeks of May should produce the maximum number of Honey Buzzards.

General Information

Although many parts of this site are inaccessible to wheelchair users, there are areas that can be adequately viewed from the comfort of a car and I would recommend this site to any person with mobility problems.

Bird Calendar

The species of birds that can be seen here roughly corresponds with those on my list for the Playa de los Lances.

Raptor Migration

The phenomena of bird migration is a subject that has aroused human interest for hundreds of years and it is here, along the Strait of Gibraltar where two continents almost meet and two seas, the Mediterranean and the Atlantic Ocean, merge together, that this bi-annual spectacle can be best observed.

The spring migration (northward) of storks, eagles and other

Caspian Tern *(Sterna caspia)*

raptors, along with other species is by far the most spectacular and it has been estimated by experts that upward of half a billion birds could cross over from the African continent en route to their European breeding grounds during this period. At the same time, there is also significant movement through the strait involving gannets, shearwaters, skuas, terns, gulls and other seabirds.

The movement of birds generally runs from February through to November, but the periods that produce both the maximum species and numbers are undoubtedly from March to May and from August to October. Visits here during these periods can provide the watcher with good views of many interesting species, maybe including such rarities as Spotted and Lesser Spotted Eagles, Lanners, Lammergeiers, and Rüppell's Vultures. Those who are intent on seeing Honey Buzzards should plan to visit during the first two weeks of May.

A network of bird observatories has been created at strategic points throughout the region, some coastal and some inland, which are manned by volunteer recorders during the migration periods and an annual report of these records is then produced jointly by the Sociedad Española de Ornitología (SEO) and the Consejería de Medio Ambiente de la Junta de Andalucía (AMA).

Most of these observatories are a simple covered semi-circular construction of concrete and stone with bench seating and a stone table. Unfortunately they are open on all sides and offer no protection against the strong winds that often affect the area. However, on calmer days they do provide some sort of comfort for your raptor watching.

Below is a map showing the locations of some of these observatories but there are numerous others that I have yet to discover. There is, however, an ornithological centre (Estación Ornitología de Tarifa) just on the landward side of the N-340 at km 78.5, where directions to other observatories can be obtained from a notice board. Unfortunately I have never found the centre to be open and so I am unable to tell if other information is available there.

General map of bird observatories

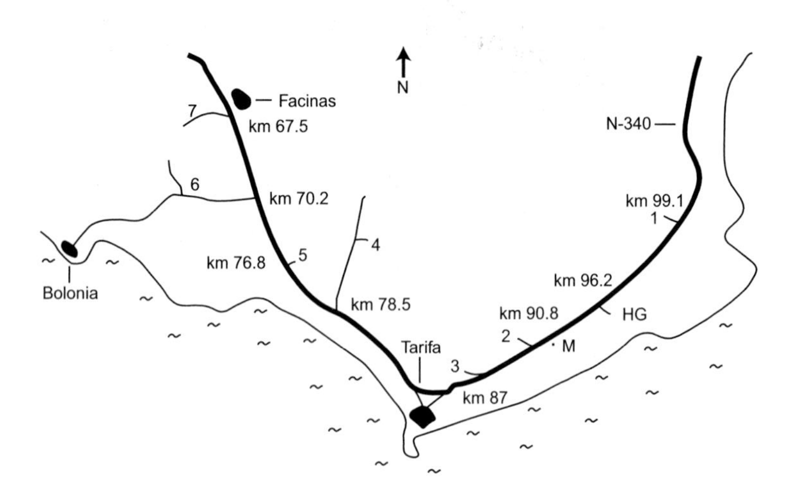

Key to the bird observatories map

1. ALGARROBO. Can be reached via a forest track on the seaward side of the N-340 at km 99.1.

2. CABRITO. Turn inland 100 metres beyond the Mirador del Estrecho at km 90.8. Cross over the cattle grid and take the second turning right. The observatory is 200 metres uphill.

3. CAZALLA. Turn off the N-340 onto a dirt-track at km 87 exactly. A large, white, flat-roofed building is the landmark.

There is no observatory but this spot offers some of the best views in the area.

4. SANTUARIO. Turn inland beside the Estacíon Ornitologia de Tarifa at km 78.5. The observatory is in open land on the right, 1.3 kms from the main road.

5. LA PEÑA. Turn inland onto a dirt-track at km 76.8. Follow the track uphill and the observatory is on the left.

6. PUERTO DE BOLONIA. Take the turning to Bolonia at km 70.2 and proceed for 2.8 kms. Turn right onto a dirt track and the observatory is about 70 metres along the track.

7. PUERTO DE FACINAS. Turn toward the sea onto an old farm track at km 67.5 and park. The observatory is a few minutes walk along the track

HG. This is the Tourist Centre and Information Office of Huerta Grande. Turn toward the sea at km 96.2 and follow the signs to the centre. A lot of useful information is available here and the office is usually open from 10am to 2pm and from 5 to 8pm.

M. This is the very touristy Mirador del Estrecho situated beside the N-340 at km 90.9. It offers good views across the strait to the Moroccan coast and there is a bar/restaurant and car-park. Due to the number of visitors it is not recommended as a serious bird watching location.

La Janda

Although much has been written about La Janda in various other bird guides, I feel that its uniqueness as a site and the wide diversity of bird species that are to be found here make it an essential inclusion in this book. I have visited the area on many occasions during different seasons and have never been disappointed by the variety it offers.

La Janda, in the province of Cádiz, was once a vast lake (*La Laguna de la Janda*) with surrounding flood plains and was one of the most important wetlands in Andalucía. Unfortunately, the land was drained about 40 years ago and much of the reclaimed land was turned over to agricultural use. Now large cotton plantations, cattle farms and fields of sunflowers take up part of the countryside, but large areas of unspoilt land still remain.

The Río Almodóvar runs through the remaining plains and numerous reed-fringed water ditches and small canals form a network through the farmland. As the area is low-lying, it often floods in wet weather, especially in the winter, giving you a view of how it looked in its natural state many years ago. When flooding does occur, thousands of waterfowl, waders, and gulls, for which the site is noted, are attracted here.

Both Great and Little Bustards can be found in the general area, the latter breeding locally and maintaining a reasonable population. However, the Great Bustard numbers, which were never very high, have diminished to such an extent that in the winter of 2000/01 it was suspected that only one pair remained. On the brighter side, two Great White Egrets had taken up residence on the plains and hopefully these may become a regular feature. Wintering flocks (November-February) of Common Cranes are regular visitors and at peak times the numbers can reach 3,000, although 200-500 is normal in most years. As many as 23 species of eagles, vultures and other raptors have been recorded here, including Lanner Falcon, together with six owl species.

To the south of the site is the Sierra de Retín (316 mts above sea level), whilst to the east the Sierra Blanquilla towers 634 metres above the plains. This is the domain of the vultures, eagles and Ravens.

To the north of the plains the Río Barbate flows from the Embalse de Celemín and streams from two smaller reservoirs flow into the river. This area also floods in winter, attracting similar species to those found at this site. Also in this area there is an unsurfaced road which runs from Benalup de Sidonia to the N-340, near to the village of Facinas. This road leads along the eastern side of the plains and offers a different aspect of the site, but in wet weather this also can become flooded and impassable.

The whole of the general area is directly below the main migration flight paths and is, therefore, very productive in the spring and autumn passage periods, when many birds land here to recover from their sea crossing from Africa, or to rest before beginning their journeys across the strait.

Access

The main point of entry to the site is from the N-340 highway, directly opposite the Venta de Retín and the road to Zahara de los Atunes, at km 56. There is also another entry point at km 47, signed for Presa de Celemín. The surfaced and unsurfaced roads that lead through the area are all in a bad state of repair and extreme care should be taken when driving around the site.

In the winter, the central track (see map) can sometimes be impassable due to subsidence. If you have entered the site at km 56, you need to return to the N-340 and drive to the entry point at km 47 to visit the rest of the site and vice versa if you entered at km 47.

The track opposite the Venta de Retín leads downhill for approximately one kilometre with pastures and marsh areas on the left and a large field, usually planted with sunflowers, on the right. At the bottom of the hill the track turns left and runs alongside the Río Almodovár. Park here and scan the surrounding countryside. White Storks, herons and egrets are prominent throughout the year and Common Cranes, waders and waterfowl are regular winter visitors. The reeds and scrub on both sides of the river hold finches, warblers, larks and pipits.

Also present, during the passage periods and in the summer, are Purple Heron, Squacco Heron, Little Bittern and Black Stork. Marsh and Hen harriers can be seen in the winter and Montagu's Harrier, Black Kite, Short-toed Eagle, Booted Eagle and Egyptian Vulture are all regularly present in the summer.

Continue along the central track, making several stops en route, until, after about 5 kms you reach a bridge that crosses the river. Turn here and follow the road for about 7 kms, again making stops anywhere along the route. This will lead you to the unsurfaced road that passes the eastern edge of the plain and gives a slightly elevated view of the area.

General map of the La Janda area

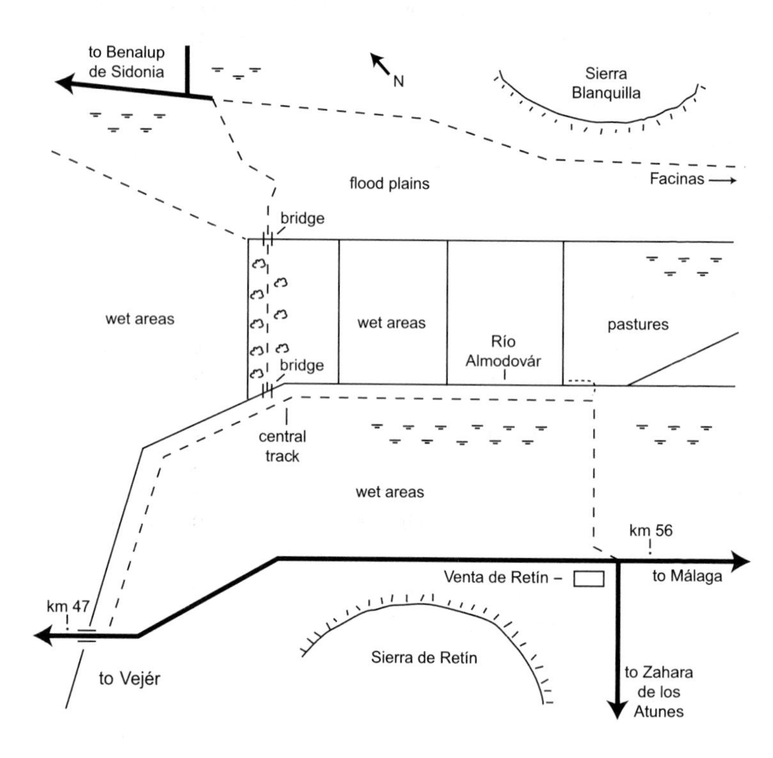

Return along the track until you reach the surfaced road that leads to Benalup de Sidonia. After about 100 metres you cross over the Río Barbate. Turn right here and view the river and marsh areas beside the road. This is a particularly good spot for gulls and waders in the winter. Regular visitors include Lapwing, Kentish, Grey and Golden Plovers, Dunlin, Ruff, Snipe, Black and Bar-tailed Godwits, Curlew, Whimbrel, Redshank, Greenshank, Green Sandpiper and Common Sandpiper.

After visiting this area, retrace the route back to the central area and after crossing over the Río Almodóvar turn right. This road leads back to the N-340 at km 47. Once again, you should make several stops along the route. Check the electricity pylons and cables for raptors and Great Grey Shrikes as these are very popular perches in what is otherwise a very flat and featureless area.

This end of the site has large expanses of dense gorse, broom and scrub and it is here that you are most likely to find Fan-Tailed, Sardinian, Spectacled, Olivaceous and Dartford Warblers, Hoopoe, European Nightjar, Woodchat Shrike, Bee-eater and Black-eared Wheatear.

Once you have left the site, take the road to Zahara de los Atunes (km 56). The first few kilometres of this road passes between pastures to the right and large fields of cereal on the left and is a fairly reliable place to find the Little Bustards, Short-toed Larks, Calandra Larks and Stone Curlews.

When to Visit

The site is of interest at all times but without doubt the winter and passage periods produce the greater variety of species and northern visitors increase the population numbers of many of the resident birds. Visits in the height of summer are not recommended as the temperatures can be very oppressive at this time. Also, most of the area will have dried out and the cultivated crops will have grown so high that you have very little chance of seeing whatever birds may be present. Heat haze will also be a problem at this time.

Due to the open and exposed nature of the site it can also be extremely uncomfortable on windy and rainy days.

General Information

This is a vast area and a telescope is a big advantage, although on very windy days it can be as much a hindrance as a help.

The majority of the tracks around the site are elevated above the surrounding areas, offering excellent views out across the plains. The tracks are, for the most part, fairly even, although there are a few areas that are rutted. I would therefore class this site as being fully wheelchair accessible.

Bird Calendar

Resident

Little Grebe, Cattle Egret, Little Egret, Grey Heron, White Stork, Mallard, Griffon Vulture, Marsh Harrier, Sparrowhawk, Buzzard, Bonelli's Eagle, Peregrine, Kestrel, Pheasant, Red-legged Partridge, Water Rail, Moorhen, Great Bustard, Little Bustard, Stone Curlew, Black-headed Gull, Yellow-legged Gull, Rock Dove, Wood Pigeon,

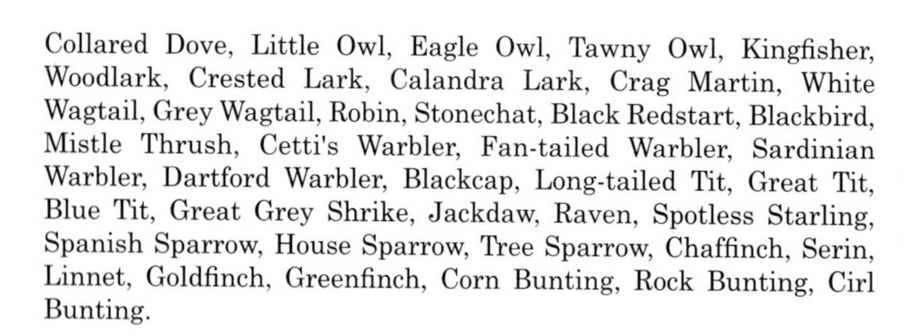

Collared Dove, Little Owl, Eagle Owl, Tawny Owl, Kingfisher, Woodlark, Crested Lark, Calandra Lark, Crag Martin, White Wagtail, Grey Wagtail, Robin, Stonechat, Black Redstart, Blackbird, Mistle Thrush, Cetti's Warbler, Fan-tailed Warbler, Sardinian Warbler, Dartford Warbler, Blackcap, Long-tailed Tit, Great Tit, Blue Tit, Great Grey Shrike, Jackdaw, Raven, Spotless Starling, Spanish Sparrow, House Sparrow, Tree Sparrow, Chaffinch, Serin, Linnet, Goldfinch, Greenfinch, Corn Bunting, Rock Bunting, Cirl Bunting.

Summer / Breeding

Little Bittern, Black Kite, Short-toed Eagle, Egyptian Vulture, Montagu's Harrier, Booted Eagle, Lesser Kestrel, Quail, Black-winged Stilt, Collared Pratincole, Little-ringed Plover, Kentish Plover, Turtle Dove, Cuckoo, Scops Owl, Barn Owl, European Nightjar, Red-necked Nightjar, Little Swift, Alpine Swift, Common Swift, Pallid Swift, Hoopoe, Bee-eater, Short-toed Lark, House Martin, Red-rumped Swallow, Barn Swallow, Tawny Pipit, Yellow Wagtail, Nightingale, Rufous Bush Chat, Redstart, Black-eared Wheatear, Reed Warbler, Olivaceous Warbler, Melodious Warbler, Spectacled Warbler, Spotted Flycatcher, Woodchat Shrike, Ortolan Bunting.

Winter

Great White Egret, Greylag Goose, Wigeon, Teal, Pintail, Shoveler, Osprey, Red Kite, Black-winged Kite, Black Vulture, Hen Harrier, Golden Eagle, Spanish Imperial Eagle, Merlin, Common Crane, Avocet, Ringed Plover, Grey Plover, Golden Plover, Lapwing, Dunlin, Sanderling, Little Stint, Ruff, Snipe, Black-tailed Godwit, Bar-tailed Godwit, Curlew, Whimbrel, Redshank, Greenshank, Green Sandpiper, Common Sandpiper, Great Spotted Cuckoo, Long-eared Owl, Skylark, Meadow Pipit, Water Pipit, Bluethroat, Iberian Chiffchaff, Penduline Tit, Starling, Siskin, Reed Bunting.

Passage Migrants

Squacco Heron, Night Heron, Purple Heron, Black Stork, Garganey, Honey Buzzard, Curlew Sandpiper, Wood Sandpiper, Short-eared Owl, Roller, Lesser Short-toed Lark, Tree Pipit, Whinchat, Northern Wheatear, Sedge Warbler, Willow Warbler, Pied Flycatcher, Golden Oriole.

Rarities

Cream Coloured Courser. One recorded at nearby Tahivilla in Sept. 1987.

Lanner Falcon. One recorded at the site in Oct. 1994.

Black-Crowned Tchagra. One recorded nearby in July 1995.

Sociable Plover. One recorded nearby in Feb. 1996.

Little Swift. There have been five separate sightings in the area since 1983. Each of these occured in the months of April or May.

Common Crane *(Grus grus)*

Laguna de Medina

The Laguna de Medina is a vast lake situated 10 kms south-east of Jerez de la Frontera in the province of Cádiz. The lagoon has an area of some 120 hectares and forms part of a Reserva Natural. The reserve is warden controlled and the warden's office can be found beside the car-park. Like many of the other lagoons in the area, this is seasonal and can dry up in high-summer if there has been insufficient winter/spring rainfall.

Direct access to the water's edge and the surrounding extensive reedbeds is not possible due to fencing that encircles the reserve but much of the lagoon can be seen from an observation point near to the parking area and from a trail which leads alongside the south-western perimeter. Unfortunately, dense growths of buckthorn between the trail and the reedbeds have been allowed to grow too high and views over these are becoming increasingly difficult, not to say downright frustrating, at certain points along the route.

The lagoon is notable for the wide range of wintering species that can be found here. Wildfowl numbers are always high and usually include Mallard, Shoveler, Wigeon, Teal, Pochard, Red-crested Pochard, Pintail and occasional Tufted Ducks. The lagoon is also a stronghold for two of the scarcer ducks in Spain, the White-headed and Marbled Ducks, whose numbers can reach over 300 and 100 respectively in good years. Also on the water you can see Moorhens, Coots and Great Crested, Black-necked and Little Grebes. Very small numbers of Crested Coots (2-3 pairs) live and breed here but they are elusive and are more easily seen in the breeding season after the wintering hordes of Common Coots have left.

Other birds that are attracted to the water, some resident and some seasonal visitors, include Greater Flamingo, Avocet, Black-winged Stilt, storks, herons, egrets, plovers, shanks and a good selection of other waders. Obviously with so much activity going on, there are bound to be birds of prey on the look-out for easy meals and these are represented by Buzzard, Kestrel, Peregrine, Sparrowhawk, Red Kite, Black Kite, Marsh Harrier, Hen Harrier and Montagu's Harrier. Occasionally, Short-toed and Booted Eagles may be seen overhead and the Black-shouldered Kite, which is a fairly scarce bird, is now being recorded much more frequently.

During the summer/breeding season, the lagoon is visited by a very wide range of species. Typical breeders include Little Bittern, Red-crested Pochard, Collared Pratincole, Avocet, Little-ringed Plover, Kentish Plover, Bee-eater, Hoopoe, Rufous Bush Chat,

Black-eared Wheatear, Cetti's Warbler, Reed Warbler, Great Reed Warbler, Nightingale, Woodchat Shrike, Great Grey Shrike and Cirl Bunting. Many other breeding species can also be found in addition to those that can be seen as they pass through the area on migration.

Access

From all points along the coast of the Costa del Sol, the easiest way to reach the site is via the N-340 highway and taking the turn-off to Los Barrios (km 110) and following the A-381 for Jerez de la Frontera. The lagoon can be seen on the right as you pass by the km 10 marker and the entry point is 500 metres further on.

Travelling from further east, ie. Tarifa, Barbate or Vejer de la Frontera, you drive through Medina Sidonia and join the A-381 for Jerez. Be careful travelling towards Jerez from either of these two routes when you come to a new stretch of dual-carriageway. The kilometre markings on this stretch of road bear no resemblance to those on the old road and you should disregard all the km markers until you rejoin the old A-381, some 14 kms from Jerez.

If you are travelling from further inland and your trip involves passing through Jerez, you should first follow the directions for Málaga on the C-440 before taking the A-381 to Medina Sidonia/ Los Barrios. You will then find the entry point to the site midway between kms 9 and 10.

At the parking area of the lake you will find the warden's office. He is a young Spaniard who speaks hardly any English but he knows the names of some of the birds and will try to help you. If you have a bird book, you can show him the pictures of the birds you particularly wish to see and he will probably be able to tell you if there are any present at that time. He also knows where to look for most of the species, which can save you a lot of time and effort.

Gates, barriers and tall vegetation surrounding the lagoon prevent wheelchair users from seeing most of the area, except from a distance.

From the parking area, cross the road and enter through a gate. From this position you have views of the far end of the lagoon and also of the reedbeds directly ahead. A trail leads downhill to the right which passes along the entire southern perimeter of the reserve. The reeds and scattered shrubs inside the fence hold good numbers of Cetti's, Reed, Great Reed, Willow, Fan-tailed and Sardinian Warblers at the appropriate times of the year. Purple

Gallinules, Purple Herons, Little Bitterns and occasional Squacco Herons, along with duck and grebe species, can also be found in the reeds. The White-headed Ducks are commonly seen in the north-western corner and the Crested Coots prefer the sheltered area to the west, just below the warden's office.

Map of the Reserva Natural - Laguna de Medina

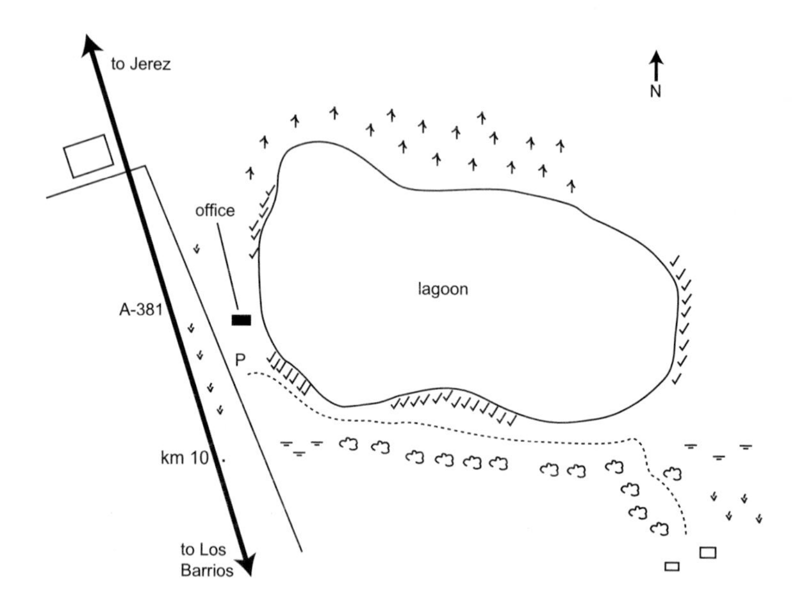

To the right of the track there are trees and fields of cereal crops. The trees hold the usual array of finches, tits and leaf warblers, whilst in the fields you can find Red-legged Partridge, Quail, Crested Lark, Woodlark, Skylark, Meadow Pipit and both White and Yellow Wagtails. Great Grey and Woodchat Shrikes can often be seen perched on any prominent post or fence.

At the far end of the lagoon, the trail turns right and leads down, through a small rocky area, to an expanse of farmland, much of which is quite marshy. Both Cattle and Little Egrets are often found here and Snipe feed on the marshy edges. Birds of prey, including owls, regularly hunt over this area, especially near to the farm buildings. This point marks the end of the site and you have to retrace your steps back toward the parking area. On the way back, spend time to scan the reeds at the bottom corner of the lagoon.

It is here that you are most likely to see wintering Penduline Tits, Bluethroats and Reed Buntings. In the spring/summer this is also the best spot to see Reed and Great Reed Warblers. The dense growth of prickly pears and other cacti that surround the warden's office has been productive in the past for Rufous Bush Chats and shrikes.

When to Visit

As the lagoon may dry up in the summer you should not consider making a long journey to this site between August and the end of November as it might prove to be disappointing. December to February is the prime time to see the wintering species, although many may remain for a long time after that. The summer visitors usually start to arrive from mid-February and the breeding season is in full swing by mid-April. This is the time I prefer as the weather is warmer, the days are longer and the maximum number of species are present.

Bird Calendar

Resident

Little Grebe, Great Crested Grebe, Black-necked Grebe, Cattle Egret, Little Egret, Flamingo, Mallard, Shoveler, Red-crested Pochard, White-headed Duck, Black-winged Kite, Marsh Harrier, Sparrowhawk, Buzzard, Peregrine, Kestrel, Red-legged Partridge, Water Rail, Moorhen, Purple Gallinule, Common Coot, Crested Coot, Stone Curlew, Kentish Plover, Common Sandpiper, Yellow-legged Gull, Rock Dove, Wood Pigeon, Collared Dove, Little Owl, Barn Owl, Kingfisher, Great Spotted Woodpecker, Woodlark, Crested Lark, White Wagtail, Grey Wagtail, Robin, Stonechat, Black Redstart, Blackbird, Cetti's Warbler, Fan-tailed Warbler, Blackcap, Sardinian Warbler, Dartford Warbler, Long-tailed Tit, Great Tit, Blue Tit, Great Grey Shrike, Spotless Starling, House Sparrow, Chaffinch, Serin, Linnet, Goldfinch, Greenfinch, Corn Bunting, Cirl Bunting.

Summer / Breeding

Little Bittern, Purple Heron, Ferruginous Duck, Montagu's Harrier, Short-toed Eagle, Black Kite, Red Kite, Quail, Black-winged Stilt, Avocet, Collared Pratincole, Little-ringed Plover, Black Tern, Whiskered Tern, Turtle Dove, Cuckoo, Nightjar, Common Swift, Pallid Swift, Hoopoe, Bee-eater, Sand Martin, Red-rumped Swallow, Barn Swallow, Yellow Wagtail, Nightingale, Rufous Bush Chat,

Black-eared Wheatear, Savi's Warbler, Reed Warbler, Great Reed Warbler, Sedge Warbler, Olivaceous Warbler, Melodious Warbler, Orphean Warbler, Willow Warbler, Spotted Flycatcher, Woodchat Shrike, Ortolan Bunting.

Winter

Grey Heron, Spoonbill, Greylag Goose, Shelduck, Gadwall, Wigeon, Teal, Pintail, Marbled Duck, Tufted Duck, Pochard, Hen Harrier, Ringed Plover, Lapwing, Dunlin, Curlew Sandpiper, Sanderling, Little Stint, Ruff, Snipe, Jack Snipe, Black-tailed Godwit, Bar-tailed Godwit, Whimbrel, Spotted Redshank, Redshank, Greenshank, Wood Sandpiper, Green Sandpiper, Black-headed Gull, Mediterranean Gull, Skylark, Meadow Pipit, Bluethroat, Song Thrush, Chiffchaff, Penduline Tit, Siskin, Reed Bunting.

Passage Migrants

Squacco Heron, White Stork, Black Stork, Garganey,Curlew, Roller, Wryneck, Tree Pipit, Whinchat, Northern Wheatear, Wood Warbler, Pied Flycatcher.

White-headed Duck *(Oxyura leucocephala)*

Rarities

Goldeneye. January 1989,

Scaup. March 1991

Ring-Necked Duck. December 1996

Blue-Winged Teal. February 1997

Ruddy Duck. December 1988, February 1991, March 1991, February 1997.

Parque Natural Sierra de Grazalema

This large natural park covers an area of 51,695 hectares and is situated partly in the north-eastern corner of the province of Cádiz and at the western end of Málaga province. Within the boundaries of the park, there is a "reserve" area where access is limited and can only be entered with a permit. It is mainly a mountainous limestone region with altitudes ranging from 250 metres above sea-level to the highest point of 1,654 metres at the "El Torreón" peak of the Sierra del Pinar.

The region records the highest annual rainfall in Spain with an average of over 2,100 mm per year, and because of this much of the area is very well vegetated at the lower levels and on the forested hillsides where cork-oaks, Holm oaks, round-leaved oaks, wild olives, strawberry trees, carobs and a range of pines, including the Spanish fir (*Pinsapo*), grow profusely. In stark contrast there are towering rock formations that are devoid of any form of vegetation.

The animal life in the park is extremely varied and includes Roe Deer, Red Deer, Foxes, Genets, Ibexes and a vast range of amphibians and reptiles. To date there have been 146 bird species officially recorded in the park and it is that list that I shall supply as the bird calendar for this site.

Numerous streams and rivers flow through the area but many of these are seasonal and dry up in the early summer. There is a large reservoir beside the village of Zahara de la Sierra which holds permanent water and offers good birdwatching where many interesting species can be found.

Throughout the park there are walking routes and driving itineries that form part of the Rutas Ornitológicas (bird-watching routes) that are recommended by the park's management as good places for any visiting birder. Some of these locations will form part of this site description.

To simplify any tour of the park, I recommend that you start at the town of Grazalema as it is central to all of the sites and there is a very helpful tourist information office in the centre of the town where maps and leaflets on the park and surrounding areas can be obtained. One map that I have found very helpful is the "Plano topográfico del macizo de Grazalema". This has lots of information about the park and is written in Spanish, English, French, German and Esperanto. It can be purchased at the information office for about seven Euros. There is also a very handy book called "Aves del

Parque Natural Sierra de Grazalema" (Birds of the natural park) that contains information and illustrations on the birds and the sites within the park. This is written in Spanish, English and German.

Access

There are numerous routes to Grazalema and your starting location should determine your best route. Travelling up from the coast from between Estepona to beyond Málaga, take the San Pedro-Ronda-Sevilla road (A-376) and turn off where signed for Grazalema between kms 107 and 106. From areas such as Sotogrande, Gibraltar, Algeciras and Tarifa, your best route is the A-369 Algeciras-Ronda road and then proceed as above. From further west, ie. Cádiz, Jerez etc., take the A-382 Jerez-Antequera road, turning off at Villamartín or Algodonales, following signs for Grazalema.

On arrival at Grazalema, pass through the centre of the town to a large car-park and walk back into the town where you will find the information office on the left, directly opposite the Plaza de España. Cut diagonally across the plaza and take any of the small roads to the right leading to the mirador at the Plaza de Asomadores, which offers views of the valley below and the surrounding hills and mountains.

This position often produces views of Blue Rock Thrushes, Rock Buntings, Bonelli's Warblers, Black Redstarts and Serins. During the breeding season there are always many swifts, swallows and martins flying over the town and these include both White-rumped and Alpine Swifts and Red-rumped Swallows. Passing vultures, eagles and other raptors can be viewed, along with occasional Ravens and Red-billed Choughs.

In the left-hand corner of the plaza there are numerous information boards, one of which gives details of all the sites that are included in the Rutas Ornitológicas, complete with a map showing their locations.

As this is such a vast area it would be impossible to describe it in its entirety. I will describe my preferred route which takes in some of the best locations and usually produces a long and varied bird list.

From the car-park, return back through the town and after one kilometre you reach a turning on the left, signed for Algodonales, where you turn and follow the road for about 7 kms until you reach a bridge over the Río Guadalete. Parking anywhere here should enable you to see Hoopoes, Bee-eaters, larks, pipits, finches, tits and warblers, depending on the season. This valley is often overflown by birds of prey and a watchful eye should be kept on the sky.

Continuing along the road for about another kilometre, you come to a road junction where you turn left, following the signs for Zahara. The road now runs beside the Embalse de Zahara for about 10 kms. Unfortunately there are no kilometre markers along the way, so I cannot give you any specific distances. However, stopping at any point and scanning the reservoir, scrubland and the wooded areas should reveal some interesting species, such as Black-eared Wheatears, Rufous Bush Chats, Great Grey and Woodchat Shrikes, Dartford Warblers, Rock Sparrows and both Rock and Cirl Buntings.

As you approach Zahara, there is a turning to the left which takes you up to the town but I prefer to keep to the lower road leading to the dam, before driving up to Zahara. There is an ancient Roman castle and a mirador that looks out over the reservoir and the surrounding areas. Red-billed Choughs are often seen around the castle and swallows and swifts are prominent in the spring and summer. Egyptian Vultures breed close by and good views, both from above and below, can be had as they pass by. The water birds that can be found in and around the reservoir include Great Crested and Black-necked Grebes, Cormorants, Coots, Grey Herons and gulls during the winter and Night Herons, White Storks and Little-ringed Plovers in the summer. Mallards, Moorhens and Common Sandpipers can be seen throughout the year.

On leaving Zahara do not go back down to the reservoir but instead take the higher road (C-531) back to Grazalema. This is a forest route where you can stop virtually anywhere to search for Jays, Short-toed Treecreepers, Nuthatches, woodpeckers, flycatchers, finches, warblers and tits. Four kilometres along the road you come to the Puerto de los Acebuches where there is a mirador with good views and where passing raptors can be seen.

A further 6.5 kms along the road you reach the Puerto de las Palomas (Pass of the Doves). Park at the highest point for outstanding views and the opportunity to find Blue Rock Thrushes and Black Wheatears. There is a walk that starts from this area that leads to the Monte Prieto and there are also a few driveable track.

Continue for another 3.5 kms and you reach the Grazalema-El Bosque road where you should turn right. Within two kilometres you come to the Puerto del Boyar where again you can stop and look out over the valley below. There is a long walk that can be taken from here that leads to the Salto del Cabrero (Leap of the Goatherd) which is a wide cleft in a limestone hill where many of the previously mentioned bird species can be found.

From here it is simply a choice of going further or returning back through Grazalema. I prefer to follow the circular road through El Bosque, Ubrique and Villaluenga to reach the connecting road to the A-376, making several stops along the way, but this is totally dependent on time.

General map of the Grazalema area

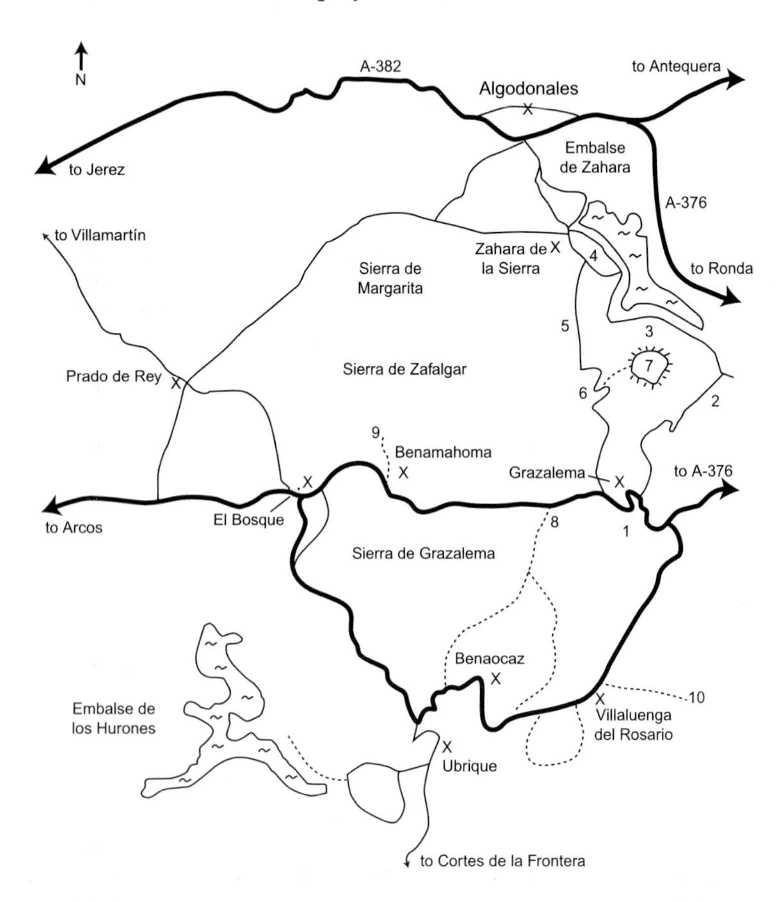

1. The mirador at Grazalema. 2. Bridge over the Río Guadalete. 3. Embalse de Zahara. 4. Embalse and the village of Zahara. 5. Puerto

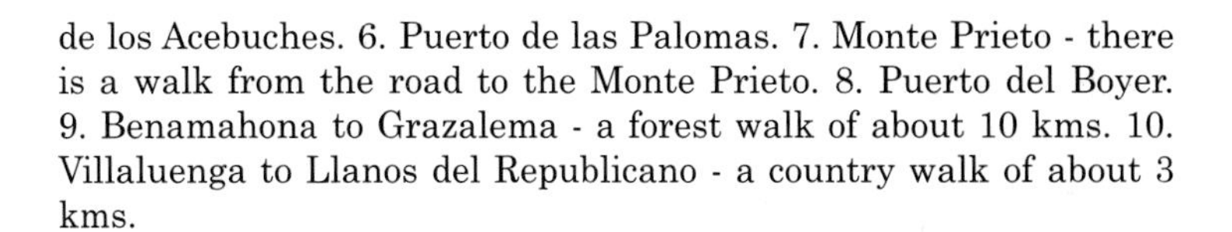

de los Acebuches. 6. Puerto de las Palomas. 7. Monte Prieto - there is a walk from the road to the Monte Prieto. 8. Puerto del Boyer. 9. Benamahona to Grazalema - a forest walk of about 10 kms. 10. Villaluenga to Llanos del Republicano - a country walk of about 3 kms.

When to Visit

The site is of interest at all times, with many resident species, but without doubt the breeding season produces the greater variety and visits here between mid-March and the end of June should prove to be the most rewarding.

Please remember that this site is at altitude and much cooler than the coast, so it is advisable to take a few items of protective clothing with you.

General Information

Although this is a mountainous area, I do not see this as a problem for any wheelchair birder. There are plenty of opportunities to park off-road, as well as at the miradors. In areas that are not suitable for wheelchairs the birdwatching can be done from the car.

If you suffer from any form of heart disease or breathing disorder that may be aggravated by the rarer air at altitudes over 1,000 metres you should think carefully about visiting this site as medical assistance is a long way away.

Bird Calendar

Resident

Cattle Egret, Mallard, Griffon Vulture, Goshawk, Sparrowhawk, Golden Eagle, Bonelli's Eagle, Kestrel, Peregrine, Red-legged Partridge, Moorhen, Common Sandpiper, Rock Dove, Wood Pigeon, Barn Owl, Eagle Owl, Little Owl, Tawny Owl, Kingfisher, Hoopoe, Green Woodpecker, Great Spotted Woodpecker, Woodlark, Crested Lark, Thekla Lark, White Wagtail, Grey Wagtail, Crag Martin, Wren, Robin, Black Redstart, Stonechat, Blue Rock Thrush, Blackbird, Mistle Thrush, Black Wheatear, Cetti's Warbler, Fan-tailed Warbler, Dartford Warbler, Sardinian Warbler, Blackcap, Iberian Chiffchaff, Firecrest, Long-tailed Tit, Crested Tit, Coal Tit, Great Tit, Blue Tit, Nuthatch, Short-toed Treecreeper, Great Grey Shrike, Jay, Red-billed Chough, Raven, Jackdaw, Spotless Starling, Rock Sparrow, House

Sparrow, Chaffinch, Serin, Linnet, Goldfinch, Greenfinch, Hawfinch, Corn Bunting, Rock Bunting, Cirl Bunting.

Summer / Breeding

Little Bittern, Night Heron, Purple Heron, White Stork, Black Kite, Egyptian Vulture, Short-toed Eagle, Montagu's Harrier, Buzzard, Booted Eagle, Lesser Kestrel, Quail, Black-winged Stilt, Little-ringed Plover, Turtle Dove, Cuckoo, Red-necked Nightjar, Scops Owl, Common Swift, Pallid Swift, White-rumped Swift, Alpine Swift, Bee-eater, Wryneck, Tawny Pipit, Yellow Wagtail, Sand Martin, House Martin, Barn Swallow, Red-rumped Swallow, Nightingale, Rock Thrush, Black-eared Wheatear, Olivaceous Warbler, Melodious Warbler, Subalpine Warbler, Orphean Warbler, Grasshopper Warbler, Spectacled Warbler, Whitethroat, Lesser Whitethroat, Bonelli's Warbler, Willow Warbler, Spotted Flycatcher, Woodchat Shrike, Golden Oriole.

Winter

Great Crested Grebe, Red-necked Grebe, Cormorant, Grey Heron, Monk Vulture, Hen Harrier, Osprey, Coot, Lapwing, Common Snipe, Woodcock, Redshank, Yellow-legged Gull, Meadow Pipit, Dipper, Dunnock, Alpine Accentor, Great Spotted Cuckoo, Ring Ouzel, Song Thrush, Redwing, Tree Sparrow, Brambling, Siskin, Crossbill.

Passage Migrants

Black Stork, Honey Buzzard, Roller, Redstart, Whinchat, Northern Wheatear, Garden Warbler, Willow Warbler, Pied Flycatcher.

Although this is the official list of the park's birds I can add Merlin, Rufous Bush Chat, Starling and Ortolan Bunting to the list, birds that I have seen during my visits to the Parque Natural Sierra de Grazalema.

Bonelli's Eagle *(Hieraaetus fasciatus)*

Doñana

This is probably one of the most written about and most visited birding areas in Europe. Certainly it is the best site in southern Spain and I make no apologies for following the lead of other authors in trying to describe the wealth of sites and birds that exist in this region.

Parque Nacional de Doñana

The National Park of Doñana is situated in the south-eastern corner of the province of Huelva and consists of 50,720 hectares of protected land in which there are vast wetlands and forests of stone pines and cork-oaks. For hundreds of years it was the royal hunting grounds where kings, queens and other notable dignitaries would come to enjoy their sport. Then, in the early 1960's, a part of the land was purchased to aid the conservation of the area and in 1969 it was declared as a national park. More land was added over the years until it became what it is today. In 1981 certain areas of the park were turned into Biospheric Reserves and in 1988 it was given the status of a Special Protection Area for birds. Finally, the park was declared as a World Heritage Site in 1994.

Various ecosystems exist within the park which include the sand-dunes and lagoons, the forests and surrounding scrubland and, perhaps most importantly, the marsh areas which are considered by many to be among the finest and most important in Europe.

The park is now managed by the Ministry of the Environment of the Spanish Government and entry into the park is restricted to tours operated by a licensed company using large 22-seater safari vehicles. These tours are of four hours duration and cover some 70 kms of trails along the Atlantic sand-dunes and inside the park proper. Unfortunately, as good as these tours are, they are not an ideal way to watch birds as the drivers are on a schedule and cannot stop just because you may have caught a fleeting glimpse of a "lifer" and would like to investigate it further. The constant motion of the vehicle over rough terrain makes the use of binoculars almost impossible.

Parque Natural de Doñana

The national park is further protected by a buffer zone of some 84,200 hectares of surrounding natural parkland and by the Atlantic

Ocean to the south, where 35 kms of deserted sandy coastline forms the boundary. This buffer zone, the Parque Natural de Doñana, also benefits from protected status, but not to the same strict degree as the national park. Entry into these areas is largely restricted but there are various visitors centres with nature trails where the general public are welcomed, and all of the birds and other wildlife that exists within the park boundaries can generally be found at these sites.

The importance of the Doñana region as a conservation site cannot be overstressed. Millions of wintering birds, mainly waterfowl and waders from the north, flock to the area each year and many millions more use it as a feeding station during the migration periods. It is also of major importance as a breeding ground for some of the most endangered bird species in Europe. Over 250 different species are regularly seen here. Rarities are very often recorded and the geographical position means that it is likely to attract any vagrants or accidentals that may wander, or be blown, into the region.

There are four visitors centres within the Parque Natural, three of which are very easily accessible and should form part of any visit here. The fourth centre is many kilometres out into the Marismas del Guadalquivir and access is extremely difficult. In my opinion, the time and effort involved in getting there is not really worthwhile as you are unlikely to see anything that you have not already found at the other sites. I will, however, make reference to this site and leave you to decide whether you wish to visit it or not.

Access

From all points in the region, you head for Sevilla and then follow the signs for Huelva. Once on the main Sevilla-Huelva road (the A-49), continue until you reach junction 10, signed for Bollullos del Condado. Once you have passed through Bollullos, the road leads directly towards Doñana.

A good place to start your birdwatching visit would be the village of El Rocío, which is the most central area to the sites that are described in this guide. The village itself is reminiscent of the days of the wild west in America. There are no surfaced roads in the village, only wide sandy streets. The houses are low and are mostly painted white, complete with hitching rails for horses which are still very much used as a form of transport in this area. Those locals that have "moved up" to the automobile tend not to conform with the normal rules of driving, preferring to drive where the sand is more compacted rather than on any particular side of the road. There are no traffic lights or road signs and it is hard to know who has the right of way at any junction. The simple rule I apply is to drive slowly and to give way to everything.

General map of the Doñana area

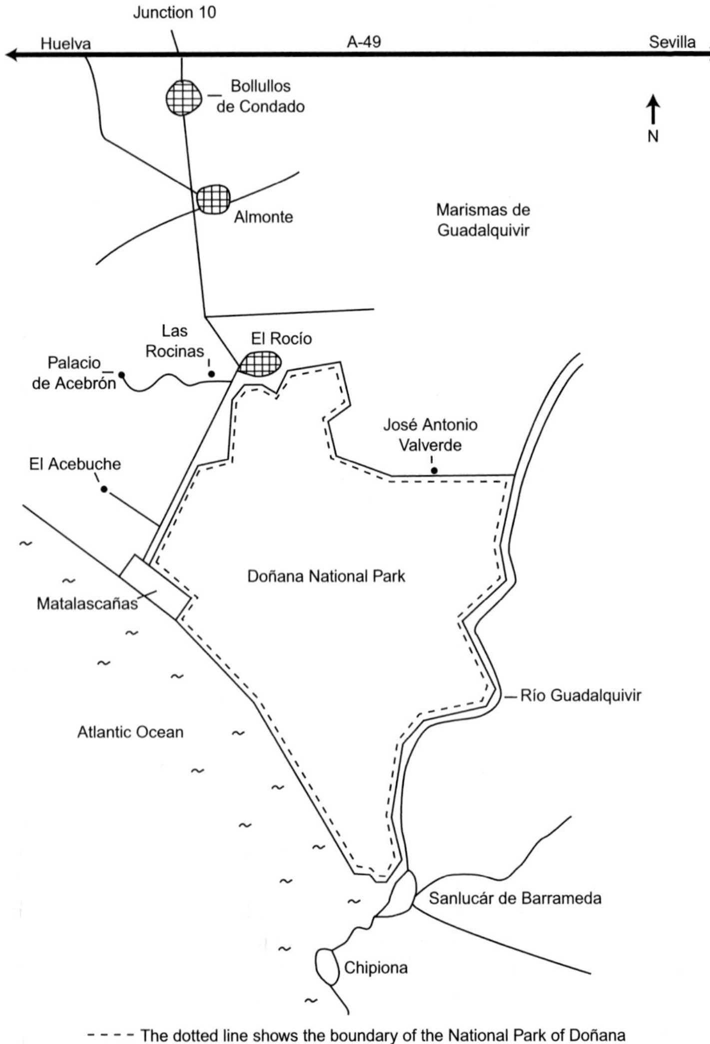

- - - - The dotted line shows the boundary of the National Park of Doñana

Site One - Madre de las Marismas del Rocío
(The Mother of the Marshes)

This is a vast shallow lagoon and marsh area right beside the village of El Rocío, known as the Mother of the Marshes. There is ample car parking space and a promenade which extends for about 500 metres alongside the marsh. The water-level in the lagoon fluctuates with the seasons and can, at times, be completely dry, especially at the end of a long hot, rainless summer. During the winter, water is virtually guaranteed and the area is an exceptional site for all manner of waterbirds including Greater Flamingos, Spoonbills, Common Cranes, White Storks, herons, egrets, ducks, geese and waders.

Many species breed out in the marshes or in the surrounding reedbeds, amongst which Whiskered Terns, Black-winged Stilts and Great Reed Warblers are the most notable, along with the more common Moorhens and Coots.

On the far bank of the lagoon, there are breeding colonies of Bee-eaters and further back in the trees there is a sizeable heronry. Some of the park's scarcest birds can appear on the marsh at times and Glossy Ibises, Crested Coots, Marsh Sandpipers and both White-headed and Ferruginous Ducks have all been recorded here. The site is constantly overflown by raptors and although the Black Kite is by far the most numerous you may also see Red Kites, Peregrines, Kestrels, Lesser Kestrels, Marsh and Hen Harriers and Short-toed, Booted and Spanish Imperial Eagles. Even the extremely rare Spotted Eagle has been recorded at this location.

Other birds that can be seen with some regularity include Avocets, Curlew Sandpipers, Purple Herons, Collared Pratincoles, Black Terns, larks, pipits, finches and a wide range of plovers, swifts, swallows, martins and all three wagtail species.

Site Two - The S.E.O. Bird Observatory

This bird observatory is run by members of the Sociedad Española de Ornitología and is located beside the marsh at the eastern end of the village of El Rocío. It can be reached by following the promenade to its end and then by a sandy road along the edge of the marsh. It is open most days from 10am until dusk and is manned by an SEO worker. A list of current bird sightings is maintained inside the building and is a useful source of information.

The observatory has large plate glass windows that give excellent views of the marsh/lagoon and there are two telescopes available for the use of the public. Use of these is free, but a donation to the SEO funds is always welcome. A small shop sells books, badges, stickers etc. and information leaflets in various languages are also available. In the winter, this is good place to watch birds in some degree of comfort. There is an upstairs open-air viewing platform which is never locked and offers good elevated views of the whole area. On sunny days, the best time for viewing is up to 2pm. On overcast days any time is good.

Black-winged Stilt *(Himantopus himantopus)*

Site Three - Boca del Lobo

This area called "The Wolf's Mouth" is east of the SEO bird observatory and can be reached by following the small track beside the fence to the left of the observatory. After about 100 metres you reach the end of the village and a track leads directly ahead. The land here is very flat and there are numerous small lagoons and marsh areas. The track leads for about 1 kilometre into the area known as the wolf's mouth. The characteristic birds of this area are scrub warblers, larks, pipits, including Tawny, finches, Hoopoes and Bee-eaters. Marsh Terns, such as Whiskered and Black are often seen here in the summer.

The many fence posts between the track and the main marsh should be checked for shrikes and raptors. To the right of the track, there is a sewage treatment plant on the edge of the marsh. This area obviously attracts birds and should be investigated. The area at the end of the track is one of the better spots for seeing Griffon Vultures and Spanish Imperial Eagles.

Site Four - Puente de la Canariega

This is the bridge just to the south of El Rocío that carries the main road over the Arroyo de la Rocina, the stream that feeds the marsh. It offers excellent elevated views of the lagoon, marshes and the flooded pastures where many of the egrets, herons and waders prefer to feed. Amongst these you are likely to find Lapwings, Redshanks, Greenshanks, Whimbrels, Curlews and both Black and Bar-tailed Godwits.

This is quite a popular spot for birdwatchers, but I must add a note of warning. Being on the bridge means you are very close to traffic passing by at quite high speeds and a certain amount of caution should be exercised here. The bridge is best visited from mid-afternoon onwards when the reflecting sunlight will not impair your views.

There is also a track that leads down to the stream beneath the bridge that you may wish to investigate. Kingfishers and resting Marsh Terns are often seen here and Red-rumped Swallows, nest underneath the bridge.

Site Five - Centro de Visitantes la Rocina

This is the La Rocina Visitors Centre and Information Office situated about 100 metres beyond the bridge on the right-hand side. It is a staffed centre where leaflets and other information can be obtained and there is an audiovisual display. Toilets and a soft drink vending machine are also available.

Drive through the gates and park in the designated area beyond the office. At the front of the office you will find the start of the nature trail, which is about 2.5 kms in length. Along this route, there are three bird hides that look out over the Charco de la Boca, which is part of the Arroyo de la Rocina. The whole of this walk is on boardwalks and you are required to keep to these. Before reaching the first hide you pass through a pine forest where Tree Sparrows, tits and finches are the most common residents, but do keep an eye out for warblers, shrikes and the Azure-winged Magpies which are often present. The first hide provides excellent close-up views of the stream and a few small islands where resting/nesting ducks and waders are commonly seen.

The second hide is really no more than a screen fence with "windows" cut into it but it looks out over a very marshy area where Squacco Herons, Water Rails and Purple Gallinules can be found. Follow the boardwalk downhill and you reach a causeway across two inlets. This gives a more open view of the marsh and often provides much better views of the birds. The trees, reeds and shrubs should be checked for Cirl Buntings, Reed, Great Reed and Melodious Warblers, Wrens, Spotted Flycatchers, Penduline Tits and other passerines.

Once across the causeway the trail leads back up into pine forests where you will find the third hide. This gives a more overall view of the stream and marshes. Most of the aforementioned birds can also be seen here but I have been lucky enough to have had very good views of a Great White Egret and Glossy Ibises (Jan. 1999), a Marsh Sandpiper (Jan. 2000), a Black-shouldered Kite (Nov. 2000) and Great Spotted Cuckoo (May 2001) from this particular hide. The marshes to the right are favoured by breeding Little Grebes and the reeds often hold Little Bitterns and Night Herons.

Continuing along the trail for a few hundred metres you reach a junction where you have the option of two routes. The trail to the left leads through the pines and a marsh area and then leads back to the car-park. My preference here is to follow the trail to the right, which leads directly through scrubland for one kilometre, where two more bird hides can be found. This does not form part of the original 2.5 km nature trail, which can be rejoined once you have visited this extension to the walk. This trail leads to a vast area of low scrub and scattered trees where Great Grey Shrikes, Woodchat Shrikes, Black-eared Wheatears, Hoopoes, Red-necked Nightjars, Rufous Bush Chats and Dartford, Spectacled, Melodious and Olivaceous Warblers can be found. The first hide is on the right after about 400 metres and looks out over the stream. On the far bank there is a row of wooden posts where harriers, kites and other raptors regularly perch to eat their prey. The trail finally ends at the last hide which overlooks marshes and small islands. White Storks nest in the trees to the left and Night Herons roost in the reeds and canes on the far bank.

Returning along the same track, take the right-hand fork at the junction. As you pass through the pines you come to a thatched shelter where you can sit and observe the reedbeds in front of you. Finches, tits, Cuckoos, Great Spotted Cuckoos, Wrens and warblers may all be seen with a little patience. Looking back into the forest you may see Great Spotted Woodpeckers, Short-toed Treecreepers and Jays.

The trail now leads across another causeway, through a marsh, where Iberian Chiffchaffs, Blackcaps and Cetti's, Melodious and Reed Warblers are commonly seen. Eventually the trail brings you back to the car-park behind the visitors centre.

Map of the Arroyo de la Rocina and the nature trails

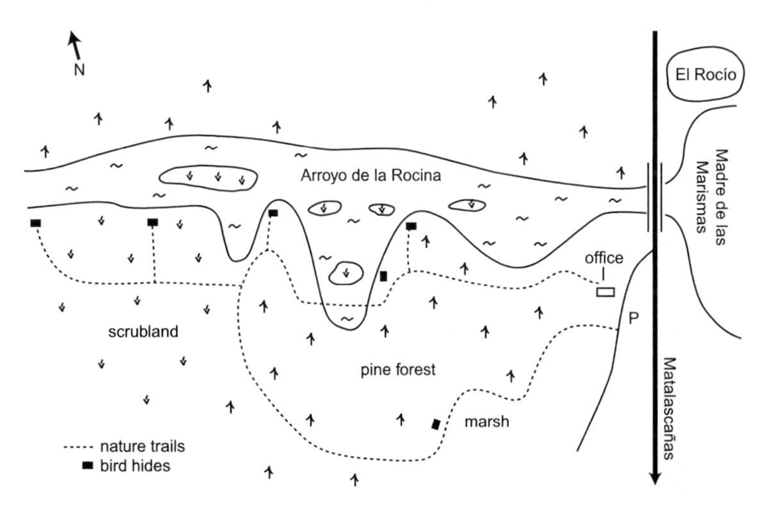

Site Six - Palacio de Acebrón

This was once a rather grand country mansion that has now been restored and turned into an exhibition centre showing the history of the rural life in the Doñana area. It is set in a mixed forest and has extensive grounds and gardens which are open to the public. There is a nature trail of some two kilometres which passes through the forest and circles the lake of Acebrón. Bench seats are scattered along the route where you can sit and observe the wide range of forest and woodland birds that can be found here.

Access is from the car-park of the previous site. Simply follow the road from the La Rocina site for about seven kilometres and you arrive at a large parking area just before the gates. This road passes through large areas of low scrub and gorse with scattered trees and is an excellent area for Hoopoes, Great Spotted Woodpeckers, Bee-eaters, Great Grey and Woodchat Shrikes, Black-eared Wheatears and scrub warblers. Overhead there are usually eagles, kites and other raptors.

From the car-park of the Palacio you can choose to either enter the gates and follow the trail around, finishing back at the car-park, or you can take the reverse route, which is my particular preference. From the bottom right-hand corner of the parking area a track leads into the wood. The trees in this area are mainly cork-oak but there are other broadleaved varieties, including poplars and strawberry trees. There is a dense floor covering of ferns and other undergrowth. The common birds to be seen here are Nightingales, Robins, Wrens, Spotted Flycatchers, Short-toed Treecreepers, Firecrests, Golden Orioles, woodpeckers, finches, tits and warblers. The Bullfinch is very scarce in Spain but there are a few pairs to be found here.

After a few hundred metres the track turns left onto a wooden causeway which takes you across a wide marsh area. Cetti's Warblers, Nightingales, Long-tailed Tits and Blackcaps are normally present at this location. Once across the marsh you come into a totally different habitat. The trees are mostly pine and the floor covering is of broom, cistus and other scrub plants. This is the most likely spot to find Crested Tits, Coal Tits and Nuthatches.

Follow the track to the left which leads downhill and back toward the Palacio. The tree canopy is more open here and you have a much better chance of seeing Jays and passing raptors. After about 500 metres turn left and cross back over the marsh area by way of another causeway. There is access to the lake half-way along but I have always found this to be very unproductive except for a few Mallards and swifts, swallows and martins.

After crossing the marsh you arrive at the Palacio and part of the gardens. The main central track leads for 400 metres back to the car-park but there are other small paths into the gardens that you can follow. At the Palacio end of the main track there is a very tall tree which, in the spring, is covered in orange flowers and attracts many birds. In May 2001, I counted at least eight Olivaceous Warblers in this one tree.

The exhibition in the Palacio may or may not be of interest to you but there is access to a roof observation platform which is ideal for watching passing birds of prey, most notably the Spanish Imperial Eagle.

Site Seven - Centro de Visitantes "El Acebuche"

The visitors centre at El Acebuche is the biggest of the centres that are open to the public. Here there is a bar, restaurant, gift shop, permanent exhibitions and audiovisual shows. It is also an excellent source of information.

The centre can be reached from the El Rocío-Matalascañas road by turning right, where signed, just before the town of Matalascañas. It would be unhelpful to give you a kilometre reading as this road is currently being up-graded and the distance markers will almost certainly change

At the entrance to the visitors centre there is a large car-park beside a picnic area. The resident Azure-winged Magpies have become very tame and will come to your table to take food if you put something down for them. They are often joined by the more common species of Magpie. White Storks nest on the roof of the visitors centre and in April and May the chicks can be clearly seen. Once inside the building that houses the shop and restaurant you may notice that Barn Swallows actually build their nests inside against the ceiling beams. Windows are normally left open at night to allow the birds access and exit. If you should decide to have a drink or meal, it is wise to check overhead before sitting down.

Inside the nature park there are about five kilometres of boardwalked trails that can be followed with eleven different bird hides. Some of these look out over the area of the "Laguna del Acebuche" which is a large expanse of reed-fringed water. Small islands are dotted about where many species of waterfowl breed. Throughout the park there are notice boards informing you of the type of trees, shrubs, herbs and grasses that are to be found.

In early 2001, an extension to the nature trail was opened, giving access to previously closed-off areas. This trail leads to two further lagoons and to hides overlooking areas of scrubland where other forms of wildlife, ie. wild boar, red deer, fallow deer, badger, fox, etc. can be found alongside the birds.

Although most of the birds that can be seen here can also be found at various other sites, this is the most likely place to find Ferruginous, Marbled and White-headed Ducks, Great Crested Grebes, Ring Ouzels, Great Spotted Cuckoos, Red-legged Partridges, Purple Herons and Siskins.

The last two hides at the eastern end of the site look out over an exceptionally reedy area where Water Rails, Savi's, Sedge, Cetti's and Moustached Warblers can all be found at the appropriate times of the year.

Map of the Acebuche Visitors Centre and nature trails

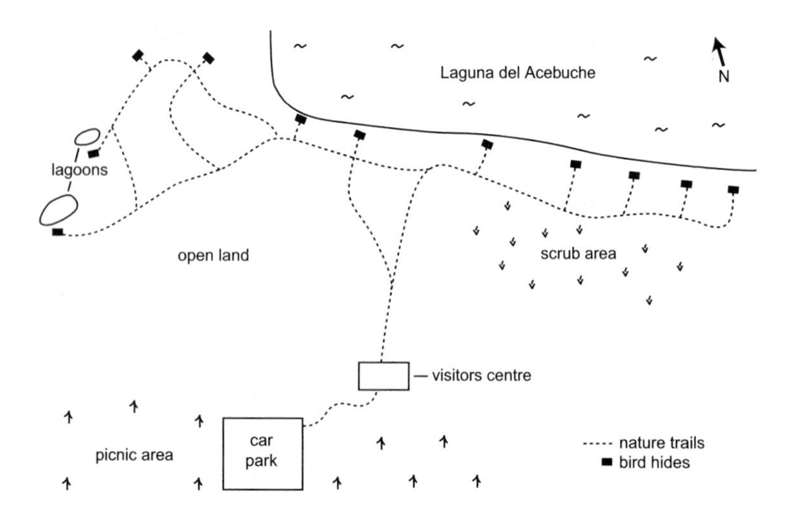

Site Eight - Matalascañas Beach

The beach is best avoided in the warmer months of the year as it is a very popular bathing resort and can get very noisy. During the winter, however, it is a good place to watch for passing gulls, shearwaters and terns. Offshore there may be Razorbills, Gannets, Red-breasted Mergansers, Black-necked Grebes and Common Scoters. The clifftop to the right of the roundabout at the seafront provides good elevated views, although reflecting sunlight can be a problem in the late afternoon. To the right of this position there is a huge rock on the beach where gulls often gather. You can turn left and drive right through the town to the far side where you will find the beach that forms part of the National Park. Here there is the entry point for the safari vehicles taking visitors into the park. Park wardens man this point and will normally deny access along the dunes but may, if asked politely, allow you to walk along the beach where waders can usual1y be found.

Site Nine - Centro de Visitantes "José Antonio Valverde" (Cerrado Garrido)

This centre is many kilometres out into the Marismas de Guadalquivir and is not easy to reach since the huge toxic waste

contamination occurred in April 1998, after which many of the old roads and tracks through parts of the marsh were changed during the clean-up operation.

The modern visitors centre has a bar/restaurant, information desk, temporary exhibitions and various audiovisual shows. Inside the centre there are large plate glass windows that look directly out over a lagoon and marshes where many species of herons, egrets, storks, ducks and waders can be seen at very close quarters. Birds of prey are always present and the Red Kite is particularly common here. Garganeys are regularly seen during the breeding season, as are Purple Herons, Montagu's Harriers, Collared Pratincoles, Red-necked Nightjars, Rufous Bush Chats and Nightingales.

There are no nature trails here although there is a raised dirt road that can be walked to either side of the centre that affords good views of the surrounding marshes, water ditches and what used to be agricultural land before the contamination. The land is very flat and the distances are great so a telescope would be a big advantage here. Directions to the site can be obtained from the other visitors centres

***Great Spotted Cuckoo** (Clamator glandarius)*

When to Visit

The whole of the Doñana region is of immense interest at any time of the year and any visit here is bound to produce a very good bird list. If your preference is for wildfowl, waders and seabirds, then October to February should suit your needs. If you are more interested in the passage migrants or the breeding population, then a visit here between March and the end of June is advisable as this is the time of maximum bird movement and breeding activity. Visits in the height of summer may prove to be a bit disappointing as many of the wet areas will have dried out completely and bird numbers can be low at such times.

General Information

Most of the sites mentioned in this chapter are accessible to wheelchair birders either in part or in whole, although I do have reservations about some of them. The following is a list of problems that may arise at each of the sites.

EL ROCÍO. The promenade is fully accessible and offers good views.

SEO BIRD OBSERVATORY. It is reached by a sandy track and steps lead down to the entrance but there is also a ramp. The upstairs viewing terrace is completely inaccessible.

BOCA DEL LOBO. This is also reached by a sandy track that may cause problems if the sand is too soft or is wet after rain. However, the track is driveable and most of the area can be viewed from a car.

PUENTE DE LA CANARIEGA. The bridge is easily accessible but the width of the hard shoulder is only about 1.5 metres, which means you are very close to passing traffic. Unfortunately, you are not allowed to park on the bridge. The track below the bridge poses the same problems as the Boca del Lobo but it is also possible to drive along the track.

CENTRO DE VISITANTES LA ROCINA. The whole of the nature trail is comprised of boardwalks which may be a bit bumpy in places. The causeways where vegetation has overgrown the track and gaps in the track to allow the safari vehicles through may be awkward to cross. All the hides have a step up or down to get in, but the third hide could also present other problems because the floor is sandy and there is very little room for a wheelchair to get between the bench seats, so you may have to sit well back from the windows.

PALACIO DE ACEBRÓN. The central track to the Palacio and some of the small garden paths are perfectly accessible but the forest walk presents many problems and safety risks. The road to the Palacio has many parking areas and much of the surrounding area can be viewed adequately from a car.

CENTRO DE VISITANTES "EL ACEBUCHE". This site is completely boardwalked and should not cause too many problems other than those described for La Rocina. The hides along the new walkway to the south of the site are ramped and have special wheelchair access viewing points.

MATALASCAÑAS BEACH. There is a track along the cliff which, although bumpy, should not cause major problems. The sandy beach is not recommended as there is a steep sand-dune to negotiate.

CENTRO DE VISITANTES "JOSÉ ANTONIO VALVERDE". Both the centre and the road walk are easily accessible.

Accommodation

Most people who visit this area find there is far too much to see in one day and spend maybe two or three days here. If you should decide to stay overnight, I suggest you find accommodation in the village of El Rocío as it is central to everything and you are right beside the marshes. There are several choices, ranging from small hostales to a very large hotel.

PENSIÓN ISÍDRO. Avenida de los Ansares. Tel. 959 442 242. This is a small but comfortable guest-house toward the back of the village. I have stayed here many times without any problems.

HOTEL CRISTINA. Calle Real. Tel. 959 442 413. A small hotel popular with birders as it is very close to the marsh. Very basic but functional.

HOTEL TORUÑO. Plaza Acebuchal. Tel. 959 442 323. A very smart little hotel and my favourite. It is reasonably priced and very comfortable. Rooms 221 and 223 are on the first floor and look out directly over the marsh, only 15 metres away.

HOTEL PUENTE DEL REY. Avenida de la Canaliega. Tel. 959 442 575. A very large hotel (237 rooms) right beside the main road and close to the marsh. It is the most expensive of all those that I have listed.

There are other hotels at Almonte and Matalascañas, where there is also a campsite.

Bird Calendar

Although my personal bird list for Doñana is pretty impressive, it cannot adequately reflect the vast range of birds that have been recorded here. I will therefore supply a list that has been compiled by searching through various records and reports.

Resident

Great Crested Grebe, Black-necked Grebe, Squacco Heron, Cattle Egret, Little Egret, Grey Heron, Spoonbill, Glossy Ibis, White Stork, Greater Flamingo, Mallard, Gadwall, Shoveler, Marbled Duck, Red-crested Pochard, Pochard, White-headed Duck, Black Kite, Red Kite, Egyptian Vulture, Griffon Vulture, Monk Vulture, Marsh Harrier, Sparrowhawk, Buzzard, Booted Eagle, Spanish Imperial Eagle, Peregrine, Kestrel, Lesser Kestrel, Red-legged Partridge, Quail, Andalusian Hemipode, Spotted Crake, Baillon's Crake, Little Crake, Water Rail, Moorhen, Purple Gallinule, Coot, Crested Coot, Little Bustard, Oystercatcher, Black-winged Stilt, Avocet, Stone Curlew, Ringed Plover, Little-ringed Plover, Kentish Plover, Grey Plover, Lapwing, Dunlin, Sanderling, Little Stint, Ruff, Black-tailed Godwit, Bar-tailed Godwit, Curlew, Whimbrel, Redshank, Greenshank, Green Sandpiper, Arctic Skua, Great Skua, Audouin's Gull, Slender-billed Gull, Blackheaded Gull, Yellow-legged Gull, Lesser Black-backed Gull, Caspian Tern, Sandwich Tern, Gull-billed Tern, Pin-tailed Sandgrouse, Rock Dove, Wood Pigeon, Collared Dove, Little Owl, Long-eared Owl, Tawny Owl, Barn Owl, Kingfisher, Hoopoe, Green Woodpecker, Great Spotted Woodpecker, Woodlark, Crested Lark, Thekla Lark, Lesser Short-toed Lark, Calandra Lark, House Martin, Barn Swallow, White Wagtail, Grey Wagtail, Robin, Stonechat, Blackbird, Mistle Thrush, Moustached Warbler, Cetti's Warbler, Fan-tailed Warbler, Blackcap, Sardinian Warbler, Dartford Warbler, Spectacled Warbler, Long-tailed Tit, Crested Tit, Coal Tit, Great Tit, Blue Tit, Nuthatch, Short-toed Treecreeper, Wren, Great Grey Shrike, Jay, Azure-winged Magpie, Magpie, Jackdaw, Raven, Spotless Starling, Spanish Sparrow, House Sparrow, Tree Sparrow, Chaffinch, Serin, Linnet, Goldfinch, Greenfinch, Corn Bunting, Cirl Bunting.

Summer / Breeding

Little Bittern, Night Heron, Purple Heron, Garganey, Short-toed Eagle, Montagu's Harrier, Hobby, Collared Pratincole, Common Tern, Little Tern, Gull-billed Tern, Black Tern, Whiskered Tern, Turtle Dove, Great Spotted Cuckoo, Cuckoo, Scops Owl, Red-necked

Nightjar, Common Swift, Pallid Swift, Bee-eater, Short-toed Lark, Sand Martin, Red-rumped Swallow, Tawny Pipit, Yellow Wagtail, Nightingale, Rufous Bush Chat, Redstart, Black-eared Wheatear, Savi's Warbler, Reed Warbler, Great Reed Warbler, Olivaceous Warbler, Melodious Warbler, Orphean Warbler, Subalpine Warbler, Spotted Flycatcher, Woodchat Shrike, Golden Oriole, Hawfinch, Ortolan.

Winter

Red-throated Diver, Mediterranean Shearwater, Gannet, Cormorant, Great White Egret, Snow Goose, Greylag Goose, Brent Goose, Barnacle Goose, Canada Goose, Shelduck, Wigeon, Teal, Northern Pintail, Ferruginous Duck, Tufted Duck, Common Scoter, Velvet Scoter, Red-breasted Merganser, Osprey, Black-shouldered Kite, Hen Harrier, Bonelli's Eagle, Merlin, Common Crane, Stone Curlew, Golden Plover, Red Knot, Common Snipe, Great Snipe, Woodcock, Spotted Redshank, Marsh Sandpiper, Wood Sandpiper, Common Sandpiper, Turnstone, Grey Phalarope, Little Gull, Mediterranean Gull, Kittiwake, Razorbill, Wryneck, Skylark, Crag Martin, Meadow Pipit, Water Pipit, Richard's Pipit, Dunnock, Bluethroat, Black Redstart, Ring Ouzel, Fieldfare, Redwing, Song Thrush, Iberian Chiffchaff, Firecrest, Penduline Tit, Starling, Siskin, Bullfinch, Crossbill, Rock Bunting, Reed Bunting.

Passage Migrants

Cory's Shearwater, European Storm Petrel, Black Stork, Honey Buzzard, Curlew Sandpiper, Temminck's Stint, Purple Sandpiper, Short-eared Owl, Alpine Swift, Roller, Tree Pipit, Whinchat, Northern Wheatear, Grasshopper Warbler, Sedge Warbler, Garden Warbler, Bonelli's Warbler, Willow Warbler, Pied Flycatcher.

Azure-winged Magpie *(Cyanopica cyana)*

Almería Province

The province of Almería is to the south-east of the country and is the driest region in Spain, holding Europe's only area to be classified as a desert. The interior of the province is sparsely populated and underdeveloped whereas the coastal strip, called the Costa de Almería, has large holiday resorts and vast expanses of agricultural land, much of the latter being under unsightly white plastic greenhouses.

Both tourism and agriculture play a very important role in the local economy and it is, perhaps, because of this that past construction had been allowed to continue without any evidence of sensible planning. Due to this, many important habitats suitable to birds and other wildlife have been sacrificed. Even so, Almería is still an important ornithological region with some of Spain's (and Europe's) scarcest birds, such as Dupont's Lark, Trumpeter Finch, Marbled Duck and White-headed Duck, being present in varying numbers, at suitable locations, throughout the year.

General map of the area and sites in Almería

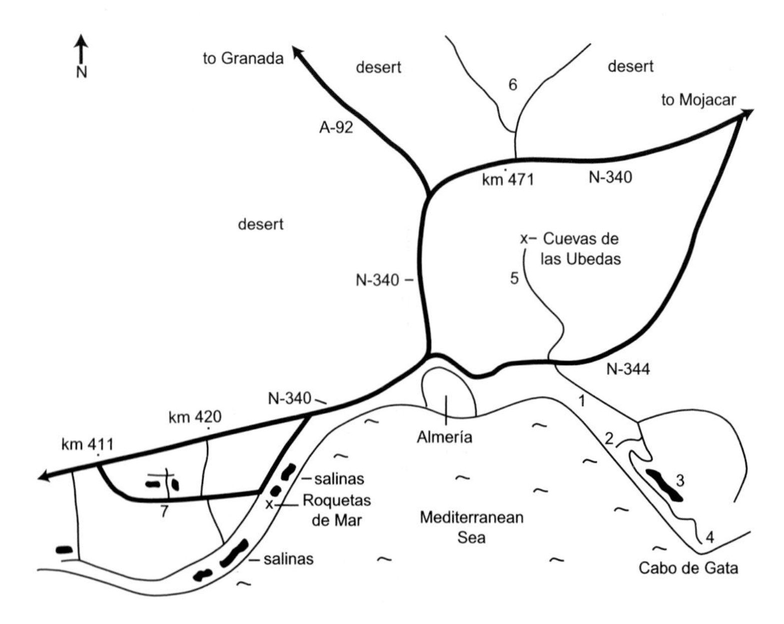

1. Centro de Visitantes de las Amoladeras. 2. Rambla de Morales

/Playa del Charco. 3. Reserva de Salinas de Cabo de Gata. 4. Reserva de Cabo de Gata. 5. The Inland Steppes. 6. The Tabernas Desert area. 7. Cañada de las Norias.

The vast range of habitats includes rivers, lagoons, salinas (saltpans), steppes, deserts, mountains, sea-cliffs, beaches and agricultural land.

Much of the area is within the boundaries of reserves or nature parks where many nature trails can be found, although this particular activity should only be contemplated in the cooler months of the year as from April through to the end of October the temperatures can be oppressively hot and regularly rise to over 40°C. during the afternoons.

I have included seven sites from Almería that I feel produces the maximum number of attractive species throughout the year.

Cabo de Gata

The Cabo de Gata is a volcanic cape on the Almería coastline that lies within the boundaries of the Parque Natural Cabo de Gata-Nijar, which covers an area of 49,547 hectares. Within the park there are numerous marine and land "Reserves".

As there are several quite distinct sites in the Cabo de Gata area, I will describe them separately, in the order which I feel is best to visit them.

Centro de Visitantes de las Amoladeras

This is a very important stop to make as it is here, at the visitors centre, where the best books, leaflets and other information concerning the park and the surrounding area can be obtained. The centre, which is run by the A.M.A. and the S.E.O. has a shop which sells a wide range of items and there are very impressive audiovisual displays, including the calls of some of the scarcer birds that can be found in the reserve and at other locations in the region.

There is a nature trail that can be taken which leads from behind the centre and crosses the road into steppe land but it is poorly marked and I do not recommend it. However, the first part of this trail, from behind the centre to the road, passes through sandy scrubland and a plantation of agaves (large spiny-leaved succulent plants) where you may find Rollers, Great Grey and Woodchat

Shrikes, Stone Curlews, Little Bustards, Short-toed and Lesser Short-toed Larks, Rufous Bush Chats, Dupont's Larks, Trumpeter Finches and Red-necked Nightjars, along with a good variety of warblers.

Access

The easiest way to reach the centre and Cabo de Gata is via the N-340, turning off onto the N-344 at junction km 448. You should then turn right where signed for Cabo de Gata just beyond km 14. At the first roundabout turn left and follow the road for about 5.5 kms until you reach the centre, which is well signposted, on the right-hand side of the road.

There is a large car park which offers good views of the surrounding scrubland, but please be aware that the area to the south, ie. toward the sea, is a "reserve" area and you should not enter into this land. The only accessible walk is indicated by arrows on small wooden posts at the front right and rear right corners of the centre and runs diagonally toward the road in a north-easterly direction.

When to Visit

The centre is open every day between 10am-2pm and from 5.30-8.30pm.. Many of the bird species that can be found in the reserve are resident but obviously the spring/summer periods hold more in both numbers and species.

General Information

The car-park, centre and the viewing areas beside the centre are all easily accessible by wheelchair. The nature trail is sandy in some places and unevenly rocky in others and is unsuitable for wheelchair birders or for those with other mobility problems.

Rambla de Morales - Playa del Charco

This is a river/lagoon situated on the Playa del Charco where a good number of interesting species can be found at any time of the year. The shallow lagoon is formed when the river ceases to flow and measures some 800 metres in length by 150 metres in width. At the beach end there is mainly tamarisk and other scrub vegetation that offers some cover and at the far end there are trees and dense reedbeds. There is the possibility that the lagoon may dry out completely in dry years but I have never known this. During my latest visit in mid-July 2001 there was plenty of water remaining and also plenty of birds. Typical species include Greater Flamingos, Black-winged Stilts, Marsh Harriers, gulls, terns, ducks, herons, egrets, larks, finches and warblers. There are no restricting fences or barriers and it is possible to get right to the water's edge, using suitable cover so as not to disturb the birds.

Access

From the previous site at the visitors centre, turn right and at the next road junction keep right, heading toward Cabo de Gata. About 500 metres beyond the junction there is a turning on the right that leads to "Camping Cabo de Gata". Turn here and follow the road for 1.5 kms. As you near the campsite there is a small crossroads. Do not turn right, toward the campsite, but instead continue straight ahead on a very poorly surfaced road between plastic greenhouses and the campsite. After 800 metres the road ends and becomes a dirt-track.

There is a junction 100 metres further on where you turn right and proceed for 200 metres until you reach the reedbeds at the top end of the lagoon/river. Turn left and follow the track, which runs beside the lagoon, to a parking area on the beach. If the river is in flow, only this side of the river will be accessible to you. If a lagoon has formed you can walk, or drive, all the way around (approximately 2 kilometres).

Greater Flamingos are present in small numbers throughout the year and Kentish Plovers, Little Bitterns, Black-winged Stilts, Marsh Harriers, Moorhens, Coots and both Great Grey and Woodchat Shrikes breed on or near to the lagoon. The scrubby sand-dunes behind the beach offer another opportunity to look for Stone Curlews, larks and warblers. This is not reserve land and there are no restrictions if you wish to walk in this area.

General map of the Rambla de Morales / Lagoon

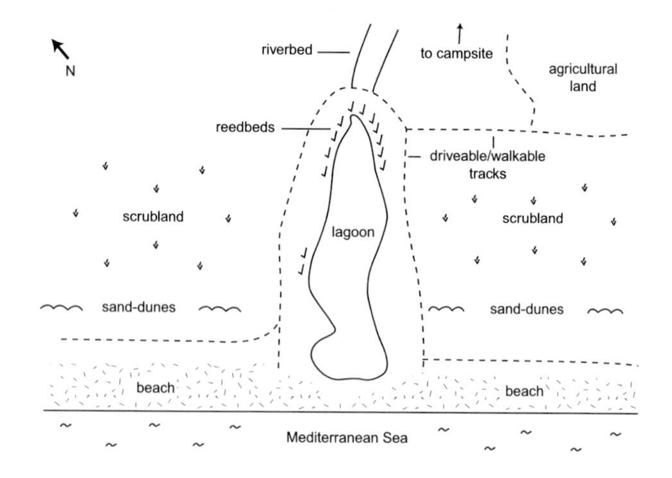

During the spring/summer there are usually Caspian, Whiskered, Little and Gull-billed Terns present and even a few waders such as Avocets, Oystercatchers, Curlew Sandpipers, Spotted Redshanks, Dunlins, Common Sandpipers and Collared Pratincoles. Obviously, both the numbers and species of waders and ducks etc. is very much higher in the winter and during passage periods, when just about anything can turn up.

The reedbeds at the top end of the lagoon shelter Cetti's, Melodious, Reed, Great Reed and Moustached Warblers, along with Nightingales, Little Bitterns, Little Grebes, Moorhens, herons and ducks.

Offshore views of Gannets, shearwaters, grebes and other seabirds may be had and gull flocks, mainly Black-headed and Yellow-legged, often form on the beach or on the lagoon. Careful scanning of these flocks may reveal Audouin's and Mediterranean Gulls and Kittiwakes. Slender-billed Gulls are also a possibility.

The river/lagoon should be checked above the reed areas for Hoopoes, Rollers, Rufous Bush Chats, Black-bellied Sandgrouse, Short-toed Larks and warbler species. This area is not very productive for birds of prey although Kestrels and Marsh Harriers are both fairly common. Ospreys are sometimes present in the winter and resident Little Owls can often be seen nearer the agricultural land.

When to Visit

Although this site can be very rewarding at any time of the year it is at its most productive during the passage periods and in the spring, once most of the breeding species have arrived. Obviously, from a birder's point of view, the site is far more interesting once the lagoon has formed as the waders' numbers are much higher then as they fly in to feed in the shallow waters.

General Information

A lot of this site is wheelchair accessible and those areas that are not can be viewed from numerous parking places along the banks of the river/lagoon. Although distances are not a great problem here, a telescope will always be an advantage. Reflecting sunlight is not a major problem but heat haze can affect views if you are looking along the lagoon from the beach end.

The Playa del Charco is a public beach which is usually very quiet in the winter months. Even in the height of summer it does not become too busy, so human disturbance is minimal.

Bird Calendar

Resident

Little Grebe, Cattle Egret, Little Egret, Greater Flamingo, Mallard, Marsh Harrier, Buzzard, Kestrel, Red-legged Partridge, Moorhen, Coot, Little Bustard, Oystercatcher, Avocet, Stone Curlew, Little-ringed Plover, Kentish Plover, Dunlin, Curlew Sandpiper, Black-tailed Godwit, Redshank, Common Sandpiper, Audouin's Gull, Black-headed Gull, Yellow-legged Gull, Sandwich Tern, Black-bellied Sandgrouse, Rock Dove, Collared Dove, Little Owl, Kingfisher, Hoopoe, Woodlark, Crested Lark, Thekla Lark, Lesser Short-toed Lark, Dupont's Lark, White Wagtail, Grey Wagtail, Stonechat, Black Redstart, Blackbird, Cetti's Warbler, Fan-tailed Warbler, Sardinian Warbler, Dartford Warbler, Great Tit, Blue Tit, Great Grey Shrike, Raven, Spotless Starling, Spanish Sparrow, House Sparrow, Linnet, Goldfinch, Greenfinch, Trumpeter Finch, Corn Bunting, Rock Bunting, Cirl Bunting.

Summer / Breeding

Little Bittern, Purple Heron, Short-toed Eagle, Booted Eagle, Black -winged Stilt, Collared Pratincole, Common Tern, Little Tern,

Gull-billed Tern, Whiskered Tern, Turtle Dove, Red-necked Nightjar, Common Swift, Pallid Swift, Bee-eater, Roller, Short-toed Lark, Calandra Lark, Sand Martin, House Martin, Red-rumped Swallow, Barn Swallow, Yellow Wagtail, Nightingale, Rufous Bush Chat, Black-eared Wheatear, Reed Warbler, Great Reed Warbler, Moustached Warbler, Olivaceous Warbler, Melodious Warbler, Spectacled Warbler, Spotted Flycatcher, Woodchat Shrike.

Winter

Great Crested Grebe, Black-necked Grebe, Gannet, Cormorant, Grey Heron, Shelduck, Gadwall, Wigeon, Shoveler, Red-crested Pochard, Pochard, Common Scoter, Osprey, Ringed Plover, Grey Plover, Golden Plover, Lapwing, Sanderling, Ruff, Common Snipe, Bar-tailed Godwit, Green Sandpiper, Turnstone, Mediterranean Gull, Little Gull, Lesser Black-backed Gull, Kittiwake., Razorbill, Skylark, Crag Martin, Meadow Pipit, Ring Ouzel, Blackcap, Iberian Chiffchaff.

Passage Migrants

Cory's Shearwater, Mediterranean Shearwater, Red Knot, Little Stint, Curlew, Whimbrel, Marsh Sandpiper, Greenshank, Wood Sandpiper, Great Skua, Arctic Skua, Slender-billed Gull, Caspian Tern, Black Tern, Tree Pipit, Whinchat, Willow Warbler.

Slender-billed Gull *(Larus genei)*

Reserva de Salinas de Cabo de Gata

The "salinas" are a vast area of wetlands created by a natural lagoon, which stretch for over 4 kms between the villages of San Miguel del Cabo de Gata and La Almadraba de Monteleva (San Miguel and Almadraba for short). There used to be a full scale salt producing operation here but nowadays the craft only continues on a much smaller scale. There are two distinct aspects of this site. To the north-west, near to San Miguel, there are major wetlands surrounded by low sand-dunes, scrubland and reedbeds. To the south-east there are the saltpans that are currently in use, an area greatly favoured by large flocks of gulls.

Two-thirds of the way along the salinas there is a bird observatory which overlooks parts of both the lagoon and the saltpans. This offers the opportunity to view many of the resident, breeding and migratory species that are to be found here.

The sand-dunes and scrubland between the lagoon and the coast road are also of interest and clearly defined paths run through this part of the site. There is also a walkable track to the far side of the lagoon which can be found behind the saltpans in Almadraba.

Access

From the previous site at the Playa del Charco, return to the road and turn right, passing through the village of Pujaire, toward the cape. As you approach San Miguel the salinas are evident on the left. There is only one very small parking spot on this road but there is parking further along the road opposite the Hotel Mediterraneo. From here you can walk across the dunes to view the north-western area where waders, herons, egrets and wildfowl are usually to be found, either in the reedbeds or on the many small islands.

Continue into San Miguel and turn left at the first roundabout, which will lead you right along the beach. Just before the large stone tower (*Torre de San Miguel*) you may notice an information board which advises you that the bird hide (*Observatorio de Aves*) is 4 kms along the road. Ignore this information as the distance to the turn-off to the hide is only 2.9 kms from this board. The actual turn-off is on the left-hand side of the road and it is a dirt track directly opposite the second metal observation tower on the beach. The hide is 150 metres down the track and is surrounded by a screen fence.

To the left the hide offers views of the end of the lagoon and some of the islands where Greater Flamingos, herons, egrets, waders and wildfowl can be seen at close quarters. To the right there are the saltpans where gulls, including many Audouin's, usually congregate. However, the view here is restricted and you would be advised to walk 50 metres to the right of the hide where a little knoll gives a much better view. The surrounding scrubland should be checked for finches, larks, warblers, wagtails and chats.

When to Visit

Any visit to this site, irrespective of the time of year, will produce a very good bird list. Distances are great and heat haze can be a major problem in the warmer months of the year when morning or evening visits should be considered.

General Information

The area surrounding the salinas is mostly sand-dunes and scrubland which would be difficult to negotiate with a wheelchair, though the central tracks are much firmer and should not present too many problems. The bird hide is of an awkward construction which involves climbing a step to sit on the bench seats. The windows are above wheelchair height and the bench seats do not allow enough room for a wheelchair to get between them. If the hide proves unsuitable, you can drive to the little knoll to the right of the hide and get almost as good views from there, although you are an extra 50 metres away from the main area of bird activity.

General map of the Reserva de Salinas de Cabo de Gata

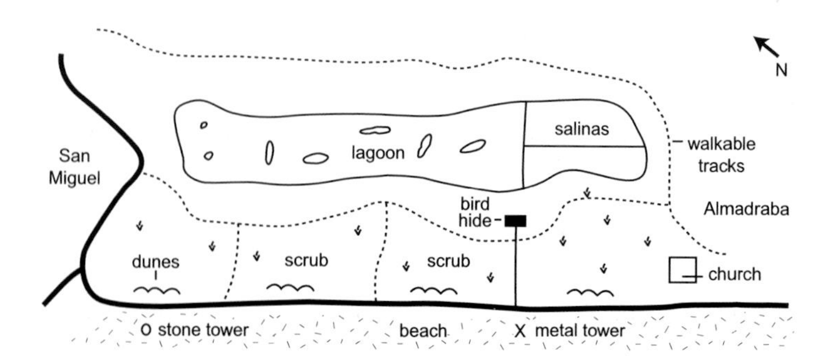

Bird Calendar

Resident

Great Crested Grebe, Little Grebe, Gannet, Cattle Egret, Little Egret, Grey Heron, Greater Flamingo, Mallard, Pochard, Marsh Harrier, Buzzard, Peregrine, Kestrel, Red-legged Partridge, Water Rail, Moorhen, Coot, Avocet, Stone Curlew, Kentish Plover, Dunlin, Curlew Sandpiper, Blacktailed Godwit, Redshank, Common Sandpiper, Audouin's Gull, Black-headed Gull, Yellow-legged Gull, Sandwich Tern, Rock Dove, Collared Dove, Little Owl, Kingfisher, Hoopoe, Woodlark, Crested Lark, Lesser Short-toed Lark, Crag Martin, White Wagtail, Grey Wagtail, Stonechat, Blackbird, Cetti's Warbler, Fan-tailed Warbler, Sardinian Warbler, Dartford Warbler, Great Tit, Blue Tit, Great Grey Shrike, Jackdaw, Spotless Starling, Spanish Sparrow, House Sparrow, Serin, Linnet, Goldfinch, Greenfinch, Corn Bunting, Cirl Bunting.

Summer / Breeding

Little Bittern, Purple Heron, Short-toed Eagle, Booted Eagle, Lesser Kestrel, Black-winged Stilt, Collared Pratincole, Little-ringed Plover, Common Tern, Little Tern, Gull-billed Tern, Black Tern, Whiskered Tern, Turtle Dove, Red-necked Nightjar, Common Swift, Pallid Swift, Bee-eater, Roller, Sand Martin, House Martin, Red-rumped Swallow, Barn Swallow, Yellow Wagtail, Nightingale, Black-eared Wheatear, Reed Warbler, Great Reed Warbler, Olivaceous Warbler, Melodious Warbler, Spotted Flycatcher, Woodchat Shrike.

Winter

Black-necked Grebe, Cormorant, Shelduck, Gadwall, Wigeon, Teal, Shoveler, Red-crested Pochard, Osprey, Merlin, Oystercatcher, Ringed Plover, Grey Plover, Golden Plover, Lapwing, Sanderling, Little Stint, Ruff, Common Snipe, Bar-tailed Godwit, Whimbrel, Greenshank, Green Sandpiper, Turnstone, Little Gull, Mediterranean Gull, Lesser Black-backed Gull, Kittiwake, Skylark, Meadow Pipit, Ring Ouzel, Iberian Chiffchaff.

Passage Migrants

Squacco Heron, Spoonbill, White Stork, Black Stork, Garganey, Pintail, Red Knot, Curlew, Spotted Redshank, Marsh Sandpiper, Caspian Tern, White-winged Black Tern, Tree Pipit, Whinchat, Redstart, Willow Warbler.

Reserva de Cabo de Gata

The area around the cape is of great interest as there is a wide, but scarce, range of birds to be found here. The mountain range of the Sierra de Cabo de Gata, along with the steppes, lighthouse, mirador, rocks, cliffs and of course the sea, all offer opportunities to watch for birds. There are parking places at the Playa del Corralete and at the lighthouse.

A road to the left just before the beach leads towards the town of San José but you can only drive for about 1.5 kms as the road is closed to vehicles by a barrier. Stopping anywhere along this road and surveying both the hills and sea-cliffs and also the surrounding scrub areas may produce birds of prey, notably Peregrines, Kestrels, Lesser Kestrels and both Booted and Bonelli's Eagles. Black Wheatears, Blue Rock Thrushes and Great Grey Shrikes are fairly common residents and there are small populations of Trumpeter Finches and Dupont's Larks amongst the more common finch and lark species. Seasonal visitors include Red-necked Nightjars, Calandra Larks, Spectacled Warblers, Black-eared Wheatears, Woodchat Shrikes and Rufous Bush Chats.

The mirador at the lighthouse is a good vantage point to watch for passing and offshore seabirds such as Razorbills, Shags, Cormorants, Gannets, gulls, skuas, terns and shearwaters. Unfortunately, the mirador is a very popular tourist attraction and you may find it more peaceful to move to another cliff-top location where you can watch without being disturbed.

Access

This is very straightforward as you simply follow the road from the previous site, through the village of Almadraba, to reach the cape. Walking along the beach and near to the rocks can often produce a few waders, such as Sanderlings, Turnstones, Whimbrels and plovers. The mirador gives you good elevated views out over the sea and time spent here may prove rewarding for raptors as well as seabirds.

The rocky hillsides are where you are most likely to see the Blue Rock Thrushes, Rock Buntings and wheatears whilst the scrubland and dry watercourses can produce a good variety of warblers and chats.

General map of the Reserva de Cabo de Gata

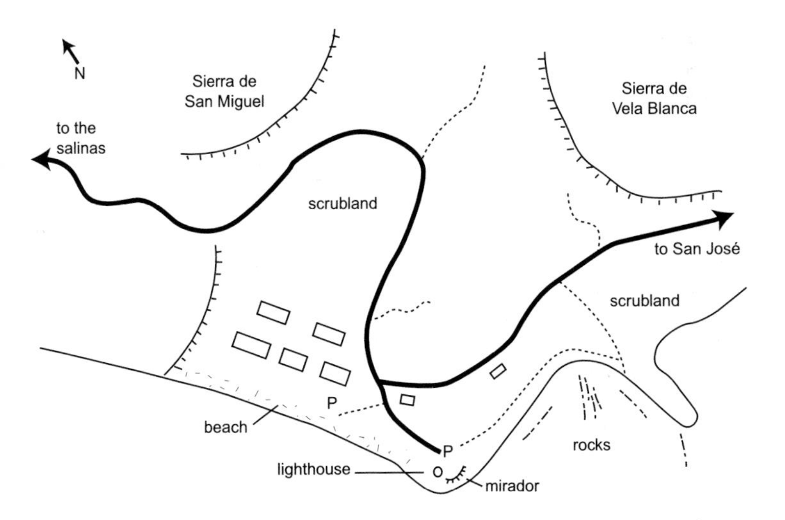

When to Visit

The site is of interest at any time, as far as birding is concerned, with numerous resident species being present. The spring and early summer should produce the maximum number of land birds whilst the autumn to spring period will produce more seabirds, either offshore or as they pass along the coast.

The best times of the day are mornings and evenings when the birds are most active.

General Information

This is not a particularly good site for disabled birders, although various off-road parking places will enable you to see parts of the site without leaving the car.

The road from Almadraba to the cape is very narrow with many sharp bends. It is also quite busy with tourist traffic so care needs to be taken here.

Bird Calendar

Resident

Gannet, Shag, Buzzard, Bonelli's Eagle, Peregrine, Kestrel, Red-legged Partridge, Audouin's Gull, Black-headed Gull, Yellow-legged Gull, Sandwich Tern, Rock Dove, Little Owl, Eagle Owl, Hoopoe, Crested Lark, Thekla Lark, Dupont's Lark, Crag Martin, White Wagtail, Stonechat, Black Redstart, Black Wheatear, Blue Rock Thrush, Blackbird, Fan-tailed Warbler, Sardinian Warbler, Dartford Warbler, Wren, Great Grey Shrike, Jackdaw, Raven, Spotless Starling, Rock Sparrow, House Sparrow, Serin, Goldfinch, Greenfinch, Linnet, Trumpeter Finch, Rock Bunting.

Summer / Breeding

Short-toed Eagle, Booted Eagle, Lesser Kestrel, Little Tern, Red-necked Nightjar, Alpine Swift, Common Swift, Pallid Swift, Bee-eater, Roller, House Martin, Red-rumped Swallow, Barn Swallow, Nightingale, Rufous Bush Chat, Black-eared Wheatear, Olivaceous Warbler, Spectacled Warbler, Woodchat Shrike.

Winter

Black-necked Grebe, Cormorant, Osprey, Oystercatcher, Ringed Plover, Sanderling, Whimbrel, Redshank, Common Sandpiper, Turnstone, Great Skua, Arctic Skua, Little Gull, Mediterranean Gull, Lesser Black-backed Gull, Kittiwake, Razorbill, Meadow Pipit, Ring Ouzel, Iberian Chiffchaff.

Passage Migrants

Cory's Shearwater, Mediterranean Shearwater, European Storm Petrel, Shelduck, Eleonora's Falcon, Caspian Tern, Common Tern, Gull-billed Tern, Whinchat, Redstart, Northern Wheatear.

The Inland Steppes

This is an open arid expanse of steppe country and semi-desert situated some 5-15 kms inland from the coast. It is here, in this barren wilderness, that many of the "prize" bird species may be found. The area is very large and any stopping points that I mention in the description may prove successful or disappointing. At this site it really is a case of being in the right place at the right time if you are going to "tick" the more elusive species, such as Little Bustard, Dupont's Lark, Trumpeter Finch and Black-bellied Sandgrouse.

The countryside is riven by dry ramblas which are created by the effects of flash-flooding that occasionally occurs following torrential rain storms. Some of these riverbeds are worth investigating for any of the above mentioned birds, especially if water is still present.

Other attractive residents of the site include Stone Curlew, Lesser Short-toed Lark, Great Grey Shrike, Rock Sparrow, Rock Bunting and Dartford Warbler. During the breeding season you should find Bee-eater, Roller, Black-eared Wheatear, Woodchat Shrike and possibly, both Spectacled and Subalpine Warblers.

Toward the end of the site the road runs into the foothills of the Sierra de Alhamilla where Ravens, eagles and other birds of prey can be found along with Blue Rock Thrushes and Black Wheatears.

Access

If you are travelling to the area on the N-340, turn onto the N-344 at km 448. From here, turn left onto the ALP-209 just before km 14, where signed for Centro Penitenciario and Cuevas de los Ubedas.

If you are coming from the Cabo de Gata, return to the Almería-San José junction and turn left towards Almería, passing the visitors centre. At the first roundabout, follow the signs for Almería N-344. This is a connecting road that leads for just over a kilometre to the N-344, where you turn left towards Almería. After 600 metres turn right onto the ALP-209.

The road now leads into the plains and steppe lands, passing the penitentiary after 1.8 kms. After 3 kms you pass under the motorway bridge and a kilometre further on you reach a large pull-off area on the right. Park here and survey the surrounding area before walking down to the river/riverbed to the right and then walking upstream towards the cliff-faces and farm buildings. This area, as with so many other spots along the route, can produce wheatears,

warblers, larks and finches. Little Owls, Great Grey Shrikes and Kestrels are quite common around the farmland, and in the summer you may see both Short-toed and Booted Eagles.

Further along the road, on the left, there is a large road leading uphill. This is of no interest as it leads directly to a new waste disposal plant where many hectares of land have been scraped and levelled for what, I assume, will become a land-fill rubbish dump. If this is the case then, in common with other rubbish dumps, it may attract birds once it is operational.

Continue along the road until you reach the village of Cuevas de los Medinas. Follow through the village taking the left-hand fork to Cuevas de los Ubedas. You can stop anywhere along the road to search the immediate area but the next stopping point that I can recommend is at the bridge which crosses over a rambla. Once again, a walk up the river/riverbed to the left may prove productive as Black Wheatears, Rollers, Bee-eaters, Hoopoes and Trumpeter Finches can all be found here.

General map of the Steppe lands

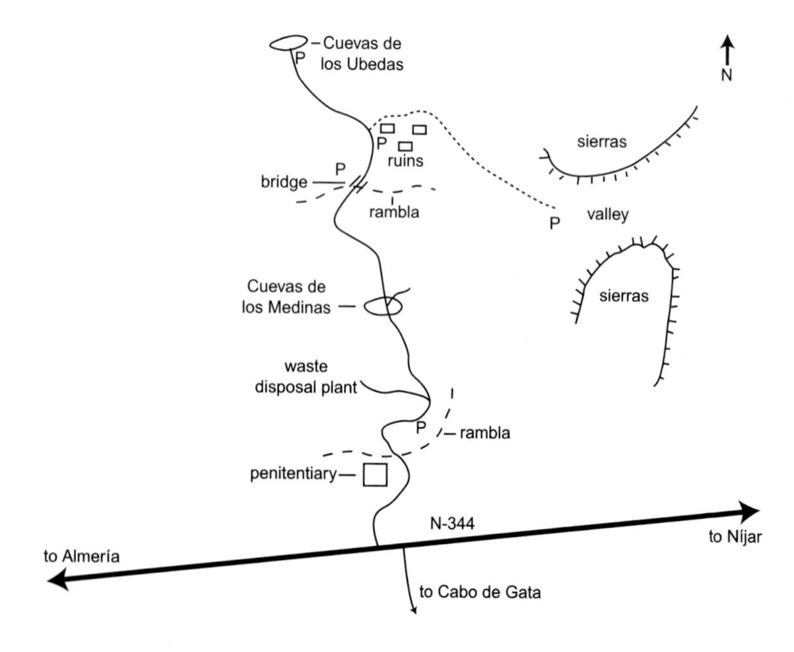

A further 800 metres along the road there are some ruined buildings on the right where the surrounding land has been terraced. This area often produces a good bird list and is exceptional for Rock Buntings, Rollers, shrikes and larks. The sparse orchards in the valley to the left of the road should also be checked for Rock Sparrows, warblers and finches.

Behind the ruins there is a track which will lead you down into a very dry and windless valley on the right where you stand a reasonable chance of finding Black-bellied Sandgrouse, Hoopoes, Black Redstarts, Blue Rock Thrushes, buntings, wheatears and larks. This track is driveable but care needs to be taken. If you decide to walk the track, be sure you take a supply of liquids with you.

The road now continues for another 1.5 kms before ending at the very small village (just a few houses really) of La Cuevas de los Ubedas. At the end of the road there is a deep crater where the earth is a purple shade. In the crater there are a few fruit trees where warblers, finches and larks can be viewed from above. This marks the end of the site and you have to turn around and return the way you came.

When to Visit

The site can be of interest at any time with a good number of resident species always present. The breeding season adds a touch of colour to an otherwise drab area, with Bee-eaters, Rollers, Woodchat Shrikes and Black-eared Wheatears all being prominent.

Please note that this is a particularly dry and hot region and you should ensure that you carry an adequate supply of water with you.

Morning and evening visits should be considered to coincide with peak bird activity and to avoid the hottest temperatures.

The Tabernas Desert Area

The "Desierto de Tabernas" is the only area in Europe to be officially classified as a desert region. The area records an average annual rainfall of about 200mm and most of this falls in a few torrential downpours which cause flash-flooding. The many gullies and ramblas are a testament to the power of the water's movement. Generally the region is extremely arid and summer daytime temperatures can climb to well over 40°C. Even during the winter period, visits here can be uncomfortably warm. To combat the effect of the heat you should plan to visit the site in the morning or evening, and even then it is wise to take an adequate water supply with you.

The desert is very sparsely vegetated with low scrub plants such as broom and tamarisk. Vision, therefore, is quite good and it is fairly easy to spot any birds that may be in the vicinity. However, the desert is so vast that it is possible to walk quite long distances without seeing anything. Birding here really is down to luck and being in the right place at the right time.

Access

The best and most accessible area of the desert can be reached directly from the main N-340 highway by turning off onto the A-349, signed for Macael, Castro de Filabres and Velefique, at km 471.4. After about one kilometre, turn left toward Castro de Filabres and explore the area up to that village. It would be difficult to identify any particular place along the route as one spot can be as equally good, or bad, as any other. However, one site that should be investigated is around a large abandoned building which is about 2 kms along the road on the left. This has proved reliable in the past for Rollers, Bee-eaters, Trumpeter Finches, Stone Curlews, Great Grey Shrikes, Little Owls and various warblers. Alas, not all at the same time. Apart from this, any rambla or gully can prove profitable.

To find the Black-bellied Sandgrouse or Dupont's Larks usually involves a trek of at least a few hundred metres into the desert or along a rambla, but even this may not prove successful. You should therefore plan to make numerous stops along the route. I recommend you do not proceed beyond Castro de Filabres as the roads are in poor condition and you should return the way you came. You can, of course, take the road to Velefique, again returning along the same road. On the return trip I suggest you explore the small orchards and the dense cacti growths near to the junction where you turn right, back toward the N-340. This area can provide you with

a few seasonal visitors which can include Rufous Bush Chats, Rollers, Woodchat Shrikes and Orphean, Olivaceous and Melodious Warblers.

General map of the Tabernas Desert

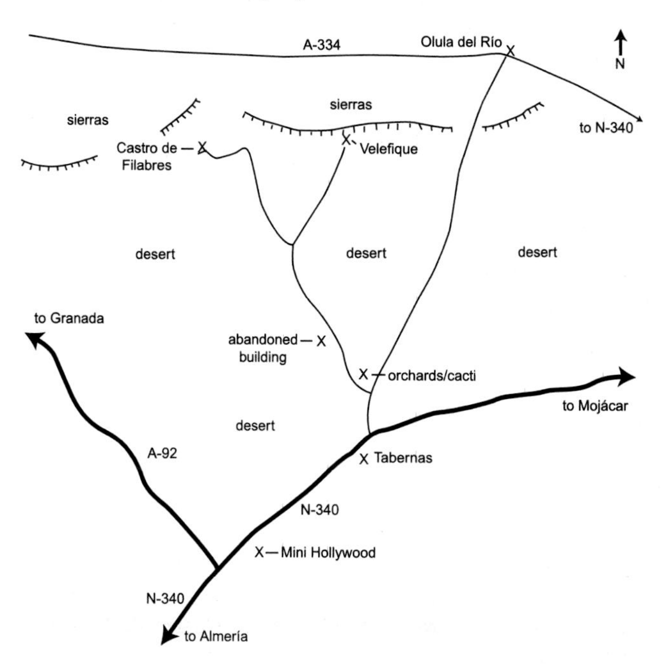

Obviously there is a great deal more to the desert than this route and you may wish to explore further areas. Turning left at the junction previously referred to will take you through the desert, passing through Noria, Tahal, Macael and Olula del Río, where you can turn right onto the A-334. This road will then eventually take you back to the N-340 near to the town of Huércal Overa. This part of the region is more mountainous and you stand a reasonable chance of seeing Blue Rock Thrushes, Black Wheatears, Rock Buntings and a few eagles and other birds of prey, amongst which both Golden and Bonelli's Eagles are distinct possibilities.

When to Visit

Although there is a very interesting resident population of species to be found here, there is also a very attractive list of summer visitors that can be found. To see the complete range of species, or to at least have a chance of seeing them, you should try to plan your visit in April or May, before

the summer temperature becomes too oppressive. All visits, regardless of the season, would be better undertaken in the morning or evening as this would coincide with the maximum bird activity.

General Information

As this is a desert area with many gorges, gullies and ramblas, it would be very difficult for disabled birders to really get off-road to look for birds. However, much of the area is very flat and the road only attracts minimal traffic. This gives the opportunity to at least see parts of the surrounding countryside and hopefully some of the better bird species. Other areas can be adequately viewed from within a car, either from the road or from various pull-off areas. I should stress that once you have entered the desert there are no petrol stations, so make sure you have adequate fuel in your car before leaving the main road.

Bird Calendar

Resident

Buzzard, Bonelli's Eagle, Golden Eagle, Peregrine, Kestrel, Red-legged Partridge, Stone Curlew, Black-bellied Sandgrouse, Collared Dove, Little Owl, Eagle Owl, Hoopoe, Crested Lark, Thekla Lark, Dupont's Lark, Crag Martin, White Wagtail, Stonechat, Black Redstart, Black Wheatear, Blue Rock Thrush, Blackbird, Sardinian Warbler, Dartford Warbler, Wren, Great Grey Shrike, Jackdaw, Raven, Rock Sparrow, House Sparrow, Serin, Linnet, Goldfinch, Greenfinch, Trumpeter Finch, Rock Bunting.

Summer / Breeding

Short-toed Eagle, Booted Eagle, Lesser Kestrel, Turtle Dove, Great Spotted Cuckoo, Scops Owl, Red-necked Nightjar, Common Swift, Pallid Swift, Bee-eater, Roller, House Martin, Red-rumped Swallow, Barn Swallow, Tawny Pipit, Nightingale, Rufous Bush Chat, Black-eared Wheatear, Olivaceous Warbler, Melodious Warbler, Orphean Warbler, Spectacled Warbler, Subalpine Warbler, Spotted Flycatcher, Woodchat Shrike, Ortolan Bunting.

Winter

Meadow Pipit, Iberian Chiffchaff, Cirl Bunting.

Passage Migrants

Whinchat, Redstart, Northern Wheatear.

Cañada de las Norias

This wetland site was originally created by the large scale excavation of the area to provide soil for the vast expanse of plastic greenhouses in the 1970's and '80's. It then became a local dumping ground for all manner of waste and rubbish. It has since become flooded and is now a very mature site with dense reedbeds and large areas of tamarisk and oleander cover around the edges of the lake.

At the present time (July 2001) the site is being upgraded and prepared by the Sociedad Española de Ornitología as an ornithological Reserve of Special Importance. An entry point is being made and, I suspect, a perimeter fence may be erected. It is also possible that bird observation hides may be built in the future.

Although only small in comparison to some other sites in the area it is, in my opinion, one of the finest sites for bird variety that I have visited and is bound to produce an excellent bird list at any time of the year. Typical resident species include Hoopoes, Gadwalls, Pochards, White-headed Ducks, Marbled Ducks, Purple Gallinules, Lesser Short-toed Larks, herons, egrets, gulls, waders, warblers, finches, tits and doves. Amongst the summer visitors there are Rollers, Bee-eaters, Woodchat Shrikes and Black-winged Stilts.

Access

The easiest routes to the site are from the main N-340 highway. If you are travelling from the east you should leave the N-340 at km 420, signed for Mojonera and turn right once you have reached the town. This is the new A-358 Berja-Roquetas de Mar road. Continue until you have passed the km 29 marker and 700 metres further on there is a small turning to the right, beside a large factory building with two prominent silver gas cylinders. Turn here and the entry point to the site is 100 metres along on the left, directly opposite the "Denplax" plastic waste recycling plant entrance.

Travelling from the west you should leave the N-340 at km 411, signed for Las Norias and follow the A-358 through that town where you will see the lake on the left beside the road. The small turning to the entry point is 300 metres beyond the km 28 marker.

Before entering the main part of the site walk along the road toward the greenhouses checking the agricultural land on the left and the rather scruffy small lake on the right. White-headed Ducks, Pochards, Mallards, Gadwalls, Little Grebes, Black-winged Stilts,

Moorhens, Coots, herons and egrets are all common here and the small marsh area at the far end often produces waders such as Ringed, Little-ringed and Kentish Plovers, Redshanks and Green and Common Sandpipers.

Entering into the main site you will notice a large banked causeway that runs to the right which enables you to walk the entire width of the lake and view it from an elevated position. The reed and scrub area to the left, as you start across the causeway, is a favoured breeding spot for both Little Grebes and Purple Gallinules. The dense giant reeds surrounding the water canal on the right hold Cetti's, Reed and Great Reed Warblers.

Out on the open water you will find various ducks, grebes and other waterfowl. In the spring and summer there is always a good selection of terns, with up to 200 Gull-billed and lesser numbers of Whiskered, Black, Common, Sandwich and Little Terns.

Hoopoes and Rollers (summer) breed in the area and are a fairly common sight. Little Bitterns, Purple Herons and Squacco Herons are also summer visitors with the former, at least, breeding in the reedbeds. Wader and wildfowl numbers are always highest in the winter months although there is still plenty to see during other times of the year. My latest visit here was in July 2001 and I recorded Common, Green, Wood and Marsh Sandpipers, Little-ringed and Kentish Plovers, Ruffs, Black-tailed Godwits, Black-winged Stilts, Ferruginous, Marbled and White-headed Ducks, Little and Black-necked Grebes, Squacco Herons, Cattle and Little Egrets, Purple Gallinules, Reed and Great Reed Warblers, Hoopoes, Rollers, Great Grey and Woodchat Shrikes and Little, Black, Whiskered and Gull-billed Terns, together with over 20 other more common species.

After visiting the main part of the site drive along the road toward the greenhouses and turn left. Follow the road for 550 metres until you reach a pull-off area beside a greenhouse on the left. This point overlooks part of the site that cannot be seen from elsewhere and the elevated position gives excellent views of a few small islands, inlets and marsh areas. This is the main roosting/resting area for most of the terns and it is also the best place to find Marbled Ducks, which like the cover of the tamarisks near to the bank. Waders also favour this spot and various species can always be found here.

Apart from the ducks and waders there are several other interesting and attractive wintering species which have included Bluethroats, Reed Buntings and Penduline Tits.

General map of the Cañada de las Norias

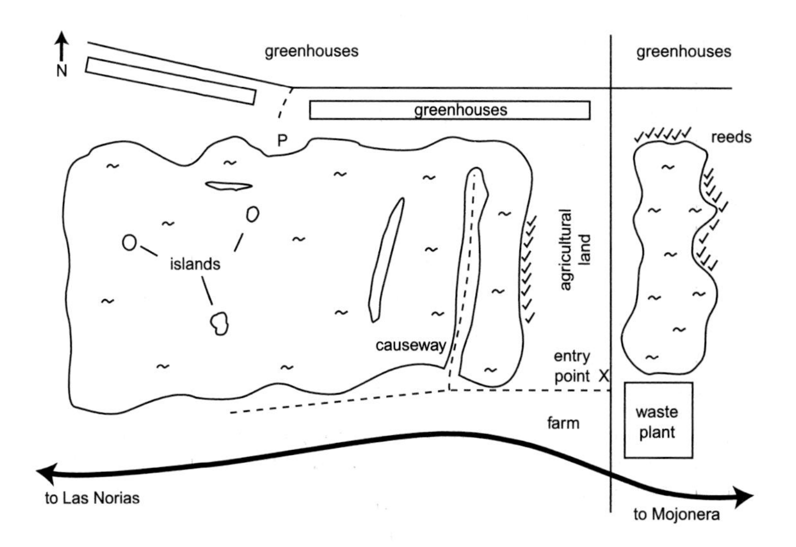

When to Visit

The site is of great interest at any time of the year and will always produce a good bird list. The autumn and winter is the best time for wildfowl and waders whilst the spring/summer produces many of the more attractive breeding species.

Although the A-358 road passes directly beside the southern end of the site this is generally a very quiet site where you can enjoy your birdwatching in peace.

General Information

Although much of the site is rather bumpy in places it is wheelchair accessible and should not pose too many problems for disabled birders. The central causeway is crumbling in one or two places and a certain amount of care should be exercised if you intend to walk along it.

The map shows the site as I know it at the present time, but various aspects may change once the SEO begin their work to turn the area into an ornithological reserve.

Bird Calendar

Resident

Little Grebe, Black-necked Grebe, Cattle Egret, Little Egret, Mallard, Gadwall, Marbled Duck, Red-crested Pochard, Common Pochard, White-headed Duck, Marsh Harrier, Buzzard, Kestrel, Water Rail, Moorhen, Purple Gallinule, Coot, Stone Curlew, Kentish Plover, Black-headed Gull, Yellow- legged Gull, Rock Dove, Collared Dove, Little Owl, Hoopoe, Crested Lark, Lesser Short-toed Lark, White Wagtail, Grey Wagtail, Stonechat, Blackbird, Cetti's Warbler, Fan-tailed Warbler, Sardinian Warbler, Great Tit, Blue Tit, Wren, Great Grey Shrike, Jackdaw, Spotless Starling, House Sparrow, Serin, Linnet, Goldfinch, Greenfinch.

Summer / Breeding

Little Bittern, Squacco Heron, Black-winged Stilt, Avocet, Little-ringed Plover, Common Tern, Little Tern, Gull-billed Tern, Black Tern, Whiskered Tern, Turtle Dove, Common Swift, Pallid Swift, Bee-eater, Roller, Short- toed Lark, Calandra Lark, House Martin, Red-rumped Swallow, Barn Swallow, Nightingale, Black-eared Wheatear, Melodious Warbler, Spotted Flycatcher, Woodchat Shrike.

Winter

Great Crested Grebe, Grey Heron, Shelduck, Wigeon, Teal, Pintail, Shoveler, Sparrowhawk, Ringed Plover, Lapwing, Dunlin, Curlew Sandpiper, Little Stint, Ruff, Snipe, Redshank, Greenshank, Green Sandpiper, Turnstone, Kingfisher, Skylark, Meadow Pipit, Bluethroat, Black Redstart, Blackcap, Iberian Chiffchaff, Reed Bunting.

Passage Migrants

Night Heron, Purple Heron, White Stork, Garganey, Osprey, Black Kite, Short-toed Eagle, Bonelli's Eagle, Booted Eagle, Collared Pratincole, Grey Plover, Golden Plover, Red Knot, Sanderling, Black-tailed Godwit, Bar-tailed Godwit, Whimbrel, Spotted Redshank, Marsh Sandpiper, Wood Sandpiper, Common Sandpiper, Sandwich Tern, Yellow Wagtail, Whinchat, Olivaceous Warbler, Willow Warbler.

Other Sites

To the north and north-east of Roquetas de Mar there is a series of three lagoons (Salinas de San Rafael) that can be visited. To the

south-west of Roquetas there are two more lagoons (*Salinas Viejas and Salinas de Cerrillos*) that can be easily reached from the town by taking the coast road.

Further west there is another lagoon at Guardias Viejas, which can also be reached via the coastal road. All of these lagoons hold good numbers of wader and waterfowl species but, having only visited these sites once, very briefly, I do not feel I am in a position to write an accurate description of them. However, I am aware that an increasing number of rarities are being recorded at these sites and you may wish to discover these for yourself.

Roller *(Coracias garrulus)*

Birds of the Southern Coast

It must be stressed that this is not a comprehensive list of Spanish birds. It contains those species that can normally be found at the sites described in this book. The status given to each bird (ie. common, scarce or rare) relates only to this particular part of the country and not to Spain as a whole.

Although many of our birds are migratory, small numbers of some of the species may, in fact, remain throughout the year. Therefore, some of the information contained within this section may conflict with the information given in your own bird books and field guides.

The English names that I have used here are those that are currently used in the official British birds list that is compiled by the British Ornithologist's Union. I have also included the Spanish names that are currently recommended by the Sociedad Española de Ornitología (SEO).

Great Crested Grebe
Podiceps cristatus
Somormujo Lavanco

A common resident, breeding on lakes and reservoirs. Scarcer in winter.

Black-necked Grebe
Podiceps nigricollis
Zampullín Cuellinegro

Scarce breeding resident. More often seen at sea in the winter.

Little Grebe
Tachybaptus ruficollis
Zampullín Chico

A common resident, breeding on lakes, rivers and reservoirs.

Cory's Shearwater
Calonectris diomedea
Pardela Cenicienta

Present offshore throughout the year but more commonly seen in the summer.

Mediterranean Shearwater**
Puffinus yelkouan
Pardela Yelkouan

Present offshore throughout the year but more commonly seen in the summer.

Northern Gannet
Morus bassanus
Alcatraz Atlantico

Present offshore all year but more numerous from September to March.

Great Cormorant
Phalacrocorax carbo
Cormorán Grande

A common winter visitor with large populations at Soto-grande and Palmones.

European Shag *Phalacrocorax aristotelis* Cormorán Moñudo	A scarce resident, usually only seen at Gibraltar and Almería.
Little Bittern* *Ixobrychus minutus* Avetorillo Común	A common summer visitor breeding in reedbeds. A few remain in winter.
Squacco Heron* *Ardeola ralloides* Garcilla Cangrejera	A scarce but regular summer visitor. More often seen during passage.
Black-crowned Night Heron* *Nycticorax nycticorax* Martinete	Scarce summer visitor. Mainly noctunal but some are active in the daytime.
Cattle Egret* *Bubulcus ibis* Garcilla Bueyera	A very common resident. Roosts communally in trees and reed-beds.
Little Egret *Egretta garzetta* Garceta Común	Common resident. Found on coasts, rivers, lakes and most other wetlands.
Grey Heron *Ardea cinerea* Garza Real	A very common winter visitor. Small numbers remain through-out the year.
Purple Heron *Ardea purpurea* Garza Imperial	A common breeding summer visitor. Usually at marshes and in reedbeds.
Great Egret* *Ardea alba* Garceta Grande	A very scarce but regular winter visitor.
Eurasian Spoonbill *Platalea leucorodia* Espatúla Común	A scarce resident. More numerous during the winter at wetland sites.
White Stork *Ciconia ciconia* Cigüeña Blanca	A very common resident in the west of the region. Scarcer elsewhere.
Black Stork* *Ciconia nigra* Cigüeña Negra	Common on passage in the west, otherwise scarce in the area.

Greater Flamingo* *Phoenicopterus ruber* Flamenco Común	A very common resident. Liable to turn up on any lake, river or estuary.
Greylag Goose *Anser anser* Ansar Común	A scarce winter visitor although thousands overwinter in Doñana.
Common Shelduck *Tadorna tadorna* Tarro Blanco	A scarce winter visitor. Small numbers may appear at any wetland site.
Mallard *Anas platyrhynchos* Ánade Azulón	A very common resident that can be found almost anywhere where there is water.
Gadwall *Anas strepera* Ánade Frisco	Scarce in summer but more numerous in winter. Small resident population.
Eurasian Wigeon *Anas penelope* Ánade Silbón	A common winter visitor. Small flocks are often seen on the sea.
Eurasian Teal *Anas crecca* Cerceta Común	A common winter visitor to suitable wetlands.
Garganey *Anas querquedula* Cerceta Carretona	Scarce. Usually only seen during the spring passage period.
Northern Pintail *Anas acuta* Ánade Rabudo	A scarce winter visitor but small numbers may appear anywhere.
Northern Shoveler *Anas clypeata* Cuchara Común	Very common in the winter. Small numbers remain throughout the year.
Marbled Duck* *Marmaronetta angustirostris* Cerceta Pardilla	A scarce resident species. Numbers increase during the winter periods.
Red-crested Pochard *Netta rufina* Pato Colorado	A common breeding species. Mainly resident.

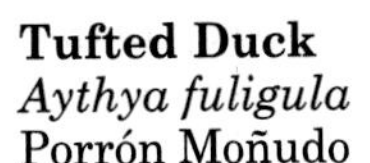

Tufted Duck
Aythya fuligula
Porrón Moñudo

A scarce but regular winter visitor. Mainly found on the larger lakes.

Common Pochard
Aythya ferina
Porrón Común

A fairly common winter visitor. Small numbers remain throughout the year.

Black Scoter
Melanitta nigra
Negrón Común

Scarce winter visitors which are sometimes seen in rafts offshore.

Red-breasted Merganser
Mergus serrator
Serreta Mediana

Fairly scarce winter visitor. Mostly seen off the Atlantic coastline.

White-headed Duck**
Oxyura leucocephala
Malvasía Cabeciblanco

A fairly scarce resident but occasional birds can turn up anywhere.

Osprey
Pandion haliaetus
Águila Pescadora

A scarce resident whose numbers increase in the winter.

Black Kite*
Milvus migrans
Milano Negro

A common summer visitor. Small numbers may remain throughout the year.

Red Kite
Milvus milvus
Milano Real

A scarce resident whose numbers increase in the summer.

Short-toed Eagle*
Circaetus gallicus
Culebrera Europeo

A very common summer visitor throughout the region.

Egyptian Vulture*
Neophron percnopterus
Alimoche Común

A fairly common summer visitor. A few may overwinter.

Monk Vulture*
Aegypius monachus
Buitre Negro

Very scarce. Occasionally seen on passage near the strait of Gibraltar.

Griffon Vulture**
Gyps fulvus
Buitre Leonardo

A very common resident. Can be found in most mountain ranges.

Eurasian Marsh Harrier *Circus aeruginosus* Aguilucho Lagunero	Common in suitable areas during the winter. Scarcer in the summer.
Hen Harrier *Circus cyaneus* Aguilucho Pálido	A scarce but regular winter visitor.
Montagu's Harrier *Circus pygargus* Aguilucho Cenizo	A common summer visitor. Often seen over orchards and farm-land.
Eurasian Sparrowhawk *Accipiter nisus* Gavilán Común	A fairly common resident. Northern visitors increase numbers in winter.
Northern Goshawk *Accipiter gentilis* Azor Común	A fairly scarce resident. Normally found in large forests.
Common Buzzard *Buteo buteo* Busardo Ratonero	A common resident. Winter visitors increase the numbers.
European Honey Buzzard *Pernis apivorus* Abejero Europeo	Scarce except on passage when thousands pass through the western areas.
Bonelli's Eagle** *Hieraaetus fasciatus* Águila-Azor Perdicera	Fairly common resident in the mountains. Summer visitors increase numbers.
Booted Eagle** *Hieraaetus pennatus* Águililla Calzada	A very common summer visitor. A few remain throughout the winter.
Golden Eagle *Aquila chrysaetos* Águila Real	A scarce resident but can be found in many mountain ranges.
Spanish Imperial Eagle** *Áquila adalberti* Aguila Imperial Iberíca	A scarce resident. Prefers lowland forests rather than mountainous regions.
Peregrine Falcon *Falco pereginus* Halcón Peregrino	A fairly scarce resident population. Migrants increase numbers in winter.

Eleonora's Falcon* *Falco eleonorae* Halcón de Eleonor	Very scarce summer visitor. Usually seen near Gibraltar and the strait.
Eurasian Hobby *Falco subbuteo* Alcotán	A scarce summer visitor to the area.
Merlin *Falco columbarius* Esmerejón	A very scarce visitor during winter periods.
Common Kestrel *Falco tinnunculus* Cernícalo Vulgar	A very common resident species that can be found anywhere.
Lesser Kestrel* *Falco naumanni* Cernícalo Primilla	Some resident birds but mainly summer visitors. Quite common.
Red-legged Partridge *Alectoris rufa* Perdiz Roja	A very common resident species throughout the region.
Barbary Partridge** *Alectoris barbara* Perdiz Moruna	Resident in Gibraltar, which is the only place in Europe to see them.
Common Quail *Coturnix coturnix* Codorníz Común	A common summer visitor but very seldom seen.
Water Rail *Rallus aquaticus* Rascón	An elusive resident that is probably more common than it seems.
Common Moorhen *Gallinula chloropus* Gallinela Común	A very common resident throughout the region.
Purple Swamp-hen** *Porphyrio porphyrio* Calamón Común	A scarce resident. Usually found in dense reedbeds. Common in Doñana.
Common Coot *Fulica atra* Focha Común	Common resident. Numbers greatly increase in the winter.

Common Crane *Grus grus* Grulla Común	Fairly scarce. A few hundred overwinter at La Janda and Fuente de Piedra.
Eurasian Oystercatcher *Haematopus ostralegus* Ostrero Común	A scarce but regular winter visitor. Usually along the coasts.
Black-winged Stilt* *Himantopus himantopus* Cigüeñuela Común	A common and widespread summer visitor throughout the region.
Pied Avocet *Recurvirostra avosetta* Avoceta Común	A fairly scarce resident whose numbers increase during the winter.
Stone Curlew *Burhinus oedicnemus* Alcaraván	A fairly scarce resident population but winter visitors increase numbers.
Little Bustard* *Tetrax tetrax* Sisón	Fairly scarce residents but can be found in Almería and at La Janda.
Collared Pratincole* *Glareola pratincola* Canastera Común	A fairly common summer visitor. More often seen during passage periods.
Ringed Plover *Charadrius hiaticula* Chorlitejo Grande	Small resident population whose numbers greatly increase in the winter.
Little Plover *Charadrius dubius* Chorlitejo Chico	A small resident population whose numbers are increased by summer visitors.
Kentish Plover *Charadrius alexandrinus* Chorlitejo Patinegro	A fairly common resident species throughout the region.
Grey Plover *Pluvialis squatarola* Chorlito Gris	Common between autumn and spring. Small numbers remain throughout summer.
Golden Plover *Pluvialis apricaria* Chorlito Dorado Europeo	A fairly scarce winter visitor

Northern Lapwing *Vanellus vanellus* Avefría Europeo	A small resident population. Winter numbers increase greatly.
Dunlin *Calidris alpina* Correlimos Común	A few resident birds and a very common winter visitor.
Curlew Sandpiper *Calidris ferruginea* Correlimos Zarapitín	Fairly common on passage. Some birds may remain throughout the year.
Red Knot *Calidris canutus* Correlimos Gordo	Fairly common during pasage periods and in the winter. Scarce in summer.
Sanderling *Calidris alba* Correlimos Tridáctilo	Common winter visitor and passage migrant. Small numbers remain in summer.
Little Stint *Calidris minuta* Correlimos Menudo	Quite common on passage and in the winter.
Purple Sandpiper *Calidris maritima* Correlimos Oscuro	A very scarce winter visitor to rocky coasts.
Ruff *Philomachus pugnax* Combatiente	Mainly seen in the winter and on passage. Fairly Scarce.
Common Snipe *Gallinago gallinago* Agachadiza Común	A small resident population whose numbers are increased by winter visitors.
Eurasian Woodcock *Scolopax rusticola* Chocha Perdiz	A very scarce winter visitor and passage migrant.
Black-tailed Godwit *Limosa limosa* Aguja Colinegra	A fairly common winter visitor. Some remain all year at suitable sites.
Bar-tailed Godwit *Limosa lapponica* Aguja Colipinta	Fairly common on passage and in the winter.

Eurasian Curlew
Numenius arquatta
Zarapito Real

Fairly common. Some residents but numbers increase in the winter.

Whimbrel
Numenius phaeopus
Zarapito Trinador

A common resident whose numbers are increased by winter visitors.

Spotted Redshank
Tringa erythropus
Archibebe Oscuro

Fairly common on passage and in the winter.

Common Redshank
Tringa totanus
Archibebe Común

A common breeding resident. Numbers greatly increase during the winter.

Wood Sandpiper
Tringa glareola
Andarríos Bastardo

Fairly common in the winter and on passage. Usually near fresh water.

Green Sandpiper
Tringa ochropus
Andarríos Grande

Common on passage and in the winter, usually by fresh water.

Marsh Sandpiper*
Tringa stagnatillis
Archibebe Fino

A very scarce passage migrant but is regulary seen at suitable sites.

Common Sandpiper
Actitis hypoleucos
Andarríos Chico

Very common in the summer but numbers decrease during the winter months.

Ruddy Turnstone
Arenaria interpres
Vuelvapiedras Común

Very common in the winter. A few birds may remain throughout the year.

Great Skua
Catharacta skua
Págalo Grande

Fairly common offshore during the passage periods and in the winter.

Arctic Skua
Stercorarius parasiticus
Págalo Parásito

Present offshore all year but most numerous on passage and in the winter.

Audouin's Gull**
Larus audouinii
Gaviota de Audouin

Very common on passage in spring and autumn. Some remain all year.

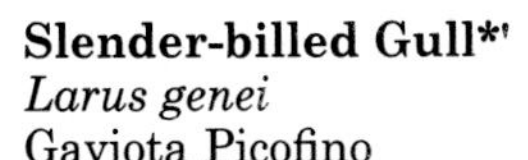

Slender-billed Gull*
Larus genei
Gaviota Picofino

Scarce resident that is sometimes seen on passage along the coast.

Black-headed Gull
Larus ridibundus
Gaviota Reidora

A fairly common resident species whose numbers increase greatly in winter.

Little Gull
Larus minutus
Gaviota Enana

A fairly common winter visitor, especially in the west of the region.

Mediterranean Gull
Larus melanocephalus
Gaviota Cabecinegra

Very common during the winter months. Small numbers remain in summer.

Yellow-legged Gull**
Larus cachinnans
Gaviota Patiamarilla

A very common resident that can be found just about everywhere.

Lesser Black-backed Gull
Larus fuscus
Gaviota Sombría

Fairly common. Can be seen all year although more numerous in the winter.

Black-legged Kittiwake
Rissa tridactyla
Gaviota Tridáctila

A scarce but regular winter visitor. More often seen on Atlantic coast.

Caspian Tern*
Sterna caspia
Pagaza Piquirrojo

A scarce but regular winter visitor and passage migrant.

Lesser Crested Tern*
Sterna bengalensis
Charrán Bengalí

Very scarce in the area but is sometimes seen on passage near the strait.

Common Tern
Sterna hirundo
Charrán Común

Fairly common on passage in spring and autumn.

Little Tern
Sterna albifrons
Charrancito Común

Fairly common along the coast in the summer and during passage periods.

Sandwich Tern
Sterna sandvicensis
Charrán Patinegro

The most common tern in the area. Passing birds can be seen at any time.

Gull-billed Tern* *Sterna nilotica* Pagaza Piconegra	Fairly common summer visitor to selected inland waters where they breed.
Black Tern *Chlidonias niger* Fumarel Común	Fairly common on inland waters and on passage. Summer visitors.
Whiskered Tern* *Chlidonias hybridus* Fumarel Cariblanco	Fairly common on inland waters. A breeding summer visitor. Some overwinter.
Razorbill *Alca torda* Alca Común	Fairly common offshore during the winter.
Atlantic Puffin *Fratercula arctica* Frailcilo Común	Very scarce except on passage through the strait.
Black-bellied Sandgrouse** *Pterocles orientalis* Ortega	Common resident in Almería province. Extremely scarce elsewhere.
Rock Pigeon *Columba livia* Paloma Bravía	A very common resident species.
Stock Pigeon *Columba oenas* Paloma Zurita	Very scarce in this area but may occasionally be seen in the winter.
Common Wood Pigeon *Columba palumbus* Paloma Torcaz	A very common resident. Winter visitors greatly increase the numbers.
Eurasian Collared Dove *Streptopelia decaocto* Tórtola Turca	Expanding its range and is now a fairly common resident in the region.
European Turtle Dove *Streptopelia turtur* Tórtola Común	A common summer visitor and passage migrant. Can be found almost anywhere.
Monk Parakeet** *Myiopsitta monachus* Cotorra Argentina	Fairly common resident of the western Costa del Sol. Breeds communally.

Rose-ringed Parakeet *Psittacula krameri* Cotorra de Kramer	A fairly scarce resident. Sometimes found alongside the Monk Parakeets.
Great Spotted Cuckoo* *Clamator glandarius* Críalo Europeo	A fairly scarce summer visitor to the area but is quite common in Doñana.
Common Cuckoo *Cuculus canorus* Cucu Común	A fairly common summer visitor which is more often heard than seen.
Little Owl *Athene noctua* Mochuelo Europeo	A very common resident species that is often seen during the daytime.
Eurasian Scops Owl* *Otus scops* Autillo Europeo	A common summer visitor to much of the area.
Eagle Owl** *Bubo bubo* Búho Real	A scarce resident that is usually found in rocky, wooded hillsides.
Long-eared Owl *Asio otus* Búho Chico	A fairly scarce resident species.
Short-eared Owl *Asio flammeus* Búho Campestre	A scarce winter visitor. Sometimes heard but seldom seen.
Tawny Owl *Strix aluco* Cárabo Común	A common woodland species. Resident.
Barn Owl *Tyto alba* Lechuza Común	A common resident species throughout most of the region.
European Nightjar *Caprimulgus europaeus* Chotacabras Europeo	A fairly common summer visitor to suitable habitats.
Red-necked Nightjar* *Caprimulgus ruficollis* Chotacabras Cuellirrojo	A common summer visitor to much of the area.

White-rumped Swift** *Apus caffer* Vencejo Cafre	A scarce summer visitor that is more often seen in the west of the region.
Alpine Swift* *Apus melba* Vencejo Real	A fairly common summer visitor. Usually found in mountainous areas.
Common Swift *Apus apus* Vencejo Común	A common summer visitor throughout most of the region.
Pallid Swift* *Apus pallidus* Vencejo Pálido	A very common summer visitor to all coastal areas.
Common Kingfisher *Alcedo atthis* Martín Pescador	A common breeding species. Resident but more numerous in the winter.
Hoopoe *Upupa epops* Abubilla	A common summer visitor although small numbers remain throughout winter.
European Bee-eater *Merops apiaster* Abejaruco Común	A very common summer visitor throughout the region. Nests in colonies.
European Roller* *Coracias garrulus* Carraca	Fairly common in the eastern areas but scarce except on passage elsewhere.
Green Woodpecker *Picus viridis* Pito Real	A fairly scarce resident species.
Great Spotted Woodpecker *Dendrocopos major* Pico Picapinos	A fairly common resident that is found throughout the region.
Eurasian Wryneck *Jynx torquilla* Torcecuello	A fairly scarce resident population.
Wood Lark *Lullula arborea* Totovía	A common resident species whose numbers are increased during the winter.

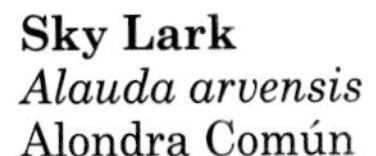

Sky Lark
Alauda arvensis
Alondra Común

A fairly scarce resident population. Winter visitors increase numbers.

Crested Lark*
Galerida cristata
Cogujada Común

A very common resident. Usually found at lower levels.

Thekla Lark**
Galerida theklae
Cogujada Montesina

A common resident usually found in the hills and mountains.

Greater Short-toed Lark
Calendrella brachydactyla
Terrera Común

A common summer visitor to various parts of the region, mainly in the east.

Lesser Short-toed Lark*
Calendrella rufescens
Terrera Marismeña

A fairly scarce resident species that can be found in suitable habitats.

Dupont's Lark**
Chersophilus duponti
Alondra de Dupont

A very localised species only found in the steppe areas of Almería.

Calandra Lark*
Melanocorypha calandra
Calandria

A fairly scarce resident. More often seen in large wintering flocks.

Sand Martin
Riparia riparia
Avión Zapador

A common summer visitor. Individual birds may remain through the winter.

Eurasian Crag Martin*
Ptyonoprogne rupestris
Avión Roquero

Common resident in hills and mountains. Lower down during the winter.

House Martin
Delichon urbica
Avión Común

A very common summer visitor throughout the region.

Red-rumped Swallow*
Hirundo daurica
Golondrina Dáurica

A fairly common summer visitor. A few individuals may sometimes overwinter.

Barn Swallow
Hirundo rustica
Golondrina Común

A very common summer visitor. Small numbers remain through the winter.

Tree Pipit
Anthus trivialis
Bisbita Arbóreo

Mainly seen during the passage periods, when it is reasonably common.

Meadow Pipit
Anthus pratensis
Bisbita Común

Very common on passage and throughout the winter. Often in large flocks.

Water Pipit
Anthus spinoletta
Bisbita Alpino

A very scarce winter visitor and passage migrant.

Tawny Pipit
Anthus campestris
Bisbita Campestre

A fairly common summer visitor and passage migrant.

White Wagtail
Motacilla alba
Lavandera Blanca

Small resident population whose numbers are greatly increased in winter.

Grey Wagtail
Motacilla cinerea
Lavandera Cascadeña

A fairly common resident species.

Yellow Wagtail
Motacilla flava
Lavandera Boyera

The Spanish race (*iberiae*) is a fairly common summer visitor.

Alpine Accentor*
Prunella collaris
Acentor Alpino

A very scarce resident usually only seen in the region during the winter.

Hedge Accentor
Prunella modularis
Acentor Común

A scarce resident usually only seen in the region during the winter.

Common Nightingale
Luscinia megarhynchos
Ruiseñor Común

A very common summer visitor to all parts of the region.

Rufous-tailed Scrub Robin*
Cercotrichas galectotes
Alzacola

A fairly scarce but regular summer visitor to many parts of the region.

European Robin
Erithacus rubecula
Petirrojo

A fairly common resident whose numbers are increased in the winter.

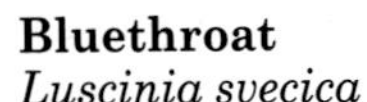

Bluethroat
Luscinia svecica
Pechiazul

A fairly scarce winter visitor to reedbeds, lagoons and marshes.

Stonechat
Saxicola torquata
Tarabilla Común

A large resident population whose numbers increase even more in winter.

Whinchat
Saxicola rubetra
Tarabilla Norteña

Very common during the passage periods, especially during late summer.

Black Redstart
Phoenicurus ochruros
Colirrojo Tizón

A very common resident species of the hills. At lower levels in winter.

Common Redstart
Phoenicurus phoenicurus
Colirrojo Real

Fairly scarce summer visitor that is more commonly seen on passage.

Northern Wheatear
Oenanthe oenanthe
Collalba Gris

Fairly common during passage periods but very few remain in the area.

Black-eared Wheatear*
Oenanthe hispanica
Collalba Rubia

A fairly common summer visitor to suitable habitats throughout the region.

Black Wheatear**
Oenanthe leucura
Collalba Negra

A fairly common resident. Usually found at higher, rocky habitats.

Rufous-tailed Rock Thrush*
Monticola saxatilis
Roquero Rojo

A very scarce resident species usually only found at very high altitudes.

Blue Rock Thrush*
Monticola solitarius
Roquero Solitario

A fairly common resident species normally found in hilly countryside.

Common Blackbird
Turdus merula
Mirlo Común

A very common and widespread resident.

Ring Ouzel
Turdus torquatus
Mirlo Capiblanco

A fairly scarce winter visitor to the region. More often seen on passage.

Fieldfare *Turdus pilaris* Zorzal Real	An extremely scarce winter visitor.
Redwing *Turdus iliacus* Zorzal Alirrojo	Fairly scarce winter visitor.
Song Thrush *Turdus philomelos* Zorzal Común	A fairly common winter visitor.
Mistle Thrush *Turdus viscivorus* Zorzal Charlo	A fairly scarce resident species. Usually found in the higher forests.
Common Grasshopper Warbler *Locustella naevia* Buscarla Pintoja	A very scarce passage migrant.
Savi's Warbler* *Locustella luscinioides* Buscarla Unicolor	A scarce summer visitor usually only found in the west of the region.
Eurasian Reed Warbler *Acrocephalus scirpaceus* Carricero Común	A very common summer visitor to most large reedbeds.
Great Reed Warbler* *Acrocephalus arundinaceus* Carricero Tordal	A fairly scarce summer visitor to reedbeds throughout the whole region.
Moustached Warbler* *Acrocephalus melanopogon* Carricerín Real	A scarce resident of reedbeds. May appear at any suitable site.
Sedge Warbler *Acrocephalus schoenbaenus* Carricerín Común	A fairly scarce summer visitor. More often seen during migration periods.
Cetti's Warbler *Cettia cetti* Ruiseñor Bastardo	A very common and widespread resident. Usually to be found near to water.
Fan-tailed Warbler *Cisticola juncidis* Buitrón	A very common resident species. Can be found throughout the region.

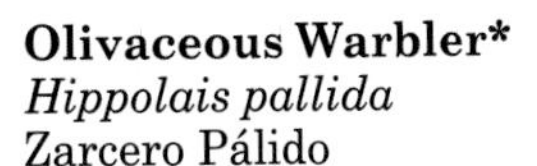

Olivaceous Warbler*
Hippolais pallida
Zarcero Pálido

A fairly scarce summer visitor that is becoming more commonly seen.

Melodious Warbler
Hippolais polyglotta
Zarcero Común

A common summer visitor to much of the region. Abundant on passage.

Garden Warbler
Sylvia borin
Curruca Mosquitera

A fairly scarce summer visitor usually only found in the western areas.

Common Whitethroat
Sylvia communis
Curruca Zarcera

A fairly scarce summer visitor favouring the west of the region.

Blackcap
Sylvia atricapilla
Curruca Capirotada

A common resident species whose numbers greatly increase in the winter.

Sardinian Warbler*
Sylvia melanocephala
Curruca Cabecinegra

A very common resident species appearing throughout the whole region.

Orphean Warbler*
Sylvia hortensis
Curruca Mirlona

A fairly common summer visitor to woodland habitats throughout the region.

Dartford Warbler
Sylvia undata
Curruca Rabilarga

A fairly common resident of heathland and gorse throughout the region.

Spectacled Warbler*
Sylvia conspicillata
Curruca Tomillera

A fairly scarce but widespread summer visitor throughout the region.

Subalpine Warbler*
Sylvia cantillans
Curraca Carrasqueña

A fairly common and widespread summer visitor to open hilly areas.

Western Bonelli's Warbler*
Phylloscopus bonelli
Mosquitero Papialbo

A fairly common summer visitor to hilly woodlands. A few may overwinter.

Wood Warbler
Phylloscopus sibilatrix
Mosquitero Silbador

A scarce migrant that is usually only seen on passage in the west.

Iberian Chiffchaff* *Phylloscopus brehmii* Mosquitero Ibérico	A small resident population whose numbers greatly increase in the winter.
Willow Warbler *Phylloscopus trochilus* Mosquitero Musical	Very abundant passage migrant in spring and autumn in western areas.
Firecrest *Regulus ignicapillus* Reyezuelo Listado	Fairly common resident of forests throughout the region.
Spotted Flycatcher *Muscicapa striata* Papamoscas Gris	A very common summer visitor to all parts of the region.
Pied Flycatcher *Ficedula hypoleuca* Papamoscas Cerrojillo	A scarce summer visitor but fairly common on passage across the region.
Long-tailed Tit *Aegithalos caudatus* Mito	The Spanish race (irbii) is relatively common in the west of the region.
Eurasian Penduline Tit* *Remit pendulinus* Pajero Moscon	A scarce but regular winter visitor to reedbeds throughout the region.
Crested Tit *Parus cristatus* Herrerillo Capuchino	A fairly common resident of mixed woodlands across most of the region.
Coal Tit *Parus ater* Carbonero Garrapinos	A fairly common resident in hilly and mountainous woodlands.
Great Tit *Parus major* Carbonero Común	A common and widespread resident throughout most of the region.
Blue Tit *Parus caeruleus* Herrerillo Común	A common and widespread breeding resident.
Wood Nuthatch *Sitta europaea* Trepador Azul	A fairly common resident of mixed woodlands, especially in the west.

Short-toed Treecreeper* *Certhia brachydactylata* Agateador Común	A fairly common resident of forests. Can be found throughout the region.
Winter Wren *Troglodytes troglodytes* Chochín	A fairly common resident which can be found throughout the region.
White-throated Dipper *Cinclus cinclus* Mirlo Acuático	A very scarce resident usually only found by mountainous rivers.
Southern Grey Shrike* *Lanius meridionalis* Alcaudón Real	A common and very widespread resident. Can be found almost anywhere.
Woodchat Shrike *Lanius senator* Alcaudón Común	A very common summer visitor that can be found throughout the region.
Eurasian Jay *Garrulus glandarius* Arrendajo Común	A fairly common and wide-spread resident of forests and orchards.
Black-billed Magpie *Pica pica* Urraca	Surprisingly scarce in the region except for in the far south-west.
Azure-winged Magpie** *Cyanopica cyanus* Rabilargo	A scarce resident confined to a few small areas, more so in the west.
Red-billed Chough *Pyrrhocorax pyrrhocorax* Chova Piquirroja	A fairly common resident of mountainous areas throughout the region.
Eurasian Jackdaw *Corvus monedula* Grajilla	A common resident. Often seen on old bridges and coastal watchtowers.
Common Raven *Corvus corax* Cuervo	A common resident of the mountains. Can be found throughout the region.
Eurasian Golden Oriole *Oriolus oriolus* Oropéndola	A fairly common and widespread summer visitor. Prefers woods near rivers.

Spotless Starling* *Sturnus unicolor* Estornino Negro	An extremely common resident that can be found almost anywhere.
Common Starling *Sturnus vulgaris* Estornino Pinto	A fairly common winter visitor to the more south-western areas.
Rock Sparrow* *Petronia petronia* Gorrión Chillón	A fairly scarce resident in hills and mountains with scattered trees.
Spanish Sparrow* *Passer hispaniolensis* Gorrión Moruno	Fairly scarce but can be found at both extremities of the coast.
House Sparrow *Passer domesticus* Gorrión Común	An extremely common and wide-spread resident.
Eurasian Tree Sparrow *Passer montanus* Gorrión Molinero	A fairly scarce resident species. Usually found in small isolated flocks.
Avadavat** *Amandava amandava* Bengali Rojo	Very scarce except near to the Río Velez (Málaga) where they are quite common.
Common Waxbill** *Estrilda astrild* Pico de Coral	A very scarce resident species that may show up at any reedbed location.
Black-rumped Waxbill** *Estrilda troglodytes* Estrilda Colinegro	This species is classed as a Spanish rarity but there is a very large resident breeding population (300+ birds) around the Río Velez (Málaga).
Brambling *Fringilla montifringilla* Pinzón Real	A scarce but regular winter visitor. More so to woods in the south-west.
Chaffinch *Fringilla coelebs* Pinzón Vulgar	A very common resident species whose numbers are increased in the winter.

European Serin *Serinus serinus* Verdecillo	A very common resident throughout the region. Large flocks form in winter.
Common Linnet *Carduelis cannabina* Pardillo Común	A common resident found throughout the region. Numbers increase in winter.
Eurasian Siskin *Carduelis spinus* Lúgano	A fairly common winter visitor to the south-west of the region.
European Goldfinch *Carduelis carduelis* Jilguero	A very common resident species that can be found all across the region.
European Greenfinch *Carduelis chloris* Verderón Común	A common resident species that appears across the region.
Common Bullfinch *Pyrrhula pyrrhula* Camachuelo Común	Very scarce winter visitor occasionally reported in south-western areas.
Hawfinch *Coccothraustes coccothraustes* Picogordo	A scarce resident species usually found near orchards or in woodlands.
Trumpeter Finch* *Bucanetes githagineus* Camachuelo Trompetero	Very scarce resident except for the steppe and desert areas of Almería.
Common Crossbill *Loxia curvirostra* Piquituerto Común	Common resident across much of the region. Usually found in pine forests.
Corn Bunting *Miliaria calandra* Triguero	A common resident across the region. Prefers agricultural and open land.
Rock Bunting* *Emberiza cia* Escribano Montesino	Common and widespread resident of hilly, rocky ground. Lower in winter.
Cirl Bunting *Emberiza cirlus* Escribano Soteño	Fairly common and widespread resident of open land.

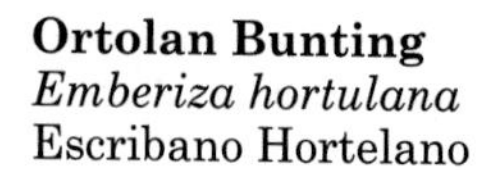

Ortolan Bunting
Emberiza hortulana
Escribano Hortelano

A fairly common summer visitor to much of the region.

Reed Bunting
Emberiza schoeniclus
Escribano Palustre

Fairly scarce resident population. Winter visitors increase numbers.

* The species marked with a star are considered as British rarities.

** The species marked with two stars do not appear on the British list.

Rare Birds of the Region

This section deals with the rare birds that have been recorded in this region since 1980. Each of these records have been ratified by the Iberian Rarities Committee (IRC), or are currently under consideration by them.

I have also included certain species that, although not classed as rarities for Spain as a whole, are considered by me to be rarities for the described region. For those that are classed as Spanish (SR) or European (ER) rarities, I have included the times of the year and the locations of these sightings. For those that I class as regional (RR) rarities, I have made general notes.

Although the whole of the region is likely to produce rarities at any time, the nearer the Strait of Gibraltar the greater are your chances of finding rare birds, especially storks, cranes, eagles and other raptorial species. The geographical location of the strait and its close proximity to both the African continent and the Atlantic Ocean means that the area is pefectly placed to receive both overshooting migrants and storm-blown vagrants.

Unfortunately, birdwatchers here tend not to report their sightings with the same enthusiasm that birders in Britain and some other northern European countries do, and there is no doubt that many rarities have gone unreported. This may be due, in part, to the fact that many rarities have been seen by birdwatching holidaymakers who have not known who to report their sightings to, so have returned home taking that knowledge with them. If you should be fortunate enough to discover a rare bird in the region, or indeed, anywhere else in Spain, I strongly urge you to submit a report to the Iberian Rarities Committee.

Any reports can be made in English and should give as full a description of the bird as possible. A sketch of the bird would be of assistance as would a size comparison with another species. The time, date, location, habitat and weather conditions will all help the committee in their deliberations. The use of any field aids, such as binoculars, telescope, books etc, should also be stated. In all cases your reports should be addressed to:

Dr. Eduardo de Juana.
Comite Iberico de Rarezas.
Dept. de Biologia, Animal 1.
Univ. Complutense.
E-28040 Madrid.

Slavonian Grebe (SR) *Podiceps auritus* Zampullín Cuellirrojo	Four old records exist from Málaga in the winter of 1981-82. There is a more modern record of a single bird at Doñana in January 1990.
Bulwers Petrel (ER) *Bulweria bulwerii* Petrel de Bulwer	One offshore record in February 1982.
Little Shearwater (SR) *Puffinus assimilis* Pardela Chica	Five records. Málaga Bay in November 1981. Sotogrande in May 1982 and May 1986 and Gibraltar in August 1988 and 1989.
Wilson's Storm Petrel (SR) *Oceanites oceanicus* Paíno de Wilson	One recorded at Doñana in June 1988.
Brown Booby (ER) *Sula leucogaster* Piquero Pardo	Two records from Málaga Bay in May 1983 and September 1986.
Masked Booby (ER) *Sula dactylatra* Piquero Enmascarado	Two records. Sotogrande in October 1985 and Málaga Bay in December 1985.
Cape Gannet (ER) *Sula capensis* Alcatraz de El Cabo	One report under consideration from Estepona in October 2000.
Great White Pelican (SR) *Pelecanus onocrotalus* Pelícano Común	One record from Tarifa in August 1996 and one in the Doñana area during September 1998. Three birds photographed near Doñana in January 1999.
Glossy Ibis (RR) *Plegadis falcinellus* Morito	A regular winter visitor to Doñana and perhaps other sites in the western areas. A few remain throughout the year.
Sacred Ibis (ER) *Threskiornis aethiopica* Ibis Sagrado	A single bird recorded at the Río Guadalhorce (Málaga) in February 1997.

Marabou (ER)
Leptoptilus crumeniferus
Marabu Africano

One recorded at Doñana in July 1989.

Mute Swan (SR)
Cygnus olor
Cisne Vulgar

Three records from Almería in April 1991, June 1992 and May 1993.

Ruddy Shelduck (SR)
Tadorna ferruginea
Tarro Canelo

Five accepted records in recent years. From Doñana in December 1987, Laguna Dulce (Campillos) in June 1991, Cabo de Gata in June 1993, Salinas Guardias Viejas (Almería) in May 1994 and the Río Guadalhorce in December 1997.

Egyptian Goose (SR)
Alopochen aegyptiacus
Ganso del Nilo

One accepted record from Estepona in January 1999 and a further report from Estepona in June 2000 is under consideration by the IRC.

Fulvous Whistling Duck (ER)
Dendrocygna bicolor
Suiriri Bicolor

One recorded at Laguna de Fuente de Piedra during May, June and July 1998.

Blue-winged Teal (SR)
Anas discors
Cerceta Aliazul

There are records from Doñana in May 1988, the Río Guadalhorce from October- December 1990 and from Laguna de Medina in February 1997.

Ring-necked Duck (ER)
Aythya collaris
Porrón de Collar

One record from Laguna de Medina in December 1996.

Greater Scaup (SR)
Aythya marila
Porrón Bastardo

One record from Laguna de Medina in 1991.

Ferruginous Duck (RR)
Aythya nyroca
Porrón Pardo

These are regularly reported from various sites throughout the region.

Long-tailed Duck (SR) *Aythya hyemalis* Havelda	There are records from Salinas de Cerrillos (Almería) in October 1987 and December 1988, Málaga in February 1992, Salinas de Guardias Viejas (Almería) in November 1993 and from the Doñana area in November 1993.
Common Goldeneye (ER) *Bucephala clangula* Porrón Osculado	One recorded at Laguna de Medina in January 1989.
Ruddy Duck (SR) *Oxyura jamaicensis* Malvasía Canela	Three records from Laguna de Medina in December 1988, February 1991 and February 1997. One record from Laguna Dulce in February 1997.
Black-winged Kite (RR) *Elaneus caerruleus* Elanio Común	Occasional sightings of this species occur annually, especially in the central and south-western areas.
Bearded Vulture (RR) *Gypaetus barbartus* Quebrantahuesos	Small numbers of this species are recorded annually near to the strait.
Rüppell's Vulture (SR) *Gyps rüppellii* Buitre Moteado	There have been numerous reports of this species from the Montes de Tarifa and the surrounding areas in the autumns of 1997, 1998 and 1999.
Long-legged Buzzard (SR) *Buteo rufinus* Ratonero Moro	Small numbers of this species are recorded almost annually from the areas near to the Strait of Gibraltar.
Greater Spotted Eagle (SR) *Aquila clanga* Águila Moteada	Numerous records exist for this species, mainly from the strait area or from Doñana.
Lesser Spotted Eagle (SR) *Aquila pomarina* Águila Pomerana	Two were recorded in the Montes de Tarifa during the autumn migration in 1999.

Lanner Falcon (SR)
Falco biarmicus
Halcón Borni

Recorded at La Janda in October 1994, Tarifa in October 1997 and three were recorded in the Montes de Tarifa in spring 1999.

Red-footed Falcon (SR)
Falco vespertinus
Halcón Patirrojo

One recorded in Doñana in January 1987 and one in the Montes de Tarifa in spring 1999.

Allen's Gallinule (SR)
Porphyrula alleni
Calamón de Allen

One recorded at Laguna Salada (Cádiz) in March 1990 and one at the Río Guadalhorce in December 1994.

Baillon's Crake (RR)
Porzana pusilla
Polluela Chica

At least one pair bred at the Río Velez (Málaga) in May 1999.

Little Crake (RR)
Porzana parva
Polluelo Bastardo

A few are reported as being resident in Doñana and may also appear in other locations.

Crested Coot (RR)
Fulica cristata
Focha Cornuda

One or two pairs regularly breed at Laguna de Medina and probably at a few other lagoons in the south-west. They are also to be found at Doñana.

Great Bustard (RR)
Otis tarda
Avutarda.

A small population exists at La Janda but this is diminishing gradually

Cream-coloured Courser (ER)
Cursorius cursor
Corredor

Recorded at Cabo de Gata in August 1985, Roquetas de Mar in May 1987 and at Tahavilla, La Janda, in September 1987. Black-winged Pratincole.

Black-winged Pratincole (SR)
Glarreola nordmanni
Canastera Alinegra

One record from Torremolinos in October 1982.

Dotterel (SR)
Charadrius morinellus
Chorlito Carambolo

There have been a few reported sightings of this species, especially in the south-west but there are no definite records that I can find.

American Golden Plover (ER)
Pluvialis dominica
Chorlito Dorado Chico

One record from Málaga in 1982.

Pacific Golden Plover (ER)
Pluvialis fulva
Chorlito Dorado Siberiano

One old record from the Río Guadalhorce in August 1980.

Sociable Lapwing (SR)
Vanellus gregarius
Chorlito Social

One record from Doñana in February 1984.

Temminck's Stint (SR)
Calidris temminckii
Correlimos de Temminck

Numerous reports exist for this species from throughout the region.

White-rumped Sandpiper (SR)
Calidris falcinellus
Correlimos Culiblanco

One record from Cabo de Gata in September 1980 and one from the Río Velez (Málaga)in November 1996.

Broad-billed Sandpiper (SR)
Limicola falcinellus
Correlimos Falcino

One record from Doñana in May 1988 and one from the Río Velez (Málaga) in May 1994.

Pectoral Sandpiper (SR)
Calidris melanotos
Correlimos Pectoral

One record from Laguna de Medina in October 1999.

Buff-bellied Sandpiper (SR)
Tryngites subruficollis
Correlimos Canelo

One record from Tarifa in October 1998.

Terek Sandpiper (SR)
Xenus cinerus
Andarríos del Terek

There are records from Cabo de Gata, September 1980 and October 1994, Río Guadalhorce in September 1981 and May 1991 and also from Tarifa in May 1995.

Lesser Yellowlegs (SR)
Tringa flavipes
Archibebe Patigualdo Chico

One record of a bird at the Río Guadalhorce estuary between October and December 1998.

Long-billed Dowitcher (SR)
Limnodromos scolopaceus
Agujeta Escolopácea

Three records. Río Guadalhorce, May 1987, Doñana in April 1988 and Tarifa in August 1988.

Spotted Sandpiper (SR)
Actitis macularia
Andarríos Maculado

One record from Málaga in May 1982.

Long-tailed Skua (SR)
Stercorarius longicaudus
Págalo Rabero

One record from Málaga in August 1981 and one from the strait area in October 1987.

Sabine's Gull (SR)
Larus sabini
Gaviota de Sabine

One record from Benalmadena in October 1988.

Grey-headed Gull (ER)
Larus cirrocephalus
Gaviota Cabecigrís

Reported from Doñana in June and August 1997.

Franklin's Gull (SR)
Larus pipixcan
Gaviota de Franklin

Two records from the Río Guadalhorce in October 1983 and May 1989.

Laughing Gull (SR)
Larus atricilla
Gaviota Guanaguanare

Five records. Fuengirola, May 1981. Río Guadalhorce, July 1985 and June 1989. Benalmadena, August 1988. Gibraltar, November 1988.

Ring-billed Gull (SR)
Larus delawarensis
Gaviota de Delaware

Two records from Río Guadalhorce, January 1986 and January 1991. One from Benalmadena in January 1991. One from Gibraltar in June 1992. One report from Sotogrande in November 1999 currently under consideration by the IRC.

Iceland Gull (SR)
Larus glaucoides
Gaviota Polar

One record from Gibraltar in January 1987.

Royal Tern (ER)
Sterna maxima
Charran Real

Two records from Río Guadalhorce, June 1986 and April 1991. One rom Tarifa, September 1996. Two from Doñana, July 1987 and August 1992. One from Salinas de Cerrillos in August 1997.

Little Auk (SR)
Alle alle
Mérgulo Marino

One record from Gibraltar in March 1986.

Black-hooded Parakeet (RR)
Nandayus nenday
Aratinga Ñanday

This species can be found in small numbers throughout the region.

Palm Dove (SR)
Streptopelia senegalensis
Tortola Senegalesa

One reported as being resident at the Río Guadalhorce since May 1997.

Blue-cheeked Bee-eater (ER)
Merops persicus
Abejaruco Papirrojo

One record from Fuengirola of three birds in April 1999.

Little Swift (ER)
Apus affinus
Vencejo Moro

At least thirty records for this species ranging from Almería to Doñana.

Chimney Swift (ER)
Chaetura pelagica
Vencejo de Chimenea

Two birds reported over the Paraje Natural, Sotogrande on the 27th of October 1999, following Hurricane Irene in the Atlantic. This report is currently under consideration by the IRC.

Black Woodpecker (RR)
Dryocopus martius
Pito Negro

Two records from Málaga in August 1986 and August 1990.

Blyth's Reed Warbler (SR)
Acrocephalus demetorum
Carricero de Blyth

One record from Doñana in October 1988.

Marmora's Warbler (SR)
Sylvia sarda
Curruca Sarda

Numerous reports from the central part of the region. A breeding pair recorded in Doñana in May 1986.

Yellow-browed Warbler (SR)
Phylloscopus inornatus
Mosquitero Bilistado

Two records from Doñana in October 1985 and November 1999. One from Los Barrios, January 1993. One from Málaga, October 1999.

Red-breasted Flycatcher (SR)
Ficedula parva
Papamoscas Papirrojo

One record from Doñana in October 1999.

Collared Flycatcher (SR)
Ficedula albicollis
Papamoscas Collarino

One record from Torremolinos in April 1989.

Wallcreeper (RR)
Tichodroma muraria
Treparriscos

Various records and reports of winter sightings throughout the region.

Common Rosefinch (SR)
Carpodacus erythrinus
Camachuelo Carminoso

Records from Río Palmones, November 1986. Doñana, September 1988. Alhaurin de la Torre (Málaga), September 1995.

Isabelline Shrike (SR)
Lanius isabellinus
Alcaudrón Isabel

One record from Roquetas de Mar in November 1999.

Richard's Pipit (SR)
Anthus novaeseelandiae
Bisbita de Richard

Records from Río Guadalhorce, December 1980. Doñana, November 1988. Torremolinos, April 1996. Cabo de Gata, January to March 1998.

Desert Wheatear (ER)
Oenanthe deserti Collalba Desértica

One record from Gibraltar in September 1987.

Red-billed Quelea (ER)
Quelea quelea
Quelea

One record from Facinas (Cádiz) in July 1995.

Black-crowned Tchagra (ER) *Tchagra senegala* Chagra del Senegal	Two records from Gibraltar in August 1989 and May 1991.
Pine Bunting (SR) *Emberiza leucocephala* Escribano de Gmelin	One record of a pair at Gibraltar in May 1987.
Black-headed Bunting (SR) *Emberiza melanocephala* Escribano Cabecinegro	One record from the Río Guadalhorce in October 1996.
House Bunting (ER) *Emberiza striolata* Escribano Sahariano	One record from Algeciras in January 1987.
Little Bunting (SR) *Emberiza pusilla* Escribano Pigmeo	One record from Doñana in October 1986 and two records from Málaga in November 1991 and November 1999.
Yellowhammer (SR) *Emberiza citrinella* Escribano Cerillo	One record from Gibraltar in March 1984.
Bobolink (ER) *Dolichonyx oryzivorus* Charlatán	One record from Gibraltar in May 1984.

In addition to these, most northern species of geese are also regularly recorded during winter periods, primarily from the Doñana region. Individuals or small groups of any goose species can turn up at any wetland.